Jean Ternant and
the Age of Revolutions

Jean Ternant and the Age of Revolutions

A Soldier and Diplomat (1751–1833) in the American, French, Dutch and Belgian Uprisings

FRANK WHITNEY

McFarland & Company, Inc., Publishers
Jefferson, North Carolina

LIBRARY OF CONGRESS CATALOGUING-IN-PUBLICATION DATA

Whitney, Frank, 1942– author.
    Jean Ternant and the age of revolutions : a soldier and diplomat (1751–1833) in the American, French, Dutch and Belgian uprisings / Frank Whitney.
        p.   cm.
    Includes bibliographical references and index.

    ISBN 978-1-4766-6213-8 (softcover : acid free paper) ∞
    ISBN 978-1-4766-2322-1 (ebook)

    1. Ternant, Jean Baptiste, chevalier de, 1751–1833. 2. United States—History—Revolution, 1775–1783—Biography. 3. United States—History—Revolution, 1775–1783—Participation, French. 4. Soldiers—France—Biography. 5. Diplomats—France—Biography. I. Title.
    E207.T39W48 2015
    973.3092—dc23
    [B]   2015033773

BRITISH LIBRARY CATALOGUING DATA ARE AVAILABLE

© 2015 Frank Whitney. All rights reserved

No part of this book may be reproduced or transmitted in any form or by any means, electronic or mechanical, including photocopying or recording, or by any information storage and retrieval system, without permission in writing from the publisher.

Front cover image of Jean Ternant by Charles Wilson Peale, from life, ca. 1781–1784 (courtesy Independence National Historical Parks)

Printed in the United States of America

McFarland & Company, Inc., Publishers
   Box 611, Jefferson, North Carolina 28640
      www.mcfarlandpub.com

To
Ann and Christina

Ternant Family Genealogy

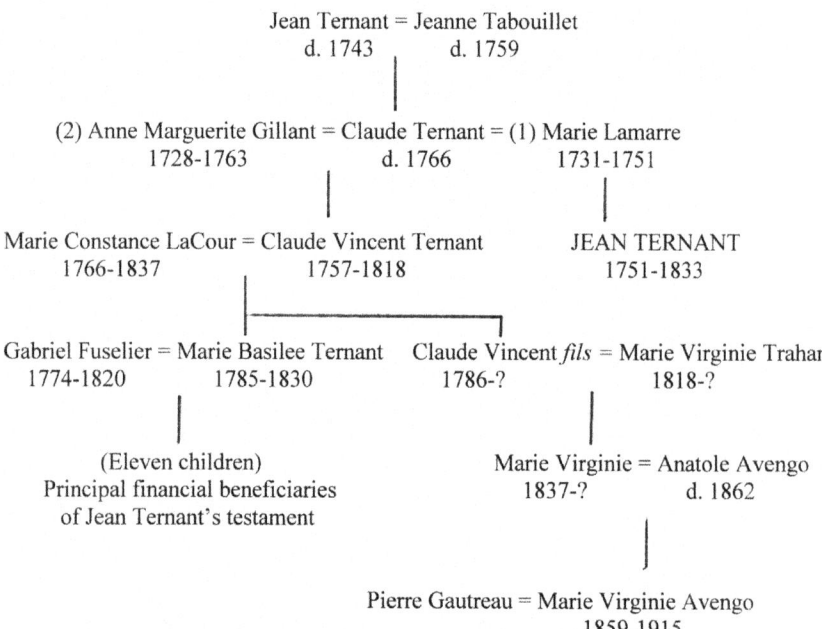

Table of Contents

Acknowledgments	ix
Introduction	1
I. Damvillers—Mézières 1751–1772	11
II. New Orleans—Versailles—Cap-Français 1773–1777	22
III. Valley Forge—Philadelphia March 1778–September 1778	36
IV. Charlestown—Savannah—Philadelphia October 1778–December 1779	60
V. Charlestown—Havana—Philadelphia January 1780–February 1782	73
VI. Monticello—Fuller's Plantation—Philadelphia March 1782–June 1784	93
VII. Versailles—Amsterdam—London August 1784–March 1788	111
VIII. Paris—Darmstadt—Bitche March 1788–August 1791	133
IX. Philadelphia—Mount Vernon—Goodstay August 1791–July 1801	163
X. Paris—St. Germain-en-Laye—Contrexéville August 1801–November 1833	188
Chapter Notes	209
Bibliography	231
Index	247

Acknowledgments

In the research for this study I am pleased to acknowledge the contributions of numerous individuals and institutions. Early on I had the benefit of several conversations with Francis Dallett, a former archivist at the University of Pennsylvania and a vice president of the French Benevolent Society of Philadelphia, who had a long-standing interest in Jean Ternant. For his insights and encouragement I am extremely grateful. Richard Boijen, at the Musee Royal de l'Armée in Brussels, Daniel Lamblat and Mary Kergall, acting on my behalf, obtained copies of manuscript and related material from various European archives and I am in their debt for their generous and indispensable assistance. I am equally appreciative for the assistance of Diane May and the staff of the interlibrary loan department at the Kent State University Library for their diligence in tracking down and obtaining hard to find material.

Throughout my research I have benefited enormously from the kind efforts of individuals at many libraries and museums in both the United States and France. Marjorie McNinch, reference archivist at the Hagley Museum and Library, Ward Childs at the Philadelphia City Archives, Earl Spamer at the American Philosophical Society, Mary Dyleski in the Luzerne County Recorder's office, Edward Richi with the Delaware Historical Society, Bruce Kirby at the Library of Congress and Joseph Rubinfine at American Historical Autographs all provided copies of material pertaining to Ternant. In addition, I also benefited from the efforts of the staffs at the Massachusetts Historical Society, the New York Public Library, the National Archives, the Cleveland Public Library and the William L. Clements Library at the University of Michigan. I was likewise aided by the generous assistance of Madame Lydiane Ghet-Montchal at the Archives Departmentales de la Meuse and Monsieur Bruno Galliard at the Archives Nationale. Finally, my research was also greatly aided by being able to view books long out of print on the Internet. The on-line genealogical records from the archives of the Church of Jesus Christ of Latter-day Saints were particularly helpful.

While the translations from French material are my own, I owe an immense debt of gratitude to Françoise Massardier-Kenney, director of the Institute for Applied Linguistics at Kent State University. Her graduate students, Ania Kurowska and Edward Asare, provided transcriptions of Ternant's correspondence and the documents pertaining to his final testament. Françoise Becquey was also of enormous help with my correspondence with various French archives. In addition, Baily Dumaine was kind enough to provide me with some translations of material in Spanish. For the generous efforts of all the individuals and institutions listed above I remain profoundly grateful but I alone bear the responsibility for any error of fact or mistaken interpretation.

Finally I wish to thank Christina Whitney for her considerable assistance in guiding me through the mysteries of the computer.

Introduction

... It is required of a man that he should share the passion and action of his time at peril of being judged not to have lived.
—Oliver Wendell Holmes, Jr.,
in a Memorial Day Address, 1884

Jean Ternant, chevalier of the Royal and Military Order of Saint-Louis, member of the Society of the Cincinnati, general officer and former minister-plenipotentiary to the United States from the court of Louis XVI, passed away at his home in Paris in the autumn of 1833, just a few weeks short of his eighty-second birthday. He was unmarried with no immediate family, and so except for his *valet de chambre*, Louis Martin, and his housekeeper and cook, Anne Bardou, the neighbors on rue des Petits-Hôtels, his few remaining friends and some distant relatives in the United States and the Department of the Meuse, the old man's death and the ceremonies that accompanied it attracted little public attention.[1] During the preceding forty years the chevalier de Ternant had been content to pursue an unobtrusive, completely private life and what little prominence he once may have enjoyed had faded away long before he died. It was not surprising therefore that few people in Paris of the July Monarchy were aware of either the old gentleman's history or his recent demise.

Notwithstanding his many years spent in undisturbed obscurity, Ternant's death did not pass entirely without notice. Eventually, perhaps inevitably given his history and his many friends in the Franco-American community, the news reached the United States. In Philadelphia the American Philosophical Society, to which Ternant had been elected as a foreign member more than half a century before, noted his recent passing in the minutes of its 18 April 1834 meeting.[2] It was a brief announcement and few present at the Friday session would have had much knowledge of the deceased. The society's president, Peter Duponceau, however, had served with Ternant at Valley Forge and the news of his former comrade's death must have brought back memories of a man who had risked everything in his youth to help the country win its independence and who ever since that time had maintained an abiding affection for it.

For most people today, either American or French, Jean Ternant remains an unknown figure, one of history's countless footnotes. He is neither prominent in the history of the United States nor does he occupy a position of much importance in the history of his native land and his impact on the events of his time has been judged marginal at best. Consequently, even those few individuals who recognize his name and are aware of his military service during the American war for independence and his brief career later as a diplomat are unlikely to know anything more about his life.

Unlike some of his more consequential fellow foreign volunteers who either obtained high rank in the Continental Army or became noteworthy later, Ternant has received little attention from historians. Johann de Kalb, Kazimierz Pulaski, Tadeusz Kosciuszko, Louis Le Begue de Presle Duportail and Pierre Charles L'Enfant, his comrades-in-arms, have all been favored with biographies. Friedrich Wilhelm von Steuben, the celebrated "drill master" of Valley Forge, who was Ternant's patron and friend, has had several studies devoted to his remarkable career. And the most famous of the volunteers, Gilbert du Motier, marquis de Lafayette, the "hero of two worlds," has been the subject of an ever-increasing number of books and articles dedicated to his life and influence.[3] The only works that pertain directly to Ternant however are a few brief biographical sketches included in larger collections and a short journal article that is limited to a review of his service as an inspector in the south during the American war for independence.[4] There has been no detailed study of his life.

This neglect has been encouraged by several factors. In contrast to his long life Ternant's public career was brief, lasting a mere sixteen years, and although he was admired by his peers and often praised by his superiors, he never achieved either widespread recognition or high office. For most of his military career Ternant was a mid-level officer. He did hold positions of trust and responsibility but the authority he exercised was always limited. In the Continental Army, where he began his career, most of his time was spent as a staff officer; he did not obtain a field command until several years after the victory at Yorktown when most of the fighting had ended. Consequently, although he was involved in several major battles, he had few opportunities to lead troops in combat. Ternant's later experience in the Royal Army was similar to his service in the American military. He never rose above the rank of colonel while on active duty, his authority was restricted to his regiment and he had the misfortune to miss the only military action that involved his unit.

Ternant's brief diplomatic career was the high point of his public service. He began as an unofficial agent acting as liaison between the French ministry of foreign affairs and groups of revolutionaries, initially in the United Provinces and later in the Austrian Netherlands. In the spring of 1791, largely through the influence of his patron, Anne-Cesar, chevalier de La Luzerne, Ternant was appointed minister-plenipotentiary to the United States, a post of secondary importance for the French foreign ministry, but for Ternant the posting represented a major advance. As the official representative of the court of Louis XVI he proved to be both responsible and effective under increasingly difficult circumstances, but his diplomatic career was soon overtaken by events. The steadily increasing political chaos in France that resulted in the overthrow of the monarchy undermined Ternant's standing in political circles and in the spring of 1793 he was replaced as minister. With his diplomatic career ended Ternant quickly disappeared from public view. His dismissal marked the beginning of his historical oblivion as well.

If his lack of celebrity, the limited time he spent in the public arena and his minor historical significance have been the principal factors in explaining Ternant's obscurity, his subsequent neglect also has been aided by the scarcity of source material. His papers have disappeared and other material pertaining to him is limited and scattered. Once more, the documents that are extant are distributed in an uneven manner over the course of his life. From his birth in 1751 until 1777 few documents have been uncovered and the record of his activity is difficult, indeed almost impossible, to trace with any degree of certainty. The period from his involvement in the American war for independence through his service as minister to the United States however, is more fully documented. Letters, official reports and diplomatic dispatches pertaining to his activities exist in sufficient number to allow his public career to be studied in some detail.

The final forty years of his life extending from his replacement and recall in 1793 until his death in 1833 is similar with regard to the lack of material as the period of his youth. Public records, with the exception of some pension papers and those documents that pertain to his last testament and the division of his estate, are few in number, especially after 1816, the year often mistakenly given for his death. For this period the principal source of the small amount of information available is personal letters, a collection of some fifty pieces of private correspondence written by Ternant mostly to various members of the Dupont family between 1792 and 1826. These letters provide the few details we have regarding his activities during these years but they also accord some insight into Ternant's personality, his financial interests and his circle of friends. Until additional documents are discovered a more complete biography of Ternant, one that links his thoughts and motivation with his actions or provides additional information on his youth or the period after 1793, remains problematic. At present the most that can be accomplished with the material available is a narrative of his activities; an investigation supplemented with some, I hope, plausible speculation regarding his activities during the undocumented periods.

Ternant's adult life falls neatly into two distinct periods. From his first attempt to enter the Royal Army in 1772 until his replacement as minister-plenipotentiary to the United States in the late spring of 1793, Ternant was involved in the public arena and his life was dominated by his efforts to advance his career. It was an active, often exciting twenty years, a period of solid achievement and some distinction. His remaining forty years, until his death in 1833, were anticlimactic and substantially different. With the termination of his diplomatic position Ternant suddenly found himself adrift, without a career to follow. And, when his efforts to regain it failed, he chose to abandon the world of public affairs, to retire and devote himself to purely personal concerns.

Worn out physically and disillusioned by his experiences, Ternant followed Voltaire's advice and his own inclinations and sought relief in the cultivation of his own interests; content to be "obscurely good" in a private station.[5] In choosing to retire Ternant was not unique. Every French bourgeois dreamed of being able to live without having to work. Almost every public figure in the period also longed to escape the cares of public life and enjoy the pleasures and tranquility associated with domestic affairs. In a letter to Arthur Young written in 1788 for example, George Washington declared, "I wish most devoutly to glide silently and unnoticed through the remainder of my life."[6]

Measured by both his achievements and the standard of living he enjoyed later in life Ternant experienced a modest degree of success. In the course of his long life he became, if not wealthy, certainly comfortable and financially independent. At the time of his death he owned a house in one of the new residential neighborhoods being developed in Paris during the Restoration, and had filled it with fine furniture, numerous works of art and an eclectic collection of books. He owned a barouche, a large expensive carriage with seats for four. He also provided room and board in addition to salary for two servants. For recreation he hunted, played chess and traveled on a regular basis to many of the spas scattered throughout the country. His time, including that devoted to managing his investments, was entirely his own. For his last forty years Ternant lived a life of unpretentious leisure, pursuing his interests, free from the need to earn a living, and experienced, in most respects, the hope of every eighteenth century bourgeois; to retire early and live nobly.

To a significant degree Ternant, as a commoner, owed his professional career to the influence of prominent members of the ruling elite in both America and France who acted on his behalf. Intelligent, personable and prudent, Ternant possessed the qualities that his social and political superiors found attractive and worthy of their support. Henry Laurens, Frederick von Steuben, the chevalier de La Luzerne, the comte de Montmorin de Saint Herem and the marquis de Lafayette at different times helped advance Ternant's career and in return Jean repaid them for their friendship and patronage with deference and loyalty.

One of the striking features of Ternant's story is the large number of important people he knew personally. In the course of his rather short career he formed numerous professional relationships and won the respect of some of the leading figures of his day on both sides of the Atlantic. At the very beginning of his American adventure Ternant met Benjamin Franklin. George Washington, Thomas Jefferson and Alexander Hamilton knew him well, as did most of the political and military leaders of the American rebellion. Ternant became an especially close friend of John Laurens, one of Washington's aides-de-camp and the son of Henry Laurens, a president of the Continental Congress. In addition, Jean counted Gouverneur Morris, one of the most intellectually gifted of America's founding fathers, among his friends for more than twenty years. While campaigning in the South Ternant met the engaging but ill-fated English officer, John Andre, and during Jean's many months spent as a paroled prisoner of war in Philadelphia after the fall of Charlestown, he came to know most of the staff of the French legation. Anne-Cesar, chevalier de La Luzerne, the French minister to the United States, became a close friend and patron and La Luzerne's secretaries, François Barbe-Marbois and Louis Guillaume Otto, became long-standing associates.

In later years Ternant became personally acquainted with many of the principal figures in the French ministry of foreign affairs and *corps diplomatique*; Joseph-Mathias Gerard de Rayneval, Charles Gravier, comte de Vergennes, Armand-Marc, comte de Montmorin, François Barthelemy and Charles Maurice de Talleyrand, to name just a few. After La Luzerne and the comte de Montmorin no Frenchman was more important in promoting Ternant's career than the marquis de Lafayette. During the early years of the revolution in France he was Ternant's most celebrated acquaintance and the lack of correspondence between these two like-minded liberals following Jean's return to France in the summer of 1801 remains one of the most perplexing mysteries of Ternant's story.

Ternant's personal relationships were not limited to the world of public affairs. He also enjoyed long-term friendships with important figures in the American business community. Stephen Girard, a prominent Philadelphia merchant on his way to becoming the richest man in the

United States, became a close friend and confidant, as did the merchant and banker John Nixon. Ternant's American agent and financial advisor until the early 1820s was George Simpson, head teller at the First Bank of the United States, a man recognized by many of his contemporaries as one of the Republic's foremost authorities on banking and international finance.

During the course of his career Ternant had the honor of being presented to the reigning monarchs of both France and England. Louis XVI decorated him for service to the crown while England's George the Third, in an incident that caused comment at the time, publicly snubbed him. Finally, and of particular importance for Ternant, there was his forty-year friendship with the French liberal economist, Pierre Samuel Du Pont de Nemours, and members of his extended family. This long-term relationship, begun during the early years of the revolution in France, formed the centerpiece of Ternant's social network in the second half of his life and provided Jean with his most intimate friend, Gabrielle Josephine Du Pont.

What sort of man was this patriot soldier and diplomat? Given his ambition for a military career it is perhaps somewhat surprising that Ternant was not a man of impulse and action. Instead, more than anything, he was by inclination an intellectual, a man contemplative by nature and one drawn to liberal ideas. In his youth he had the good fortune to acquire a solid education and throughout his life Jean continued to pursue a variety of intellectual interests, foremost among them, natural history and art. He also exhibited a talent for languages and was praised for his fluency in English.

As many educated people of his time, Ternant was influenced by the political ideas and the progressive humanitarian concepts advanced by the leading figures of the Enlightenment. Exposed to the realities of slavery in Saint Domingue and in the United States he later became an early member of the anti-slave trade movement and his personal involvement in the armed struggle for American independence and the Dutch "Patriot" movement is ample evidence of the strength of his political convictions. Finally, included among his personal effects brought from France to the United States in 1791 was a small but nevertheless telling aesthetic testament to his ideals, a pair of Carrara marble busts of the Enlightenment's two great adversaries, Voltaire and Rousseau.[7]

Well educated and studious by nature, Ternant was also, as one might expect, well read. The inventory of his library taken at the time of his death revealed a wide variety of scholarly material. Among the more than five hundred books contained in his collection were works by the leading naturalists of the day, Pierre Sonnerat's two-volume study, *Voyage aux Indies orientales et Chine*, a copy of *Dictionnaire raisone universal de l'his-*

toire naturale by Jacques Christophe Valmont-Bomare and Georges-Louis Leclerc, comte de Buffon's multi volume classic, *Histoire Naturelle générale et particuliere*.

Other books included were studies by the art historian Johann Wincklemann, the complete works of Voltaire, Montesquie's classic work, *Spirit of the Laws*, works by Jean Jacques Rousseau, dramas by Jean Racine and Pierre Corneille, Samuel Johnson's *Dictionary of the English Language*, the works of Henry Fielding and studies and drawings by Charles de Wailly, one of the leading architects of the period. Finally, there were numerous mathematical studies, most notably those by Joseph Louis Legrange and John Landen; the writings of the essayist and moralist, Luc de Clapiers, marquis de Vauvenarge, Stendhal's travel book, *Rome, Naples et Florence*, and works by the Roman poets Horace and Juvenal. All these studies testify to the varied nature of Ternant's interests and his commitment to the ideals of the Enlightenment.[8]

In terms of personality Ternant was reserved, easygoing and well mannered with a quiet, self-deprecating sense of humor. He had few pretensions and it is easy to understand why many people of both sexes found him charming and a good companion. His letters show him as temperate in his habits and very prudent in financial matters. Sober and dedicated to his duties, Jean exemplified in many respects the ideals of eighteenth century French bourgeois culture by being ambitious, hardworking and determined to improve his material circumstances and social standing; to make a better life for himself.

Although most of his close associates found Ternant's personality congenial, his character admirable and were impressed by his intelligence and diligence, Ternant was not without critics. Louis-Guillaume Otto, a member of the French legation in Philadelphia from 1779 until 1792, thought him cold and unsociable.[9] Ternant was also reputed by some Americans to be "hypochondriac and discontented," a characterization that persisted long enough to be repeated by Thomas Jefferson in 1789, while in Paris.[10] In spite of being as fluent in English as in his native tongue and serving in the Continental army, Ternant, as a Frenchman, was still viewed as an outsider; a member of a national group and religion that the majority of Americans disliked and feared. As with many such negative whisperings there was just enough evidence to give these unflattering opinions and accusations some validity.

Otto's opinion, for instance, was based upon his comparison of Ternant's reserved personality with the conviviality of the former minister-plenipotentiary to the United States, the chevalier de La Luzerne, who was famous for his hospitality, largess and sociability. Having served under both men, Otto appreciated the value of La Luzerne's outgoing personality and thought Ternant's reserve had a negative effect on French diplomatic efforts.

Regarding the charge of being a hypochondriac, throughout his life Ternant often experienced bouts of debilitating illness, which suggest that at some point in his travels he contracted malaria and consequently suffered reoccurring spells of fatigue and high fever. And he did in fact use poor health, but quite legitimately, as a reason for requesting leave on several occasions during his service in the Southern Department. If he was overly anxious regarding his health it may have been the result of poor health experienced as a child. His later letters often contained general references to his well-being and to that of his correspondents.

The more unflattering and condescending charge of being discontented was almost certainly linked to the views Ternant occasionally expressed during the war for independence. Jean's letters from that period often show frustration, much of it directed at what he viewed as congressional ignorance, especially regarding the formal establishment of the Inspectors Department and at the lack of American military efficiency. None of his complaints were concerned however, with his personal promotion. Later grumbling regarding the failure to be exchanged in a timely fashion when he was a prisoner of war was also less an example of special pleading on his part than a reflection of his desire to serve.

Officers in the Continental Army in general and the foreign officers in particular were often dissatisfied and outspoken regarding their grievances. Hard dangerous duty, the perceived lack of recognition and appreciation, the often acknowledged inadequacy of their compensation, and the Congress's continuing refusal to address their concerns regarding pensions caused most officers to voice frustration and anger. Everyone complained and many officers simply resigned in disgust. Jean, always anxious about the state of his personal finances and the future of his military career, was no exception.

In 1783 the financially embarrassed Congress arbitrarily ignored its own military regulations and deprived Ternant of an important promotion in rank. And it was only after some complaining on his part and the influence of his former commanders, Benjamin Lincoln and Friedrich von Steuben, that the Congress was finally persuaded to approve his advancement. Ternant's refusal to accept his being unfairly treated undoubtedly upset some members of Congress and may well have contributed to his reputation for being dissatisfied.

Thanks to the work of the American artist Charles Willson Peale, we have a portrait of Ternant as a young man. A committed patriot, former soldier and someone personally acquainted with many of the leaders of the Continental Congress and its army, Peale created a portrait gallery devoted to men he considered heroes of the struggle for independence.[11] Ternant was one of eleven foreigners whose portraits were included among the initial collection of forty-four paintings. Executed sometime between June 1780 and the spring of 1784 but most probably during the summer of 1780, the painting shows Ternant in either his late twenties or early thirties; a thin handsome young soldier with an oval face, high forehead, hazel eyes and a fair complexion. His light chestnut hair is tied back according to the fashion of the day, and he is elegantly attired in the regulation blue and buff colored uniform with epaulets of a commissioned officer. With the lapels of his coat unbuttoned and slightly askew, Ternant's pose is informal yet with no hint of carelessness. His facial features are regular and he gazes straight to the front with a calm countenance suggestive of both intelligence and a reserved personality.[12]

Unlike his compatriot and friend, Lafayette, Jean Ternant has no monument to commemorate his participation in the war for independence. No American city, street or square bears his name and except for his portrait in the Independence National Historical Park there is no reminder of his service to the United States, except perhaps, the United States itself. He has been similarly ignored in France as well. This study is an attempt to remedy this lack of recognition by telling his story; by tracing with as much detail as possible the many twists and turns he experienced in his long life and present a more full and rounded portrait of this modest man. It is also an effort to correct some of the errors that have crept into the historical record over the years. In 1796 Elizabeth Nixon, the daughter of the prominent Philadelphia banker John Nixon, wrote in a letter to a friend that Ternant was "surely one of the best men in the world."[13] I believe he was.

I

Damvillers—Mézières
1751–1772

Jean Ternant was born in Damvillers, a small provincial city in the diocese of Verdun on the northeast border of France, on a winter Sunday, 12 December 1751, and as was often the case with newborns, he was christened on the same day.[1] Although most of the details concerning his birth, his early years and his family remain unknown, several facts are clear. Jean was the first child born to his parents, Claude Ternant and his twenty-year-old wife, née Marie Lamarre, and he was named after his paternal grandfather. His father was a retail merchant and shopkeeper, the son of Jean Ternant, and his wife, née Jeanne Tabouillot. Jean's mother was the emancipated daughter of Pierre Lamarre and Jeanne Pierre from the nearby village Sivry-sur-Meuse.[2] Of more significance to Jean however, was the fact that he proved to be his mother's only child and that he never knew her. A little more than two years after his birth, in February 1754, Claude Ternant married again, taking for his second wife a twenty-six-year-old woman from Champneuville, Anne Marguerite Gillant.[3]

While neither the cause nor the date of Jean's mother's death have been discovered, Marie Lamarre's demise at such a young age was not unusual. In matters regarding health the eighteenth century was a dangerous age. Local epidemics were a regular occurrence in every European community. Dysentery, typhus, malaria, tuberculosis, smallpox and a host of other diseases plagued society. During the winter months pneumonia and other pulmonary infections were especially deadly. Any of these afflictions could have been responsible for Marie Lamarre's death, at any time. Another explanation for her death however, could be puerperal fever or other complications connected with Jean's birth. Along with smallpox and bad water, pregnancy represented the greatest threat to women of all classes. Midwives were mostly ignorant, there were no techniques available for dealing with postpartum hemorrhaging or other complications during delivery, hygienic concerns were seldom considered and life threatening infections were common. Modern studies estimate that perhaps as many as one woman in ten lost her life to childbirth-related causes and given the normal five or six pregnancies experienced by a woman during the course of her life, the odds of her dying giving birth increased significantly.[4]

Little is known about Anne Gillant. Her appearance, her disposition and personality and the nature of her relationship with Jean are unrecorded. What is a matter of record however, is that in January 1757, three years after her marriage, she gave birth to the first of five children, a son, Claude Vincent Ternant. Then at regular intervals were born Barbe in 1759, Marie-Françoise in 1760, Nicolas-Maurice in 1761 and on 31 January 1763 a daughter, Jeanne. One week later Anne Marguerite Gillant died, almost certainly because of difficulties associated with the birth of her fifth child.[5]

A widower for the second time, but now with six children ranging in age between eleven and one week to care for, it was a second and much more serious domestic situation for Claude Ternant. In response he followed convention and took the sensible practical course; he married for a third time. Although the date of his marriage to Therese Lolot has not been determined, in September 1766 a son, Nicolas, was born. At some point in that same year however, Claude Ternant died and in December Jean turned fifteen.[6]

Claude Ternant's experience of fathering seven children by three wives over the course of fifteen years was a common one among families of all classes in the eighteenth century. Life expectancy was short and marriages lasting more than fifteen years were rare. Multiple spouses and numerous children from different unions therefore was often the case. Such situations almost always guaranteed a complicated if not tense and difficult domestic environment. Favoritism and expectations regarding inheritance rights would often strain both extended and immediate family relationships. What effect multiple stepmothers and six half-brothers and sisters had on Jean is impossible to know but as the firstborn and the eldest male his inheritance rights at least would have been recognized and his future well-being a primary concern for the extended Ternant family.

Damvillers during Jean Ternant's youth was a town with only local significance; populated by small businessmen, artisans, lawyers, notaries and *rentiers* of modest incomes. Located in the valley of the Thinte River and surrounded by rolling wooded hills on the edge of the great Argonne forest, the town was situated midway between Verdun and Montmédy, about twenty miles from the border with Luxembourg and 150 miles from Paris.

First mentioned in charters dating from the eleventh century, Damvillers in 1334 had become part of Luxembourg by the terms of the marriage contract between Beatrix de Bourbon and Jean, King of Bohemia and Count of Luxembourg; an event reflected to this day by the city's coat of arms.[7] During the sixteenth century the city became a major strategic factor in the region, constantly changing hands in the contest between the Valois Kings of France and their Hapsburg rivals. In 1526 Charles V's Italian engineers constructed a modern fortress at Damvillers to protect Luxembourg's western border. Furnished with five bastions capable of supporting artillery, several demi-lunes, a dry ditch, covered way and glacis, the city became a primary focus of the struggle in the disputed area of northern Lorraine. For Damvillers that struggle finally ended in October 1637. After a lengthy and fiercely contested siege the city's Spanish garrison capitulated to a French army and by terms of the Treaty of the Pyrenees signed in 1659 Damvillers, along with the neighboring *prevotes* or jurisdictions of Montmédy, Marville and Chauvency, became part of the Kingdom of France.[8]

For Damvillers the change in sovereignty inaugurated a reversal of fortune. The next forty years witnessed a slow decline in both the town's status and its physical appearance. Immediately following its capture many of the town's inhabitants emigrated eastward into Hapsburg territory. The city's population declined in number but thanks to its new garrison became increasingly French. In 1661 Damvillers and the other cities in the area were placed under the authority of the Governor of Metz and included in the Generality of Metz for the purpose of taxation. Finally, and most significant, in 1678 as part of a reorganization of the region's defenses, the city's walls and bastions were razed and its military importance ended.[9]

Jean Ternant was born into a petit bourgeois or lower middle class family and he was therefore a *roturier* or commoner. His father, Claude, the son of a *marchand-tanneur*, was a retail merchant and shopkeeper who sold hides, raw leather and possibly finished leather goods. He may well have owned a tannery as well.[10] In addition to Jean's immediate family there was another branch of the Ternant family in Damvillers, one headed by Nicolas Ternant who was most likely either Jean's uncle or a cousin. By 1762 Nicolas had married and also had begun to raise a family. Between the two branches the Ternant name figured prominently in Damviller's parish register during this period.

In spite of its lower middle class status, Jean's family was connected by marriage to some of the more prominent families in the region; a fact that may explain any assistance with his education and financial support that Jean received as a young man. His mother's family, the Lamarres, while not particularly distinguished, was numerous, prosperous and included among its members a local seigneur and a minor tax collector in Verdun.[11]

Much more important to Jena's future however, was the kinship with the family of his paternal grandmother, Jeanne Tabouillot. A large wealthy family with branches in Marville, Damvillers, Verdun and Metz, the

14 • Jean Ternant and the Age of Revolutions

Tabouillots by the mid eighteenth century had become well established in the legal profession, the church and as local government officials. Hubert Tabouillot, a *marchand tanneur*, later served as a notary and eventually became mayor of Marville. His younger brother, Claude, a resident of Damvillers, succeeded Hubert in both positions and later was ennobled for his service to the crown.[12] Jeanne Tabouillot, his daughter, married Jean Ternant and their son, Claude, was the father of the subject of this study.

Although the geographical origin of his father's side of the family remains a mystery, it most likely came from the Côte-d'Or region of Burgundy and took its name from that of a small hamlet located in the wine country between Beaune and Dijon.[13] From there Jean's paternal ancestors migrated north into the Meuse Argonne area sometime during the seventeenth or early eighteenth century and by the time of Jean's birth the family had become a respected part of the Damvillers community. It is also likely that the family had been involved in tanning for several generations before it expanded into the retail business in an effort to improve its economic position and social standing.

Some indication of the Ternant family's economic condition can be gained from its involvement with the production and marketing of leather. Throughout history tanning has been a basic industry, essential to every society's clothing, transportation, agricultural and military needs. This fact insured that successful tanners might expect to enjoy a respectable standard of living. For merchants dealing in leather products the opportunity existed for an even better life. Most leather was produced locally in small-scale operations. It was a difficult, malodorous and lengthy process but tanning was an important part of many local economies.[14] Damvillers today has its rue des tanneries, a reminder of the importance that tanning played in the city's early economy.

As most other economic activities in the Meuse-Argonne region, the tanning industry had been devastated by the wars during the seventeenth century. By the middle of the eighteenth century however, it along with the rest of the local economy had recovered. Damvillers and most other towns and villages in the area benefited from an upsurge of new tanning enterprises. By 1756 nearby Metz had sixty-one such ventures.[15] Unfortunately so rapid an expansion could not continue and by the early 1760s an economic decline had set in and the imposition of new taxes only added to economic stagnation. The worsening economy combined with the death of Jean's father in 1766 hastened the decline of the family business.

Information pertaining to Ternant's childhood and adolescence is non-existent. On his childhood experiences and friends, his role in the family business, his relationship with his parents and siblings, and where and how he was educated the historical record is blank. It is in regard to this period of Ternant's life that the disappearance and apparent loss of his papers following his death is so keenly felt. Ternant, as an adult, was exactly the type of individual who would have carefully preserved and cataloged his papers. He was well educated and comfortably well off, intellectually active, cultured and well traveled. He had been personally involved in many of the important events of his time and was acquainted with a large number of prominent and influential people. His papers if extant would be a rich source for information on his life and times.

Ternant's collection of papers would have included a *livre de raison*, a detailed record of a family that was usually passed from father to eldest son. Notebooks of this type were a fount of information on a family's origin and history, its genealogy and usually contained a wealth of detail regarding the family's property and other economic interests. Most families regardless of class kept such books, recording the most trivial and intimate information. Ternant's *livre de raison* would have provided the answers to many of the questions regarding his early years and the fate of his family.[16]

As later events proved, Jean had little interest in following family tradition and becoming a shopkeeper. With the death of his father parental authority ended, Jean's independence was assured and it became possible for him to plan a future based on his own interests and ability. Nothing had prepared Jean more for this opportunity than his education. As most bourgeois boys he attended the communal school in Damvillers where he learned the rudiments of reading, writing, arithmetic and music. At some point he then passed to a secondary school, probably, if only for convenience, the college established by the Jesuits at nearby Verdun. There he would have mixed with the sons of the local elite and been introduced to a wide variety of technical and academic subjects; classical literature, Latin, algebra, drawing, geography, perhaps foreign languages and equally important for an ambitious bourgeois, cultural skills and manners. Colleges were windows on the larger world, which tended to encourage independence and many a student was tempted to abandon his father's occupation and follow his own interests.[17] In Jean's case this meant a military career which he later would describe as stemming from a "natural inclination to military matters."[18]

Over the course of his adolescence Jean's interest in the military and his aptitude for study reinforced each other. His academic ability and his enthusiasm for the army came together and encouraged him not merely to join the Royal Army but to use his academic talent to become a military engineer and gain a commission. Jean's fondness for study and his intelligence cannot be accounted for, but the reasons for his interest in the army in general and the engineers in particular are more easily explained.

The eastern border region of France has always been a military zone, heavily fortified and garrisoned. In an arc of territory stretching from the imposing fortress, Charlemont, at Givet in the north, through Lorraine and Alsace to Huningen on the border of the Swiss Cantons, French territory was protected by an elaborate system of seventeen major and a number of minor fortresses, strategically located to block the roads leading to the plain of Champagne and Paris. No other area in the Kingdom could match the east in its level of military presence. In addition to the large number of fortresses, approximately one third of the Royal army was stationed in the region, and consequently, nowhere in France did the army have a greater impact on the local economy. As a major consumer of both raw materials and finished goods, and a reliable source of specie the royal army exerted enormous economic influence. Once more, over time the royal army also exerted an "emotive impact" on the civilian population in the region, helping to foster identification with France and a sense of pride.[19] In addition, because regiments usually recruited in the area where they were stationed, men from Lorraine, the Three Bishoprics (Toul, Verdun and Metz) and Alsace made up a significant proportion, some 40 percent, of troops in the royal army. Finally, with regard to Damvillers, although no longer a fortress it had regained a measure of military importance. In 1741 the Governor of Metz, Charles Fouquet, Marshal Belle-Isle, had the city's ditch cleared of rubble, the covered way repaired and palisades erected to establish a *place de moment*, a fortified position for a field army to use as a temporary refuge if necessary.[20]

In addition to being born into a region with a large and constant military presence Jean grew into his early teens during the period when France was involved in the Seven Years' War (1756–1763). At an age when boys are most impressionable, his world was crowded with columns of troops and equipment moving from staging areas to join armies in the field and the news of the day was filled with reports of military operations. It would have been very strange for a small boy not to be captivated and want to be a soldier.

Jean's interest in the engineers was a later development. At some point during his adolescence, probably after his father's death, he became determined, and perhaps encouraged, to seek a commission in the Royal Army by gaining admission to the *l'École du Génie*, the school for military engineers, located at Mézières. This marked Jean's first attempt at a military career and it was one of the most important decisions of his life. To prepare for Mézières required him to continue his schooling but it also helped mold his self-image. A career in the engineers would also provided him with an acceptable alternative to remaining in the family business. For the French bourgeoisie, to have a son become an officer in the king's service opened the way for a family to be ennobled. It brought honor and prestige to both the individual and his family and more important, a commission in the army was a reliable source of money.[21] With these advantages to be gained, Jean's family would have supported him wholeheartedly in his ambition.

Several aspects regarding the engineers naturally appealed to Ternant. One was the importance of mathematics in their work. Ternant must have had an affinity for numbers and have been recognized by his teachers as having the academic skills necessary for advanced study. He may also have been attracted by the engineer's reputation as a *corps des savants* or scholars. Although often paid the backhanded compliment of being called Jesuits, because of their dogmatism and habit of argument, the engineers were recognized as the most intellectual group in the Royal Army.[22]

The fact that most attracted Jean and his family however, was the knowledge that admission to Mézières remained open to non-nobles. In spite of the traditional prejudice against commoners in general and the sons of retail merchants in particular, serving in positions of military leadership, *roturiers* who were able to meet the academic requirements faced no statutory restriction to their attending the school at Mézières; between 1748 and 1777 some forty-three percent of engineers serving with the Royal army were commoners.[23]

One of the reasons for this open admission policy was that until 1744 military engineers, along with their fellow specialists in the artillery, had not been included in the Royal Army. Not considered as part of the military, they were viewed instead as " a kind of superior camp follower."[24] Historically most engineers had served as volunteers without rank and lacked the authority to command troops. Moreover, there also tended to be a considerable difference in the degree of technical competence among them. It was also a fact that until the reforms in the middle of the eighteenth century nepotism reigned supreme, indeed family "dynasties" of military engineers were not unusual; a situation that while it reflected the corporate nature and social arrangements of French society failed to provide the army with a consistent or reliable source of engineering competence. The school at Mézières was founded in part to correct these problems and did so. By 1770 the number of engineers with relatives in the *génie* had been substantially reduced and the level of technical expertise among the corps of engineers much improved.

Located approximately seventy miles northwest of Damvillers on a bend of the Meuse River, the small fortress city of Mézières had been selected as the site for the military engineering school in 1748. In the ensuing twenty years a two-year course of instruction had been developed, the student body fixed at fifty and a two-step procedure for admission put in place.²⁵ After successfully completing a preparatory course of study with a heavy emphasis on mathematics, prospective candidates applied for a *lettre d'exame*, a certificate issued in the king's name by the Secretary of State for War that granted official permission to take the entrance examination.

Although neither the means nor the manner of Jean's preparation for the entrance examination to Mézières are known, there were a variety of venues that offered preparatory courses of study for young men interested in an engineering career. The royal military academy was an obvious source of instruction. Colleges at Nanterre, west of Paris, at Rhiems, at Soreze, east of Toulouse or at Clamecy near Dijon in Burgundy were also well regarded. If a student's family could afford it there were also several boarding schools in Paris that catered to students requiring advanced mathematics. Berthaud's, Bouffet's and Longpre's had excellent reputations. Private tutors were also an option.

Although it was the easier of the two hurdles for applicants to Mézières to cross, obtaining a *lettre d'exame* was not without its own difficulties. The candidate submitted a dossier, certified by four nobles, which included a copy of his baptismal record indicating his age (at least fifteen) and his place of birth, information regarding his family's good standing and the names of any relatives that had served in the Royal Army. The file also included a statement regarding the family's ability to contribute financially to the applicant's living expenses should he be admitted. Students at Mézières were paid 720 livres a year but it was almost impossible for candidates to survive on this sum alone.²⁶

Even with the absence of regulations against non-nobles being admitted, obtaining the required *lettre d'exame* was not a certainty. Many commoners were refused the certificate and as the century wore on it became increasingly difficult to obtain. In 1763 and 1767 renewed emphasis was placed upon restricting access to the school to members of the lesser nobility and the sons of physicians, notaries or counselors were routinely refused admission. To circumvent these new developments it became a common practice for a non-noble candidate to obtain the support of an influential sponsor or patron, someone to vouch for their fitness and to pull strings. Any noble was acceptable but the higher placed the better. A letter of recommendation from a government official, a Bishop or a marquis would lend weight to a student's application and family connections and personal contacts with the right government official were often more important to an aspirant's chances than his social status or academic ability. Lazare Carnot, from Nolay in Burgundy, who as a member of the Committee of Public Safety gained fame as the "organizer of victory" during the period 1793–94, obtained his *lettre d'exame* because of the recommendation on his behalf from a local dignitary and family friend, the duc d'Aumont. It is very likely that Jean received a letter of recommendation from a member of his grandmother's family, the locally prominent Tabouillots.

After receiving the required certificate the candidate then faced the second part of the admission process, the entrance examination. Given in Paris once each year in the fall, the examination was a demanding test of a student's academic ability. It covered an array of technical subjects including algebra, geometry, hydraulics, mechanics and drawing and was proctored by Abbe Charles Bossut a noted mathematician, a former instructor at Mézières and a member of the Academy of Science.[27] Following the examination Bossut prepared a *dossier d'exame* for the Secretary of State for War placing each candidate in a class according to his performance and with his recommendations. The Secretary for War then selected which candidates would be admitted to Mézières. Only those students who scored highest were selected but young students who showed promise or were well connected, often were permitted to retake the test after further study, in fact it was quite common. Lazare Carnot, for example, took the exam twice. Claude Joseph Rouget de l'Isle, another graduate from Mézières who later gained fame as the composer of the *Chant de Guerre de l'armée du Rhin*, today the *La Marseillaise*, took the exam five times.[28]

Upon the successful completion of the rigorous two-year course of instruction a graduate became an officer engineer and was awarded a brevet as a retired second lieutenant in the infantry. This retired status in the infantry was clear evidence that the engineers, in the third quarter of the eighteenth century, still had not yet been completely integrated into the Royal Army.[29]

In a document prepared in 1787 that listed his past military service and that was part of his request for induction into the Royal and Military Order of Saint Louis, Ternant, in an effort to meet the length of service required for eligibility, indicated that he had begun his military career in 1772 as a student in the engineers.[30] His claim for beginning his service in 1772 was rejected, but he nonetheless gained membership in recognition of his political service to the crown. There are no records in his dossier in the military archives that indicate he ever attended Mézières or that he ever served in the royal army prior to the spring of 1788. In reality Jean's brief association with the *Corps du Génie* ended when he failed to score high enough in the examination to be selected.[31]

For Ternant and the other candidates in 1772, the timing was unfortunate. The engineers during this period were undergoing a major downsizing; one designed both to reduce government expenditures and to match engineering personnel with the army's changing needs. As part of this reform, student enrollment at Mézières was in the process of being reduced from fifty students to thirty. To accomplish this end, the entrance examination for 1771 had been cancelled and for future tests the number of candidates chosen for admission was to be linked with the number of graduating students. For the examination in 1772 the number of admissions was reduced from the usual twenty to twelve.[32] In these circumstances, every applicant's chance was greatly reduced and Ternant was among the vast majority of unsuccessful candidates.

One of Jean's later acquaintances who experienced the same disappointment was Guillaume Mathieu Dumas. In 1770, two years before Jean, Dumas had taken the entrance examination for Mézières and also failed to be selected. When the examination for the following year was cancelled Dumas ended his attempt to become an engineer. A few years later however, his family arranged for him to join a regiment of infantry and he began what was to be a long and distinguished military career that included service in America under Rochambeau, assisting Lafayette in the organization of the National Guard in Paris and participation in Napoleon's retreat from Moscow. In October 1787 Dumas and Ternant would meet in Amsterdam during the Prussian siege. For both men the failure to become an engineer had proved a blessing. By the summer of 1789 and the beginning of the revolution in France each had risen to the rank of colonel in the Royal Army, a development that would have been impossible had they become engineers.[33]

It is some indication of Ternant's mind set and character however, that in spite of his failure to gain admission to Mézières and the tenuous nature of his association with the *Corps du Génie*, he continued to identify with the fraternity of military intellectuals. Throughout his military career and later in life many of his closest friends had either been engineers or were related to one. Jean-Baptiste Joseph de Laumoy, one of four military engineers sent by Louis XVI to serve in the Continental Army and Ternant's companion in arms during the campaigns in the American south was a close friend for many years and Laumoy's widow, Agathe Louise Bocquet de Chantereine, would be a beneficiary in Ternant's last testament.

Jean-Xavier Bureaux de Pusy, a close friend of Lafayette and the son-in-law of Dupont de Nemours, became an associate of Ternant for a brief period. He had graduated from Mézières in 1774 and his daughter, Françoise-Josephine, who was married to a brother of an engineer, was also included in Ternant's will. There were many others. Bureaux de Pusy's brother-in-law, Jacques-Antoine de Reveroni de Saint-Cyr, another graduate of Mézières and a noted military author, popular playwright and novelist was a member of Ternant's social circle in Paris, as was Jean-Rene Guerin de Foncin, the engineer who both designed and supervised the construction of Fort McHenry at Baltimore.[34]

Jean Ternant's failure to gain admission to the *École du Génie* and begin a career in the Royal Army marked the end of his early hopes and changed the course of his immediate future. For the next five years, from the autumn of 1772 until March of 1778, he would struggle to find an acceptable alternative to a military profession. It would prove a long adventure, one that entailed almost continual travel. For Ternant, an educated, ambitious twenty-one-year-old that had been to Paris, a life spent as a shopkeeper in rustic and unsophisticated Damvillers had little appeal. His future and his fortune would lay elsewhere.

II

New Orleans— Versailles—Cap-Français
1773–1777

Ternant's activities beginning in 1773 and continuing until his arrival at Valley Forge in March of 1778 are not well documented and are only slightly better known than his activities during his childhood and adolescence. There are no references to his experiences during this period in his later letters and he likewise ignored any mention of these years in his numerous applications for a military pension. For the most part these five years seem to have been marked by almost continuous travel; journeys often to foreign destinations and undertaken for entirely personal reasons; prompted perhaps by a sense of adventure, intellectual curiosity or wanderlust.

The chronology of Jean's travels during the early part of this period is impossible to establish with any certitude, and no evidence regarding the circumstances under which they occurred has been uncovered. Ternant's earliest forays, for instance, may have included visits to England, Italy and perhaps Spain, but in what capacity he traveled or how he managed to finance his journeys remain a mystery. The little information that pertains to this period and these matters that has been found is contained in several documents that date from early in 1777, only hint at past events and are open to a variety of interpretations.

In a brief note written from Bordeaux to Benjamin Franklin in January (the first letter from his hand that we have) Jean reiterated his enthusiasm for the American cause. "If I can be of any use to you in anything whatever, you may depend upon my ardent desire of defending the rights of humanity and supporting with all my might those who have so generously stood in defense of them." He also wished the American commissioner success in the latter's forthcoming negotiations with the Spanish court and claimed that he knew Conde de Floridablanca, the then recently appointed Spanish court's principal minister, who Jean insisted "will undoubtedly serve your cause with an unremitted ardour."[1]

Floridablanca was born Jose Monino y Redondo in 1728. A graduate of the University at Salamanca, Monino by the late 1760s had established a reputation as a liberal economic reformer, with interests in agriculture and banking and someone familiar with the writings of French intellectuals. Following a successful period of service as a magistrate and a *fiscal* on the Council of Castile, in March 1772 he had been sent as an emissary to Pope Clement XIV, charged with insuring that the Jesuit order, after its recent expulsion from Spain, did not re-establish itself in Italy under the protection of the Vatican. As a reward for his success in this mission Monino, in 1773, was awarded the title, Conde de Floridablanca. Three years later the forty-eight-year-old attorney turned diplomat was recalled to Spain and in February 1776 appointed Secretary of State for Foreign Affairs and first minister. An effective administrator, if extremely sensitive to criticism, Floridablanca was generally hostile to aristocrats and favored well-educated individuals from the middle class for positions in the government.[2]

If Ternant had become personally acquainted with Floridablanca as he claimed, he must have met the Spaniard sometime during 1773 or shortly thereafter, in Italy. This claim on Jean's part and his interest in art may be some evidence for a visit to Rome. It may be however, especially given Jean's optimistic but completely mistaken evaluation of Floridablanca's enthusiasm for the cause of American independence offered in his note to Franklin, that he had only been introduced to the Spanish diplomat and did not know him in any meaningful way. Or, perhaps Jean only knew the Spanish foreign minister by reputation and therefore his mention in the letter is no evidence of an early journey to Italy.

Although Ternant's visits to Italy or Spain during this period remain speculation derived from his letter to Franklin, there is another, somewhat more reliable document that clearly establishes he made several voyages to North America and the French colonies in the Caribbean. Several days before writing to Franklin, Ternant signed a *certificate d'identité et de catholique* required of all French travelers leaving the country that identified him as already a resident of Louisiana.

At some point between 1773 and 1777, Ternant made the first of at least two journeys to the French islands in the Caribbean and the former French colony, Louisiana. Although there is no other documentation for this initial trans Atlantic voyage, it is quite possible that Jean had decided to emigrate and seek his fortune in the New World. Why he chose Louisiana is also unknown, but perhaps it was because as a former French colony with a French population and legal system, the cultural environment would have made starting a career there less difficult. He may also have been attracted because of the region's reputation.

Early in the century John Law's Mississippi Company, in an effort to attract investors to the area, had promoted Louisiana, praising its economic potential. Although Law's banking and commercial empire soon collapsed Ternant may have been encouraged by the old stories to visit the region, establish its potential for himself and if it measured up to the earlier claims, make preparations for a permanent move at a later date. Jean's interest in natural history may also have been a consideration.

As claimed by France in the seventeenth century, Louisiana had been an enormous ill-defined expanse of territory that stretched from the Great Lakes and the *pays des Illinois* to the Gulf of Mexico, encompassing the lands bordering the Mississippi river and its tributaries. As part of the series of treaties that marked the end of the Seven Years' War however, France surrendered its claim to the Louisiana territory east of the Mississippi to Britain and transferred its rights to the territory on the west bank of the river and the city of New Orleans to Spain in a secret treaty signed at Fontainebleau in the winter of 1762. By the time of its acquisition by Spain, Louisiana had been considerably reduced in size and was of little economic importance. Notwithstanding its central role in Law's investment ventures and later having been lauded for its climate and agricultural potential by Voltaire, the colony remained isolated, undeveloped and expensive to administer.[3] Its principal immediate attraction for the Spanish crown lay in its strategic location as a buffer zone protecting Spain's Mexican territories.

Although the Spanish government was initially reluctant to accept sovereignty over a European colony it had not settled and took nine years for Spain to establish complete political control and to integrate Louisiana into its American Empire, the Spanish colonial regime proved a success. Louisiana's agricultural output increased and its economy expanded. From the beginning, as part of its economic development program, Spanish authorities expended considerable sums of money to encourage immigration. With its liberal policy of land grants, financial assistance and offers of free tools and livestock, Spanish Louisiana quickly attracted a wide variety of new settlers from the Canary Islands, the English colonies and Malaga. Between 1765 and 1768 more than 1,500 Acadians, previously displaced from their homes in eastern Canada also arrived in the region of the lower Mississippi. They were the first of what became a steady stream of French immigrants that would continue for the next twenty years. Thanks to the influx of new settlers, between 1766 and 1788 the white population of Louisiana increased from 11,000 to over 42,000.[4] Ternant was likely an early participant in this influx of French immigrants, attracted by the opportunity to acquire land at little or no expense and begin a new life.

The details of Ternant's first visit to the Caribbean and Louisiana, his itinerary, how long he spent in any one location or his activities, if they exist, have yet to be uncovered, but it seems likely given his great interest in natural history that he used some of his time to explore as much of the region as possible, in search of new specimens of plants and animals or to investigate the many strange peoples native to the area. In Louisiana such wanderings would have taken him north up the Mississippi, past the Alsatian communities on the German Coast, beyond Pointe Coupee, and perhaps even as far as the French settlement on the Arkansas river. Wherever he traveled and whatever his experience however, Ternant was impressed enough with the colony's potential that later he would return with his younger brother.

One result of these years spent in traveling and one that would have important consequences for Ternant in the future, was his increasing fluency in English. By the spring of 1777, a full year before he arrived at Valley Forge, Jean had acquired a through command of the language. He both spoke and wrote it with ease. In large measure this fluency was the result of an interest in languages but also of the opportunity to use English on a regular basis afforded by his wide ranging travels. During the period between 1770 and 1776 English merchants dominated trade with New Orleans and Jean may have used any early instruction and familiarity with the language to facilitate business dealings with them and in the process improve his conversational skill. His interest in foreign languages was not limited to English however. Years later, during his military service in the United Provinces, Ternant would again use the occasion of his extended stay in that country as an opportunity to learn Dutch.[5]

How Ternant may have managed to finance his journeys during this period also remains undetermined but there were numerous positions that would have facilitated his travels. He could very well have served as a clerk to a merchant, or as a secretary to a government official. Given his talent for mathematics, his language skills and his experiences in the family business during his adolescence, Ternant would have been well placed to act as an agent for any company dealing in international trade. In this capacity, using whatever financial resources he may have received from the settlement of his father's estate, he could have invested in commodities or products for shipment and then served as cargo master, responsible for the sale of the cargo at its destination and the purchase of freight for the return voyage. In this fashion, and if successful, Jean would have provided himself with a respectable return on his investment. At the same time he would have been in a position to establish numerous business and personal relationships in the commercial community, travel widely with little expense and gain valuable experience in the wider world.

While Ternant was exploring Louisiana, improving his English and becoming more self-reliant, the decade long political dispute between England and its North American colonies grew evermore contentious and finally, exploded into armed conflict. Beginning with the Stamp Act controversy in 1765, the English Parliament's efforts to assert its legislative authority in the American colonies met increasing resistance. The collision of imperial and local interests that had been marked in the beginning by letters of protest and organized boycotts of British goods escalated over ten years time into mob violence directed against both individuals and property and by the spring of 1775 into a military confrontation that rapidly became a war for independence with serious international implications. For Ternant the rebellion of England's North American colonies was not only an inspiration, it also encouraged him to make a second attempt for a military career. In a very real sense the American conflict would change the course of Jean's life.

As relations between England and her North American colonies deteriorated and armed resistance became almost certain, colonial leaders quickly realized that the colonies had little in the way of military resources. If hostilities erupted they would find themselves at a distinct disadvantage. Arms, ordinance and especially gunpowder were all in short supply and there were few domestic sources. To meet this urgent need, as early as the summer of 1774, the leaders of local patriot groups in the various colonies prepared for the coming conflict. They seized government arsenals and storehouses and organized a secret trade with European merchants to purchase military supplies. The clandestine international commerce in arms and gunpowder that developed was widespread and on a large scale. It involved merchants from all across Europe; Amsterdam and Rotterdam, Hamburg and Liège, Nantes and Bordeaux, Lisbon and Cádiz and their respective agents in Saint Domingue, St. Eustatius, Martinique and Louisiana. Between 1774 and the end of 1775 French merchants alone had provided 32 million livres worth of military supplies.[6] With his political leanings, fluency in English and his presence in the Caribbean, it is not difficult to imagine that Ternant was well aware of the illicit arms trade and may well have been an active participant. However, even if not directly involved, he certainly was in a position to have acquired reliable and current information of events taking place during the first two years of the rebellion.

At some point in 1776 Ternant returned to France to put his affairs in order and make the necessary arrangements regarding both returning to Louisiana with his younger brother and for enlisting in the American rebellion. His plan called for him to first escort his nineteen-year-old half-brother, Claude Vincent Ternant, to New Orleans, introduce him to the region and insure that he was properly settled. Then with Claude Vincent safely established, Jean would have the freedom to join the American cause and pursue his dream of becoming a military engineer. If it proved impossible for Ternant to achieve his ambition he could always return to Louisiana and rejoin his brother or if events proved deadly, Jean would at least have had the satisfaction of knowing that his brother's future was secure and that he had fulfilled his family responsibilities.

Upon his return to France and following a brief visit to Damvillers, Jean, accompanied by his younger brother, traveled to Paris and then Versailles where he successfully obtained meetings with two of the royal government's leading ministers, Claude-Louis, comte de Saint Germain, the Secretary of War and Jean-Frederic Phelypeaux de Pontchartrain, comte de Maurepas, Louis XVI's mentor and principal advisor. Although the means whereby he gained access to these particular officials remains a mystery (most likely he carried letters of introduction from someone with social significance or political connections), Ternant certainly would have been a welcomed source of up-to-date information on the course of the American rebellion and this fact may have been the deciding factor in explaining his success.

In what were probably separate meetings Ternant received both sympathy and encouragement. Both ministers, though advanced in years, were determined to promote France's strategic interests and as Anglophobes were in favor of France taking advantage of England's difficulties in North America by providing assistance to the American insurgents. Maurepas in particular would also have been interested in the details of Ternant's recent experience in Louisiana. As a former Secretary of State for the Marine, he had been directly involved in promoting French maritime trade and advancing colonial interests. He would have been predisposed to lend his support to Ternant.

During the interviews at either the imposing *Hôtel de la Guerre* or the palace itself, Ternant informed the ministers of his plan to return to Louisiana and his intention afterward to join the American rebellion, and he requested their approval. He also volunteered his services to the royal government. According to Ternant's later account, Maurepas and Saint Germain both approved of his ambition and zeal, and accepted his offer of service by engaging him to use his connections in North America to obtain information regarding the course of the rebellion and convey it to the then recently appointed French trade commissioners at New Orleans, who were in charge of coordinating the secret assistance being provided to the American rebels. Finally, both ministers assured Ternant that the king would look with kindness on his efforts and indicated that after the war he could expect to obtain a rank in the service of France comparable to that which he had held in the army of the United States.[7] Unfortunately, by the time Ternant returned to France in the summer of 1784 both Maurepas and Saint Germain were dead and whatever promise they had made would not be not honored.

In spite of Ternant's inability to benefit from the promises made to him there is little reason to doubt his account. Agreements of this nature were standard practice in the royal government of the period and it was expected that individuals would request either monetary or career advancement rewards for service. Numerous agents asked for and received such benefits. Julien-Alexandre Archard de Bonvouloir, a twenty-six-year-old former soldier, who was sent in secret to Philadelphia in 1775 to meet with the members of the Committee of Secret Correspondence made several requests prior to his mission. For his effort Bonvoulior requested payment of 200 *louis d'or*, a brevet as lieutenant in the infantry and a letter acknowledging that the king was aware of his service. Vergennes granted the requests and in addition gave Bonvouloir permission to join the Continental army if he so desired.[8]

Another agent with an even more extensive list of demands was Michel Chartier Lotbiniere. In April 1776 this French Canadian volunteered to serve as the representative of the royal government to the American Congress in return for being commissioned colonel, given the cross of the Royal and Military Order of Saint-Louis, awarded the title of marquis and provided with enough money to fund his journey to Philadelphia.[9] In spite of having almost nothing to show for his effort Lotbiniere's requests were later granted. The promise made to Ternant was quite modest by comparison and moreover, its fulfillment was entirely dependent upon the degree of his success.

The rebellion in America, which was to provide Ternant with another opportunity for a military career, had come as no surprise to the leaders of France's *corps diplomatique*. Even before the conclusion of the Seven Years' War French policy makers had viewed England's North American possessions as an area of potential difficulties and had begun making preparations to take advantage of any future developments there to restore France's great power status. In addition to refurbishing and enlarging the royal navy and reinforcing its colonial possessions, an important part of the Bourbon monarchy's preparedness program also included sending secret agents to visit North America, to report on the political situation and collect information concerning the possibility of a rebellion. Etienne-François, comte de Stainville, later duc de Choiseul, the Secretary of State for Foreign Affairs, began the program in the 1760s and Charles Gravier, comte de Vergennes, the Secretary of State for Foreign Affairs after 1774, continued the policy as he prepared France to take a more active role once fighting between England and its colonies had begun.[10] Following the battles at Lexington and Concord and the siege of Boston Vergennes initiated a dual policy of maintaining diplomatic relations with England while at the same time engaging French merchants to provide much needed military supplies and equipment to the American rebels.

From the very beginning of the war for independence the American Congress had viewed France, Britain's traditional adversary, as the most likely source of assistance and in the summer of 1776 dispatched Silas Deane, a Connecticut lawyer and merchant with business links to the French merchant community, as its secret representative to Versailles with instructions to purchase military supplies. Deane not only enjoyed ties to French commercial firms in Bordeaux, Nantes, Harve and L'Orient that were already involved in providing supplies to the American rebellion, he was also part of an international commercial and land-speculating group that included among its numbers such influential figures as the Parisian banker, Ferdinand Grand, Conrad Alexandre Gerard, the under-secretary for foreign affaires who would become Vergennes's liaison for dealing with American agents and Jacques-Donatien Le Ray Chaumont, a wealthy, well connected merchant who would later provide lodging for Franklin and Deane at his estate at Passy.[11]

Deane had arrived in Paris in July of 1776 alone, unable to speak a word of French and armed only with a bundle of paper currency issued by the Congress and several letters of introduction from Benjamin Franklin. During the next five months however, he worked to foster and coordinate French assistance with considerable success. The ever-cautious Vergennes, taking care not to compromise French neutrality, soon arranged a series of secret meetings between the American agent and entrepreneurs anxious to provide military supplies and make a profit in the process. In August Deane met with the secret government agent, arms merchant and principal advocate for French assistance, Pierre Augustin Caron de Beaumarchais and two prominent officers of the royal artillery, Lieutenant-General Jean-Baptiste Vaquette de Gribeauval and his aide, Lieutenant-Colonel Philippe-Charles-Jean-Baptiste Tronson du Coudray, to arrange for the acquisition and transfer of ordinance from royal arsenals. In addition to obtaining munitions, military stores and artillery, Deane also was persuaded by his French collaborators of the necessity to recruit technical specialists from the artillery and engineers to accompany the equipment. Although Deane's authorization from Congress was limited to acquiring the service of several engineers, he gave in to the pressure from other officers and began to enlist increasing numbers of military personnel and provide them with commissions. Later, Deane's efforts would become a source of embarrassment and controversy, but at the time the Congress itself had already engaged in such enlistments. By December 1776 at least nineteen French officers had been commissioned, eight of them in the artillery and engineers.[12] In Paris the news that Deane was recruiting individuals with engineering experience spread quickly and provided Ternant with the opportunity his was looking for.

Having already obtained the approval of Maurepas and Saint Germain for his plan to join the American insurgency, Ternant made the effort to establish contact with the American representatives in Paris and if possible, gain their support as well. Once again he somehow succeeded. In spite of police surveillance and government arrest orders for individuals openly declaring they were joining the American rebellion, Jean was able to obtain an interview with the recently arrived international celebrity, Benjamin Franklin.

At the time of their meeting Franklin, a thickset, balding and bespectacled septuagenarian, was still recuperating from the hardships of his resent early winter crossing of the North Atlantic. He was one of three commissioners appointed by the Committee of Secret Correspondence of the Continental Congress charged with negotiating treaties of alliance and commerce with France and with continuing Silas Deane's work of acquiring material aid and financial assistance for the war effort.[13]

The most well known of the three commissioners; Franklin's reputation was well established on both sides of the Atlantic. In Europe, in addition to being hailed as an inventor, scientist, philosopher and an "American Prometheus" the New World's preeminent figure of the Enlightenment, Franklin was also viewed as the embodiment of his country's struggle for liberty and independence. As news of his arrival spread it caused a sensation at every level of French society.

After a three-week journey from the coast Franklin had arrived in Paris on the early afternoon of Saturday, 21 December 1776 and settled into rooms at the Hôtel d'Entragues on rue de l'Universite, where his friend and fellow commissioner, Silas Deane had an apartment. Almost at once he was besieged by visitors and confronted with requests for letters of introduction from young French officers, eager to take advantage of the fighting in North America to advance their military careers. Irritated by the surveillance of both English spies and the French police and hoping to escape the flood of petitioners as well, Franklin, sometime between Christmas and the first week of January moved to the Hôtel d'Hambourg on rue Jacob in the *faubourg* Saint Germain.

Although the details surrounding Ternant's interview with Franklin were not recorded, the little evidence that does exist suggests that the meeting occurred in Paris at Franklin's apartment at the Hôtel d'Entragues and that it took place sometime between the 22nd and the 29th of December and prior to Franklin's secret meeting with the Spanish ambassador.

The well-mannered young man who arrived at Franklin's door that winter day had turned twenty-five only a few weeks before and was completely unknown. He had no social prominence, little wealth, and unlike his famous host, had no accomplishments to his credit. Nevertheless, at a time when practically everyone of note in Paris was queuing up at Franklin's door and most were being turned away, Jean's request for an interview was granted.

There can be little doubt that Ternant owed his good fortune to a recommendation from a prominent figure, probably someone associated with the royal government and most likely either Maurepas or Saint Germain; an introduction from either minister would have commanded Franklin's immediate attention. Always maneuvering to curry favor with influential individuals, Franklin was usually inclined to endorse requests from those who were highly placed.[14] An equally reasonable explanation for Ternant being received however must also be that he claimed some knowledge of military engineering. The American commissioners had been specifically authorized to enlist the services of at least two officers with such experience and Ternant's reception was undoubtedly aided by Franklin's belief that he might be a candidate for an engineering post in the Continental army. Discovering in the course of their meeting that Ternant spoke fluent English, was already scheduled to travel to Louisiana as an agent for the royal government and was committed to the cause of liberty and American independence gave Franklin additional reasons to agree to the young Frenchman's request for letters of introduction.[15]

Ternant's meeting with Franklin was an early and minor incident in the ever-expanding program of enlisting volunteers to serve in the Continental army. By late December 1776 several other much more significant agreements had already been arranged. Beaumarchais's liaison to the royal arsenals, the well-connected Tronson du Coudray, had successfully arranged with Silas Deane for the transfer of numerous pieces of artillery and had been rewarded for his effort with a commission as a major general in the Continental army. He also had been named director of its artillery and engineers. Along with a contingent of forty officers and specialists, Du Coudray had already sailed for America in company with the first of Beaumarchais's arms shipments.

During the same period Johann de Kalb, a veteran with considerable military experience and a client of the comte de Broglie, also had successfully negotiated a contract with Deane for commissions for himself and a group of fourteen officers that included the marquis de Lafayette. Finally, by mid December the Secretary of War, Saint Germain had selected Colonel Louis Lebgue Duportail to head a four-man group of engineers and had recommended him to the American commissioners. In February 1777, following a series of meetings with Deane and Franklin, Duportail accepted the terms of a contract for himself and his three companions that provided each with one rank higher in American service than that which they currently held in the royal army.

Unfortunately for Ternant, almost immediately after his meeting with Franklin, he fell "dangerously ill" and was not alone in his misfortune. Shortly after Christmas Silas Deane also became sick, afflicted with flu-like symptoms and a high fever that disabled him into the New Year. Ternant's illness incapacitated him as well and it came at an inopportune moment, delaying his departure and hindering his effort to purchase the supplies necessary for the voyage to Louisiana. More important, his sickness, and perhaps Deane's as well, may also have contributed to his failure to obtain the letters of introduction promised by Franklin. It was a setback that a year later would have serious consequences for Jean.

As soon as he was sufficiently recovered and able to travel Ternant and his brother left Paris for Bordeaux. Three hundred miles southwest of Paris and depending upon the weather or other circumstances a five- or six-day journey by stagecoach, Bordeaux in the 1770s was France's principal Atlantic port for international trade, especially that with the French islands in the Caribbean.[16] Situated on the Garonne River some sixty miles from the sea, the city was a rapidly expanding commercial center, with 100,000 inhabitants, among them some 1200 merchants and traders.[17] Because of Bordeaux's strong commercial ties to the Caribbean and the fact that his previous voyage to Louisiana probably originated there, it is quite likely that Ternant was already familiar with commercial interests in the city. Upon arrival he immediately established contact with "friends" at Messrs. Pecholiers freres Negotiants and began to make the necessary arrangements for his voyage.[18] On 9 January Jean, claiming to be a resident of Louisiana, signed the *Certificate d'identité et de catholique* required of all subjects leaving France. In addition to recognizing the supremacy of the Catholic religion the document also provided a physical description of the two brothers and the reason for their travel (on business). In addition, the certificate also indicated that they had secured passage to Cap-Français in Saint Domingue on Captain Louis Gruillocheau's 330-ton merchant vessel, *Prudent*.[19]

On the eve of his embarkation Ternant, in a short note to Franklin, informed the American commissioner of his departure and indicated that he would wait for six weeks at Cap-Français. Franklin was requested to send the promised letters of introduction to the Pecholier brothers and they would forward them on the next ship. On Wednesday, 15 January 1777 *Prudent*, with a cargo of 800 barrels of flour and five passengers that included Jean and his brother, sailed for Saint Domingue.[20]

On its voyage to the West Indies *Prudent* followed the traditional route and standard procedures. Avoiding the Marguerite shoals at the entrance to the Garonne and dropping the pilot south of the Cordouan lighthouse, the ship worked its way across the Gulf of Gascony, passed along the coast of Portugal and eventually reached the Canary Islands. From there the North Equatorial currant and trade winds from the northeast pushed the merchantman across the wide expanse separating the coast of Africa from the islands in the West Indies. Sometime in mid to late March Ternant reached Cap-Français, the first stage on his voyage to Louisiana.[21]

Often referred too as the "Paris of the Antilles," Cap-Français by 1777 was the largest and most impressive French city in the Caribbean. With a quarter of its 1,300 buildings multi-storied and in stone with tiled roofs, wide straight streets with sidewalks and numerous squares, the city was as much European as it was colonial. Located on the north coast of Hispaniola at the head of the *Plaine de Nord*, a densely populated and rich agricultural area devoted to the production of sugar cane and coffee, Cap-Français was the colony's most important entrepot. The city was also a rapidly growing administrative and judicial center.[22] As Saint-Domingue's principal port, Cap-Français was also strategically positioned to act as a major staging area for the transfer of supplies sent from France to aid the American rebellion. Beaumarchais's trading company, Roderigue Hortalez and Co. maintained an agent there as did the Secret Committee of the Congress.[23] By the time Ternant and his brother arrived the brisk business in secret aid to America begun in 1774 was flourishing.

It was at Cap-Français during the first week of April that Ternant encountered the individual who later would become his comrade in arms and closest American friend, John Laurens. The son of a prominent South Carolina merchant and plantation owner and an ardent supporter of the American cause, Laurens was on his way home from Europe and eager to join the fighting.[24] Although their chance meeting seemed of little importance at the time, Laurens came away impressed by Ternant's knowledge of military matters, his easy manners and fluency in English; so much so that a year later at Valley Forge he would recall their earlier conversations and champion Ternant's effort to obtain a commission in the Continental army.[25]

That Ternant and Jack Laurens later became close friends is easy to understand. Although they had very different personalities the two men had much in common. They shared an interest in natural history. Both had benefited from overseas travel and years spent outside their own country. They spoke each other's language with ease and they were close in age, Laurens was twenty-two and Ternant three years older. They were well educated and committed to many of the progressive social and political ideals associated with the Enlightenment. Finally, their recent experiences were almost identical. Both men had recently met with Franklin in Paris, traveled to Bordeaux and sailed for Cap-Français; Laurens embarking on January 28, only two weeks after Jean. Shortly after their meeting Laurens and Ternant went their separate ways. Laurens left Cap-Français for Charlestown and home, while Jean made arrangements to continue his voyage to Louisiana.

By the time Jean and his younger brother reached Louisiana, probably in the early summer before the onset of the hurricane season, both the economic and political situation in the Spanish colony had changed dramatically. The economy was much improved. In July of 1776 France and Spain had finally concluded a convention that reduced trade restrictions between the French Antilles and Louisiana and provided for the appointment of two French trade commissioners at New Orleans to supervise the increased commercial activity. They would also coordinate French and Spanish efforts to aid the American insurgents.

During the same summer the governor of Louisiana had responded to an urgent request from Virginia and sent 9,000 pounds of gunpowder to Fort Pitt, inaugurating a program of Spanish aid to the American rebels that would continue to grow in importance. Finally, in the spring of 1777, governor Bernardo de Galvez moved directly against English mercantile interests in the colony by capturing English vessels on the lower Mississippi, a measure that marked the end of their commercial dominance in the region. Galvez then began to collect a military

John Laurens, miniature by Charles Willson Peale, 1780. The impulsive, glory-driven son of Henry Laurens, a president of the Continental Congress, John was Ternant's first American advocate and closest friend during the war for Independence (National Portrait Gallery, Smithsonian Institution/Art Resource, New York).

force that would enable him to take a more active role in any future conflict with England.²⁶

After fulfilling his official duty and delivering whatever information he had recently acquired to the trade commissioners and provided them with the current news regarding the American rebellion that he had learned in Saint Domingue, Ternant devoted the remainder of his time in Louisiana to introducing his brother to the region and ensuring that Claude Vincent would be able to take care of himself after he departed.

At some point, probably sometime in the late fall of 1777, Ternant left Louisiana and there is no evidence that indicates that he ever saw his brother again. Several comments contained in letters to his American agent, George Simpson, written in the early 1820s reveal that Jean had corresponded with Claude Vincent but none of the letters from either of the brothers to the other have been discovered.²⁷ After being replaced as minister and recalled in 1793, Ternant elected to remain in the United States and didn't return to France until the summer of 1801. During those eight years he had both the opportunity and the ability to return to Louisiana and may have done so but once again there is no record to confirm it.

After his brother's departure Claude Vincent Ternant took up residence at False River on the west bank of the Mississippi north of New Orleans, in what later became Pointe Coupee parish. He married in 1784, and over time became a successful planter and one of the principal landowners in the area.²⁸ Purchasing property one small parcel at a time, by 1803 and the acquisition of Louisiana by the United States, Claude had grown wealthy through the production of indigo and cotton and had emerged as one of the leading citizens in the False River community. Moreover, by 1788 he also had become the father of three children, a daughter, Marie Basilee, born in 1785, and two sons, Claude Vincent *fils* born in 1786 and St. Ville in 1788.

Every bit as ambitious, enterprising and diligent a bourgeois as his older brother, Claude Vincent was determined to better his condition and succeeded in doing so. When he died in January 1818, shortly before his sixty-first birthday, his estate, which included 159 slaves, was valued at over one hundred and forty-eight thousand dollars. In the 1830s the Ternant family was still prominent in the Pointe Coupee area and the eleven children of Claude's daughter, Marie Basilee, would become, as Jean's grand nieces and nephews, the principal financial beneficiaries of his final will and testament.²⁹

III

Valley Forge—Philadelphia
March 1778–September 1778

After leaving Louisiana Ternant made his way northward and ultimately found his way to the winter encampment of the Continental army at Valley Forge. His path there and the circumstances of his journey are not known, but by the first week of March 1778, at the latest, he had made his appearance.[1] By the time of his arrival conditions in the camp were beginning to improve and the worst of the supply shortages that had plagued the army from December through February had been partially relieved. The controversies however, that had swirled around Washington regarding his leadership during the 1777 campaign remained unresolved and the much-needed reorganization of the army had still not been initiated. Since late January, at Washington's request, a committee from the Congress had been in camp reviewing plans to correct the administrative failures that had caused so many of the problems during the winter and there was a general consensus regarding the appointment of an Inspector General who would be delegated to develop new training procedures and standardize army drill. In late February the first drafts of new recruits began to arrive and the army slowly began to increase its numbers and prepare for the campaign season to come. The weather however was wretched. Rain beginning in late February became almost continuous during the first two weeks of March.[2] Under these weather conditions both logistics and travel were difficult and living conditions at Valley Forge uncomfortable at best.

Although historians have usually linked Ternant's appearance in America with either Lafayette or Steuben, Jean, in fact, arrived at the Valley Forge encampment alone and independent of an association with any particular individual.[3] As a man of some means he probably arrived on horseback and given the fact that he was an experienced traveler, Jean almost certainly carried bills of exchange to be drawn on merchants in nearby Philadelphia. Plainly dressed and speaking English, there was little to distinguish him from other visitors to the camp. Unfortunately, he arrived without the letters of introduction from Franklin that would have established him as a "man of character" and facilitated his reception.[4]

The lack of a recommendation from a known source was a serious social liability for travelers during the period and for Ternant it was one of several factors that combined to undermine his effort to obtain a position as an officer in the Continental army's corps of engineers. Other than his slight acquaintance with Jack Laurens, now serving as one of General Washington's aides de camp, there was no one at Valley Forge who could personally vouch for him.

Fortunately for Jean, Laurens remembered him from Cap-Français and worked to persuade his fellow officers of his friend's good character and merit. Laurens also was probably responsible for introducing Ternant to another recent arrival that had impressed Jack with his military knowledge, the Prussian veteran and soon to be Inspector General of the Continental army, Friedrich Wilhelm von Steuben. Equally important as well, Jack recommended Ternant to his father, Henry Laurens, then serving as president of the Continental Congress.[5] Over the course of the next seven months it would be the influence of these three that enabled Ternant, after many disappointments, to finally obtain a commission in the Continental army and begin a military career.

In truth, Ternant was most fortunate in the stature of his supporters. Steuben's professional expertise was unmatched and his recommendations regarding Ternant's abilities were highly regarded in both the army and Congress. Jack Laurens was a prominent member of Washington's military family, distinguished for his courage and loyalty and his friendship with Ternant also worked to Jean's advantage. Finally, Henry Laurens was well placed to assist with his influence. The fifty-four-year-old president of Congress was a well-respected figure. One of the wealthiest men in North America, Laurens's social status and political prominence provided Ternant with a friend in high places that could hardly be equaled. A successful wholesale merchant, former slave trader and an owner of eight plantations spread over South Carolina and Georgia, Henry Laurens was both sober and hardworking, and his favor and patronage were of considerable value.

As was the case years earlier when he attempted to gain admission to *L'École du génie* however, the timing of Ternant's arrival at Valley Forge proved unfortunate. He was among the last of the foreign volunteers to offer his services and by the spring of 1778 an atmosphere of resentment and hostility toward foreigners already existed among American officers. With the experience of recent events fresh in their minds most of the leaders of the Continental army, Washington among them, were opposed to employing foreigners in positions of authority. And it wasn't only army officers that were angry. For the past two years the Continental Congress had been embarrassed by the steadily increasing number of mostly French officers demanding conformation of their commissions and positions in the Continental army granted them by the American emissaries in France. James Lovell, one of the representatives from Massachusetts who had been designated chairman of the Committee of Foreign Applications primarily because he was fluent in French, had exhausted his patience and claimed to have ruined his health dealing with their demands.[6]

Although there had been numerous foreign volunteers at Morristown in the winter of 1776-1777, the first large contingent of foreign soldiers, a group of more than fifty individuals under the general direction of Tronson du Coudray, arrived in Philadelphia in the late spring of 1777. Several individuals from this group would go on to serve with distinction, but there were many others whose actions and attitudes would only antagonize American sensibilities and generate increasing resentment. Tronson du Coudray, before his untimely death in September, had proved a divisive figure, clashing with the Congress, Washington and other French officers. It was Thomas Conway however, that would prove the most repugnant to American officers. A forty-four-year-old Irish-born French colonel and a determined disciplinarian who had proven his worth in the fighting at Brandywine and Germantown, Conway nevertheless managed to alienate American officers with disparaging remarks, a condescending attitude and his outspoken criticism of Washington's military abilities that bordered on insubordination. At Valley Forge he would be identified as one of the central figures among a group opposed to Washington's leadership of the army.[7]

In early July a second group of French officers headed by Johann de Kalb that included Lafayette arrived. Because of the problems with Tronson du Coudray's company however, the new arrivals, with the exception of Lafayette, found the environment already inhospitable; the Congress refused to honor their commissions and encouraged them to return to France. The vast majority of both groups of "volunteers" were ill equipped by both attitude and education for service in America. Few spoke English with any competence, many were condescending toward Americans in general and American officers in particular, considering them ill-disciplined amateurs, and almost all of them were confounded by the American culture of equality.[8] American officers, acutely sensitive regarding questions of seniority and status, responded to the newcomers with outrage and threats of resignation.

Notwithstanding the poisoned atmosphere regarding foreigners among members of Congress and American officers at Valley Forge, Ternant's immediate concern was to persuade both General Washington and the head of the army's engineer corps, Brigadier-General Louis Lebgue Duportail, of his military abilities.

Since November 1777 the engineers in the Continental army had been under the direction of a thirty-four-year-old graduate of the engineering school at Mézières, Louis Le Begue de Presle Duportail. Born into a family of the minor nobility, Duportail in 1776 had gained prominence by helping to prepare new regulations for the *corps du génie* that were part of Saint Germain's program of military reform. Primarily because of his work, in January 1777 the Secretary of War recommended that Duportail head a four-man contingent of royal engineers that would be granted official leave to serve in the American army. In March, two months after Ternant had sailed from Bordeaux, Duportail and his three companions, Jean-Baptiste-Joseph de Laumoy, Jean-Baptiste Gouvion and Louis-Guillaume-Servais Deshayes de La Radiere, traveling under assumed names, embarked from Nantes on their journey to North America. In mid May they arrived at Cap-Français and by early July had presented their credentials to the Congress at Philadelphia.[9]

Socially conservative by inclination and austere, serious, remote and not overly friendly with fellow officers by nature, Duportail nevertheless proved an excellent choice for service in America. Highly intelligent, with the ability to communicate in English, he was an experienced engineer with pronounced, if somewhat controversial, ideas regarding the proper role for engineers in military operations; concepts that emphasized engineers being actively employed in field operations rather than with the construction and defense of fortresses.[10] He and Washington were well matched by both temperament and their sense of duty; together they provided the Continental army a high level of leadership and military expertise.

The most pressing problem Duportail faced at Valley

Portrait of Louis Le Begue de Presle Duportail by Charles Willson Peale, probably from life, ca. 1781–1784. Stern, austere and jealous of his prerogatives, Duportail was a graduate of L'École du génie at Mézières and commanded the Corps of Engineers in the Continental army (courtesy Independence National Historical Park).

Forge and one which at first portended positive for Ternant, was the small number of qualified engineers in service; far to few to meet the demands for their special talents. In January, shortly before Ternant arrived in camp. Duportail had begun a search for individuals with some of the necessary expertise that would permit them to serve as engineers. He soon discovered that an officer at nearby York, formerly a member of Tronson Du Coudray's group and listed as an engineer was available and requested that this individual be added to his command. In a letter to Washington, Duportail related that although the officer in question, Jean Louis Ambroise de Genton de Villefranche, was not an engineer and did not pretend to be one, he had "studied geometry, understood surveying and drawing and therefore ought to be useful to us."[11] A thirty-year-old noble and former officer in the cavalry, de Villefranche was eventually commissioned and served as an engineer for the remainder of the war, mostly at West Point.

During the same period Duportail also acquired the services of another individual with much better qualifications. In spite of being a *roturier*, Jean-Bernard Bourg Gauthier de Murnan had considerable military and engineering experience. He had prepared for the entrance examination to Mézières, served in the *garde de corps* of the comte d'Artois, Louis XVI's youngest brother, and with a recommendation from Voltaire no less, spent three years as an engineer in the Russian army.[12] In a letter written on 23 February, recommending him for Washington's consideration, Duportail explained:

> M. de Murnan ... has gone through the necessary studies for entering into the corps of engineers in France—he even obtained his license for examination, which is never granted until satisfactory papers are delivered at the war office setting forth that the person is of a noble family. France does not receive into the corps, which is charged with the precious trust of her fortified places and everything relative to the defense of our frontiers, any other subjects than those whose birth and education are pledges of their sentiments and conduct. This license is at the same time proof of his studies, because it can only be had in consequence of certificates given by professors who are liable to be called upon—The reason this gentleman was not admitted was because the arrangement of the minister underwent a considerable change at that time—and that after having intended to make a considerable promotion in the Corps of Engineers, he confined himself to making a very small one—This officer may be very useful here, he possesses sufficient theoretical knowledge to make him an exceedingly good Engineer.[13]

As both his own history and the above letter indicate, Duportail was extremely sensitive on the subject of an engineer's social status.[14] It seems however that in this case at least, Duportail did not concern himself that de Murnan was a commoner. He simply accepted the *lettre d'exame* as proof that de Murnan was a gentleman.

While de Murnan's social status was clouded and seems never to have been questioned, such would not be the case regarding Ternant. In spite of the need for additional engineers Duportail was unwilling to recommend Ternant for a commission. Jack Laurens's explanation that "party differences were an invincible obstacle" is vague but must be a reference to the social prejudices that were so much a part of French thinking during the period and point to the strong feelings that Duportail harbored against *roturiers* becoming officers in the engineers.[15]

Unfortunately for Ternant, Washington also had serious misgivings. Usually quite formal in his dealings with most individuals and ever mindful of social proprieties and the importance of correct behavior, Washington's suspicions were aroused by Ternant's lack of letters of introduction. In 1775 he had confided to a friend that "no gentleman that is not well known, ought to come here without letters of introduction as it puts me in an awkward situation with respect to my conduct towards them."[16] Without letters of introduction Washington found it difficult to evaluate a person's capabilities and in his role of Commander-in-chief he was concerned about Ternant's lack of practical experience. On 21 March, in response to what appears to have been a letter from Steuben in support of Ternant's application for a commission, and quite likely already aware of Duportail's objections, Washington outlined his own reservations regarding the appointment of the young Frenchman as an engineer.

> Knowing it to be the intention of Congress to employ no more foreigners except such as come under special engagements or whose recommendations and former services speaks so powerfully as scarce leave a choice, I could not undertake to give Mr. T any assurance of a permanent appointment, much less the promise of rank without authority of Congress. Nor could I stand justified upon any principal for employing a stranger without recommendations on any other acct. than his profound knowledge in the business intended for him to execute.... Mr. T—informed me that he had never been in any other Service than in the Engineering departmt. If so I think he must be much at a loss in practice let his theoretical knowledge be what it will, and if this should be the case would lay us both open to censure....[17]

In spite of these objections however, Washington ended his letter by offering to appoint Ternant to another position, that of sub-inspector or assistant drill instructor, under Steuben's direction, with the pay of about 60 dollars, the monthly salary of a Lieutenant colonel of infantry at the time and far above the 6 dollar a month pay for a soldier in the infantry.[18] Jean may not have received an appointment as an officer but his pay definitely established him as a gentleman.

Five days later, after what appears to have been a week of confusion in Ternant's mind regarding his future, Washington informed him that he was fully prepared to appoint Jean to a position as a sub-inspector and added as a mark of encouragement, that he was "persuaded it will afford much relief to Baron Steuben and benefit the Service."[19] Washington later informed the President of Congress of the hiring of "Mr. Ternant, a French gentleman" as a sub-inspector, "the reason for employing him apart [from] his intrinsic merit and abilities, was his possessing the French and English languages equally, which made him a necessary assistant to the Baron de Steuben; he is content to serve without rank, until after an experiment of his abilities, Congress shall determine what he is entitled to."[20]

Friedrich Wilhelm von Steuben, Ternant's benefactor, was a forty-seven-year-old former Prussian officer with an impressive military record. A veteran of the Seven Years' War in Europe, Steuben had experienced a wide variety of military duties, service as a company officer in the Lestwitz infantry regiment, as a staff officer in Johann von Mayr's free battalion, later on staff service at the brigade level under General von Hulsen and finally as a *Quartermeister-lieutenant* on the staff of Frederick the Great. Twice wounded, Steuben had participated in many of the most famous and hard fought battles of the period; Prague, where he survived his regiment's wreck and rout, the victory at Rossbach, and the disasters at Kay and Kunnersdorf. For a brief period in 1761 he also had been a prisoner of war at Saint Petersburg. At the conclusion of the war Steuben's service in the Prussian army ended and for the next fourteen years he tried and failed to find an alternative career. The spring of 1777 found him unemployed and attempting without success to restore both his reputation and his finances.[21]

Thanks to an old acquaintance, the French Secretary of State for War, Saint Germain, who recommended his services to the American commissioners in Paris; to Beaumarchais, who paid for his passage to America, to an exaggerated resume and letters of introduction from Benjamin Franklin, and to his own open manner and willingness to serve, the Baron von Steuben had arrived in America with several companions and received an uncommonly positive reception from both members of Congress and Washington. He had arrived at Valley Forge in late February shortly before Ternant, at an opportune moment, when his training and staff expertise was most in demand and also to find in Jack Laurens and Alexander Hamilton, two of Washington's aides de camp who spoke French, individuals who appreciated his military knowledge and urged his appointment to the post of Inspector General.

It was Ternant's luck that Steuben was unable to communicate in English. To overcome this obvious handicap to an American appointment, Beaumarchais in Paris had introduced Steuben to a seventeen-year-old, English speaking student, Pierre Etienne Duponceau, who had agreed to accompany the Baron to America and serve as his secretary. Duponceau's work as an interpreter proved insufficient to Steuben's needs however and the fact that Duponceau was injured and sick for much of the time in March and April forced Steuben to seek additional help. Introduced to Ternant at Washington's quarters, Steuben recognized Jean's linguistic talent as a solution to his most immediate problem. He was also impressed by Jean's military knowledge and manners. Influenced perhaps by the fact that Ternant had anglicized his name and his belief that Ternant was already a citizen, Steuben requested that he be appointed to his staff.[22] Coming after the failed negotiations with Duportail and the apparent end of any chance for a military career, the offer of a position with Steuben was an opportunity Jean could not ignore. Although he would remain a civilian and serve on a strictly trial basis, there was an implied understanding that if he performed well he might be considered for a commission sometime in the near future.

The details of Ternant's early association with Steuben prior to his appointment as a sub-inspector are not known. Between March 6 and March 28 however, Ternant gained Steuben's confidence and friendship and as early as 16 March there was some discussion regarding Ternant becoming a member of Steuben' military family. It was a consideration that was helped no doubt by Ternant's frequent visits to the convalescing Duponceau during the same period. Eventually, on 14 April, Ternant took up lodging at Steuben's quarters; by this date he had been actively involved with his duties as a sub-inspector for two weeks.[23]

In addition to Ternant, Washington chose three prominent and well-educated Lieutenant Colonels from the line who were willing to serve

Frederick William Augustus, Baron von Steuben by Charles Willson Peale after Charles Willson Peale, ca. 1781–1782. The renowned "drill master" of Valley Forge and Inspector General of the Continental army, Steuben was Ternant's military mentor, patron and friend (courtesy Independence National Historical Park).

as sub-inspectors under Steuben's direction; men "whose character and abilities will give them the influence and ensure their success."[24] Francis Barber from the 3rd New Jersey regiment was a graduate of the College of New Jersey (Princeton) and as rector of the Academy at Elizabethtown had Alexander Hamilton as a student. The second officer was William Davies, from the 5th Virginia regiment. He also had graduated from the College of New Jersey and before the war had been an attorney in Norfolk, Virginia. Finally, there was John Brooks from the 8th Massachusetts. Trained as a physician, Brooks had commanded a militia company at Concord and later distinguished himself in the fighting at Saratoga.[25] Together with Ternant these three experienced officers formed the first link in Steuben's chain of military instructors.

Accepting Washington's offer to temporarily fill the office of Inspector General without rank, Steuben began his duties as a drillmaster on 17 March, personally instructing the soldiers of a "model company" in the basics of how to stand and form ranks. These lessons were then taught to other units in the army by the sub-inspectors and brigade inspectors. No part of Steuben's reforms was more important to improving the performance of the Continental army however, than his replacement of the 60 pace per minute cadenced common step with one of 75 steps per minute and his introduction of a quick step of 120 paces per minute.[26] During the 1740s the Prussian army had instituted similar cadenced marching and the speed and precision of its maneuvering became a major factor in its success under Frederick the Great.[27] A decade earlier Maurice de Saxe, Louis XV's most successful general, had observed that "the foundation of training depends upon the legs and not the arms, all mysteries of maneuver and combat is in the legs and it is to the legs that we should apply ourselves."[28]

Steuben's work at Valley Forge and his famous manual, *Regulations for the Order and Discipline of the Troops of the United States*, it must be noted, only represented the culmination of the Continental army's training however. Prior to his reorganization the militia and regular army units had utilized a variety of military exercises and tactical formations garnered from a number of handbooks. The official British Army Manual of 1764 was one source. It had been introduced throughout the colonies soon after it was published and Americans were already familiar with two other training studies, Humphrey Bland's 1727 study, *A Treatise of Military Discipline* and the *Norfolk Discipline*, a manual also produced in the 1760s for use by England's County militias. Americans also produced instructional guides for military drill. In 1776 a Philadelphia shopkeeper and former British officer, Lewis Nicola, published *A Treatise of Military Exercise calculated for the use of the Americans* for the local militia. An equally popular manual was *An Easy Plan of Discipline for a Militia*, published in 1775 by Timothy Pickering, an officer in the Salem, Massachusetts's militia. Simple, with detailed instructions pertaining to forming ranks, firing and maneuvering, and illustrated with twelve plates of diagrams Pickering's book had been adopted by Massachusetts and was also used by many units from other colonies.[29]

In addition to introducing a more rapid step for marching and maneuvering, Steuben also established a more flexible two rank battle formation and a much simpler cadenced manual of arms. Equally important he mandated the use of a column formation for marching and maneuvering and drew up instructions to govern the rapid deployment from column to line of battle. Finally, as a battlefield veteran, Steuben insisted on training in the use of the bayonet and argued for the formation of light infantry units.

During the period from mid March through the end of May, under the direction of Steuben and his team of inspectors, the Continental army's organization was recast and its tactical efficiency much improved.[30] It was in all, a remarkable achievement. Ternant's contribution to Steuben's success however remains undocumented, and given his lack of military experience, he was probably as much a student as he was an instructor. In the evenings he most likely worked along side Duponceau copying instructions for the next day's exercise. But whatever his task, Jean's intelligence, diligence and enthusiasm won de Steuben's praise.

As a civilian drill instructor employed on a trial basis and as an interpreter for Steuben, Ternant's position in the military hierarchy of the Continental army was ambiguous. He was not a common soldier and never contemplated becoming one, but neither was he an officer. His authority, if he had any at all, was limited to the drill field and to a certain degree he remained outside the regular chain of commend. As a member of Steuben's military family however, Ternant's standing as a gentleman was recognized and as a "man of character" Jean was included in the social activities of officers when off duty.

It was during evening dinners and entertainments hosted by either Washington or his various commanders that Ternant had the opportunity to make the acquaintance of and an impression on, the army's leaders, their families and any civilians visiting the camp. Able to converse easily in both English and French and talk on a variety of subjects, polite and a man of some means and experience in the world, Jean was likely well received in the mixed companies of those occasions. After dinner conversations would have provided him the ideal opportunity to establish his reputation and confirm his gentlemanly status. And for a young ambitious individual such as Ternant, being viewed as a gentleman and a man of honor with integrity and self control was the key to being accepted and eventually becoming an officer.[31]

Except for Steuben Ternant's most important ally at Valley Forge and later his closest American friend was Jack Laurens. When Jean arrived at the winter encampment Laurens was already a highly regarded member of Washington's staff and a veteran of the 1777 campaign in which he had been wounded several times and distinguished himself. Eager for a field command and the laurels victorious combat bestowed, Laurens in January 1778 had become interested in the idea of enlisting slaves as a means whereby the continuing manpower problems of the continental army might be alleviated and at the same time provide a source of troops for him to command. Laurens, influenced by friends in London, his father and the workings of his own conscience, had for sometime been uncomfortable with the moral contradictions involved between the fight for liberty and the "peculiar institution."[32] Ternant, either from his own reading or under the influence of Jack, agreed with his friend regarding the contradictions of slavery in a free society, and he became an ardent supporter of Laurens's proposal to employ former slaves as soldiers. In addition to his friendship with Jack Laurens and his increasingly close relationship with Steuben, Ternant made the acquaintance of two other individuals at Valley Forge that would later become close associates, Gouverneur Morris and Gilbert du Motier, marquis de Lafayette.

Recently turned twenty-six, Gouverneur Morris was the same age as Jean, and from February through April was one of a five member Congressional committee at Valley Forge working with Washington to reorganize the army. An energetic, intelligent lawyer from New York and an ardent admirer of Washington, Morris, in addition to his age, had much in common with Ternant. He spoke French with some skill, appreciated French culture, enjoyed society and was well educated with a fondness for mathematics. Although somewhat conservative in his political thinking, Morris's patriotism and commitment to American independence by 1778 matched those of Ternant. In addition, he also was opposed to slavery.[33] A few years later in Philadelphia and still later in Paris during the early years of the French revolution, Ternant and Morris would become close friends and colleagues and as fate would have it, both men would hold the identical diplomatic post of minister plenipotentiary of their respective governments to each other's country at the same time.

Gilbert du Motier, marquis de Lafayette, the other of Ternant's new acquaintances was not present at Valley Forge when Ternant arrived. He had returned to the camp from Albany on 23 April, after the cancellation of an ill-conceived plan to invade Canada that he had been selected to command. Six years younger than Jean and already a Major General, Lafayette was the most socially prominent and wealthiest of the foreign volunteers in the Continental army. A well-known figure at the royal court and related by marriage to one of the more prominent families in France, he was, in spite of his military inexperience also easily the most influential foreigner in American service. His close relationship with Washington in time came to symbolize the alliance between France and the United States.

Although both served for the remainder of the war, the fact that Ternant and Lafayette did not fashion anything more than a casual acquaintance during their time in America is hardly surprising. Jean was already a member of Steuben's military family when Lafayette returned to Valley Forge. Moreover, the great gulf in social standing, wealth and the military rank that separated them, added to Jean's lack of a prior military position in the Royal army precluded any close friendship. But the lack of any reference to Ternant in Lafayette's correspondence, which was filled with recommendations for French soldiers and requests for their promotion may also indicate that Ternant was a victim of his association with Steuben.

As the most experienced veteran in the Continental army Steuben had little regard for Lafayette, and the feeling may have been mutual on Lafayette's part even if not openly displayed. Lafayette's youth and lack of military experience combined with his high rank violated Steuben's sense of military propriety, an attitude that was mirrored by his aides and many others. On his part Lafayette saw Steuben as a threat, a competitor for Washington's favor, someone whose success and influence would be achieved at Lafayette's expense.[34] Lafayette's suspicions of Steuben may have made Ternant suspect in his eyes as well. It was only in the late 1780s therefore, in France and under different circumstances, that Ternant and Lafayette would establish a relationship, one based upon

Marie Joseph Paul Yves Roch Gilbert du Motier, marquis de Lafayette by Charles Willson Peale after Charles Willson Peale, ca. 1779–1780. The most famous foreign volunteer of the American war for independence and later the influential commander of the Paris National Guard during the early years of the French Revolution, Lafayette became an important supporter of Ternant's diplomatic career. (courtesy Independence National Historical Park).

being former comrades in arms and having similar political ideals. In Paris during the early years of the revolution Ternant would be identified as a member of Lafayette's circle. By then the differences in class, wealth and military rank no longer precluded the two men becoming close associates.

In May, as the ground dried and the temperature rose, the pace of activity at Valley Forge quickened. Unit drills on brigade and division level continued, additional huts were built to accommodate the increase in new recruits arriving daily and the camp's fortifications were strengthened. Official word of the formal alliance with France arrived and was celebrated on 6 May with a grand parade of the entire army using Steuben's new maneuvers. Following the ceremony Washington announced Steuben's temporary appointment as Inspector General with the rank of Major General. In early May as well, procedures for administering oaths of allegiance to "every officer who held or should thereafter hold a commission or office from the Congress" that had been ordered in February were instituted and at Washington's headquarters planning for the coming campaign began in earnest.[35] And it was also in May and as part of this increased activity that Ternant had his first combat experience in the affair at Barren Hill.

Beginning in early May the British army in Philadelphia also began to prepare for the coming campaign; troop movements and attacks on American positions increased. On 1 May a body of Pennsylvania militia numbering about six hundred was surprised and scattered and a week later a British force raided up the Delaware River and destroyed shipping between Bristol and Bordentown. In response to these developments, on 17 May, Washington ordered a reconnaissance in force to cross the Schuylkill River to gain information regarding British troop movements and re-establish an American military presence in the area. Under the command of Lafayette, a picked force of 2,200 men and five cannon was dispatched. Included in the expedition were a number of enthusiastic volunteers eager for adventure. Among them, probably chosen for their ability to serve as interpreters, were Ternant and Jack Laurens.

On 18 May Lafayette moved to a position at Barren Hill, an open plateau twelve miles north of Philadelphia and ignoring Washington's orders to not linger in one place, established a camp. Almost immediately his presence was reported to the British in Philadelphia and plans were made to surround and destroy the American force. On the evening of 19 May a force of between 5,000 and 6,000 men under General Grant marched out of the British lines. Grant was directed to place his troops in the rear of Lafayette's force and prevent it from retreating. The next morning an equally large column commanded by Lord Howe marched toward Germantown to attack the American position. In spite of the excellent plan that employed almost the entire British army in Philadelphia, its execution proved unsuccessful. Lafayette was warned in time and was able to retreat across the Schuylkill River to safety and the British returned to Philadelphia.[36] At most the incident at Barren Hill was an inconsequential skirmish with few casualties on either side and of little importance to future operations. Ternant's role in the affair or if he came under fire is not documented but he and Laurens were part of a small group of scouts that shadowed the British on their return to Philadelphia.[37]

By the time of Ternant's Barren Hill adventure, Steuben had become more confident in his protégé's loyalty, dedication and good sense and he began to take a more personal interest in Jean's career. As a mark of his increasing appreciation of his young assistant's work, Steuben charged Ternant to deliver proposals regarding arrangements for the Inspectors Department to the Congress at York and to personally represent him before the Board of War. "I wish," he wrote to Henry Laurens,

> the hon[ble] Congress would get personally acquainted with this Gentleman, whom I can't sufficiently praise, and who by his zeal and application to the service, deserves a peculiar consideration.
> I beg at the same time your Excellency would be so good as to procure him the necessary audiences without delay, not to stop operations he is charged of, and that he may join the Army as soon as possible.[38]

On 23 May, Ternant signed the required certificate of loyalty, administered by Steuben, and a week later, on 28 May, he set out from Valley Forge on the eighty mile, three day journey to the village of York.[39] Arriving on 31 May, Ternant delivered the letters he was carrying, met with Henry Laurens, the President of Congress, and gave him a detailed account of the "honorable retreat" from Barren Hill.[40] He next met briefly with the Board of War and then, since he had not been away from Valley Forge and his military duties for three months, Jean appears to have taken the opportunity and turned his attention to his own affaires. He may have met with Lazare Jean Baptiste Theveneau de Francy, Beaumarchais's personal agent to the Congress, to either borrow money or to make some other financial arrangements, but neither his official nor personal business took much time, and complying with Steuben's request, by 4 June he was on his way back to camp.

Although his journey to York brought no immediate change in his military status, Ternant's visit proved valuable. In the course of his brief stay he showed himself to be a gentleman, worthy of consideration and made himself known to those individuals who had the authority to make him an officer. In spite of the strong prejudice against foreigners among members of Congress, Ternant experienced a cordial reception. The officials he met were impressed, especially Henry Laurens. His son had previously informed him of Ternant's good character and ability and now, in a letter dated 27 May, Jack added, "you will find him a person who had read enough in books to store his mind with knowledge of various kinds ... upon the whole I am persuaded his conversation will please you, and that if you are not too much overwhelmed with business you will not regret granting him a little of your time."[41] Laurens came away from his meeting with the young Frenchman equally affected. Although he was disappointed that he had been unable to personally introduce Ternant to other delegates and was surprised by the suddenness of Jean's departure, Laurens promised Steuben that he was ready to render Ternant "any service in my power."[42]

Already pleased by early reports of Steuben's success on the drill field, the members of the Board of War were likewise impressed with Ternant's poise and articulate presentation of the Inspector General's proposals. In his letter to the Board of War describing his work to date, Steuben commended his sub-inspectors and insisted that it was "to the assistance of these gentlemen I owe the little success I have had." He was especially marked in his praise of Ternant, "who in addition to considerable military knowledge, has the greatest zeal and activity, and being already settled in this country may be regarded as a citizen. He has undertaken the department of inspection as a volunteer, and has not yet demanded rank, though he has merited it by the pains that he has taken and the progress of the brigades committed to his care."[43] Writing to Steuben in response, the Board's secretary, Richard Peters, informed him that the Board "had much and very satisfactory conversations" with Mr. Ternant "on the subject of the inspection."[44]

On his return to Valley Forge Ternant learned that

Henry Laurens by Charles Willson Peale from life, ca. 1784. A wealthy and cosmopolitan merchant from Charlestown and John Laurens's father, Henry Laurens, while servicing as a President of the Continental Congress, was a major supporter of Ternant in his effort to obtain a commission in the Continental army (courtesy Independence National Historical Park).

for the approaching campaign the sub-inspectors had been attached to the army's various divisions. His civilian status notwithstanding, Jean was assigned to Lafayette's division and instead of sub inspector duties he would act in the office of Adjunct General for the division and be responsible for the transmission of all orders.[45] Until the army abandoned its winter encampment however, Ternant continued as a member of Steuben's military family and given the Inspector General's difficulties with English, it was probably in the capacity as an interpreter that he accompanied de Steuben to a council meeting on the evening of 17 June. At the meeting Washington informed his commanders that at last the British had begun their evacuation of Philadelphia and although their plan of campaign was not yet apparent, he requested his commander's written opinions regarding what should be the Continental army's response. As is often the case when a consensus is sought, the division and brigade commanders were almost unanimous in recommending a conservative policy of wait and see.

After the meeting Ternant prepared what appears to be a first draft or a working copy of Steuben's response. The document, currently part of a private collection, is unsigned, undated but has been judged to be in Ternant's handwriting. Most curiously however, considering it was for de Steuben's consideration, it also was written in English.

> My opinion relative to the matter agitated yesterday in the Board is as follows; 1 That the intelligence received of the enemy's motions are so uncertain and so far from being satisfactory about his designs, that it would be highly imprudent to trust so far to appearances & undertake a march with the whole army, especially in several columns, whilst the enemy has according to reports such a numerous cavalry as to enable him to move rapidly & carry his point of attack either upon our position or upon one or two columns of lesser strength & to get the advantage of us by detail. Therefore I think it advisable to send out between us & the enemy a detachment of observation, which on our part will supply us with better & more positive intelligence, & on the other hand oblige the enemy to discover his intentions. That detachment consisting of 2,000 troops supported by all the cavalry that can possibly be gathered, will keep up an immediate, direct & constant correspondence with the small detachment under Gen. Maxwell & leave us no doubt about what is a passing.... This detachment can at any time join the main army in case it is likely to be engaged by any motion of the enemy; it will favor desertion which is an important object at this present juncture; & when the enemy has completed the evacuation of the city, & does not seem to lean anything else but a retirement to New York, I think it likewise advisable to follow that detachment which will be our advance guard and make a sudden and rapid march into the Jersey, with the whole army, collected in one body and without baggage which may be sent by any road on our left, & thus will always be covered. The army by keeping together will be able to follow the enemy closer, prevent his spreading & laying waste the country and lastly favor and protect desertion, which in this retreat of the enemy from such a place as Philadelphia, becomes an object of the greatest importance

for the American army & will undoubtedly prove so if duly attended to.... Nothing from the knowledge I have of the country can prevent our joining afterwards the northern army if found necessary, or taking some advantageous part of observation about Middlebury & keeping up an open correspondence with that army.... Celerity being the main object of what the army is to undertake, I think it is indispensable to remove the sick & as soon as possible, & I should say immediately.[46]

The final draft of Steuben's response followed the main points of Ternant's draft and used much of the same language but was more concise and detailed.[47]

On 18 June the British army evacuated Philadelphia, crossed the Delaware River below the city and began its march to New York City. Encumbered by a baggage train that stretched for twelve miles and plagued by sweltering heat and high humidity, a sullen and hostile countryside and the delaying tactics of a numerous American militia, Sir Henry Clinton's force could only move at a measured pace. The American army on the other hand, free of the restraints imposed by its baggage and eager for a fight, had little difficulty in catching up with the slow moving British col-

I *John Ternant Inspector of the army* do acknowledge the UNITED STATES of AMERICA to be Free, Independent and Sovereign States, and declare that the people thereof owe no allegiance or obedience to George the Third, King of Great-Britain; and I renounce, refuſe and abjure any allegiance or obedience to him; and I do *swear* that I will, to the utmoſt of my power, ſupport, maintain and defend the ſaid United States againſt the ſaid King George the Third, his heirs and ſucceſſors, and his or their abettors, aſſiſtants and adherents, and will ſerve the ſaid United States in the office of *Inspector of the army* which I now hold, with fidelity, according to the beſt of my ſkill and underſtanding.

Sworn before me Camp Valley Forge, May 23, 1778. Ternant
Steuben Maj. Genl.

John Ternant's Oath of Allegiance certificate, 1778. Sworn to at Valley Forge and signed by General von Steuben, the document verifies that Ternant anglicized his name during his service in the Continental army (National Archives and Records Administration).

umn. At this point, certain of the British army's intention to return to New York City and encouraged by his more offensive minded commanders to take advantage of the opportunity provided by Clinton's lagging withdrawal, Washington gave in to his own aggressive impulses, ignored the earlier agreed upon program of caution and made plans to attack, and if possible, bring on a general engagement.

Ternant's role in the ten days of maneuver that culminated in the battle at Monmouth Court House on 28 June 1778 was limited and unremarkable. Assigned previously to Lafayette's division, he departed from Valley Forge on the afternoon of 20 June and moved with it by easy stages into central New Jersey. Several days later on 25 June Jean was included in a contingent of 5,000 troops under Lafayette's command that was dispatched as the advance guard of the intended American attack on the retreating British, and on the morning of the 28th he was caught up in the confused retreat of the Continental troops that characterized the first stage of the battle. Later, in the afternoon, he helped Steuben rally and reform the disorganized portions of Maxwell's New Jersey brigade and Scott's detachment at Englishtown and accompanied the brigades when they returned to the battlefield in the evening.[48] Following the battle Ternant remained with the army on its march north into New York State; assigned along with another member of Steuben's staff, Pierre Charles L'Enfant, to assist the division quartermaster in establishing camps for the army. In this role he crossed the Hudson River at Kings Ferry and on 22 July camped at White Plains.

During the campaign the exercise of the inspectorship had been suspended but the complaints that had been raised in early June concerning the authority of Steuben and his sub-inspectors to command during drills, the Inspector General's place in the army's chain of command and the extent of his authority remained unresolved and continued to cause concern and discontent among the army's line officers. Already distrustful of foreign officers, the brigadier generals, in particular, were outspoken in their opposition when Steuben was employed as a temporary field commander after Monmouth. For his part Steuben had been delighted by the opportunity for a field command. Mindful of the authority exercised by staff officers and inspectors in the Prussian army and dissatisfied with being limited to a strictly administrative position on Washington's staff, he was determined to obtain the right for the Inspector General to command in the field. On 22 July Steuben departed for Philadelphia to present his case to Congress and if not satisfied with its decision, determined to resign his commission. In Steuben's absence, drill instruction was resumed under the direction of line officers but supervised by the sub-inspectors. Ternant however, was no longer a part of the department.

It was while Ternant was at White Plains that his career in the Continental army temporarily change course. After four months of being included in Steuben's military family and serving as a sub-inspector Jean was offered and he accepted a new position. On 23 July 1778 his appointment as a deputy quartermaster general was announced.[49]

At the time of Ternant's appointment the Quartermaster's Department was under the command of Major General Nathanael Greene. During the winter of 1777–78 the lack of an energetic and able Quartermaster General and the failure of Congressional oversight had been responsible for much of the hardship suffered by the army at Valley Forge. Because it was responsible for providing transportation services for the army and supplying its clothing, equipment and fuel needs, the reform of the Quartermaster operations had been the primary focus of the Congressional committee sent to Valley Forge in late January. In March General Greene had reluctantly agreed to assume the duties of Quartermaster General and immediately began to reorganize the department. By 1780 there were almost three thousand employees serving in a wide variety of offices scattered throughout the thirteen states; a large bureaucracy that included 28 deputy quartermasters general, 109 assistant deputy quartermasters general and an ever increasing number of clerks, shopkeepers, express riders, wagon masters, barracks managers and bargemen.[50]

The Quartermaster Generals operations were expensive and very inefficient under the best of conditions and with the exception of General Greene, who retained his military rank; it was almost entirely staffed with civilians. Similar to their opposition to foreigners being given commissions, officers in the Continental army also objected to Congress giving military rank to employees in the Quartermaster Generals Department and Washington agreed. On 29 May 1778 the Congress made it official and "resolved that no person thereafter appointed in the civil staff of the Continental army were to be entitled to any rank in the army by virtue of such a staff appointment."[51]

Ternant's official title was Deputy Quartermaster General for field operations, which signified that he remained attached to the army and was not assigned to any specific geographical location. As deputy he supervised the collection and distribution of supplies and consequently was in constant conflict with regimental officers whose interests were limited to their own unit's well being and were difficult for civilians to control.

Two days before Ternant's appointment General Greene had written to Washington complaining of the difficulties he faced managing the Quartermasters department and bemoaning the fact that it was "almost impossible to get good men for the conducting all parts of so complex a business."[52] It was an effort therefore to address Greene's concerns that Ternant and

III. Valley Forge—Philadelphia • 55

Robert Forsythe, one of Greene's aides de camp, were appointed.[53] Both men were well-known to Greene and neither would have been offered the appointment had there been any question regarding their ability to perform the duties of the office. As a civilian Ternant's appointment presented mo difficulties and Forsythe's rank as major, it appears, was simply disregarded.

For Ternant conditions at White Plains in August were depressing. His closest friends were absent and in spite of his determination to do his best he found little satisfaction in his new duties. Two days after Jean's appointment as deputy quartermaster, Steuben had departed for Philadelphia to present his views on the duties of the Inspector General to the Congress and he would not return until 1 September. During the first week in August Jack Laurens also left camp, accompanying a contingent of troops commanded by Generals Greene and Lafayette to Newport, Rhode Island. Ternant's letter to Steuben, two weeks after he assumed his new duties described the confusion and lack or order that reigned in the army, his growing dissatisfaction and his continuing hope for a commission.

> I visit sometime the camp of Mars which has been open since the 1st of this month. Davies and Brooks have been nominated by general orders to preside over the exercises, and it is under their auspices that your former apprentices in tactics cover themselves twice a day at least with—dust. I need not tell you that everybody acts just as he thinks proper, that the uniformity is more neglected there than ever before, and that for want of method the soldiers and officers are the more unmercifully fatigued, as no real benefit results from their drill. I hope that you will soon with your wonted success resume the direction of this department, to which you have already given the organization which it wanted so much. I should also wish that you would render to the army the important service of putting the department of marechal general de logis on a good footing. Bad order and confusion are more prevailing there than in any other have been unsuccessful and they do not even think of palliating the evil. I am always department. I continue to make observations, complaints and proposals; but hitherto I disposed to do good; to live, however, longer in this anarchy, and work much but to accomplish little, while there is so much to do if order succeeded to the confusion, I can not longer afford, and therefore, I am decided to ask General Greene, after his return from Rhode Island, either to put my department on a better footing or to look after another person to fill my place.
>
> The council of war in the case of General Lee have finally finished their work. I have read a part of his defense; it is the most stupid piece of literature and dialectics that has ever been written. His statements of facts, as well as the observations and reasoning which he develops from them, do not show an eloquent man nor a good judgment, and still less a consummate officer. As to his refutation of witnesses, it only consists in bad, would-be witty remarks, unintelligible quibbles and mean sarcasms which he tries to make stronger by declamation, so that nobody is spared.
>
> Good-bye, my dear general. Be careful in regard to your health. Continue to

enlighten Congress about their military constitution and the establishment of the inspectorship, and do not forget your promise to retain myself, the oldest of your inspectors, for whom it would be very cruel to see another man reap what he has sown."[54]

Unable to obtain any satisfaction regarding his civilian status from General Greene, Ternant at the end of August wrote his Commander-in-Chief. Committed to a well regulated and uniformly disciplined army and prevented in his own mind from contributing effectively to such an end by his civilian status, Ternant argued that without military rank he could not do his job. "Reason and persuasion," he wrote, were "useless and impractical" as a means of accomplishing anything in the army. Everything depended upon rank and as a civilian inspector and a civilian deputy in the Quartermasters department he expressed doubts about his ability to be effective.

Ternant also asked Washington for an opinion regarding his past services, advice on his future in the army and for "a testimony of my having behaved in the service of the offices entrusted to me as a well meaning member of the communities, who had used his utmost exertions, both in an out of action, to be useful, in order that after having retired to a private and rural life, nobody might question the uprightness of my public one in the army.... If on the contrary your Excellency ... should think proper to continue me in the service of those or one of these offices, I hope you'll consider the indispensable necessity of my being supplied with a rank by commission and such other means as will enable me to do the greatest good in my power." Jean closed his letter by requesting leave for a few days to attend to his private affairs in Philadelphia.[55]

Washington's response arrived four days later. He rejected Ternant's assertion that military rank was necessary in order to function effectively as a deputy quartermaster general and insisted instead that Ternant's authority "must be found in the nature of your office, not in the degree of rank you may hold." He also offered little encouragement to Jean of ever returning to the post of sub-inspector; informing him that under the plans now being considered inspectors would have to be chosen from among line officers. Washington closed by acknowledging that Ternant had distinguished himself "as an officer of intelligence, zeal and activity and have rendered valuable services" and that he would be agreeable to Ternant's continued service as a deputy quartermaster general.[56]

Ternant was now faced with a dilemma. He could not expect to return to being a sub-inspector because he was not a line officer and he was ineligible for a commission because he was serving in an office that required a civilian. His only choice was to resign and make a last appeal to the Congress in person. His reply to Washington announced his decision.

III. Valley Forge—Philadelphia • 57

White Plains, Sept. 4, 1778

Sir,

Your Excellency's kind answer was handed to me yesterday evening.... From the fervor I entertain of a good military constitution I am and have always been sensible of the necessity of limiting rank to the Line of the army, and of the dangerous impropriety of lavishing it to men more likely otherwise civilly employed in the staff departments, nor did I ever think of proposing any direct or indirect deviation of this principle in favor of myself or anybody else.... It is true I spoke of having military business transmitted by military men, and so far your Excellency seemed to be aware of the distinction that should be made between the civil and military branches of the department I have lately acted in.... If the familiar grown ideas of this army about the matter are a sufficient ground for not satisfying what is so different in other services and so opposite in this, to the principle of military science, your Excellency knows best.... I am very sorry to find that arrangements of Congress or any body else will prevent my being any longer employed in the inspection. After having cheerfully encountered and surmounted the difficulties which opposed its success and gone through the most toilsome and fastidious details of it....

As for my continuing any longer in the line I am at present in; was the office a military one and on the proper footing, I would.... And had it not been reported and offered to me as such, I would not have accepted it; for when I undertook the laborious task of the inspection; when I exposed myself to danger on several occasions; when I took pains to exercise the office of Deputy Quarter Master upon military principle, my intention was to share the toils and glory attached to the defense of the cause of America; which glory I could not aspire to but by being a military man and deserving by real service what constitutes him.

I am sorry all my endeavors could not get me any other reward but a kind of clerkship in the Quarter Masters department. If I must assume a civil employment I'll try to get one which may be more honorable or profitable to me and if possible more beneficial to the community. I'll have the honor to call tomorrow evening at Headquarters to take leave of your Excellency and beg the necessary papers for my journey to Philadelphia.

I have the honor to be with respect,
Your Excellency's most humble and
Obedient servant.
John Ternant[57]

On 6 September, bearing a letter of recommendation from Steuben to Henry Laurens, Ternant began his journey to Philadelphia and upon his arrival began a final attempt to gain congressional approval for a commission. Steuben's letter in support of Jean was direct and laudatory.

From White Plains, Sept 5, 1778

Monsieur de Ternant who sets off tomorrow for Congress will have the honor to deliver this letter in the hands of your Excellency. I am indeed extremely sorry for his leaving this army dissatisfied.... The merit of this officer is not unknown to your Excellency. I have often expiated on his zeal and activity in performing the duties of sub-inspector which employment he [illegible] for a long time with success. He was afterward entrusted with the Military part of the Quarter Master General's Department and has not yet been appointed to any Military rank.

It is the subject of his going to Congress, and I take the liberty to recommend him warmly to your Excellency, hoping you will represent to the House his past services and his great merit and abilities.

If the Plan I have proposed with regard to the Department of the Inspection should be accepted of, I think Mr. Ternant might be usefully employed as inspector of the Light Troops but thou I must own that it is to his assistance that owe great part of the success I have met with. I would be myself against his being given that employment if he was not at the same time appointed to the same rank as the other inspectors, I mean that of Lieutenant Colonel. His merit is I dare say such as the Commander in Chief will acknowledge as well as I do, and to his opinion I take the liberty to refer your Excellency.[58]

Henry Laurens, the President of Congress, and Richard Peters, the secretary of the Board of War had both been impressed by Ternant during his visit to York in May and they remained his strongest supporters among the delegates in Philadelphia. Laurens exerted his limited influence as best he could, invited Ternant to dinner frequently but was embarrassed that he was unable to assist Jean more effectively.[59] In addition to supporting Ternant's appeal, Peters may also have provided lodging for Ternant at his family estate, Belmont, west of the Schuylkill River. Steuben had resided with Peters during his August sojourn in the city and may have informed his young assistant of Peter's hospitality.

For three weeks Ternant made the rounds, lobbied members of Congress, met with the Board of War and when not so engaged, attended to his private affairs. It is vary likely that during this period he called upon the recently arrived French minister, Conrad-Alexandre Gerard and renewed his association with Thevenau de Francy.

Although Steuben's letter recommending Ternant for an appointment was presented to the Congress on 11 September, the delegates failed to act on the Inspector General's endorsement. A week later Laurens wrote to Steuben that "Nothing, I extremely sorry to say it, is yet reported respecting Mr. Ternant. I am grieved to see this meritorious Officer kept in suspense."[60] It was only on the afternoon of Friday, 25 September that the Congress finally acted.

After considering a report from the Board of War prepared by Peters, the Congress accepted the Board's recommendation and agreed to Ternant's appointment.

Resolved, That Mr. John Ternant be appointed a lieutenant colonel in the service of the United States, and be ordered to repair to South Carolina forthwith, to perform the duties of inspector to the troops in the service of these states in South Carolina and Georgia; that he report his proceedings as inspector from time to time, to the Board of War and inspector general, conforming himself to such regulations as are or shall be established by Congress for the inspector general's department; and until he shall be duly Notified of the plan of the department being arranged and confirmed by Congress, that he govern himself as near as may be by the rules and practice pursued by the Baron Steuben, during his having executed the office of inspector general with the grand army, procuring the approbation and authority of the officer commanding the troops of the United States in the said states of South Carolina and Georgia, in all matters relative to the discipline of the troops, and the police of the camps, garrisons or quarter, previous to their being put in practice by him as inspector.

Resolved, That Mr. Ternant be allowed the pay and subsistence of a lieutenant Colonel from the 26 March last.[61]

Following his appointment Ternant spent the remainder of September and the first week of October attending meetings of the Board of War, writing letters expressing his gratitude to the people that had provided recommendations on his behalf and preparing for his journey to Charlestown. He thanked Steuben for his help in obtaining a commission and asked for a copy of Steuben's code of discipline to use in the south. He also informed Steuben, somewhat naively as it turned out, that he was confident of congressional approval for the Baron's proposals concerning the inspector's department in the near future.[62] To Washington he pledged his best efforts in his new office and offered his "warmest & sincerest thanks" for "the favorable testimony you were pleased to give of my past services and conduct."[63] On the same day that he wrote to Washington Ternant also wrote to Henry Laurens expressing his gratitude and to request that the Congress make financial arrangements to fund his upcoming journey.[64] Three days later the Congress advanced lieutenant colonel Ternant $1,000.00 to cover his traveling expenses.[65] With his personal affairs in order, his orders and letters to be carried south in hand and finally wearing a uniform, Ternant departed Philadelphia for Baltimore, the first stop on the road south.

IV

Charlestown— Savannah—Philadelphia
October 1778–December 1779

Jean Ternant's commission as a lieutenant colonel and his appointment as inspector to the troops in South Caroline and Georgia were the direct consequences of not only his personal dedication and the influence of friends but also the changes that were taking place in the autumn of 1778 in both the nature of the war and its geography. Congressional approval establishing a Department of Inspection and the standardization of military procedures and regulations was in the offing; recognition on the part of the members of Congress of the need for a more efficient standing army. Ternant's appointment as inspector to the Southern Department was part of the process of extending Steuben's reforms to Continental troops deployed elsewhere and that had not yet been exposed to the new maneuvers instituted at Valley Forge.

In the spring of 1778, with the Franco-American alliance and France's recognition of American independence, the geography of the war was also dramatically altered. The subsequent declaration of war in the summer, the growing threat of French intervention in the American fighting and the distinct possibility that Spain would follow France's example compelled the British government to change its strategy. Imperial defense requirements in other areas, India, the West Indies, Gibraltar, and England itself, insured that the financial and military resources necessary to restore royal authority in the rebellious American colonies would not be available. As a consequence British efforts in the American theater of operations were shifted to the former colonies in the south where it was long believed that loyalist support for the restoration of royal authority was strong and where large numbers of Tories could be recruited to assist the royal army. Georgia, North and South Carolina and Virginia became the focus of British efforts and the principal theatre of operations for the remainder of the war.

In response to the new British strategy the Congress strengthened its army in the region by ordering reinforcements from North Carolina and Virginia for the defense of Georgia and South Carolina, It also appointed a new department commander. Among the documents entrusted to Ternant to deliver on his journey south was an order replacing Major General Robert Howe as commander in the southern department.

Leaving Philadelphia on 7 October Ternant traveled first to Baltimore. On the 10th he left there, taking what was then called the middle road or eastern route by way of Petersburg, Virginia, through Halifax, North Carolina to New Berne, Wilmington, Georgetown and finally Charlestown.[1] In a letter to Henry Laurens Jean remarked that although unsure of his route, he had been informed that it was the best. He also repeated his thanks for Laurens' support and expressed his attachment to Jack.

> Permit me to take this opportunity of expressing my sincere & most grateful thanks for all your kind exertions in my favor, & to assure your Excellency of my utmost endeavors, upon all occasions, to answer, & exceed, if possible my friend's & the public's expectations.... I wrote to my good friend Col. Laurens from Philadelphia by a gentleman whom I found going off at the same time as I.... If there is anything to be done to the southward, I sincerely wish he may take the resolution of visiting his native country as soon as the army goes into winter quarters ... he is the virtuous & sensible citizen I wish for my friend, the gallant & intelligent officer I desire for my fellow soldier; & I shall be very happy if I can succeed in deserving & securing your Excellency's friendship & his.
>
> I have the honor to be with the most respectful
> Gratitude & attachment,
> Your Excellency's
> most humble
> servant John Ternant[2]

Ternant's progress south however, proved difficult. Somewhere between Baltimore and Petersburg, Virginia, he was struck with a "violent fever." Once more, the weather was horrendous, heavy rains had caused massive flooding which destroyed bridges and ferry crossings, making travel difficult and time consuming. In addition to being sick, Ternant also lost one of his two horses and had difficulty finding a replacement. Though alone and sick Jean nevertheless maintained his good humor, referring to his physician as "my Hippocrates," making light of the benefits of having been bled several times and being nonchalant about his fate.[3] Thanks to his weakened condition and his other difficulties however, Ternant did not reach Charlestown until 18 November, after a journey that lasted forty-three days.

Unlike his experience at Valley Forge Ternant arrived at Charlestown armed with letters of introduction from Henry Laurens to his political allies and friends among the city's wealthy and socially prominent planters and merchants. Laurens assured the Governor, Rawlins Lowndes, that "South Caroline and Georgia ... will in Mr. Ternant receive the acquisition of an excellent officer, and will in turn experience in him a valuable Citizen—His conduct and manners will speak more in his favor than I can express."[4] Christopher Gadsden, an early and ardent proponent of American independence and a leading political figure in the city, was also impressed with Ternant. In a letter written to Samuel Adams several months later, Gadsden reported that Colonel Ternant "seems to be an active, sensible and spirited officer entirely devoted to his Duty. He was in town only a week or two after his arrival when he seemed very poorly. He has been here once since for a few Days, sent up by Genl. Lincoln on Business. I had the pleasure of seeing him at my house each time and think myself happy to have been introduced to him."[5]

Ternant also would have received a warm reception among the leaders of Charlestown's French community. Many of the city's wealthiest citizens were the descendents of Huguenots that had fled France in the last century and settled in Protestant countries. Henry Laurens was a member of this group and his connections with the Manigault, Ravenal, Huger and Gaillard families would have been of considerable value to Ternant.

Located on the neck of land formed by the convergence of the Ashley and Cooper Rivers, Charlestown, at the time of Jean's arrival, was the largest and wealthiest city south of Philadelphia and prior to the war it had waxed rich on trade with the West Indies and its favorable balance of trade with England. But in the autumn of 1778 it was a city filled with rumors and a rising level of apprehension. Its economy had been disrupted by the war, inflation was mounting and it was experiencing a frenzy of speculation and profiteering. It required 17 to 20 dollars a day for an individual to survive.[6] In January a major fire had devastated a sizable portion of the town destroying over 250 homes and large quantities of material stored in warehouses.

The political environment was also highly charged. Controversies surrounding changes in the State's constitution, the question of loyalty oaths, and anti–Tory animosities inflamed political feelings. In June mobs made up of members of the Sons of Liberty roamed the city's streets and in September clashed with French sailors.[7] In August the city had been treated to the spectacle of a duel between two of its most prominent leaders, General Robert Howe and Christopher Gadsden. Concern regarding an imminent British invasion was widespread.

Three days after he arrived Jean's membership on General Howe's staff became official. The order announcing his appointment declared, "He shall train, Execute & Discipline the Army in this Department in the manner Introduced and Practiced in the Grand Army by the Inspector General" and that "He is to be respected & obeyed accordingly."[8] Ternant's stay in Charlestown however, was brief and there was little time for orientation let alone taking up his duties as inspector before news arrived that a British force from East Florida had crossed into Georgia. Although still not fully recovered from the "ague & fever," on 26 November Ternant accompanied General Howe and a small force to the Georgia border to meet the British incursion.[9]

Several days later, during a lull in operations following the withdrawal of the British force, Ternant wrote his first report to Steuben describing the military situation in Georgia, the difficulties involved in carrying on military operations in the region and the failure of an earlier attempt to invade East Florida. Although only in the area for a few weeks Ternant had quickly become aware of the difficulties involved in defending such a large, sparsely populated and politically divided region. In his letter he characterized American operations in the Southern Department as suffering from "negligence, slowness and a spirit of indecision," the last a reference to the ongoing disputes between civilian officials and the continental commander for control of militia units in the field; personal feuds that undermined military operations. Jean closed his letter however, on a note of optimism, reporting that General Howe "seems to have a lot of confidence in me and I do my best always to be useful. As soon as our troops are assembled I will give them a military organization according to our principals."[10]

True to his word, during the next four weeks Ternant began his efforts to establish a degree of uniformity among the continental units that made up Howe's force and to instruct the troops in some of the basics of de Steuben's reforms. Once again however, events intervened and there was little time for drill and instruction. On 23 December a British fleet from New York bearing an invasion force of some 3,000 troops under Lieutenant General Archibald Campbell appeared off Tybee Island and began to ascend the Savannah River toward the capital of Georgia. Six days later Gen Howe and his tiny force of militia and regulars attempted to defend the city. Outnumbered almost four to one, the brief engagement was a debacle for the Americans. Howe's force was scattered, Savannah captured and Royal government reestablished in Georgia. The defeat at Savannah was a serious setback and the subsequent loss of the State of Georgia created bitter animosities on the part of many Georgian civil and military leaders toward Howe that would culminate three years later in courts martial proceedings against the General in Philadelphia, a trial in which Ternant would be called as a witness.

Howe's decision to defend the city, although criticized later, had been supported by the unanimous consent of his field officers in a council of war. Encouraged by this consensus Howe then selected a defensive position one and a half miles southeast of Savannah blocking the main road on a piece of open ground on the Fair Lawn Plantation and waited. The position appeared strong. A small stream covered the front of the American line and its flanks were protected on the left by flooded rice fields and on the right by a dense wooded swamp, which Howe believed to be impassible by a large body of troops in military formation. Howe's 850-man force consisted of 700 South Carolina and Georgia continentals and about 150 men from the Georgia militia and if only attacked on his front, his little army may have given a good account of itself. However, the British commander who had served under Wolfe at Quebec had no intention of accommodating the American force. Instead, learning from a slave familiar with the area of the existence of a little known path through the swamp on the American right, Campbell sent a 350-man force of light infantry and New York loyalists to turn the American position. Only when that maneuver had succeeded did Campbell launch a frontal assault.

From the time that Howe established his defensive position however, he had been apprehensive of a potential threat to his right flank and took additional measures. He posted a piquet at the exit of one of the several footpaths through the swamp and sent a group of mounted volunteers to scout the adjacent woods. He also posted Colonel George Walton's unit of Georgia militia behind his right flank as a further guard on the exits from the swamp. Finally, on several occasions, Howe dispatched aides to continue to reconnoiter the area. Ternant, accompanied by Majors Porter and Deheyser, scouted the swamp but was unable to find a passage that would enable a body of troops to circumvent the American position. Following his unsuccessful search of the swamp Ternant was sent to the rear with orders for Colonel Walton to advance his militia closer to the swamp.

Ternant found Walton's ninety-three militiamen deployed in a single line supported by a fieldpiece in the area of the new barracks, a large building near to Savannah's outskirts. Before the militiamen could arrive at their newly assigned position however, the British Light Infantry emerged from the swamp and rushed them. Taken by surprise and outnumbered, the militia fled without firing. Ternant had the presence of mind to send a rider to warn Howe and then attempted to rejoin the main force. He managed to meet General Huger's South Carolina Continentals, leading the American withdrawal at Spring Hill, southwest of Savannah, a position designated as a rallying point by Howe in his instructions prior to the fighting. Unfortunately, the troops from Georgia in the rear of the American retreat were intercepted and forced into Savannah where most were either killed or captured.[11] The next day, Ternant provided Steuben with an account of the recent engagement. Embarrassed by the defeat and his role in it, he asked Steuben to refrain from publicizing the details. According to Jean, in spite of favorable circumstances, the Americans had been unable to put up either a creditable defense or manage an orderly withdrawal. The retreat had been a rout.[12]

Following the battle Howe collected the remnants of his small force, crossed into South Carolina and on 3 January arrived at Purrysburgh, a village about twenty miles from Savannah, where he turned over his command to his replacement, Major General Benjamin Lincoln. Although Ternant had only served under Howe for little more than a month his relationship with the General from North Carolina had been a positive one. In his report to Lincoln on the battle at Savannah and the campaign that preceded it, Howe mentioned Ternant and acknowledged "Colonel Ternant, the inspector of the army, laid me under obligations, for his assistance as well as by his actions and spirit in the action and on many other occasions."[13] In a very short time Lincoln would come to rely on Jean's counsel and assistance as well.

Benjamin Lincoln was twenty years older than Jean and although from New England, a world quite distinct from that of France, Paris and the court at Versailles, he and his young inspector shared many similar traits. Both men valued good manners. Both were modest with mild, amiable dispositions, frugal and temperate (Lincoln heartily disapproved of foul language) and they were also dedicated to their duties.[14] Lincoln soon marked Ternant as someone whose judgment he could rely upon and as a person who was easy to work with. Ternant likewise found service under Lincoln rewarding, and from the beginning he was optimistic about their relationship He informed de Steuben, "In general I am very content with the manner in which he [Lincoln] treats me and I forecast much good in the future."[15]

Once at Purrysburgh Ternant resumed his efforts to organize the army and implement de Steuben's regulations that had been interrupted by the invasion of Georgia. The situation however was not conducive to training. It was winter, the campaign season in the south and with constant troop movement there was little opportunity for sustained instruction. Once more, morale was poor. Although reinforcements from North Caroline had arrived, there were only about four hundred Continentals in camp and many of them were new recruits. There were some militia from South Caroline also present but with their short-term enlistments and resistance to any military authority there was little chance of their being instructed or disciplined. Finally, Ternant's health remained questionable. He never completely recovered from the illness contracted on his journey south and he had difficulty adjusting to the southern climate. Although it was winter, he was taking quinine every morning and evening as a protection against malaria and dreaded the arrival of warmer weather.[16]

The only bright spot in all this was Jean's success in establishing a close working relationship with General Lincoln. He quickly gained the new commander-in-chief's support for changing the army's camping arrangements and for an inspector's review of all units to determine current strength levels. Presiding over the reorganization of the camp and utilizing the deputy quartermasters to supervise the work, Ternant implemented Steuben's regulations that mandated the army be placed in camp by battalion, in the same formation it would utilize in battle. Tents were to be positioned the same in all battalions and be marked and measured with uniform distances between them. Kitchens, wagons and horses were assigned specific locations as well.[17]

Once the camp was rearranged to conform to Steuben's regulations Ternant began his inspection, compiling information regarding troop strength. He also began introducing Steuben's drill, marching and maneuver formations to the army's field officers. He decided that only after the officers had an understanding of the drills would he begin, with their assistance, the instruction of the rank and file.[18]

In spite of making a start in implementing the inspection, after only three months in the field, Ternant's work schedule and responsibilities began to take a toll on him. Alone, and far from Philadelphia, Jean missed the camaraderie of Jack Laurens and the professional mentoring of Steuben. He was already bored with training troops dispersed in camps stretching from Charlestown to Augusta, Georgia and worn out by the constant travel required to establish a system of regular inspection. Once more, he was discouraged by the lack of resources of both men and material, and cooperation. In spite of his friendly reception in Charlestown, Ternant was exasperated by the divided loyalties of the general population and its lack of enthusiasm and by the reluctance of the wealthy to sacrifice some of their private interests to the public good. Finally, he was frustrated as well by the failure of Congress to grant formal approval to Steuben's proposals. Depressed, exhausted by constant travel and in poor health, Ternant began to question his own circumstances. It is some indication of the extent of his depression that although still committed to the cause of American independence, on 6 March 1779, exactly one year from his arrival at Valley Forge, Jean informed Steuben that once he had accomplished his mission he intended to request permission to resign.[19]

There was little time however for Ternant to worry about his health and the obstacles he faced regarding his professional duties. The period between March and early July was one of almost continuous campaigning, military operations that featured a British invasion of South Carolina, the successful defense of Charlestown and a major battle at Stono Ferry. Ternant's role in these events was minor, restricted to staff assignments and his duties as the army's inspector. His morale, if not his health, was improved however, by being reunited with Jack Laurens.

Recently commissioned a Lieutenant Colonel in the line and armed with congressional approval for his "black project," the plan to enlist slaves as soldiers in the Continental army, with the promise of emancipation after the war, Laurens departed from Philadelphia in early April and arrived in South Carolina in time to join in the campaign that prevented the British from occupying Charlestown. He then took his place as an elected representative in the general assembly and submitted his proposal for approval. Unfortunately, although supported by many of his colleagues in the army, especially Ternant, and the firm backing of General Lincoln, the assembly rejected Laurens's plan.[20] The plantation owners grudgingly accepted the employment of their slaves for manual labor provided they were compensated but refused to permit their slaves being armed or emancipated. As Alexander Hamilton, Laurens's close friend, predicted, "prejudice and private interest will be antagonists too powerful for public spirit and public good."[21]

Jack Laurens was not alone in his decision to journey south. By the early spring of 1779 a number of foreign officers that Ternant had previously known at Valley Forge also had arrived in Charlestown. Some had been ordered south by Congress to assist in the defense of the region while others had requested permission themselves, and in expectation of active campaigning, were seeking an opportunity to advance their military careers. Not surprisingly, the three most important of this group, Pierre Charles L'Enfant, Louis Antoine Jean Baptiste de Cambray-Digny and Jean Baptiste Joseph de Laumoy were French and were either engineers or serving in that capacity. Together with other foreign officers already present, they formed a circle of friends united by culture, outlook and ambition that made Jean's service more bearable.

Pierre Charles L'Enfant, today the most well known of the three, had been a member of Steuben's military family at Valley Forge and therefore was very well known to Jean. Initially one of Tronson Du Corduray's party, the then twenty-three-year-old L'Enfant had been made a captain at Steuben's request and assigned to the engineers, although he had no previous military experience or engineering credentials; facts that he readily admitted. L'Enfant was however, a talented artist and before traveling south he had produced the diagrams that were included in Steuben's manual of regulations. He had arrived at Charlestown in early May looking for a promotion in rank and an appointment in the infantry, and Laurens had promised him a place in the corps of Negroes he was hoping to form. By July however, with the increasing likelihood that Laurens's plan would not succeed, L'Enfant found himself in financial difficulty, without a military position and lacking the means to return north.[22]

Although Ternant and L'Enfant were well acquainted there is little evidence that they were ever anything more than colleagues. Their backgrounds, personalities and goals were quite different. Talkative, argumentative but thin-skinned and with little interest in the military as a profession, there was little about L'Enfant to encourage a close friendship with Jean. Both men would anglicize their names and spend the decade of the 1790s living in close proximity to one another in Philadelphia but they do not seem to have been anything more than acquaintances and former comrades-in-arms.[23]

Ternant's association with Cambray-Digny was also limited to one of being simply fellow officers on General Lincoln's staff. Born in Florence, Italy to French parents, Cambray-Digny had been an officer candidate in the artillery and like Jean, had failed the entrance examination for Mézières. Following service as an engineer in North Carolina and western Pennsylvania he had been assigned to Charlestown in the spring of 1779 for the express purpose of improving that city's fortifications. Although Cambray-Digny shared many of the same ambitions and experiences as Ternant, there is no record of either a close or continuing relationship.[24]

The relationship between Jean and Jean-Baptiste Joseph de Laumoy was of an entirely different nature. The two became close friends; and began a relationship that lasted for the remainder of their lives. Laumoy, twenty months Jean's senior, a noble and a graduate of Mézières, was one of the three royal engineers that accompanied Duportail to the United States in the summer of 1777, and in 1779 he was serving as the principal engineer with the Continental army in the south. Quiet and reserved by nature, Laumoy and Ternant were well matched. A decade later, in Paris during the early years of the Revolution, both men would be companions and identified as members of Lafayette's circle, both would escape the political storm of the Terror by residing in the United States and in 1801 they would return to France together. Following the death of his friend in 1832, Ternant included Laumoy's widow on the list of beneficiaries in his last testament.[25]

By the early summer military operations in the region had been suspended. Forced to retreat to Georgia, the British were too weak in numbers to do anything more than maintain control of Savannah and a small post on Port Royal Island. The American army of the south was in much the same position. The numerical advantage that Lincoln had enjoyed in the late spring had vanished with the expiration of enlistment terms for many of his militia, a high rate of desertion and the inability to attract new recruits. It was a stalemate that would only end with the arrival of reinforcements from the outside the contested area.

Under these conditions Ternant found it impossible to introduce new formations and training exercises and indicated that his continuing poor health left him with no choice but to resign.[26] It is not surprising that Jean was not alone in his discontent; many of his fellow French comrades felt the same dissatisfaction with conditions. Louis de Pontiere, Steuben's traveling companion and aide de camp at Valley Forge who had arrived in Charlestown in early June, complained of his post in what was left of Pulaski's Legion. He was convinced that the unit would soon disband due to the end of enlistments for most of its members. Pierre L'Enfant was disgusted with American "disorder and neglectfulness" and miserable due to his own lack of rank and money. "If I did a foolish thing in America" he wrote, "it was to come to this province, ... it is the worse place on the continent ... and the one in which toryism is most domineering; business is bad and people discontented." Finally, Charles François Sevelinges de Bretigney, another disappointed volunteer, was convinced that most of his regiment also would soon desert and was open in his desire to leave America as soon as possible.[27]

In mid July, citing health concerns and the need to attend to personal affairs, Ternant requested leave to return north and on 24 July, carrying a collection of personal letters from his colleagues to friends in the north and official dispatches, he left Charlestown. Among the letters Ternant carried was one from Jack Laurens to Alexander Hamilton in which after describing his own work in the south as "doing daily penance." Jack recommended Ternant. "You know my opinion of Ternant's value" he wrote, "if you can render him any services—they will be worthily bestowed—we have not hitherto availed ourselves of his zeal and talents."[28] After an uneventful journey Ternant arrived in Philadelphia on the evening of Friday, 27 August. For the next three months Jean would engage in efforts to replenish his depleted financial resources, consult with Steuben regarding his future in the army and if possible regain his health.[29]

Philadelphia in the late summer of 1779 was a troubled and divided city. Still in the process of recovering from the damage caused during the British occupation, it was also in the midst of a financial and economic crisis. Since the early spring, prices for goods had increased fivefold over the previous year. Sarah Bache, Benjamin Franklin's daughter, wrote to her father, "The prices of everything here are so much raised that it takes a fortune to feed a family in a very plain way."[30] Rising prices, scarcity and the depreciation of the government's paper currency had led to street protests, increasing militancy, price controls and the embargo of shipments of foodstuffs. By the summer radical elements in the state's militia and organized vigilante groups such as the Patriot Society, roamed the streets accosting anyone suspected of loyalist sentiments, price fixing or hording; developments that culminated in violence. On 4 October a mob attacked the home of the well-known merchant, Robert Wilson that ended with five dead and many wounded.[31]

Philadelphia's political environment mirrored that of its economy. Congress was divided over the actions and financial accounts of Silas Deane, recently returned from France, the controversies surrounding the financial dealings of Robert Morris, one of the city's most prominent merchants and patriots and the scandal of the court-martial of the city's military commander, Major General Benedict Arnold, on charges of larceny and corruption.[32]

As best he could, Ternant ignored the confusion and anger and concentrated on his own affairs. Concerned primarily with the state of his small fortune, the first order of business was to restore his shaky finances. In early September Ternant petitioned Congress for reimbursement of personal monies that he had expended in the course of carrying out his official duties. He provided an itemized list of traveling expenses incurred from December 1778 through July 1779 that amounted to $1,790.00. On 29 September the Congress responded and approved the payment of $2,000.00 to defray those costs and the expenses involved in Jean's recent journey north.[33]

While the Congress considered his request, Jean turned his attention to military matters. At the end of August he sent a report to Steuben describing his trip north, conditions in the southern department and organization problems facing the southern army stemming mainly from there being too few soldiers spread among to many regiments. He hoped that the South Carolina assembly would resolve the problems by either permitting drafts of the state's militia to fill the ranks in the state's Continental line regiments or that it would endorse Laurens's plan for the enlistment of slaves. He also indicated that he had not made any recent reviews of the troops due to the lack of permission from General Lincoln. The letter was business like and there was no mention of Ternant's complaints or that he had seriously contemplated leaving the army.[34]

In a private letter to Steuben a month later however, Ternant was more candid. He admitted that poor health and money problems had been the principal concerns that had caused him to consider retirement. But he assured Steuben, "I would never make a final determination until after having consulted you and obtained your consent. You have had too much a part of my entry into the military career for retirement to be agreeable to me without your approbation." Jean acknowledged his debt to Steuben and admitted that the Prussian's influence had both encouraged and inspired him. Finally, Jean expressed his gratitude for Steuben's expressions of esteem and friendship.[35]

It was never a secret that Ternant was dissatisfied and seriously considered leaving the service. In addition to Steuben, Jean's colleagues also were aware of his health problems and the difficulties involved in instituting the inspection. In May, following his returning to Philadelphia from Charlestown, Theveneau de Francy had informed Steuben that "Our friend Ternant" was dissatisfied with operations and had resigned.[36] Acting on the basis of both Jean's pessimistic reports and de Francy's letter, and in spite of his affection and high regard for his young friend, Steuben had informed Washington as to the possibility of Ternant's retirement and had already recommended a replacement, William Galvin, a young soldier from Martinique who had arrived in Philadelphia in August 1778 recommended by Steuben's old friend the Baron Holtzendorff. The following March, Galvin had sought congressional approval for a position as an inspector but the Board of War had rejected his petition. He then prepared a drill manual and submitted it for Washington's consideration. Although Washington rejected Galvin's offer, explaining that he preferred Steuben's manual of regulations and drill, he was impressed with the young man's effort. Two months prior to Ternant's return to Philadelphia Washington had informed Steuben, "If Mr. Ternant has resigned and no other person has been employed in his place, I should have only one objection to Mr. Galvin succeeding him, which is, that according to the establishment of your department, the appointment would naturally devolve on an officer already in the line."[37] Ternant however, had already decided against resigning and it is possible that he had done so even before he began his journey northward.

Concluding his business with Congress and after suffering a malarial relapse, another bout of fever and fatigue, Ternant traveled to West Point in October for a consultation with Steuben and a reunion with his former colleagues. Then, in early November, he returned to Philadelphia and from there embarked on his second journey southward; another long trek through the pine barrens made easier this time by his familiarity with the route and his better health. As usual, letters and dispatches were entrusted to his care. Of greater importance, he also carried a copy of Steuben's recently published, *Regulations for the Order and Discipline of the Troops of the United States*, soon to be better known simply as the "Blue Book."

During his first tour of duty in the southern department Ternant's effort to implement Steuben's system of drills and regulations had been hampered by the lack of officially authorized reference material. He had been forced to rely on his own experiences as a sub inspector and some notes he composed from what he remembered from Steuben's daily instructions at Valley Forge. As part of the process of establishing the Inspector General's Department, in the winter of 1778/79 Steuben and his military family had settled in Philadelphia and prepared a manual for publication that would serve as the official regulations for the Continental army. Although Steuben's book received congressional approval on 29 March there were numerous delays in getting it printed and it wasn't until early summer that it became available for distribution. In consequence, no copy had reached Ternant before he traveled north in late July.

V

Charlestown— Havana—Philadelphia
January 1780–February 1782

While Ternant was in the north recuperating physically and attending to his personal affairs, the campaign of 1779 in the south had ended in defeat and disappointment. In September a French fleet commanded by Vice-Admiral Charles Henri Hector, comte d'Estaing arrived off the coast of Georgia and a combined Franco-American force, with a decided advantage in numbers over the British forces in the region, attempted to recapture Savannah. In spite of their numerical superiority however, the effort ended in failure. From the beginning the expedition was plagued by the usual problems inherent in most allied operations, indecision and a lack of cooperation on almost every operational level. The Americans and French were mutually suspicious. Regular troops in both armies clashed with their respective militia and there was friction between Vice-Admiral d'Estaing and his commanders, and between French naval officers and their counterparts in the royal army. In addition, it was hurricane season and wet weather further complicated operations.

After considerable delay the allies finally opened their trenches before Savannah on 23 September. Pressed for time by the lateness of the season and confronted by the refusal of the British garrison to surrender however, the French and Americans attempted to storm the city. On 9 October they launched an early morning assault that was repulsed with heavy casualties. Comte d'Estaing was seriously wounded, Kazimierz Pulaski, at the head of his American Legion cavalry, was killed and Pierre L'Enfant was among the many wounded. Jack Laurens, as usual, had played a conspicuous part in the attack but fortunately was not among the casualties. Disorganized and staggered by their heavy losses the allies raised the siege; d'Estaing returned to the Caribbean and Lincoln retreated to Charlestown.[1]

At New York, Sir Henry Clinton, the commander in chief of the

British army in North America, was enormously relieved when news arrived of the success at Savannah and in spite of his misgivings regarding the wisdom of the government's southern strategy, he pressed ahead organizing an expedition to capture Charlestown and restore royal authority in South Carolina. On 26 December a large British fleet carrying Generals Clinton and Cornwallis and almost nine thousand troops sailed from Sandy Hook.

Following the failure at Savannah, Lincoln spent the next three months in preparing for a widely anticipated British invasion; reorganizing his army, attempting to increase its numbers, marshalling his resources and improving Charlestown's defenses. Any hopes he had of obtaining additional troops from South Carolina had been quickly dispelled however. The state's General Assembly refused his request to draft militia for enlistment in the state's Continental regiments and it also rejected Lieutenant Colonel Laurens's proposal for enlisting slaves for military service. The most the Assembly would do was to recommend enlisting 2,000 slaves between the ages of 18 and 40 to be employed in work on Charlestown's fortifications.[2] Lincoln was forced, in the name of military efficiency, to consolidate the five under strength South Carolina regiments of Continentals into three stronger more uniform units; the 5th and 6th regiments were disbanded and their 270 troops added to the ranks of the 1st, 2nd and 3rd regiments.[3]

Fortunately, the Congress had responded to Lincoln's repeated requests for assistance and ordered troops from North Carolina and the Continental brigade from Virginia serving with the main army, south as reinforcements. In addition Congress dispatched a shipment of military supplies and equipment from Philadelphia by sea and ordered three frigates of the Continental Navy to Charlestown to aid in the defense of its harbor.[4] Lincoln also had the good fortune to be able to draw on a bill of exchange for $140,000 provided by the Spanish merchant and Spain's unofficial agent residing in Philadelphia, Juan de Miralles y Trajan.[5]

Charlestown's defenses in the winter of 1779–80, especially its landward fortifications, were incomplete and weak. The centerpiece, indeed the only permanent work that existed guarding the land approaches to the city, was a small hornwork that dated from 1757. It consisted of a curtain wall containing the city's gate, flanked by two half bastions; the entire work protected by a twelve foot wide ditch crossed by a stone bridge. Mounting only eighteen guns, by itself the hornwork was entirely inadequate to defend the city.[6]

Spurred by the British threat to the city in the summer of 1779 additional efforts had been initiated to improve Charlestown's land defenses but they remained unfinished. Building on that effort, after the return from Savannah, the army's two French engineers, Joseph de Laumoy and Cambray-Digny, assisted by Ferdinand de Brahm, an engineer employed by South Carolina, laid out and began to construct a more extensive system of field fortifications that included several earthen redoubts and batteries connected by trenches covered by an abattis of tree limbs. They also began to dig a canal across the Charlestown peninsula linking the Ashley and Cooper Rivers.[7] The work however was slowed by the lack of workers and the absence of building tools and materials and by the opening of the siege in April the fortifications remained incomplete. Ternant arrived in Charlestown in late December in the midst of the continuing preparations.

In contrast to first visit, Jean's return to Charlestown was a more agreeable occasion. In the autumn of 1778 he had arrived during a period of economic crisis and political instability, alone and in poor health, with only Henry Laurens's letters of introduction to aid his reception. Now, his health restored, rested and already well known and highly regarded, he was welcomed back with enthusiasm. General Lincoln wrote to Steuben regarding Jean's return: "We parted from Lieutenant Colonel Ternant with reluctance, and are made happy in his return to this department, for his attention and zeal rendered him highly agreeable to us while here, and from our knowledge of his abilities we now promise ourselves from him the most essential services."[8]

In addition to rejoining his numerous French colleagues, Laumoy, Cambray-Digny, L'Enfant, François Malmady, Charles François Sevelinges de Bretigny, Pierre François (Paul) Vernier, Louis Antoine Magallon de la Morliere and Monsieur Plombard, the French consul at Charlestown, Jean was also reunited with Jack Laurens and his father, Henry.

After resigning his presidency of Congress and experiencing a tumultuous summer of discord and discontent in Philadelphia, Henry Lauren, in November 1779, had been appointed commissioner to the United Provinces and had returned to Charlestown in early December to put his affaires in order before sailing for Holland. With his stately town house and large garden in the Ansonborough district of the city's northern suburbs and his 3,000-acre plantation, Mepkin, thirty miles away on the Cooper River, Laurens was relieved to be home and more than happy to extend his largess and hospitality to Jean. Following a mission to Philadelphia with dispatches in the fall, Jack also had returned and by mid–January he had been posted as the commander of the marines assigned to the frigate, *Providence*.

Furnished at last with a copy of Steuben's *Regulations*, Ternant was anxious to begin his work, a task made easier by his delivery of a letter from Washington to General Lincoln regarding compliance with what were now the Continental Army's official regulations.

My dear Sir:

Lieutenant Colo.Ternant, who will have the honor of delivering you this, returns to the Southward to execute the duties of his Office of Inspector to the troops in South Carolina and Georgia. He is furnished with the "Regulations for the order and discipline of the troops of the Unites States" approved by Congress on the 29th. March and by them directed to be generally observed. He is also furnished with the extracts from General Orders, with the forms of the returns required, and all other matters relating to the Inspectorship.

I am well persuaded that it is needless for me to express a desire that you should give this Gentleman your countenance and assistance in forming the troops under your command upon the plan laid down in the Regulations. I shall only tell you, that we have already experienced a very pleasing change in the face of our military affairs by a steady adherence to the system.[9]

With Lincoln's support and his own renewed enthusiasm, Jean resumed his duties as chief inspector. His work was complicated however, by the slow pace of Lincoln's reorganization efforts and by the General's need to disperse his forces over a wide area. When Ternant returned to the Southern Department he found that army units had been posted at a number of widely separated locations; at Fort Moultrie on Sullivan's Island across the bay from Charlestown, at Sheldon, near Port Royal, some 70 miles away and at Augusta, Georgia, almost 150 miles distant. To implement the inspection and conduct the required reviews would necessitate considerable travel; much as a Justice of the Peace riding his circuit or an itinerate preacher making his rounds.

In his first report to Steuben announcing his arrival at Charlestown Ternant described the military situation in the Southern Department, Lincoln's reorganization efforts and promised to personally conduct the reviews. Jean also indicated that "as soon as the brigade majors are appointed" he would "immediately give them the necessary instructions for disciplining the troops." He looked forward to being even more effective once the army was collected in a single body.[10]

At the end of January the military situation in the Southern Department suddenly became more serious. Jean reported to Steuben that elements of a British fleet that had been scattered by recent storms had appeared off the coast of Georgia. It would take some time for it to reassemble and its destination was unknown but an invasion of South Carolina by a direct attack on Charlestown could not be ignored. In the same letter, Ternant also indicated that after a month's time he still had nothing satisfactory to report regarding the inspection, as the army's reorganization remained incomplete. His most positive news was that in spite of everything he was preparing for a review of the troops in early February.[11] A few days after writing to Steuben however, Jean's immediate plans were interrupted and postponed indefinitely. He received notification he had been chosen for a special assignment, a mission to Cuba.

Ever since 1778 informal discussions regarding combined Spanish-American operations had been under consideration. The Spanish monarchy's unofficial observer in Philadelphia, Juan de Miralles, had encouraged members of Congress to consider a joint operation against St. Augustine but the Congress, while generally favorable to the idea, insisted that its resources were too limited and the best that it could do was to reinforce its southern army. Nothing could be done regarding American participation in an attack on East Florida, the delegates insisted, until the British had been driven from Georgia. In December 1779 however, Lincoln was authorized to correspond with Spanish authorities in Havana and discuss the possibility of Spanish assistance in an attack on Savannah.[12]

On 2 February Lincoln notified Ternant that he had been selected to deliver letters from Congress and the Governor of South Carolina to the Governor of Havana, present an American request for assistance and act as liaison for any future joint operations. In his letter Lincoln indicated that Jean had been chosen both for his military knowledge and his "intimate acquaintance ... with our forces and resources." Moreover, he was empowered "to meet with the governor ... and agree upon such plans as shall be thought best calculated to assure first the reduction of the enemy's force in the State of Georgia and afterwards, the conquest of East Florida."[13] The choice of Jean was a clear indication of the warm personal relationship that had developed between Lincoln and Ternant and the confidence Lincoln had in Jean's character and abilities. Some familiarity with Spanish and his staff status were also likely considerations. Two days later Ternant received from Lincoln a more detailed document that listed American military needs and proposals for future combined operations.

In addition to the above items and an indication of the mounting threat to South Carolina posed by the recent appearance of the British fleet, Lincoln concluded his instructions by requesting Ternant to "immediately solicit the governor of Havana to give us, as speedily as possible, the aid of a number of men covered by some line of battle ships." He also urged Ternant to remind the governor that such aid was for their mutual benefit and warned that "if Britain should possess herself of this town and harbor it would be difficult, if not impossible, to regain it."[14] Shortly after receiving these instructions, on 7 February or soon thereafter, Ternant boarded the schooner *Eagle*, which had been provided for his use, and sailed for Havana.

Successfully avoiding British frigates, Ternant arrived in Havana's harbor on Monday, 21 February and the next day presented his credentials to the Captain General of Cuba, Don Diego Joseph Navarro Garcia de Valladares, and delivered the letters and documents from General Lincoln, the Governor of South Carolina, James Rutledge, the President of Congress, Samuel Huntington, and a copy of the 16 December 1779 Resolution of Congress.[15]

The administrative capital of Cuba, Havana in 1780 was the third largest city in Spain's American empire, and with 40,000 inhabitants it was similar in population to Philadelphia. The city was strategically situated on Cuba's north coast and controlled much of the maritime traffic into and out of the Gulf of Mexico. Its large roadstead, modern port facilities and massive fortifications made it the principal base for most Spanish military operations in North America during the American war for independence.[16]

In addition to being Spain's main military facility and a major commercial hub, since 1775 Havana also had served as the center of an intelligence-gathering network, designed to provide the Spanish government with reliable information on the course and strength of the American rebellion. Under the direction of the Captain General, a number of individuals, many of them members of Havana's merchant community with trading links to the American colonies, had been engaged as secret observers. The most important of these agents was Juan de Marilles, a merchant with strong business connections with a numbers of Philadelphia merchants, including Robert Morris.[17]

Although never as important as French aid, Spanish assistance to the American cause proved significant. In 1776 Spain had joined France in secretly providing financial aid to the American rebels and later established secret letters of credit with Dutch banks that allowed American agents to purchase supplies in Europe.[18] At New Orleans, the governors, initially Don Luis de Unzaga y Amezaga and then his successor, Don Bernardo Vincente Polinarde de Galvez y Gallardo, secretly provided Americans with much needed powder and supplies. Spain also permitted France to use New Orleans as an entrepot for supplying the American rebellion and facilitated the operation by easing trade restrictions between Louisiana and the French Caribbean Islands; developments in which Ternant had been personally involved. Later, in 1781, Spanish financial contributions would play a pivotal role in enabling the French fleet under de Grasse to participate in the Yorktown campaign.[19]

Notwithstanding its clandestine financial aid and commercial support, the Spanish monarchy was unwilling to officially recognize the United States or, despite French urging, declare war on Great Britain. Until the early summer of 1779 Spain remained neutral, pursued a policy of delay and caution and when it did finally enter the war in June, it did so only as an ally of France and with entirely Spanish strategic objectives that had nothing to do with the success of the American rebellion; the recovery of Florida, the elimination of an English presence in the Gulf of Mexico and the eastern bank of the Mississippi and in Europe, the recovery of Gibraltar. Both Charles III and his principal minister, Conde de Floridablanca, disapproved completely with the very idea of rebellion and viewed any success of the American rebels as a potential threat to Spain's American empire.[20]

In spite of his cordial reception, Ternant's mission to Havana was a failure before it began. He was immediately informed by his hosts that they had received no instructions from the government in Madrid to cooperate in military operations with American forces and Navarro admitted to being surprised by Ternant's visit and the American proposals. Acknowledging the diplomatic impasse, Ternant nevertheless requested a planning session with the Captain General, his chief engineer and the commandant of the Spanish fleet to consider possible operations, if and when the Spanish government gave its approval.

During the conference that followed, Ternant described the military situation in South Carolina, the impending British assault on Charlestown, and explained both the mutually disastrous consequences if the city was taken and the equally important advantages that would result from a British failure. To divert British attention he proposed that a Spanish invasion force being assembled in Havana to attack the British at Pensacola in west Florida, be diverted to east Florida to threaten British shipping and be in a position to act in concert with American naval and military forces if the occasion should arise.

With regret Navarro and his staff rejected Ternant's proposal. Without specific orders from Madrid they were helpless to act. Moreover, they explained, the strength of the Spanish squadron was inadequate to the task of challenging the larger more powerful British fleet. One part of the fleet had already sailed for Mobile on 10 February and the main force had been scheduled to follow on the 15th but had been delayed. Navarro, as a favor however, permitted Ternant to remain in Havana pending the arrival of any new instructions that would approve joint operations. When by 8 March no dispatches from Spain had been received and the Spanish expedition to reinforce Galvez in west Florida preparing to sail, Ternant requested permission to leave; by 20 March, after a dangerous passage, he was back in Charlestown.[21]

Although disappointed by the failure to obtain Spanish assistance, General Lincoln, true to his usual good nature, attached no blame to Ternant and was gracious and appreciative of Jean's effort. "I am perfectly satisfied," he informed his young inspector, "with the manner in which you conducted this business—and as the circumstances did not admit of the wishes and expectations of your embassy, yet I am persuaded no exertion of yours was wanted to effect it—and I beg you to accept my best thanks for the diligence, address and attachment which you have manifested through the whole transaction."[22]

Ternant returned to Charlestown just in time to aid in its defense. The British, already ashore on the islands south of the city since 12 February, had been engaged in a slow but steady advance. Nine days after Jean's return, elements of the British army crossed the Ashley River at Drayton Hall, effectively blocking routes to the north and in the face of only minimal resistance, began the final approach to the American lines. The next day, 30 March, the British advance guard reached Gibbes' Plantation, two miles from Charlestown and was heavily engaged there by a force of 200 Continental light infantry under the command of Jack Laurens.

Slowly retreating in the face of superior numbers, Laurens's command took cover in a small redoubt and was reinforced by a covering force of militia and continental troops that included Ternant and which were commanded by the army's Adjunct general, Major Edmund Hyrne. Instead of retiring as ordered, Laurens resumed the uneven struggle and only retreated late in the afternoon.[23]

Although the skirmish at Gibbes' Plantation was of little military significance, the fight nevertheless, had considerable personal consequences for Jean. Seriously wounded in the fight, Major Hyrne was unable to continue his duties and forced to resign his post as the army's adjutant general. In his place Lincoln appointed Ternant to the office, pending congressional approval.[24] As inspector of the southern army for over a year, Jean was already familiar with both the routine of Lincoln's headquarters and the requirements of his new position. Respected by Lincoln for his intelligence and dependability, well regarded in the army and not part of any line unit, Ternant was the obvious candidate for Hyrne's office.

As acting adjutant general Jean became the principal administrative officer on Lincoln's staff, responsible on a daily basis for the transmission of orders to the army. He also became one of Lincoln's advisors. Throughout the coming siege Ternant would be at Lincoln's side, dealing with the paperwork that the Commander needed to direct the defense and later Jean would be personally evolved in the events relating to the surrender of the garrison.

The siege of South Carolina's capital began in earnest on the night of 30 March 1780. British troops began digging the first parallel and during the next five weeks they slowly, methodically and inexorably pushed their trenches and batteries closer to the American lines. On 15 April they opened their second parallel and the bombardment of the city and the

American defenses became almost continuous, day and night. Eleven days later the third and final parallel, only thirty yards from the ditch and the location for a possible assault on the American lines, was begun and musketry from the trenches became as deadly as the fire from the numerous batteries.

At the same time that the British were advancing their siege works toward the city Clinton also moved to close off Charlestown from the surrounding countryside and prevent Lincoln's army any opportunity to escape. On the morning of 14 April the largest force of American cavalry outside Charlestown was destroyed at Monk's Corner and by 28 April all American positions on the eastern side of the Cooper River opposite the city had been occupied by British troops Finally, on 7 May Fort Moultrie which guarded the harbor entrance, surrendered.[25]

From the very beginning Lincoln's defense of Charlestown was hampered by a number of factors. His army was badly outnumbered, and he lacked sufficient troops to man the defense perimeter and at the same time protect his line of communications. The militia from the countryside, using the presence of smallpox in the city and the need to defend their home districts, refused to serve. In addition to strictly military problems, the municipal and state officials in Charlestown refused to continence any consideration of retreat by the Continental units and the abandonment of the city. Lincoln, cooperative by nature and deferential to civilian authority, decided to defend the city rather than retreat while there was still time, pinning his hopes for success on the arrival of reinforcements from the north. Except for the arrival of General James Hogan's 600 man brigade of North Carolina continentals that arrived on 3 March, General Woodford's 1,000-man detachment of the Virginia line that arrived on the afternoon of 7 April and the arrival of General Duportail and a small party that successfully slipped through the British lines at the end of the month however, he was disappointed. After Woodford's contingent arrived Lincoln's army totaled approximately 5,000 including militia. According to Ternant's records compiled two weeks following the surrender however, Lincoln could only count on about 3,000 troops fit for duty at any time.[26]

Following the loss of Fort Moultrie, negotiations regarding the terms of surrender of the city and its garrison began in earnest. With the militia refusing to man the defenses and resisting orders, food, except for rice, no longer available, and civilian population demanding an end to the siege, Lincoln in a series of communiqués between 8 and 11 May, finally agreed to Clinton's terms. Throughout the process Lincoln strove to protect the status of the militia, the property of Charles town's citizens and to obtain from Clinton, a clear recognition of the honorable nature of the American defense.

In twelve articles of capitulation, while accepting the inevitability of surrender and that his Continental troops would become prisoners of war, Lincoln submitted for consideration terms that allowed the militia to return to their homes and that allowed the merchants twelve months in which to make arrangements for their property. Regarding the formalities of surrender, Lincoln was equally unrealistic. He proposed that the garrison march out with flags unfurled, drums beating and with shouldered arms; that his officers should be permitted to keep their personal effects, horses, swords, baggage and servants, and finally, that a ship be made available to send his unopened dispatches to Philadelphia.[27]

Clinton would have none of it. Assured of victory and all too aware of the opportunity to acquire considerable prize money as a result of Charlestown's capture, he rejected both the substance of many of Lincoln's proposals as well as the implication that the military situations of the two forces were equal. Clinton did accept some of Lincoln's articles but changed their wording and therefore their meaning. The militia would be permitted to return to their homes, but only as paroled prisoners of war. The twelve-month period regarding personal property was rejected out of hand, and Clinton demanded the immediate surrender of all shipping and material stored in the city. Finally, on the subject of the surrender ceremony itself, Clinton insisted that the garrison march out with flags furled and "the drums are not to beat a British march."[28]

On 11 May Lincoln accepted Clinton's terms and the next day appointed Ternant as his commissioner to determine the details for the surrender ceremony. In response Clinton appointed Major John Andre, his deputy adjutant general to meet with Ternant.[29]

The two men who met that Friday morning were well matched and similar in social background, ambitions and habits; they even had the same first name and were close in age, Andre had just turned thirty, while Ternant was twenty-eight. Both men came from middle class families, had rejected following in their respective fathers' businesses and instead sought a career in the military. Andre had been educated in Geneva and as Ternant, was well traveled and adapt at languages. They were also united by their devotion to duty, amiable personalities and tact; both were well placed as staff officers and each enjoyed warm relations with their commanders.[30] Several years later and under quite different circumstances, Alexander Hamilton would describe Andre as having "a peculiar elegance of mind and manners, and the advantage of a pleasing person."[31]

No one could have been more sensitive to Ternant's misfortune and future prospects than John Andre. Clinton's deputy adjutant general was all too familiar with the emotional distress and physical difficulties of being a prisoner of war. In November of 1775 he had been part of the garrison that surrendered at Fort St. Jean on the Canadian border and had been marched into captivity in western Pennsylvania during the dead of winter, initially to Lancaster and then further west to Carlisle. He was only exchanged in late 1776. Fortunately for Ternant, his prisoner of war experience would be considerably less physically daunting.

The two weeks that followed Charlestown's fall were a period of frustration for Lincoln, his staff and American officers in general, as their expectations for a quick parole were disappointed. Clinton and his staff had other more pressing concerns and some initial difficulty establishing control in the city. Arrangements for imprisonment facilities for the Continental troops had to be made, the militia that had avoided the surrender had to be rounded up and disarmed and captured military stores and materials had to be secured. To complicate matters, on the evening of 14 May a crowd of American officers created a disturbance that required the use of troops to restore order. After the incident the captured officers were confined to their quarters.[32] Two days later a major explosion disrupted the calm of the city. The accidental discharge of a musket in a powder magazine caused a firestorm that destroyed several houses and killed a large number of civilians and British soldiers.

In these circumstances, much to the irritation of Lincoln, Clinton hesitated regarding the implementation of article XII of the surrender agreement, the granting of permission for a flag-of-truce ship to carry Lincoln's dispatches to Congress.[33] The delay forced Lincoln to change his plans. Unable to send his dispatches by sea, he turned once again to Ternant and selected his acting adjutant general to carry the official report concerning the surrender overland. For Jean, Lincoln's decision proved to be a most fortuitous development and saved him from months of an uncomfortable interment in Charlestown.

On 24 May, after almost two weeks of waiting, Jean finally was permitted to sign his parole certificate.

> I do hereby acknowledge myself to be a prisoner of war, upon my parole to his Excellency Sir Henry Clinton, that having his permission to go by land to Philadelphia, or wherever the Congress may be with dispatches from Major General Lincoln. I am hereby engaged within thirty days after I shall have delivered them to remain in the Province of Pennsylvania until I shall be exchanged or otherwise released there from; and that I shall not in the meantime do or cause any thing to be done prejudicial to the success of his Majesty's aims. And that upon a summons from his Excellency or other person having authority thereto, that I will surrender myself to him or them at such time and place as I will hereafter be required; to which intent my place of abode shall be made known to the Committee of Prisoners of the American Army.
>
> John Ternant, Lt. Col.[34]

The day after agreeing to the terms, Ternant departed Charlestown. In addition to Lincoln's report to Congress and letter to Washington, Jean also carried a number of letters from colleagues and friends to their associates in the north, one from Jack Laurens to his father in Philadelphia, another to Alexander Hamilton and a letter from General Duportail to the President of Congress. Ternant also carried with him 2,000 in cash paid to him by James Custer, Henry Laurens's steward, money that probably financed Jean's journey north.[35] By 13 June Ternant had reached Baltimore and on the evening of Wednesday, 14 June, after only twenty days on the road, he arrived in Philadelphia.[36]

In spite of being the bearer of bad news, Ternant was warmly welcomed and suddenly found himself the center of attention. During the next several days, in a series of meetings and private conversations, Ternant provided a detailed description of the siege and surrender, and for a brief moment he achieved a degree of celebrity that may help account for Charles Willson Peale's interest in painting his portrait and partially explain his later election to the American Philosophical Society. In his report to the President of Congress, Samuel Huntington, Lincoln took the opportunity to praise Ternant and insisted that Jean's "steady attention to duty and zeal for the cause entitle him to every respect."[37]

Ternant's arrival in Philadelphia in June 1780 marked the beginning of what turned out to be an unexpectedly lengthy, nineteen-month interruption in his military career; a period that caused Jean considerable frustration but one in which he would also expand his circle of friends and gain him the friendship and support of another well placed patron, the French minister-plenipotentiary, Anne-Cesar, the chevalier de La Luzerne.

Ten years older than Ternant, Luzerne was part of a family of well-connected Norman aristocrats. His mother was a sister of Malsherbes, a minister of state and a personal friend of Louis XVI. His older brother would become the governor of the Leeward Islands and another brother, Bishop of Langres. Luzerne himself was a chevalier of the Order of Malta and had been a soldier before being appointed minister-plenipotentiary to Bavaria in 1776. Described as "of good stature, rather large, plump, of a ruddy handsome countenance, of a delicate make, dressed very plain." Luzerne was both intelligent and amiable, an excellent diplomat who with tact and great charm won the praise of many Americans. Beginning in the summer of 1780 and over the next four years he would take an increasingly active interest in Jean's career.[38] Later, after both had returned to France in the summer of 1784, the chevalier would continue to exert enormous influence on Ternant.

From the early summer of 1780 until January 1782 however, the single overwhelming fact governing Ternant's life was his status as a prisoner of war waiting to be exchanged. All other concerns and circumstances, his financial situation, his social life, even the fragile state of his health were overshadowed by that fact.

Unfortunately for Jean and his fellow prisoners, any hope for a quick return to active duty was complicated by the lack of a general agreement or cartel between the British Government and the Congress regulating prisoner exchange. At best there were some temporary arrangements worked out between commanders in the field that established that such exchanges were to be on a rank for rank basis, with each rank assigned a value (a point system) and that officers should be exchanged according to the date of their capture.[39] In most cases however, an officer's exchange depended almost entirely upon a specific request and the degree of influence being exerted in his favor.

Jack Laurens's case is a good example. Made a prisoner along with Ternant, he had returned to Philadelphia with General Lincoln in late June and immediately appealed directly to Washington to intercede on his behalf regarding his exchange. He also lobbied the delegates from South Carolina for assistance and sought the help of his close friend, Alexander Hamilton, still a member of Washington's military family. For Laurens captivity was an "insupportable evil," and a condition "injurious to one's honor."[40]

At the time Hamilton warned his friend of the dangers of lobbying for what others might view as preferential treatment. "I have talked to the General about your exchange, but the rigid rules of impartiality oppose our wishes. I am the only one in the family who think you can be exchanged with any propriety, on the score of your relation-

Anne-Cesar, chevalier de La Luzerne by Charles Willson Peale from life, ca. 1781–1782. The minister-plenipotentiary from the French government to the Continental Congress, La Luzerne was Ternant's principal patron from 1780 until his death in 1791 and was largely responsible for the success enjoyed by Ternant in his later military and diplomatic career (courtesy Independence National Historical Park).

ship to the Commander in Chief ... but my friend let me give you a caution. Don't appear too impatient of your situation nor too solicitous of being freed from it. Though *I* should be satisfied you acted from a laudable desire to be useful; others might give your conduct a construction to your prejudice. You must not have an air of bearing captivity worse than another."[41]

Notwithstanding Hamilton's good advice, Laurens's efforts were effective and in November 1780, although only a Lietenant Colonel, the son of a former president of Congress and a former aide-de-camp to Washington, along with Generals Lincoln and Duportail, was among the first of those captured at Charlestown to be exchanged.

Ternant also immediately lobbied for his exchange. He petitioned Steuben to use his influence and also appealed to the French minister, the chevalier de La Luzerne, for assistance. At the end of July La Luzerne asked Steuben to request the Commander of the recently arrived French expeditionary force at Newport, Jean-Baptiste Donatien de Vimeur, comte de Rochambeau, to arrange for Jean's exchange for one of seven British officers he held. Unfortunately none of these early efforts on Jean's behalf succeeded. It was only in January 1782, after nineteen months of idleness that Ternant would succeed in being returned to active duty; in consequence he had no role in either the operations that resulted in the victory at Yorktown or Nathaniel Greene's successful campaign in the south.[42]

Ternant's activities while on parole are not well documented, but some evidence exists that illustrates both his actions and intentions. In contrast to many of the other officers in Philadelphia waiting for exchange, who were strangers in the city and who had not been paid in months, Jean was familiar with the city, favored by a number of important people and he had few financial problems. In addition to his own resources, Ternant had what remained of the 2,000.00 he had brought from Charlestown and in August 1780 he received 3,960.00, awarded him by Congress as reimbursement for expenses incurred during his mission to Havana. Later, in January 1781, he received an additional sum of 400.00 for uniforms and back pay. Finally, he also benefited from a congressional resolution that ordered rations of firewood for officers on parole in the city.[43]

As a Frenchman with a commission in the Continental army, it was not unusual that Ternant began to spend much of his time at the French legation. Beginning in the summer of 1780 he became a frequent visitor and a welcomed guest at La Luzerne's residence, a large townhouse with an extensive garden located on Chestnut Street between Sixth and Seventh Avenues, only one half block west of the State House.

There, Luzerne introduced Jean to several members of the legation's staff, the chevalier's personal secretary, Louis-Guillaume Otto, a young German with a law degree from the University at Strasbourg and the clever, ambitious thirty-five-year-old secretary of the legation, François Barbe-Marbois; described by John Adams as "one of the best informed and reflecting men I have known in France."[44] Both Otto and Barbe-Marbois had served on La Luzerne's staff in Munich, were fluent in English and much involved in the social activities of Philadelphia's upper class families. They would become close associates with Ternant, and years later, colleagues.

Equally important, La Luzerne also introduced Jean to a relative, Charles Adrien le Paulinier the chevalier d'Annemours; since October 1778 the consul at Baltimore. D'Annemours was well traveled, also fluent in English and the author of several studies on political and economic developments in the British colonies and the West Indies. He was particularly interested in promoting trade between France and the United States and La Luzerne had actively encouraged his employment by the French foreign ministry.[45] D'Annemours was also a friend of Thomas Jefferson and in the spring of 1782 he would provide Ternant with a letter of introduction to the former Virginia governor.[46]

It was also probably through La Luzerne that Jean made the acquaintance of John Holker, the French consul at Philadelphia and commercial agent for the French Navy. In addition to his official duties, Holker was a business partner with Robert Morris in the tobacco trade with France and the hugely profitable flour trade with Havana and New Orleans.[47]

During the chevalier de La Luzerne's term as minister, the French legation was one of the principal focal points of Philadelphia's social life and Luzerne himself one of the city's most celebrated hosts. The minister and his secretaries spent most afternoons making social calls on the city's more prominent families and the legation was often the scene of banquets and other entertainments. Jean, in due course, was invited to many of these events and although he could never be considered a member of the Philadelphia *haute Monde;* he nevertheless did have the opportunity to mingle with both the city's elite, wealthy merchants and a wide variety of government officials, and the *nouveau riche,* war time profiteers, paper millionaires and speculators in western lands or government script.

Young, quiet with good manners, an experienced traveler able to talk with some authority on a variety of subjects, a soldier with an excellent reputation and every hostess's dream, an unattached bachelor, Ternant was a welcomed addition to any drawing room or conversation. The same qualities that had enabled him to gain acceptance at Valley Forge now served to gain him a standing with some of the city's wealthiest and most influential citizens, Robert Morris, Thomas Willing, William Bingham, John Nixon and George Clymer. He also renewed his acquaintance with Gouverneur Morris.

Ternant also attracted the attention of visitors to the city. On the evening of 30 November 1780, François-Jean de Beauvoir, marquis de Chastellux, a major general on the staff of comte de Rochambeau, a member of the French Academy and an author praised by Voltaire, attended a dinner reception at the French legation and in the course of the evening met Jean and a number of his friends. In his account Chastellux described Ternant as "a young man of great wit and talent. [who] draws well, and speaks English like his own language."[48] Several years later, after returning to France, Chastellux would remember Ternant and as a favor to his friend La Luzerne, recommended Jean to the Secretary of War, Philippe Henri de Segur, as having "an excellent character," a "very fine and keen intellect" and someone experienced in a variety of military positions.[49]

On the same occasion Chastellux also noted three of Jean's companions, Jack Laurens, Gouverneur Morris and Charles Armand Tuffin, marquis de La Rouerie. At the time Laurens was Jean's closest American friend but in the months and years ahead in both the United States and France, Morris and Ternant, acquaintances from Valley Forge, would forge as close a relationship.

Colonel Armand, as he was known in the Continental army, was thirty years old and along with Lafayette, the only member of France's *haute noblesse* to serve in the Continental army.[50] As was Lafayette, Armand was a favorite of Washington. The leader of an independent mixed corps of infantry and cavalry, Armand had recently returned to Philadelphia from the Southern Department intending to return to France to secure funds and supplies necessary to rebuild his legion that had been wrecked in the American defeat at the Battle of Camden.

As a socially prominent member of the French aristocracy, Armand was naturally welcomed into the homes of Philadelphia's wealthiest and most influential families and in the course of his socializing met Ternant and came away, as did many others, impressed by Jean's experience and reputation. In need of officers, especially a second in command, Armand requested that Ternant be assigned to his legion following his exchange. "I must confess to your Excellency," he wrote to Washington, "that since my going from the Legion, a bad order has prevailed in it—I am sorry to say that my Major since in Carolina & especially since I quitted the Legion has not proved himself entirely equal to his command, and it appears many disorders have taken place from not paying his whole attention to his business ... and to recommend for that post l.c. Ternant, whose services and merit your Excellency is already acquainted with."[51]

During the autumn and early winter of 1780 many of Jean's closest friends and comrades-in-arms left Philadelphia on official duties. In August Henry Laurens finally departed on his mission to Holland; in early

November Steuben and Duponceau left for the Southern Department, and in December Jack Laurens, selected as an emissary to Versailles to solicit another loan from the French government, traveled to Boston.

In a letter to Jack, at the end of January, Ternant had little good news to relate. His prospects for exchange had not improved and he also regretted to report, "the execution of the useful plan we meditated (their project to enlist slaves in the army) seems also to be further off as ever." Jean concluded his letter on a more personal note, "I do not send you letters to my friends, for I have scarce any in the Capital; & you will not go nigh the place where the remains of my family reside ... besides, you have been so amply furnished with letters to so much greater people, that mine would rather appear insignificant. However as some individuals may chance to mention you my name, tell them, I am *un bien bon* American & mean to continue so.... Adieu my Dear friend, be sure of my warmest wishes for you & of the truest attachment that any man ever felt for another."[52]

Throughout the spring of 1781 Jean continued to petition Washington for information on his chances for exchange and future assignment. He was optimistic, eager to return to duty and as usual, ready to be of any service.

> Though I am favored with the hopes of a speedy exchange, by the kind exertions of Comte de Rochambeau and Chevalier de Barras, and wish most earnestly to return to activity immediately after, I shall beg your Excellency to honor me with your orders about my future destination in the army.... Col. Armand wrote me before he sailed for Europe that your Excellency intended I should be assigned to his legion; but I have not heard since what had been ultimately determined about it.... The Baron Steuben, before leaving Philadelphia expressed also his wish to me that I might continue in the Department of Inspection and was to propose it to your Excellency.... My knowledge of the southern states on the other hand and a certain readiness on speaking and writing the foreign languages might perhaps under the present circumstances of combined armies and fleets, render me of some further utility near your Excellency's person, and this I can assure you would be most flattering to me.... But your Excellency knows best, from my good service, in what line I can be most useful, and I shall always be disposed and happy to do whatever you may think proper to order.[53]

Washington's response was flattering but offered little hope for Jean being assigned a position in his staff.

> I ... sincerely felicitate you on the prospect of your being speedily exchanged, your desire of entering into active service immediately upon your release from captivity is truly laudable, and like your former conduct merits approbation.
> From the opinion I entertain of your abilities and zeal for the cause of America I am persuaded essentially and might be derived from your service in either of the different employments which have been suggesting but I know that Col. Armand is in full expectation that you would be arranged to his legion as the Board of War had made such a report to Congress which was referred to me and received my approbation in January last, I am sensible he would be greatly

disappointed should you when exchanged go into any other department and indeed it appears to me that while Col Armand is abroad attempting to procure clothing and equipage for his corps, it will be highly necessary for a gentleman of your rank, ability and attention to superintend and keep together the remains of it. I should therefore advise that upon your liberation from captivity and appointment to this command you would proceed and take charge of it accordingly.... If at the same time (as Virginia is now a theater of war) you can be more active or useful in the inspection or any other line, you have my entire consent and wish for your success and glory.[54]

In spite of the continued lack of success regarding his exchange, Ternant's summer was made somewhat more pleasant by his reunion with a number of colleagues from the Southern army. Jean de Laumoy, Cambray-Digny and L'Enfant returned to Philadelphia in July, on parole from their captivity at Charlestown; each of them as anxious as Jean to be exchanged and returned to active duty. L'Enfant had the good fortune to be exchanged along with Jean in January 1782, but Laumoy would have to wait until August for his release and Cambray-Digny until November.[55] It was during this period, with no interruptions caused by duties, that Ternant and Laumoy had the time to forge what became their life-long friendship.

The late summer and early fall of 1781 was also a period of heightened expectation. During the first week of September Philadelphia witnessed the arrival of the French expeditionary force on its march south to Virginia. French regiments drilling on the city's commons entertained large crowds and there were the usual accompanying social events for the officers hosted by La Luzerne at the legation. Ternant had the opportunity to meet many on Rochambeau's staff, including Mithieu Dumas, serving as one of the army's cartographers. Six years later the two would meet again, under very different circumstances, in Amsterdam.

Seven weeks later the hopes for the fall campaign were realized. On the morning of 24 October, news arrived of the surrender of Cornwallis at Yorktown and Philadelphia gave itself over to celebration. La Luzerne accompanied by the staff of the legation and likely Ternant and the members of Congress attended an afternoon thanksgiving service at the Dutch Lutheran church. Later that evening, the city was illuminated by a fireworks display and candles placed in windows.

In addition to attending numerous social engagements, victory celebrations, and continuing his efforts to expedite his exchange, Ternant also used his time to pursue his passion for natural history. In the autumn of 1781, frustrated by more than a year of captivity, Jean contemplated an expedition across the Blue Ridge Mountains and into the territories stretching to the northwest bounded by the Great Lakes and the Ohio and Mississippi Rivers. As part of his planning he initiated an exchange of letters with Bernardo de Galvez, the governor of Louisiana, informing him of his intentions to travel into the region and offering to provide Spanish authorities information on the regions population, newly formed communities and commercial activity.[56] Galvez responded in a positive manner, approved of Ternant's travel plans and indicated that with the approach of peace the fixing of boundaries between Spanish territory and the United States would be very important. The governor also assured Jean of His Most Catholic Majesty's approval for any visit into Spanish territory and recommended that Jean prepare a report of his travels.[57] Unfortunately for Jean, before he could embark on his planned excursion, the arrangements for his exchange were finally completed and he was recalled to active duty.

Ternant's release from his prisoner of war status was initiated by a letter from comte de Rochambeau to Sir Henry Clinton dated 7 November 1781. In his letter the French general proposed that among the number of French officers in American service currently in captivity "the Sieur de Ternant of the legion of Armand" be exchanged for Lt. Col. Welborn Ellis Doyle captured in July at sea along with Francis Lord Rawdon on their return voyage to England.[58] It would not be until the middle of January 1782 however, that Jean's exchange would be finalized and that he was released from the terms of his parole.

While the arrangements for his exchange were being worked out, Ternant was suddenly confronted with a situation that caused him some ethical concerns. On 10 December Jean was notified that he would be called as a witness in the court-martial of his former commander, Major General Robert Howe, charged with misconduct during the operations at Savannah in December 1778. The Georgia state assembly had long alleged that Howe's actions on 29 December 1778 had sacrificed the capital of the state, and that by retreating across the Savannah River into South Carolina and recalling all Continental troops from Georgia the general had "left the State at the mercy of the enemy."[59] It now pressed its case against him.

Howe's court-martial convened on 7 December 1781 in the long room at the City Tavern, Philadelphia's most elegant hostelry and drinking establishment. The presiding officer was Ternant's patron and mentor, Major-General Baron von Steuben; Brigadier-General Henry Knox headed the twelve-member jury and acting in the role of judge advocate was Captain Benjamin Walker, an aide-de-camp to Steuben and one of Jean's colleagues from the encampment at Valley Forge.

Apprehensive about the legality of his participation in the proceedings while still a prisoner of war and thereby violating the terms of his parole, Ternant turned to Washington for advice.[60] Washington's response is not known but two days after receiving Ternant's letter Washington informed Captain Walker that the commissary of prisoners was negotiating Jean's exchange and the issue of his participation in General Howe's trial was being resolved.[61]

According to the transcript of the trial, Ternant testified on Saturday, 12 January 1782 and was the final witness called. And by that date it appears he had already been notified of his release. In a letter to Rochambeau dated 14 January Washington informed his ally that he taken "the liberty to mention to Colo. Ternant that his exchange was completed."[62] Washington, following the victory at Yorktown, had chosen to remain in Philadelphia over the winter and Ternant certainly must have used the opportunity to visit the Commander in Chief and discuss his status and future posting.

Released from the terms of his parole and returned to active duty, Ternant immediately began to prepare for his return to the Southern Department and to assist in the recruitment and refurbishment of Colonel Armand's Partisan Corps. Throughout January and February he met with the Superintendent of Finance, Robert Morris, proposing improvements in regimental records keeping that he hoped to introduce in the Southern army, and offering other suggestions regarding economy.[63] Jean also submitted requests for money and horses for Armand's unit and petitioned for and received warrants for five thousand dollars for the purpose of recruitment.[64]

On 11 February Ternant was again appointed Inspector for the Southern army. A week later he informed Morris of his imminent departure and requested orders regarding the subsistence and future movement of Armand's regiment. Morris had nothing to offer. He had earlier estimated that it would cost fifty thousand dollars to recruit and mount Colonel Armand's legion, and with the current financial situation the expenses of any move would undermine the government's credit. He informed Jean that Armand's corps should remain where it was for the present time.[65]

Having concluded as much official business as possible, put his personal affairs in order and collected the letters from a number of officials to be delivered to General Greene, Ternant, on a winter day sometime in the final week of February, bid farewell to Philadelphia, his home for the last twenty months and set out once again for the south.

VI

Monticello—
Fuller's Plantation—Philadelphia
March 1782–June 1784

The path of Ternant's third and final wartime journey south was determined by the requirement to inspect Colonel Armand's legion at Charlottesville, Virginia, before he reported to General Greene in South Carolina.[1] Departing Philadelphia sometime during the last week of February, Jean traveled first to Baltimore where he was likely a guest in the home of the French consul, Charles François Adrien le Paulinier, chevalier d'Annemours. On 27 February Ternant left Baltimore, crossed the Rappahannock at Fredericksburg and instead of continuing on the eastern road to Richmond and Petersburg, continued westward toward the Blue Ridge and Charlottesville.

Taking advantage of Ternant's visit to Charlottesville, the chevalier d'Annemours wrote a short note to be delivered, along with several newspapers, to his friend, Thomas Jefferson, at nearby Monticello. In his letter d'Annemours recommended Jean to Virginia's former governor as "an intimate friend of mine" and further explained, "His hobby-horse is like mine, natural history; But speaks also very well upon Every other subjects, so as to mistake them for so many hobby-horses. I recommend him to the fate every man of merit meets with at *monte-cielo*."[2] That fate might well have meant an invitation by Jefferson to his home, for an evening of good food, Madeira and wide ranging conversation.

Although there is no record of Ternant's visit, Jefferson, in spite of his reserve, must have welcomed any opportunity to talk botany with a fellow enthusiast and hear the latest news from Philadelphia. With his life-long fascination for plants and his interest in lands to the west, Jefferson would undoubtedly have been intrigued by Ternant's accounts of his Caribbean travels, observations of flora and fauna in Louisiana and his recently abandoned plan to explore the territories north of the Ohio

River. Their mutual enthusiasm for botanical and zoological research and familiarity with the studies of the French naturalist, Georges Louis Leclerc, comte de Buffon, and the Swede, Carolus Linnaeus, as well as both men's interest in foreign languages, architecture and classical Roman letters, would have made for a lively intellectual feast. At the time, such an evening would have been little more than a pleasant diversion for Ternant on his long journey south and neither he nor his host could have imagined that they would meet again under quite different circumstances a decade later. Later still, in his old age, the evening at Monticello, if in fact it occurred, would have become something more for Jean, a cherished memory of the first meeting with an old and by then very famous, acquaintance.

Ternant's inspection of Armand's legion was completed by 5 March and he informed Washington that in spite of Col. Armand's desire to comply with orders, his corps would be unable to march south due to "many substantial reasons," mainly the lack of wagons and horses. Jean assured Washington however, that Armand's unwillingness to proceed south had nothing to do with the Colonel's dissatisfaction with his orders.[3] In his own letter to Washington, Armand explained in detail his situation and bemoaned the fact that Jean would not remain with the Legion. He added "permit me sir to consider him as belonging to the Legion and the proper person to command that corps if the circumstances I had the honor to mention to your Excellency while at York did force me to quit this service...."[4]

Following his examination of Armand's corps and the delivery of d'Annemour's papers to Jefferson, Ternant continued on his journey, crossed Rockfish Gap into the Shenandoah Valley and picked up the western route to the south that ran from Philadelphia and Harrisburg in Pennsylvania, through Maryland, Winchester and Staunton in the Shenandoah Valley, Salem, the Moravian settlements at Wachovia and Charlotte in North Carolina and finally to Camden in South Carolina. Also known as the Great Wagon Road or the Upper Road, it was a well-traveled 800 mile route that most settlers in the Carolina backcountry had used in their migration into the region.[5] In late March Ternant arrived at Bacon's Bridge, General Greene's headquarters, located about twenty miles northwest of Charlestown on the Ashley River.[6]

The military situation in the Southern Department that Ternant found when he arrived in the early spring of 1782 bore little resemblance to the state of affairs that had existed when he left some twenty-three months before. In May of 1780 defeat had been total and the future of the patriot cause uncertain. Now, following Yorktown, it appeared victory in the war and American independence were only a matter of time. The British continued to occupy Charlestown and Savannah, but their southern strategy for reestablishing royal authority in the region had failed, the victim of the mistaken belief that a loyalist majority in the region would support the restoration of royal government and provide the necessary manpower to maintain it.

In the Carolina backcountry, between the fall of 1780 and the spring of 1782, patriot partisans had emerged victorious after a ruthless and bitter civil war with their loyalist neighbors. During the same period Nathanael Greene's army of Continentals and militia had slowly gained the upper hand in the struggle waged by regular forces. By December 1781 British control in the south had been reduced to little more than Charlestown and Savannah and fighting in the region by the summer of 1782 had been reduced to skirmishes with British foraging expeditions.[7] In New York and London plans were already being made to evacuate both cities.

In spite of American military success however, many of the conditions in the Southern army remained remarkably similar to what Jean had known in his two previous tours of duty. On his arrival he found the same problems that had always plagued the Continental forces, too few troops, inadequate supplies of food, forage and equipment, continuing friction between military and civilian authorities and war-weariness on the part of everyone. The desertion rate was high, the troops often on the verge of mutiny and the officers discontented and angry.

For Ternant personally however, things were very different. Almost all of his former colleagues and friends were absent; Laumoy and Cambry Digny remained prisoners and L'Enfant was on furlough in Philadelphia. And, after twenty-one months of inactivity in Philadelphia, Jean was reluctant to resume his former duties; unprepared for a return to the routine and rigor of camp life or his responsibilities. It was only his strong sense of duty and commitment to the American cause that sustained him and caused him to accept a reassignment to the Southern department.

The relationship between Jean and Steuben had also changed as time, distance and altered circumstances had taken their toll. In the spring of 1779 the circle of Jean's friends and patrons was broken. Steuben and Henry Laurens had a falling out on the issue of increased salaries for officers on the former's staff, which placed Jean in an awkward position, between his mentor, Steuben, and his principal advocate in Congress and the father of his best friend. A year later, Steuben was actively employed in the defense of Virginia and confronted by a multitude of military difficulties. Distracted by his duties, he had little opportunity to respond to Jean's increasingly frequent requests for replacement. By the summer of 1782 the close relationship, based upon shared experiences and professional ideals, between Ternant and Steuben had cooled. They remained friends and Jean continued to seek Steuben's favor, but Jean increasingly looked to the more influential French minister, Anne-Cesar de La Luzerne, for advice and assistance.

In his initial report to Steuben, Ternant presented a mixed review of the army's present state. He described a "total deficiency" in materials required to conduct a proper inspection, the lack of printed forms and the absence of either regimental or company records. Jean was so apprehensive of being able to discharge the responsibilities of his office that he requested to be relieved as soon as a replacement could be found. It was a theme that continued in his subsequent letters in April and May.

The infantry, he acknowledged, although few in number and ragged in appearance, was in relatively good order. Regarding drill and training exercises however, Ternant reported a "total lack of system" in many of the corps. Most muskets and bayonets were in good condition, but there was an insufficient number of both and more than three hundred soldiers were without arms. More alarming than the shortage of muskets however, was the shortage of ammunition and the "great deficiency" in cartridge boxes.

If the state of the infantry was found to be generally acceptable, Ternant reported that the cavalry was in disarray. Horses were in short supply, hard to obtain and many of those on hand were not well maintained. Accouterments were in poor condition, most saddles and bridles were worn out and there was a lack of experienced saddlers and furriers. The army, in general, lacked everything, clothes, blankets, tools, a traveling forge, tents and camp equipment. Ternant concluded his review by relating that although the hospitals lacked bedding and medical supplies, the sick were generally well attended.[8]

In spite of the obstacles he faced and his own doubts, by mid April Ternant had completed a preliminary inspection of Greene's army and had been dispatched along with his assistant, Captain Archibald Steele, to inspect General Anthony Wayne's small command near Savannah. The review in Georgia was quickly undertaken and by 18 April, Wayne had informed Greene that Ternant, who he described as "an old friend and particular acquaintance" had finished his work.[9]

In early July, in response to increasing sickness in his army, Greene moved its camp to higher ground at Ashley Hill plantation, fifteen miles from Charlestown. Ternant at the same time took up residence at the nearby home of Thomas and Catherine Fuller. The Fullers' 500-acre plantation, Pierpoints, was located in St. Andrews parish, adjacent to Ashley Hill and it was also the quarters of Jack Laurens, who in all likelihood encouraged the Fullers to make space for his friend.[10]

After returning from his mission to France and distinguishing himself in the fighting at Yorktown, Laurens had returned home to South Carolina, joined Greene's army and continued to promote his "black project." At the Winter session of the South Carolina Assembly he had submitted a plan to enlist 2,500 slaves as soldiers and when that plan was rejected, Laurens then attempted to gain approval for using the profits from the sale of confiscated estates of loyalists to provide bounties for new white recruits. This proposal was rejected as well.[11] Disappointed in his attempts to find new recruits, Jack returned to the army determined to pursue an active role in military operations. In February, in spite of the low opinion of his abilities held by many of his colleagues, Laurens was appointed to a command in the army's Light Infantry, and later placed in charge of the army's intelligence network and the series of advanced posts surrounding Charlestown.

Without either the resources or the expertise to conduct a regular siege of Charlestown, Greene's only recourse was to establish a blockade and prevent the British from obtaining food and forage from the nearby countryside. In response the British sent out foraging parties that resulted in numerous small skirmishes with American forces. Unfortunately, while Greene's army went hungry, the blockade proved ineffective, a regular traffic in food supplies to the city soon developed; one that became impossible to prevent. Self-interest and necessity in this instance proved stronger than patriotism. Most American planters were hard pressed for money and as the British were willing to pay in hard currency, they made every effort to evade the restrictions on trade with the city. John Mathews, the Governor of South Carolina, labeled this trade as an "infamous traffic carried on by persons who will contribute nothing for the army, because they can get an enormous price, and the cash, for what they send to town."[12]

While Laurens was busy in the field attempting to enforce the blockade, Ternant spent the summer immersed in paperwork and travel; struggling to institute a system of regular inspection procedures, maintaining the army's records of discharges and transfers of personnel and in preparing a comprehensive review of the manpower status of the Southern army that included a detailed numerical abstract of all regular units and an official muster roll for each regiment. The abstract listed army personnel by rank and duty in four categories, present and on field duty, sick present or in hospital, on furlough and in captivity and on staff and menial duty. It also provided a numerical breakdown by terms of enlistment. According to Ternant's completed report the Southern army's strength at the end of September 1782 was 4,028 officers and men, of which 1,171 were sick. Along with up-to-date muster rolls that included the names of all individuals, Ternant's report provided General Greene, the Inspector General, Baron von Steuben, and the Secretary of War, Benjamin Lincoln, the statistical information necessary for strategic planning.[13]

At the end of August however, Jean's routine was interrupted and the war was suddenly brought home to him in a deeply personal way. Word was received that Jack Laurens had been killed on the 27th during a skirmish with a British foraging expedition on the Combahee River south of Charlestown.[14] There is no record of Jean's reaction to the depressing news, but Laurens had been his closest American friend, similar in both age and ideals, if not temperament, and Jean could not have helped but have been especially saddened at the news. Over the course of the past five years the two had become boon companions, shared numerous adventures and Jack had been Ternant's earliest and most ardent champion.

Laurens's replacement as the commander of the advanced posts surrounding Charlestown was the Southern army's chief engineer, Colonel Tadeusz Kosciusko. Another of the foreign volunteers, the thirty-year-old unemployed captain in the Polish artillery, had arrived in Philadelphia in August 1776 and had been engaged as an engineer. During the campaign that resulted in the American victory at Saratoga he had served as the Northern army's principal engineer and formed a close friendship with its commander, Major General Horatio Gates. Following Burgoyne's surrender, Congress had posted Kosciuszko to West Point, where between 1778 and the summer of 1780, he designed and supervised the construction of its fortifications in spite of an on-going and highly contentious disagreement with the French engineers. When Horatio Gates assumed command in the Southern Department following the surrender of Charlestown, Kosciuszko traveled south with his old friend and after the defeat at Camden and Gates's replacement, Kosciuszko chose to remain in the region. Always well-regarded by Americans for his competence, cooperative spirit and easy manners he had served with distinction during Greene's recent campaign.[15]

Kosciuszko's major responsibility in September 1782 was to gather intelligence, enforce the American blockade of Charlestown and end the contraband trade with the city. It was in this role that he became involved with Ternant regarding supplies entering the city. In an effort to assist Mrs. Fuller, Ternant requested Kosciuszko to allow her boat, loaded with beef and corn for Charlestown, to pass through the American lines. Reluctantly Kosciuszko refused, insisting that the cargo was too large and consequently forbidden. Jean recognized Kosciuszko's responsibility and accepted the necessity to prevent the Fuller's boat from proceeding.[16] The incident was one of many such occurrences at the time and was of little consequence in itself, but it provides some insight into Ternant's willingness to use what little influence he had to compensate his hostess for her hospitality and kindness.

In addition to all of its other problems, during the summer and fall of 1782 the Southern army was steadily overwhelmed by an epidemic of

Malaria; an outbreak so serious and widespread that by September one-half of the men were suffering from fatigue, chills, fever and the sweats and 370 had required hospitalization. General Greene himself and a number of his aides also became ill and he was concerned enough to send them and his wife away from camp to recuperate. By November the situation had further deteriorated; more than 200 soldiers had perished and so many others had been incapacitated by the "Intormiting and Flametory fevours" that military operations had to be curtailed. Greene acknowledged that it had been "one of the sickliest seasons known this thirty years."[17]

Jean did not escape being stricken. In late September, any fears he may have harbored regarding his own health were realized and he also experienced "a fit of the ague."[18] Already disillusioned and physically exhausted by the hardships connected with his inspection duties and now ailing as well, Ternant on 26 October requested that he be permitted to resign his office of inspector and when recovered, allowed to join Armand's Partisan Corps in Virginia.[19] A week later Greene reluctantly approved Jean's request and in a letter praised him for his work in the Southern army.

> Nothing could have been more unwelcome than your application to resign; and nothing but the reasons you urge and the state of your health could reconcile me to it. The progress and improvement you have made in the business of your department and the immense labour you have bestowed upon it to reduce it to method and order, makes me lament your leaving.... Give me leave to return you my sincere thanks for the constant zeal and unwearied attention you have paid to the service under my command; and you may be assured I shall do justice to your merit and services in my letters to the commander in Chief, the Minister of War and the Inspector General....
> Your have my consent to join your Corps when your health will permit with my best wishes for your speedy recovery and future glory.[20]

Greene's General Orders to the army was equally laudatory regarding Ternant's services. "The General would be wanting in justice to the merit and Service of Lt. Col. Ternant, was he to neglect to testify his highest approval of his conduct, both in respect to his judicious regulations as well as exact execution and mode of conducting the business under his direction...."[21]

Throughout November and December Ternant struggled to recover from his bout of malarial fever. Too weak to conduct business and enduring the painful application of plasters to the body, he notified Steuben that his replacement as inspector, Lt. Col. Francis Mentges, and his assistant, Lieutenant Reed, had taken over the duties of the inspection.[22] In spite of his wakened condition however, Jean attempted to stay intellectually active. He began a study of the role the Inspectors Department played in the army; the "branch of military establishments" according to

Ternant "instituted to preserve the original purity and energy of discipline as well as to prevent the abuses or misappropriations of public property." He also discussed with Greene his objections to the system under which he had labored; "the frequency of inspections, the tedious complications as well as dangerous multiplications of returns (the bane of every record keeper) & the too unweighty rank of the inspectors and the insufficiency of the means furnished them to discharge their almost incessant duties."[23]

On 14 December Jean had the satisfaction of learning that American control of Charlestown had been finally restored. Unable to be present during the reentry of the army, he remained at Ashley Hill and celebrated his thirty-first birthday. In a letter to Steuben a week later, he reported that he had been too ill to leave his quarters and therefore could provide no information regarding the British evacuation, but did indicate that he was sufficiently recovered and hoped to leave for Philadelphia in the next four or dive days. He hoped that Steuben had not disapproved of his decision to leave the inspectors department and asked to be remembered to Mrs. Peters and the rest of her family.[24]

On Christmas day Ternant informed Greene that he was now sufficiently recovered and was able to travel. Pleading "business of great moment requiring my personal attendance" however, Jean altered his travel plans and requested that he be allowed to visit Philadelphia before rejoining Armand's command in Virginia. In addition, short of cash, he also requested an advance of money from the army's chest to defray the expenses of his upcoming journey as well as those of his earlier journey that after ten months had yet to be paid.[25] In spite of his desire to leave, it seems highly likely that Jean remained in Charlestown at least through the New Year and participated in the round of festivities in celebration of the city's liberation. Sometime in mid–January he began his journey northward.

Ternant's itinerary is unknown but in all likelihood he took the eastern road. It was the most direct route and the one with which he was most familiar. Exactly when he arrived is also a mystery but by early March he was back in Philadelphia and had received a letter of thanks and recognition for his efforts in the Southern department from Baron von Steuben.

> The knowledge and activity, which you have shown in the exercise of your functions, could not fail to produce those good effects which are evident in the southern army, and which General Greene speaks of with the utmost satisfaction. I beg you will receive my sincere thanks for the pains you have taken to establish that order and regularity, which at present exists in that army. I am sorry you are obliged to quit a department in which your services have been so distinguished.[26]

VI. Monticello—Fuller's Plantation—Philadelphia • 101

What exactly the "business of great moment" was that required Jean's presence in Philadelphia has not been discovered. A few months later however, in a letter to Washington, Ternant revealed that "family affairs" required that he return to Europe as soon as possible.[27] Perhaps he had been in communication with his brother in Louisiana and learned that matters concerning their siblings in Damvillers necessitated his presence as the head of the family and their legal guardian. Perhaps the "business" that called him to Philadelphia and the "family affairs" were one and the same; or perhaps not. What is fairly certain however is the Ternant did not return to Europe until a year later, in June 1784.

Ternant's return to Philadelphia to deal with his personal affairs coincided with and were overshadowed by everyone's expectation of peace in the near future and the growing discontent among officers over the issues of back pay and pensions; a dissatisfaction that resulted in the affair at Newburgh in mid–March, when Washington was forced to confront the army's disgruntled officers and remind them of their duty. As someone with hopes for a continuing career in the military, Ternant was as concerned with both developments as any other long serving officer, but there is no record of him being personally involved in the officers' protest. Instead Jean attempted to promote his career in either a future American military or the Royal army, currying favor with his superiors, seeking certificates of service or letters of recommendation and keeping as many of his options open as possible. Some of his thoughts and feelings during this period were expressed in a letter to his friend, Josiah Harmar, the former Adjutant general of the Southern army.

> The war, my dear Harmar is thus no more! The noble struggle is over and that you will see by the enclosed preliminaries of peace. What you and I must feel on the occasion is so easy to guess that I shall say no more about it. The independence of America is now established, but equity to the [illegible] and union amongst states or sets of them are not yet; and in that, I hope, we may be instrumental. As the flag, which is to convey this will probably arrive sooner than either Major Burnett or Col. Brodhead, I enclose you another copy of the memorial of the army to Congress. The only resolution that past yet on that subject states to the commutation; and is contained in one of the gazettes I send you. That is only part of the business, as you will see, and a great deal more remains to be done: but my other letter will explain that to you. I have written also to our friend Dr. McDowel, to whom I beg to be remembered again, as well as to Mrs. N. Fuller etc. I should have written again by this opportunity, had I been informed sooner of the departure of the flag: but it is not two hours since I knew it, and the vessel is now dropping down. You will oblige me to inform Capt. Steele that I have given seventy dollars cash, to Maj. Burnett for him, in payment of his additional pay whilst in the inspectors department. Armand was at last promoted a few says ago, to the rank of Brigadier, and the Legion, I hope will soon be stationed at a convenient distance from the [illegible] Philadelphia.

Gen. Mifflin with whom I dined yesterday desired to be particularly remembered to you. Nobody ever spoke of another with more friendship and esteem than he did of you. Adieu. Write by the first opportunity and let us know what your Southern lads are disposed to do. JT

My health begins now to better with the Spring & I shall at last recover my former vigor and heal so far as to enable me to play some of my old pranks. [Illegible] bless you.[28]

By the time Ternant reached Philadelphia, the First Partisan Legion already had been at York, a small town some ninety miles west of the capital, for two months. Its numerical strength increased and level of training greatly improved by Armand during the summer spent in the Shenandoah Valley, the Legion had been recalled to the main army and had arrived in York on Christmas day. It would remain in garrison there until it was disbanded in November 1783.[29]

In spite of his earlier intention, it appears that Ternant never joined the Legion at York or assumed any role in its operation. If he did visit the Legion, it was only for a brief period. Judging by his correspondence from the period, Jean remained in Philadelphia and tended to his interests from the comfort of its familiar environment. But even if he was not physically present with the Legion, his position as its Lieutenant Colonel remained Jean's highest priority. Armand's promotion to brigadier general, from Ternant's perspective, was a major development that under ordinary circumstances should have had important consequences for his own career. Unfortunately for Jean however, there were complications that effectively blocked his advancement. For the next twelve months Ternant's primary concern was to correct what he saw as an injustice and a stain on his good character and reputation.

According to the 26 March resolution of Congress, Colonel Armand, with Washington's approval, had been promoted to the rank of brigadier general but continued in his command of the First Partisan Legion.[30] Usually, when an officer was advanced to the rank of general their regimental duties and affiliations ended and they surrendered their command. The case of Col. Armand was unique however.

Although by the last quarter of the eighteenth century it was slowly dying out, there was a tradition of proprietary interests concerning individuals that had raised units by their own effort and expense. Although their corps was part of the regular military establishment these individuals owned its command. Originally the troop raised, equipped and often paid by Armand had been one of several so-called "independent" units authorized by the Congress. It appears that in Armand's understanding, notwithstanding his promotion, he would continue to be the Legion's head or proprietor but the actual day-to-day command would devolve on his second in command, Lt. Col. Ternant. He also believed that his advance in rank "would not hinder either the promotion of Lt. Col. Ternant or his enjoying the emolument of a Lt. Col. Commandant."[31] This was not the view of Congress however. With the ending of the war and the pressing need to reduce expenditures, Ternant's rank and duties remained unchanged.

Two weeks after Armand's promotion and fearing the sudden disbanding of the Legionary Corps, Ternant wrote his former commander, Benjamin Lincoln, now the Secretary at War and presented his case for being appointed its commander.

> I am sorry to be under the necessity of addressing you on the injury done me by General Armand's promotion, with the rights of retaining command of the Legion. That such a privilege was inconsistent with the establishment of October 1780, as well as with the general rules and uniform practice of promotions, cannot fairly be contested.... Everybody knows, besides, that the command and duties of Brigadiers were ever different and distinct in this service from those of field officers to the rank of commandant inclusive; and unless the rank and duties of those general officers be made regimental by an express definition of the present system, General Armand's promotion, I would have felt the disappointment, but I should have had no grievance to complain of.
>
> That exception to the general rules, and deviation from the former usage of the army, not only deprives me of an advancement I had a double right to, both as senior officer of the Legion, and the oldest Lt. Col. in the line of cavalry, but it even renders my right to the emoluments and privileges of a Lt. Col. Commandant, disputed. Further, as this exception is peculiar to myself and unprecedented in the army, it may be taken as an implication of incapacity or demerit, highly injurious to my character. This last object is too insulting not to justify my earnest request that Congress may be explicit or that said I shall depend on their generosity, on the justice of the Commander-in-chief and of the general officers under whom I have been employed with the southern army, and from whom I can produce testimonies of my services.[32]

Ternant also sought the support of Washington, both for his petition to the Secretary at War as well as for a certificate of service.[33] Washington's response was measured but positive. He provided the certificate as requested but deferred to the Secretary at War's knowledge of promotion practices and his judgment regarding Jean's complaint.[34]

Benjamin Lincoln's support was immediate and direct. He forwarded Jean's letter along with his own recommendation to the President of Congress, pointing out that the Legion was without a colonel and that the Congress had recently ignored an earlier resolution not to appoint any additional colonels by promoting several officers in the department of engineers to that rank. This fact Lincoln observed "opens a door to Lt. Col. Ternant's promotion to the rank of colonel, without injury to the right of any other officer." He concluded, "Although I would not wish the promotion of Lieu. Col. Ternant to the injury of any other officer yet I can not but observe, that his services have been as honorable to himself and beneficial to the states, that the most simple justice is due him."[35]

Several weeks later Lincoln wrote again to reiterate his earlier support.

> In my report to Congress on the subject of Lieutenant-Colonel Ternant's situation, which is become peculiar by the promotion of General Armand, with the right of retaining the command of his corps, I was not so explicit as it is now become necessary I should be.
>
> I am also clearly in opinion that Lieutenant-Colonel Ternant has an unequivocal right, in common justice, and agreeable to the former usage in the army, to the same promotion and emoluments, as he would have been entitled to. Had General Armand been promoted without the indulgence of retaining the command of his corps. Otherwise the honor, intended him, will be conferred at the expense of Colonel Ternant, which I am persuaded was not the intention of Congress, and I think they will be disposed to place the matter on the most honorary footing in all respects as it relates to Lieutenant-Colonel Ternant.[36]

The initial response of Congress to Jean's grievance was to assure him that the promotion of General Armand had been made without any derogatory intention regarding his merit. It then appointed him lieutenant colonel commandant with the associated emoluments.[37] Jean's appointment however, failed to satisfy him. It was recognition that General Armand could no longer exercise command of the Legionary Corps, but Lt. Col. Commandant only pertained to a position, was limited to a specific location or unit and was not considered an advance in rank. Since a colonel had always commanded the legion, Ternant was convinced he deserved that rank as well. Most important for Jean, the rank of colonel represented the highest field command and was only one step removed from the rank of general.

Ternant's attempt to obtain a promotion was part of a widespread effort on the part of all foreign officers in the Continental army to secure the greatest possible benefit from their American service. With the ending of hostilities and while waiting for news of the formal declaration of peace, there was a flurry of petitions to the Congress regarding back pay, appeals for a final promotion in rank and requests to Washington or other high ranking individuals for certificates of service that would be used to gain either financial favors from the French government or prove an individual's suitability for a position in the Royal Army.

With the ending of the war the American Congress proved generous and numerous promotions by brevet (without the accompanying salary) were granted. In March, among the engineers, Laumoy was appointed brigadier general, and in May, Cambray Digny was advanced to colonel, Genton de Villefranche to Lt. Col. and L'Enfant to major. In the Legionary

Corps, during the winter of 1784, Captains Claudius de Bert and le Brun de Bellecourt were promoted to major and lieutenants, Jean-Georges de Fontevieux and Verdier were advanced to captain. In addition, many individuals also received rewards from the Royal government. Pierre L'Enfant, for instance, received a gratuity of 300 livres and a captaincy in a provincial regiment in June 1783.[38]

Notwithstanding his recognition as commander of the Legionary Corps, Ternant continued his campaign for promotion to colonel and he also attempted to obtain some rewards for his foreign service from the French crown. In September Ternant appealed to the chevalier de La Luzerne for a recommendation to the minister of war.

> My General,
> The rewards that the King has granted to several French officers in the American army who were not attached to his service has determined me to request the same favors from his Majesty. The services I have rendered in the American Revolution give me hope that these favors will be granted to me as well. Permit me to send you for this purpose several papers that you will find relevant. The favors which you have always given me make me hope that if you judge my service favorably, you will convey likewise to the Minister of his Majesty.[39]

A week later La Luzerne wrote to the minister of war, Philippe de Segur, requesting that the King extend the same favors to Ternant that he had earlier rewarded to Messieurs de Cambray, de Rochefontaine and L'Enfant, officers in the America Corps of Engineers. La Luzerne reported that Ternant's experiences in the Continental army would make him "extremely useful in the service of the King, either attached to a particular corps or employed on the staff of the army, functions that he had performed with great distinction in difficult situations."[40] In addition to his own recommendation La Luzerne also asked his friend the Marquis de Chastellux to write to Segur in support of Ternant.

On Monday, 13 October Ternant's hope for promotion to colonel was finally realized with the news of the committee's recommendation that he be appointed colonel by brevet. Several days later however, in a brief note to Jacob Reed, a delegate from South Carolina, Jean expressed his dissatisfaction with both the time it took and the nature of committee's recommendation.

> I have been honored with your favor of the 16th inst. inclosing a resolution related to my promotion by brevet. The reluctance, with which it appears to have been granted, is as mortifying to me as the little and delayed justice Congress have done on my application of April past.

Give me leave sir, to return you my best thanks for your attention, and the favorable sentiments you are pleased to express of me in your letter; and to assure you I shall ever entertain the liveliest and most gratefull sense of the exertions of my friends, on this occasion.[41]

One month later, after receiving word that his promotion to colonel was under consideration, Ternant's American military career came to an end. On the morning of 25 November the 340 officers and men of the 1st Partisan legion, formerly known as Armand's Legion, were paraded and officially discharged.[42] Whether Jean was present during the ceremony is not known, but with his military duties concluded he was now completely free to address his own interests and future.

The winter weather notwithstanding, and probably taking advantage of letters of introduction provided by La Luzerne to French consuls in Boston and Portsmouth, Ternant took the opportunity afforded by the ending of his military service to travel; touring the New England states and visiting his former commander, Benjamin Lincoln, at his home in Hingham, Massachusetts, and possibly General Greene at Newport, Rhode Island. By early February Jean was back in Philadelphia and wrote to his former commander describing his plans and expressing his affection for the United States and Lincoln.

Dear General,

Give me leave to beg your kind offices in favor of Mr. Vaughan, a worthy gentleman, whose character and family you are doubtless acquainted with. He is the person who quitted England last year, and came over to settle in this country. His ventures have a just claim to the attention of every good citizen; & I thought I could not recommend his interests to a more generous and benevolent patron than General Lincoln. The enclosed papers will sufficiently show the nature of the service he wishes you to render him, and therefore will need no further comment. I will only request it may be done as speedily as convenient; and in case you cannot attend to it yourself, Mr. Lincoln in Boston would be fully adequate to it.

My journey to the eastward has been of vast service to my health; & my voyage to Europe which will be towards June, will probably complete the cure. In the mean time I intend closing my travels through this country by visiting Niagara and Pittsburgh as soon as the weather permits. That will not be I imagine till the beginning of April: by which time I hope to be favored with a letter from Hingham and your command to those parts. I have not a word of news to impart, but what I suppose you already know. The weather continues to be severe in Pennsylvania. Congress are still at Annapolis and effectually nowhere. I sincerely wish the federal administration may be speedily put upon the most respectable footing. I shall always feel a particular concern for the happiness & glory of this country, from a strong attachment I have to its government, and the lively affection I shall preserve for a few friends in it. Amongst these, Dear General, you stand foremost, and I shall always delight in every opportunity to evidence it. Do present my respect and most cordial affection to Mrs. Lincoln and your family and let me hear of the mill and your other improvements.[43]

Although the record is silent regarding Jean's intended journey to Niagara, there is evidence that the chevalier de La Luzerne was planning to visit the Falls that spring and had extended an invitation to Washington to join him. If the French minister and his party did in fact make the journey to western New York, Washington was not part of the expedition, but Ternant may well have been included.[44] It is not difficult to imagine that with his love of travel, his close association with the staff of the French legation and his growing friendship with La Luzerne Jean may well have coordinated his plans with those of the French minister.

It was in the early spring of 1784 that Ternant's twelve-month campaign for an advance in rank finally ended. On 22 April the Congress endorsed its committee's recommendation and appointed Ternant to the rank of colonel, to date from 26 March 1783, the day of General Armand's promotion. Ever mindful of its financial problems, the Congress insisted however, that since the command of the Legion had not devolved upon Jean at that time "he be not entitled to any additional pay or emoluments in consequence of his promotion to the rank of colonel."[45] Several days later, Thomas Mifflin, President of Congress, personally informed Ternant.

> Sir,
> It is with great satisfaction that I transmit to you an act of congress of the 22nd instant by which you are promoted to the rank of colonel in the Legionary Corps, lately commanded by Colonel Armand; your commission to bear the date from the promotion of General Armand.
> The report of the committee accompanying the act aforementioned is highly honorable to you and it may not be improper to add that Congress was unanimous in giving you the rank you have so well merited.[46]

With Mifflin's polite note and enclosed document Ternant, at long last, gained a measure of vindication; unfortunately it was five months after his discharge. The timing of the congressional act and the lack of any resulting financial benefit however, stripped the promotion of any immediate value and it is easy to appreciate Ternant's dissatisfaction with the course of events and how it may have contributed to him acquiring a reputation as a malcontent, in the minds of some Americans.

In addition to his travels and pursuit of a promotion Ternant was also occupied during the spring of 1784 with his personal finances. Although he was not in the desperate straits that many of his fellow foreign volunteers found themselves, without any income and unable to pay for their return to Europe, Jean was as concerned with the resolution of the pay and pension question as anyone.

Through the summer and fall of 1783 Generals Duportail and Armand, as the leaders of their respective units in the Continental army, made repeated requests to the Congress for payment to the numerous French officers serving in the Corps of Engineers and the First Partisan Legion. Duportail claimed that foreign officers who were not attached to state units suffered "grave and singular hardships" and that their pay in depreciated currency was not equal to their services. Unable to look to the States for relief they were forced to depend for much of their relief, upon money from friends in France.[47]

In March 1783 the Congress had offered all officers the opportunity to exchange an earlier program of half-pay pensions for life for a one-time sum of five years full salary payable at a future date but with six percent per annum interest. The officers were then given certificates of the amount due. Most officers accepted the proposal but many were in such financial difficulties that they were forced to sell their certificate for cash at a considerable loss, in some cases for as little as 12 cents on the dollar. In early May Duportail and most of the officers in the Corps of Engineers accepted the commutation. Later, in February 1784, the Congress accepted the figures provided by Robert Morris, Superintendent of Finance, concerning the five years of salary debt owed to foreign officers and established a system of payment utilizing the bank of Ferdinand Grand at Paris. According to Morris, the total debt amounted to 1,009,740 livres or 186,988 dollars, with one year's interest at six percent, totaling 11,219 dollars The redemption of the bonds began in 1792, was based upon funds that were part of a 2,950.000 guilders loan from Holland and was to be paid in gold and not in depreciated paper currency. Until then, holders of the bonds could only collect the annual interest on their note.

Naturally those officers who had served at a higher rank received the most in compensation. Major General Duportail headed the list of forty recipients with a certificate in the amount of 86,222 livres or 15,967 dollars; Brigadier General Laumoy's certificate was for 55,530 livres. The amount due Colonel Ternant was sixth largest on the list, some 42,583 livres or 7,885.00 dollars; his one year interest, $493.10.[48] According to some calculations, the livre during the period had the purchasing power equal to 3.25 American dollars in 1994.[49] Using these figures Jean's five-year compensation package would have amounted to 138,394.75 in 1994 dollars or a yearly salary of 27,678. With his American money added to his own small fortune, some judicious investments, future income and the exercise of caution in his spending, Ternant was able to enjoy a modest level of freedom of action and a modicum of financial security in the coming years.

In addition to receiving notice of his final financial compensation for his American service and his long overdue promotion, Ternant during the same period also became a member of the recently organized Society of the Cincinnati, a fraternal order open to all officers of the Continental army and officers of the Royal army and Navy that had served in the American campaigns. Formed in May 1783 as a support to the officer's protest over pay and pensions at Newburgh, the Society was dedicated to providing assistance to officers and their families in need.[50] During the first week of May 1784 the Society held a series of meetings in Philadelphia and if Ternant was in the city, in all likelihood he attended. In addition to a diploma of membership, each officer received a medal attached to a light blue ribbon, to be worn on one's coat.

By the early spring of 1784 Ternant had decided to return to France but he was among last of the French volunteers to leave the United States. By that time most of the others had already departed. Cambray Digny had left in June 1783 and Duportail and his two colleagues, Gouvion and Laumoy had sailed in October. In early 1783 the chevalier de la Luzerne had requested and received permission to return to Paris on leave and on 21 June 1784 departed with a small group from Annapolis.[51] General Armand sailed about the same time.

Jean's decision to return to France represented a reversal of his previous thinking; it meant turning his back on his former intention to abandon the old world and make a new beginning in America. His reasons for doing so were never made explicit but he had been contemplating such a move as early as July 1780. The "family business" that required his presence he had mentioned in the spring of 1783 may have been either a fiction or an exaggeration, but his memory of the ministerial promise of an equivalent position in the King's service for any rank that he obtained in the army of the United States and the encouragement and patronage of the chevalier de La Luzerne certainly influenced him. Also, Ternant was thirty-two and had been away from France for almost eight years; *nostalgie* or homesickness may have been a factor as well. No matter his reasoning, if Ternant sailed with La Luzerne on 21 June, he was back in Paris by 29 July and anxious for a second chance at a career in the Royal army.[52]

By any estimation Ternant's military career during the American war for independence had been an unqualified success. A stranger without either companions or references, he had begun his service in 1778 as a civilian employee but ended six years later a well-respected Colonel. In the process he traveled widely; visited most, if not all of the thirteen states, their major cities, back counties and wilderness areas. He had journeyed to New Orleans and Havana, to Charlestown and Philadelphia and to Monticello and Mepkin. He had explored the entire country and met and impressed many of its most important leaders. Equally important he had met and socialized with many members of the French diplomatic community, who in future years would become his colleagues. With the patronage of the chevalier de La Luzerne and the military experience gained in six campaigns Jean could look forward to the future with some optimism.

VII

Versailles—
Amsterdam—London
August 1784–March 1788

Ternant returned to Paris and Versailles in the summer of 1784 with every expectation that he would be rewarded for his service in America with a commission as an officer in the Royal army and continue his military career. His references were excellent. He had highly complimentary letters of recommendation from his patron, the chevalier de La Luzerne and the marquis de Chastellux, testimonies from the Congress of the United States, a laudatory certificate of service from George Washington and the previously offered assurance that the king would look with favor on his foreign service, from not one, but two late ministers of state. Once more, comte de Rochambeau had recommended him for a lieutenant colonelcy in one of the forty-seven recently raised provincial regiments.[1]

At best however, Jean's hope for an appointment was unrealistic. Although it was quite common for the Secretary of War to receive requests for royal favors in the form of cash gratuities, promotions or decorations from officers who thought themselves deserving or their sponsors, in most instances such petitions were either denied or the favor awarded less than expected.[2]

Following the victory at Yorktown for example, Rochambeau had prepared a list of such recommendations for deserving officers. For his son, serving as an aide-de-camp, Rocambeau requested a colonelcy, the cross of Saint-Louis and suggested a gratuity of 6,000 livres. He asked for three months worth of wages for the expedition's officers and for himself, the blue ribbon of the Holy Spirit. The response from the Minister of War proved less than gratifying however. Rochambeau's son was refused a regiment and the decision regarding his own request for the blue ribbon was postponed. Instead, Rochambeau was granted a generous gratuity of 30,000 livres for his success.

The officers of the *expedition particuliere* were likewise dissatisfied with the Minister of War's response. Instead of a cash bonus equivalent to three months pay, they received a gratuity in the amount equal to one months wage; for *Lieutenants premiers* 75 livres instead of the expected 225 and for *captain commandants*, 165 livres instead of 495.[3]

In addition to financial rewards, some fortunate officers also benefited from promotions in rank, or were given additional appointments. As to be expected in a culture based on aristocratic privilege, individuals from the upper ranks of the nobility received the most liberal compensation; Lafayette, for instance, was promoted to the rank of *maréchal de camp* or brigadier general, and received the cross of the Order of Saint-Louis. Rochambeau, in addition to his gratuity, was later awarded the governorship of the Calaisis with an income of 10–12,000 livres. Among lower ranking officers, Ternant's good friend, Jean-Baptiste-Joseph de Laumoy, was one of twenty-one veterans who had served in America that received an appointment to a post on the recently established *Corps d'État-Major de l'Armée*. Bechet de Rochefontaine, a *roturier*, the son of a wine merchant, whose background was similar to Jean's, was another.[4] Ternant therefore, had some reason to be hopeful.

As was the case with the vast majority of petitioners however, Jean also would be disappointed. He was not included among those who were recipients of the king's generosity and there is no record in his military dossier of him benefiting from any gratuity or appointment in the Royal army prior to 1787. In spite of Ternant's recognized abilities and record of service, the odds against him being awarded a commission were too great. His timing, once again, was poor. He had arrived in Paris a year and a half after the war was over and the reform minded Minister of War, Philippe de Segur, was making every effort to reduce military expenditures by paring the number of active duty officers. More important, Jean was a commoner with no previous service in the Royal army and new regulations were under consideration to make it more difficult, if not officially impossible, for a person of his social class to receive a commission. Finally, both ministers of state who had made the promise of future consideration to Jean were dead. Each of these liabilities was enough in itself to account for his failure to obtain an appointment; taken together they proved an insurmountable barrier.[5] Jean's mentor and patron, Baron von Steuben, fared no better in his attempt to solicit a royal favor. In spite of the chevalier de La Luzerne's support, Steuben's request to Vergennes for a pension of 20,000 livres also was rejected.[6]

Jean's activities and his movements during the first months after his return are unrecorded. Where he resided, how he spent his time or the identity of his companions is unknown. It may be that Ternant was a member of La Luzerne's entourage, and that he relied upon the chevalier's largess for his accommodations, and it is not unreasonable to imagine that he may have spent a good deal of time in the corridors of the Ministry building waiting for a response regarding a royal favor. It is also quite probable that he took the first available opportunity to call upon the American diplomats in Paris, Franklin at nearby Passy and also the recently arrived Thomas Jefferson at the Hôtel d'Oleans in rue des Petits-Augustins; to renew acquaintances, offer his assistance and perhaps solicit their support. Since both ministers had already met Ternant, if only briefly, they certainly would have received him with pleasure.

At some point it also is very likely that Ternant returned to Damvillers, if only for a brief visit. He had been away for eight years and there remained that undefined "family business" to resolve. As quickly as possible however, Jean returned to Paris and joined the large number of unemployed officers searching for a position, an effort that would soon result in a second period of foreign military service and his participation in another democratic revolution, this time in the United Provinces.

Between the winter 1784/1785 and October 1787, Ternant would enhance his military credentials and his reputation, as an officer in the army of the Dutch Republic. More important, his simultaneous service as an unofficial and secret agent of the French foreign ministry involved with the Dutch revolutionaries would finally gain him Royal favor. It was also during this period and because of his role in Dutch affairs that Ternant began a closer relationship with the marquis de Lafayette, an association that after 1789 would place Jean close to the center of revolutionary activity in Paris.

By the time Ternant returned to France the political situation in the United Provinces had become increasingly unstable and the country was slowly drifting toward civil war. The Republic's century long economic decline, reflected in the growing gap between rich and poor and the lack of a national identity, exacerbated political discontent. Historical tensions between the Republic's inland provinces and its maritime provinces over matters of defense and the equally long-standing struggle for political prominence between the ruling oligarchy of regents and the stadtholder, William V, had both been embittered by the losses incurred during the recent war with England.

These traditional struggles were overshadowed in the 1780s however, by the emergence of an aggressive democratic movement with an uncompromising ideology, the Patriots; "part of an international current of democracy that had already manifested itself in England, America and Geneva."[7] Composed primarily of disaffected intellectuals, influenced by the political ideals of the Enlightenment and the recent successful rebellion in America, religious dissenters, and an urban middle-class that had been excluded from holding office, the Patriots attacked the stadtholder as a threat to Dutch liberties. Equally important, the Patriots advocated a more representative democracy and challenged the regent's monopoly on political appointments on both the local and national level. During the 1780s each of the three political groups, the Orangists, who supported the Stadtholder, the Regents, the hereditary oligarchy that controlled town councils and provincial estates, and the Patriots, the democratically inclined disaffected, contested for political power, in constantly shifting combinations.[8]

Following the example of the Americans, the Patriots organized committees of correspondence, operated a political press that was directed toward winning support among the reading public and advocated an armed citizenry as an essential ingredient in the defense of the Republic. In 1781 Joan Derek van der Capellen tot der Pol, a nobleman from the inland province, Overijssel, and an early leader of the Patriot movement, called for the creation of *vrijkorpsen* (free corps) a paramilitary organization established as a counter to both the regular army commanded by the stadtholder and the traditional militia controlled by the regents. A democratic force, the free corps elected their own officers, practiced military drills and acted as a political pressure group, adding strength to the Patriot's political demands.

The increasing political instability in the United Provinces and the revolutionary character of the Patriot movement had international as well as domestic implications. In addition to the Patriot's anti–English orientation, a response to the losses incurred during the recent war and the stadtholder's historic link to England, the Republic's most pressing problem in 1784, was a growing diplomatic dispute with Joseph II, the ruler of the Austrian Netherlands, over long-standing questions involving territory and the opening of the River Scheldt for trade; issues that threatened to evolve into a military confrontation between the Dutch Republic and the Austrian Emperor and one with the potential to embroil France and other major European powers.[9]

The dispute between the United Provinces and Joseph II and the growing importance of the Patriot movement presented the Bourbon Monarchy with both a foreign policy opportunity and a challenge; the chance to increase French influence in the Dutch Republic at the expense of England, but at the same time, how to do so without undermining the centerpiece of Bourbon foreign policy, its alliance with Austria. Immediately following the peace with England, the Secretary of State for foreign affairs, Vergennes, in spite of his misgivings regarding the democratic nature of the Dutch Patriot movement, supported efforts to coordinate

French policy with the Patriot's anti–English and anti–Stadtholder position. As one of the means of increasing French influence in the Republic, Vergennes supported the candidacy of a former French general for the position of principal military advisor to the Stadtholder.

For the past thirty-five years the head of the Dutch States Army had been a German, Louis-Ernest, duke of Brunswick-Wolfenbuttel. Appointed Captain-General in 1749 when William V was still a minor, Brunswick had maintained his position as the army's commander when William became Stadtholder in his own right in 1766. As a foreigner however, many Dutchmen resented his influence in Dutch affairs and blamed him for the disastrous results of the war with England. When the Patriot party questioned his loyalty and forced Brunswick from office in August 1784, during the crisis with Joseph II (Brunswick had remained an Austrian field marshal and was related to the Habsburgs) Vergennes responded to the vacancy and proposed a friend, Yves Marie Desmarets, comte de Maillebois, as the duke of Brunswick's replacement.[10]

Although his military career had ended in scandal some twenty-five years earlier, was in poor health and well past his prime, the sixty-nine-year-old Maillebois was part of Vergennes's social network and was looking for an opportunity to restore both his reputation and his finances. During the fall and winter of 1784–1785 as tensions between the Austrian Emperor and the States-General increased and the appointment of an experienced commander for the Dutch army became imperative, negotiations regarding Maillebois's candidacy were undertaken. Thanks to a recommendation by Frederick the Great, Vergennes's standing with Louis XVI, and the influence of the old soldier's mistress, Mme. Angelique-Dorothee de Cassini, all objections to Maillebois' candidacy at both Versailles and in the United Provinces were overcome, and on 13 December Maillebois was offered the command of the Dutch army.[11] On 22 March 1785 he took the oath to the States General at the Hague and received the title, General of Infantry.[12]

As part of the effort to prepare for a possible military confrontation with Joseph II, the *Raad van Staate* or Council of State, the executive body of the States General responsible for the military, included in its defense appropriations for 1785 authorization for the raising of a number of units of light troops to augment the Dutch army. Prince Christian-Louis of Hesse Darmstadt was given the authority to recruit a brigade of 3,000; Baron Jean-Alexander de Mattha and Baron Frederik de Sternbach, both officers already serving in the army, raised mixed bodies of hussars and infantry, as did Captain Pieter de Lega and Captain Johan Franciscus van Weyesenburg. Frederick Johan Otto, Rhinegrave of Salm-Krynburg, Colonel of the Marine regiment in the Dutch army raised several additional units, a regiment of hussars, a legion and a corps of riflemen. The comte de Maillebois, as part of his hiring contract, also was granted the right to raise a similar corps.[13]

Traditionally recruited on a temporary basis to meet wartime needs and not considered part of the regular military establishment, mixed formations of light troops were organized for *petit guerre* or small war; scouting, raids, ambushes, skirmishing, outpost duties and combat in terrain unsuitable for close order formations. Such mixed formations were designated by a variety of names, chasseurs, free battalions, volunteers or legions and identified by the names of their owners. French experience with this type of formation began during the war of the Austrian Succession. In 1742 Jean-Chretian Fischer formed the *Chasseurs de Fischer*, which distinguished itself. Later, during the Seven Years' War the number of mixed units was increased.[14]

As part of the military expansion prior to entering the war against England, Charles-Armand de Gontaunt-Biron, the duc de Lauzaun formed the *Voluntaires Étrangères de la Marine*, a mixed force of eight legions, for service in the French colonies. Later, in May 1784, the Ministry of War established, as a permanent part of the royal army, six chasseur battalions, each composed of four squadrons of *chasseurs-a-cheval* and four companies of *chasseurs-a-pied*.[15] The force raised by the comte de Maillebois was therefore an example of a standard military formation of the period and one with which he was familiar.

Known as *Legion de Troupes Légeres* or *Ligte Troeppe Maillebois Legioen*, the new unit was organized into four independent brigades, each brigade to consist of four companies of *chasseurs-a-cheval*, light cavalry, four companies of fusiliers, line infantry and one company of *chasseurs-a-pied*, skirmishers. Each company required three commissioned officers, combined for a total of twenty-seven captains and lieutenants per brigade or one hundred and eight for the legion as a whole.[16] In addition; the legion had one company of artillery with seven officers and an engineer, Henri-Marie Bellonnet.[17]

Along with the one hundred and fifteen company officers, the legion also included three officers per brigade; a colonel commandant, a lieutenant colonel and a brigade major. Finally, the staff of each brigade required an adjutant for the cavalry, another for the infantry, a surgeon and a chaplain.[18] Although Maillebois was the titular head of the Legion, his administrative duties regarding the Dutch army as a whole and his age and poor health necessitated that its day to day operations became the responsibility of the Legion's second in command, Dominique-Joseph, marquis de Cassini, the husband of Maillebois's long-time mistress.

By the early sprung of 1785 Maillebois had formed a cadre of about one hundred and fifty French officers with a variety of backgrounds and levels of experience, to accompany him to the United Provinces. Mostly young and without income, a number of them veterans of the recent fighting in America, the officers were undoubtedly relieved to secure an income and to continue their military careers. Along with Ternant, François-Marie d'Angely, Louis-Charles de Bellfonds and Jean-Baptiste-Raymond de Fenis, comte de la Prade had all participated in the American war, as had Eugene Macarthy, a *sous-lieutenant* in the Irish Regiment, Walsh-Serrant, who had served with John Paul Jones and been wounded in the celebrated fight with the *Serapis*.[19]

Another veteran of the American war included in the contingent that traveled north with the comte de Maillebois was Marie-Blaise-Jacques Segond de Sederon. Twenty-nine years old and a former officer in Pulaski's American Legion, Segond de Sederon had been taken prisoner at Charlestown in 1780, exchanged in November 1782, was attached briefly to Armand's legion and returned to France in 1784 with the rank of major. In the new formation he was appointed a captain in the infantry.[20] With his service in the American south, it is almost certain that he and Ternant were well acquainted.

While most of the officers who served in the *Legion de Maillebois* remain of little historical significance, several, in addition to Ternant, later rose to prominent positions in their native country. Pierre-Auguste Lajard, a captain in command of the 1st company of infantry in the Legion's First Brigade would serve as an aide to Lafayette on the staff of the Paris National Guard, then briefly as Louis XVI's minister of war during the summer of 1792 and later was as a member of the *Corps Legsilatif* where he supported the return of the Bourbons. Pierre-Antoine Dupont de l'Etang, a *cadet gentilhomme* in the Legion, later achieved distinction as a successful division commander in the *Grande Armée* before he fell into disfavor in 1808, after being forced to surrender at Bailen, during the invasion of Spain. During the first restoration he would serve for a time as minister of war. The most famous person that served in the Legion however, was Etienne-Jacques-Joseph-Alexandre Macdonald. Nineteen years old in 1785, the future Duke of Taranto and *Maréchal d'Empire*, who was instrumental in helping to persuade Napoleon to abdicate in 1814, began his illustrious military career in the Legion as a lieutenant in the company of *chasseurs-a-pied* of the fourth brigade.[21]

Although handbills and posters that advertised the raising of a new regiment were a normal part of the recruiting process for the rank and file, the appointment of officers took a different form. Prospective aspirants had their applications and credentials reviewed by the colonel of the unit and/or the Secretary of State for War and a list of potential candidates was drawn up, from which the required number of officers was chosen. Ternant's personal qualities and recent military experience, supported by certificates of service, made him an attractive candidate. Nevertheless, a well-placed recommendation was probably more important than an individual's qualifications. And since by his own account Jean had few friends in Paris, the influence of his patron, La Luzerne, must have been a significant, if not *the* deciding factor in his being chosen. The chevalier was still minister-plenipotentiary to the United States as well as a former officer, with influence at both the Foreign Ministry and the Ministry of War; any recommendation by him would have dramatically improved Ternant's chances for being offered a position.

For whatever reason, personal connections, his recent experience with Armand's command, or as some alternative compensation in lieu of his failure to receive a royal favor for his American service, Jean was selected and appointed Colonel commandant of the Legion's second brigade. To assist him, Louis Casimir, baron d'Holtzendorff, another veteran of the Continental army, was named second in command. Several months later, on 20 May 1785 the Stadtholder, in his role as Captain General of the United Provinces, officially appointed Ternant and his colleagues, officers in the Dutch Army.[22]

While the officers in the *Legion de Maillebois* were either French or had served previously in the Royal army, the rank and file of the regiment was recruited in the United Provinces, and was composed of a mix of various nationalities, mostly Dutch and Walloons but also with Germans from Cologne, Treves and the Palatinate. By early summer professional recruiters had succeeded in enlisting 3,100 men, divided between regimental depots located at Ryswick, Rotterdam and Nimegue. Once fully organized the Legion was stationed at Hertogenbosch, a city in Brabant, one of the three areas or generalities under the direct control of the States General, and one that shared a border with the Austrian Netherlands.[23]

Between the spring of 1785 and that of 1786 Ternant attended to brigade matters, studied the Dutch language, traveled and corresponded with La Luzerne; keeping his patron well informed concerning political developments. He also forged a relationship of trust with Maillebois, replicating the rapport he had enjoyed with his commanding officers in the Continental army. Jean also met many of the men associated with the Patriot faction, among them a German Prince serving in the Dutch army who would play a central, if controversial, role in coming events, Frederick III, Rhinegrave of Salm-Kryburg.

Born in 1746 at Kyrn, the capital of the Principality of Salm-Kryburg, Frederick Johan Otto had spent much of his youth at the French court. At eighteen, following in the footsteps of many of his family, he entered the service of the United Provinces, as a captain in the infantry and by 1772 had become Proprietary colonel of the Saxe-Gotha regiment. In 1779, upon the death of his father, Philip-Joseph, Frederick became the reigning Prince. Two years later he married a Hohenzollern princes.

Although he was an officer in the Dutch army, Frederick, similar to most colonels of the period, spent little time with his regiment, preferring in his case, the excitement and diversions of Versailles and Paris to the boredom of provincial garrisons in Holland. Wealthy, but always in debt due to gambling and lavish spending (in the mid 1780s he was building a large splendid mansion on the *Quai d'Orsay* in the fashionable *faubourg Saint-Germain,* where the marquis de Chastellux and Lafayette had homes) and well connected, Frederick posed as a military expert and proved remarkably successful in efforts to advance his interests.[24] In 1784, thanks to the support of Louis XVI, he was able to sell his regiment, even though it was against the policy of the Dutch government. In April 1786, Frederick was granted a pension of 40,000 livres from the French government, which he immediately exchanged for a single payment of 400,000 livres to pay his debts. Finally, the following June, he was appointed *maréchal de camp*, the most junior rank of general, with an additional pension of 20,000 livres.[25]

Although Thomas Jefferson later described him "a Prince without talents, without courage and without principal," Frederick III nevertheless impressed many of his contemporaries. Bizarre in dress and eccentric he may have been, but Frederick was also intelligent and confident in his own abilities. He was energetic and witty, a raconteur who could be extremely persuasive, especially when presenting his own ideas. An early opponent of both the Stadtholder, William V, and his mentor, Brunswick, and increasingly recognized as an important military advisor to the Patriots, Frederick traveled to Versailles in August 1785 to solicit French support against Joseph II, and largely due to his friendship with the *controleur-général*, Charles-Alexandre de Calonne, succeeded in winning the support of Vergennes.[26] Later, he challenged the officially appointed commander, Maillebois, for control of the Dutch army. As a loyal aide to Maillebois, Ternant's relationship with Frederick was never close and his opinion of the Rhinegrave was always guarded.

In November 1785, after lengthy negotiations orchestrated by Vergennes and considerable infighting at the French court, the issues that separated the Dutch Republic and Joseph II were resolved peacefully; and with the signing of the Treaty of Fontainebleau the Franco-Austrian alliance was preserved and the immediate threat of war avoided. While the ending of the diplomatic crisis did nothing to lessen the political discord in the Republic, it did end the need for an expanded military and the Dutch council of state moved quickly to cut military expenditures and reduce the army's numbers. Peacetime levels of enlistment in the regiments of the regular army were restored and most of the recently raised units of light troops dismissed.

As part of this reduction of force level, on 12 April 1786 the *Legion de Maillebois* was disbanded and its officers, in accordance with the terms of their contract, were compensated with a choice of pension plans, an annual gratuity equal to one half their yearly salary for those who chose to remain in the Republic or a one time payment equal to two years of pay for those wishing to return to France.[27] Most officers took the single payment. Ternant however, was among those who elected to remain in the Republic and chose the one half year's salary (1,000 florins) for life.[28]

During the next eighteen months Jean's liberal sentiments, military expertise and his commitment to the cause of American independence enabled him to establish a standing among the Patriots. He also became an effective liaison between their faction and the French government. As one of a number of unofficial French agents in the United Provinces, Ternant maintained his close relationship with Maillebois, became a reliable conduit for the distribution of French financial aid to the Patriots and a valuable source of information for both the Ministry of Foreign Affairs and his patron, La Luzerne.[29] It was during this period, in December 1786, that Ternant's presence in Amsterdam was remarked upon by Sir John Sinclair, a Scottish baronet. In the final stage of an eight month tour of northern Europe, Sinclair commented on the presence of numerous French agents in Holland and identified by name, Duportail and Ternant, as "two of the principal officers employed by France to carry on their intrigues in America" Sinclair was especially impressed by Jean, describing him as "a very insinuating and able man. He spoke English perfectly well, and is now learning Dutch." Sir John also caught some of the flavor of Patriot and Ternant's thinking when he related that they saw themselves as "citizens of the world" and talk of the "happiness of the world" and the "good of mankind."[30]

The settlement with Joseph II did not to lessen Patriot opposition to either the stadtholder's authority or the oligarchy's monopoly on political office. After a confrontation with the States General, over the authority to issue direct orders to military units, William V abandoned the capital and was soon relieved of his command of the Hague's garrison. Later, he was suspended from his duties as Captain General. The Patriots also were successful in gaining control of three of the Republic's seven provinces, Holland, Gronngen and Overijssel.

Increased political disorder and armed clashes with forces loyal to William V also caused the Patriot leaders to strengthen their military position. A military commission was established at Woerden to coordinate the activities of the free corps and a defensive parameter or military cordon to protect Holland and Patriot controlled territory in Utrecht was prepared. Efforts were also made to win over the allegiance of units of the regular army. Later, as the threat of civil war increased, the military commission requested aid in the form of military specialists from France. It also continued efforts to obtain a pledge of direct military assistance from France should either England or Prussia attempt to intervene in the Republic's internal affairs.

By the summer of 1787 French foreign policy regarding the United Provinces was in disarray; compromised by competing interests at the French court, their agents in the Republic and an increasingly open commitment to radical Patriot interests and objectives. Vergennes, the advocate of a cautious policy of limited commitments to both the Dutch government and the Patriots, had died in February. Even while alive however, his policy had been challenged and undermined by opponents on the king's council, who insisted on a more forceful program to promote French interests; one based on a formal alliance with the States-General and direct support of Patriot actions against the stadtholder.

The growing realization that French national interests were being sacrificed to those of the democratic Patriots had caused alarm at Versailles and in November 1786 Vergennes's principal deputy, Joseph Matthias Gerard de Rayneval, had been dispatched to the Hague in what proved to be a failed attempt to re-assert control over French policy and reign in the aggressive actions of the Patriots. The new secretary of state for foreign affairs, Armand-Marc, comte de Montmorin de Saint Herem, however, was no more successful in reestablishing control over the implementation of France's Dutch policy than his more influential predecessor. Increasingly, French interests were held hostage to those of the radical Patriots.[31]

Although Ternant supported the democratic goals of the Patriots, became actively involved in their military affairs and served as a liaison between them and the French foreign ministry, his activities were dictated more by his personal relationships with his patron, La Luzerne and the comte de Maillebois than his own inclinations. The chevalier's influence was the essential factor in advancing Jean's career and in return Jean did what he could to assist La Luzerne's interests. Since the chevalier's return to France on leave from Philadelphia, he had been attempting to secure another diplomatic post and showed some interest in the embassy at the Hague. Ternant's coded messages to La Luzerne kept his patron well informed.[32]

Although not Jean's patron, Maillebois also helped to advance his aide's career. Maillebois was Vergennes's most important agent in the Dutch

Republic and his principal military client; both were members of the same social network. First as one of his brigade commanders in the Legion and later as an aide, Maillebois came to appreciate Ternant's intelligence and reliability and entrusted Jean with several missions to Versailles. Through his meetings with officials, his own reports on Patriot military capabilities and his enthusiasm and intelligence, Jean acquired favorable notice among the ministers of state and other important government officials.

In no small measure Ternant's increased prominence was reflected by an event that occurred early in the summer of 1787 At some point in the spring, before he became a prominent part of the Patriot military forces, Jean submitted a petition to the Secretary of State for War requesting consideration for membership in the Royal and Military Order of Saint-Louis, the most prestigious French military fraternity of the period and the goal of every officer since its founding in 1693.

According to its charter, membership in the Order was granted to an individual in recognition for either a long career of honorable military service or for an act of conspicuous heroism in combat. Length of service requirements had been established according to rank; *mestres de camp* or colonels needed at least eighteen years for eligibility, lieutenant colonels, twenty years, majors, twenty-two years; captains and lieutenants, twenty-eight years and provincial officers forty years.[33] Since Ternant had never been a member of the Royal army however, his petition was irregular and it seems apparent that someone with influence with the secretary of state for war must have encouraged and promoted his petition.

At the time of his request Ternant held the rank of colonel commandant and claimed continuous service from 1776 until 1786. According to his calculations, of the eleven years, six (1778 through 1783) had been spent on active campaign during the American war for independence. By the rules for admission to the Order, wartime service was counted as double, so in Jean's case, the six years spent as an officer in the Continental army counted as twelve years of service. He also included as service the two years, 1776 and 1777, when he acted as an agent of the crown in Louisiana and the three years, 1784 through 1786, as years of service in the Dutch army. The aggregate amounted to seventeen years, one year short of the number required for induction at his current rank.

The remarks on Ternant's petition that were written in response to his request accepted the figure of eleven years of service. However, the official that reviewed his request counted the two years Jean had served in Louisiana as being on active campaign and doubled them. Jean was therefore officially credited with nineteen years of service; one year more than was necessary for induction into the Order.

In making the case for awarding Jean the Cross of Saint-Louis, the author of the report pointed out that Ternant's recent services in the United Provinces had been "very advantageous" to France and observed that having the Cross of Saint-Louis would increase Jean's status and enable him to be even more effective in his dealings with Dutch officials. The author also noted that people with influence in the affairs of Holland desired that Jean receive the award as compensation for his work there.

In his summation the reviewer did not ignore the obvious impediment to Jean's admission. "One is not able to hide the fact," he wrote, "that *le Sieur* Ternant was never an officer in the service of the king and his request is contrary to the regulations." But he also took note of the earlier, but undocumented, promise of comtes de Maurepas and St. Germain that the king would reward Jean for his efforts. In the end, political considerations and patronage carried the day. On Sunday, 24 June 1787 Louis XVI authorized Ternant's induction into the Order of Saint-Louis with the honorary title of chevalier and the much-coveted decoration.[34] Later, Ternant wrote a brief thank you note to the man responsible for his good fortune, his patron and friend, La Luzerne.

29 June 1787 the Hague

My Lord,

Permit me to offer you my thanks for the favor your kindness allowed me to obtain. I would have been willing to go to Versailles for you as an expression of my gratitude if the comte de Montmorin had not insisted that I leave immediately after my reception.

Be so good as to continue your kindness to me and grant me enough trust to allow me to take advantage of the opportunities in the country I find myself, all will be agreeable to you.

I am with respect my Lord,
Your very humble and very obedient servant,
de Ternant[35]

No event in Ternant's career was more important than being awarded the cross of the Order of Saint-Louis. For Jean, it was a source of enormous personal satisfaction and it served as unimpeachable evidence of his military service and in some strange sense, in spite of his eleven years of service, it marked the beginning of his professional career. In addition to being a military decoration however, the Order's cross and ribbon also served as an indication of a recipient's character and social distinction. Moreover, because both nobles and non-nobles were eligible, membership in the Order of Saint-Louis also tended to blur the social boundary between commoner and noble; it was one means by which a non-noble, such as Ternant, could begin to erase the line that separated the two classes.

Finally, although membership in the Order did not ennoble a *roturier* recipient, it did convey several social and financial advantages. It released commoners from the obligation to pay the *taille*, the principal tax paid by all non-nobles and it also exempted the sons of non-noble members from the social restrictions that prevented commoners from becoming officers.[36]

Ternant's improved social standing following his appointment as a chevalier of the Order of Saint-Louis was confirmed by the introduction of the particle *de* before his name. Although not an official designation of noble status, the *particule de noblesse* or *particule nobiliaire* was a recognized symbol of rank and distinction, of an individual worthy of respect. The French bourgeoisie viewed it as such and adopted its use as proof of social worth whenever circumstances permitted. Ternant however, except for using it on his note of thanks to La Luzerne, never made it a regular part of his signature. But other writers did; referring to him in both official documents and in other writings as de Ternant. He was also referred to by the title, *sieur*, indicating a man of honor.[37]

One day before Jean penned his letter of thanks to La Luzerne, the political struggle between the Patriot faction and the Stadtholder's supporters was dramatically altered by an incident that turned the Dutch dispute into an international crisis. The stadtholder's wife, Frederika Sophia Wilhelmina, Princess of Orange, who was also the sister of the recently crowned King of Prussia, attempted to return to the Hague in an effort to rally support for her husband. Intercepted on the road by a party of free corps she was detained for a short time and prevented from continuing her journey. Although she suffered no injury, the insult to the Princess caused a furor in Berlin; a demand for an apology from the States General and orders to prepare a military response should the Dutch government fail to disavow the action.[38]

The eleven weeks that separated 28 June, when the Princess of Orange was prevented from continuing her journey and 13 September when Prussian troops crossed into the United Provinces, was a period of escalating demands and hurried diplomacy between the foreign ministries of France, Prussia and Britain, and various Dutch governments. During the same period the Defense Commission at Woedren worked to improve Patriot defenses. The fortified line stretching from Muiden on the River Vecht in the north, to the fortress city, Gorkum, on the River Waal in the south was strengthened and the City of Utrecht's fortifications, the center piece of the Patriots defense system, was put in order.[39]

The commission also appealed to Versailles for additional military specialists and urged the concentration of a French military force at Givet, on the French border with the Bishopric of Liège, as a counter to the Prussian army being formed at Wesel. Finally, the defense commission appointed three officers to command the Patriot forces. After first considering the marquis de Lafayette for the office of commander in chief, an option favored by Ternant, the commission instead selected Frederick III, Rhinegrave of Salm-Kryburg. Although Lafayette was more famous and highly regarded by the Patriots, the Rhinegrave was supported by the French court and its ambassador at the Hague. He was also a long-serving officer in the Dutch army, well thought of and had the advantage of being present. To assist the new commander in chief, the commission also appointed a Dutch officer, Albertus van Rijssel, as General Major of the Infantry and Ternant as Lieutenant General of the cavalry.[40]

Ternant's appointment was recognition of his standing among Patriot leaders. His democratic convictions were well known, as was the fact, illustrated by his recent induction into the Order of Saint-Louis, that he was viewed with favor at both Versailles and the Hague. More important, Jean was a professional soldier with considerable experience in the organization and training of inexperienced troops.

Notwithstanding his appointment, Ternant was under no illusion regarding Patriot chances in the event of war. The free corps were few in number, poorly organized and equipped, had no combat experience, and didn't match the military resources available to the stadtholder. Once more Jean had little regard concerning the Rhinegrave's abilities. His reports to the French foreign ministry regarding the situation in the Republic were consistently pessimistic.[41]

During much of 1787 Ternant was active in organizing Patriot forces in Overijssel, one of the Republic's inland provinces and an early center of Patriot sentiment. During the war with England, Patriots from the province had been prominent in resistance to the stadtholder and its principal cities Zwolle, Kampen and Deventer had become Patriot strongholds.[42] In the spring Ternant had been supplied with 80,000 florins to assist Patriot activities in the region and later, in August, Jean was personally involved in a failed Patriot coup attempt in the adjacent province of Friesland.[43] In spite of this setback however, by September 1787 Ternant had collected approximately 4,500 troops at Deventer, representing Overijssel and the territory of Drente.[44]

Failing to obtain an acceptable response from either the States-General or the provincial government of Holland, on 13 September, 26,000 Prussian troops commanded by Charles William Ferdinand, duke of Brunswick, crossed into the United Provinces.

A nephew of Louis-Ernest, the stadtholder's former advisor, Brunswick was recognized as both a patron of Enlightenment ideals and a professional soldier of considerable ability. Initially he had been against an intervention, but once appointed to command he prepared what proved to be an excellent plan of operations. During the first days of the advance a declaration of his objectives was issued, pointing out that the intervention was only aimed at the province of Holland and that the other provinces, Gelderland, Utrecht and Oversijssel, if they offered no resistance and permitted free passage to his troops, would not be attacked. Only Oversijssel refused to cooperate and Brunswick was forced to send troops that occupied the major cities without resistance, and captured a large amount of arms and munitions.[45]

During the Prussian advance everything seemed to work to Brunswick's advantage. The weather was warm and dry, most of the population welcomed his troops and Patriot resistance was both half-hearted and ineffective. On 15 September, to the consternation of the Patriots, the Rhinegrave abandoned Utrecht, the centerpiece of the defense line, without a fight; his army retreating in disorder. Two days later the fortress city of Gorkum also surrendered. And on 20 September, the stadtholder returned in triumph to the Hague, where the Estates-General restored him to the office of Captain-General. What few Patriot hopes remained were now centered upon a prolonged defense of Amsterdam, the last bastion of Patriot strength and the arrival of French troops.[46]

Amsterdam, with a population of 280,000, was the largest city in the Dutch Republic and the center of its financial and commercial interests. Following the loss of Utrecht the Patriot Defense Commission had retired to the city and undertook the task of preparing its defenses. It called for volunteers, opened the dikes and flooded the surrounding fields, had bridges destroyed, numerous barricades erected, the villages in the area converted into strong points and every effort was made to increase the numbers of Amsterdam's defenders. The city's garrison included six battalions of regulars, the 60 companies of the city's militia; on paper numbering 11,000, the remnants of the Rhinegrave's army and a small contingent of French engineers and artillerymen. Military command was placed in the hands of the colonel of the city's militia, J.D. van Hogendorf tot Hofwegen but the Defense Commission remained the final authority.

Ternant had been in the city for several days and found disorder and confusion everywhere. He had prepared a plan of defense but was extremely pessimistic regarding a successful resistance. In almost every way possible, Amsterdam's defense had been compromised. The flooding of fields surrounding the city remained incomplete. Just as had been the case at Charlestown seven years before, workers were too few in number and tools were lacking. No effort had been made to collect provisions to support a prolonged defense. No advanced fortified positions had been prepared. Once more, Amsterdam's defenders were demoralized. There was continuing desertion among officers and troops, especially since the disappearance of the Rhinegrave. The city's militia was reluctant to leave their homes or serve outside the city walls and in any case, lacked military discipline. Finally, in addition to the military problems facing the city, Amsterdam's municipal government was divided and paralyzed by fear of the city's general population that openly supported the stadtholder. According to Jean, the French had few friends in Amsterdam, whereas the William V remained immensely popular.[47]

In spite of his recognition of the many difficulties involved in defending Amsterdam, on 23 September or the next day, Ternant accepted the general command of the city's defense. Although he was the highest-ranking member of the Patriot army in the city and was an obvious choice, Jean did so reluctantly, believing that his appointment was little more than an effort on the part of the municipal authorities to avoid their responsibilities and deflect public anger; to make him a scapegoat for any of the hardships of a protracted siege.[48] In his letter to the French embassy announcing his appointment Ternant demanded support. "You are aware that I have the right to insist that M.de St. Priest (the new French ambassador) when he arrives at the Hague will reassure me by a signed letter and positive assurance, that I will not be abandoned, *and above all that French troops are on the march*. If I do not receive this letter without delay I will seek to leave as quickly as possible.... Remember, I implore you, I must have positive assurance or I leave."[49]

Several days after writing his letter and assuming command of Amsterdam's defense, two French emissaries arrived to inspect the city's fortifications and discuss the Patriot demand for immediate French military assistance. Before proceeding to the Hague, the new French ambassador, François-Emmanuel Guignard, comte de St. Priest had met with Patriot leaders at Brede in the Dutch territory of Brabant. He was accompanied to the meeting by two officers, Henri-Joseph, marquis de Lambert, a *maréchal de camp* and former member of minister of war's military committee and the marquis's aide, Mathieu Dumas.[50] As a member of Rochambeau's staff, Dumas had been in Philadelphia in September 1781 and may have been introduced to Jean at one of the many social functions held in honor of the French alliance.

At Brede the Patriot representatives described the demoralized state of the free corps and the desperate need for money to pay them. Since everyone was ignorant regarding conditions in Amsterdam and the state of its defenses, Lambert and Dumas volunteered to travel to the city and assess the situation. Posing as merchants from Brussels and carrying a hidden letter of credit for one million livres, the two successfully passed through Prussian lines.[51] After an inspection of the city's defenses accompanied by Ternant and other French officers and meeting with the Defense committee, Lambert and Dumas came away with the same view as that of Ternant, convinced that Amsterdam could not survive without the presence of French troops. They explained to the city's authorities however, that there was no chance of French military intervention before the next spring.

Several days later, on 1 October, the Prussian attack on Amsterdam began. Brunswick launched a pre-dawn assault on the Patriot's advanced positions in the villages of Amstelveen and Halfweg, and by the end of the day, after some sharp fighting successfully forced the Dutch defenders to retreat.[52] During the course of the next nine days and with no additional fighting, the Patriot defense collapsed. The stadtholder, restored to the command of the army, ordered all regular troops cooperating with the Patriots to leave Amsterdam and march to the territory of Brabant. Deprived of the services of the most experienced and dependable part of the garrison, and rapidly loosing control of the city, the municipal government on 10 October, surrendered; agreeing to disarm the free corps and permit the stadtholder to garrison Amsterdam with Dutch troops. The Patriot revolution was ended, and along with it, Ternant's three years of service in the United Provinces By December at the latest, he had returned to Paris and Versailles and been reunited with La Luzerne.[53]

The failure of the French government to respond to Prussia's military intervention in the Dutch Republic was a major blow to the monarchy's prestige and a sharp set back to its foreign policy concerns; one that highlighted ministerial divisions, the lack of preparedness on the part of the French military and that revealed the French state's weakened financial condition. For most individuals involved in the debacle however, the embarrassment of the diplomatic defeat had little impact. In spite of it, people worked on advancing their careers and many of the men who served in the United Provinces were rewarded for their efforts in the lost cause. The French ambassador, Charles-Olivier de St.Georges, marquis de Verac, one of the architects of the failed French policy, who had been recalled in August 1787, was given a pension until his next posting.[54] General-Major van Rijssel, who had fled to Brussels and then to France, was made a *maréchal de camp* in the Royal army and a *chevalier* of the *Order de Merite Militaire*.[55] The military engineer, François Bosquillon received the cross of St. Louis in consideration of his conduct in Holland and his colleague, Henri Bellonnet was promoted to major and placed in charge of the Dutch military refugees in northern France.[56] Ternant was also rewarded. He had acquitted himself well enough to emerge with an enhanced reputation among the officials at the ministries of foreign affairs and war and five months after the fall of Amsterdam, he finally received a commission in the Royal army and was appointed colonel commandant of the newly raised Royal-Liègeois regiment.

Before being commissioned however, Jean was dispatched on a brief mission to England in the company of his patron, La Luzerne. For Anne-Cesar de La Luzerne the extended leave from his post as minister to the United States had ultimately proved rewarding. At first, in spite of his success in the United States, securing another diplomatic post had eluded his best efforts. Following the death of Vergennes in the winter of 1787 however, and the appointment of Comte de Montmorin as foreign minister, La Luzerne's chances improved. Montmorin's daughter was married to La Luzerne's nephew and the family connection helped no doubt to bring La Luzerne into favor. In the summer of 1787, as the situation in the United Provinces worsened, La Luzerne exhibited some interest in replacing Verac at the Hague, but had been warned off by Rayneval. Finally, in December, his patience and good luck were rewarded and he was appointed ambassador to the court of St. James. In addition, during the same period La Luzerne also married the sister of his older brother's wife, in a secret ceremony. Forced by his marriage to relinquish his membership in the Order of Malta and the title chevalier, La Luzerne was compensated by being made a marquis by the Louis XVI.[57] The new marquis was not the only member of the family to see his career flourish. In September, Cesar-Henri comte de La Luzerne, Anne-Cesar's older brother, a Lieutenant General then serving as Governor of Saint-Domingue, was appointed Secretary of State for the Marine and Colonies. He arrived at Versailles to take up his new duties in December.

Ternant's recent experience as an agent and secret liaison to the Patriots, along with his growing reputation for reliability and his close personal relationship with La Luzerne, were instrumental in him obtaining his next appointment. His facility with English was also important. In January 1788 the ministry of marine, now headed by his patron's brother, selected Jean to conduct a secret survey of ports and naval installations on England's southern coast.[58]

Jean's mission was nothing out of the ordinary; continuing espionage activity was normal and reflected the mutual distrust that historically existed between the governments of France and England. The recent diplomatic crisis regarding the Dutch Republic had only increased it. The English government's firm commitment to the stadtholder, its refusal to consider a French sponsored compromise settlement between the Dutch parties to forestall the threatened Prussian intervention and its naval preparations convinced French diplomats that England was determined to eliminate French influence in the United Provinces, even if it took a war between the two countries to do so. François Barthelemy, the French *charges d'affaires* in London, was convinced of England's hostile intentions. In his dispatches he denounced the English government's "outrageous lack of good faith" and portrayed England as "a haughty nation unhappy enough to know only hatred for France."[59] During the summer of 1787 he had been ordered by Montmorin to send agents to Portsmouth to spy on English naval activity.[60] Even after the ending of the Dutch crisis, Barthelemy continued to report on England's militant intentions; an idea reflected later in Montmorin's instructions to La Luzerne that "relations with England could only be regarded as an armed truce."[61] It was in keeping with these belligerent attitudes, and mutual suspicions, that Ternant crossed the channel and once more entered the twilight world of espionage, coded messages and double agents. In company with La Luzerne, Ternant reached London on 25 January 1788.

The arrival of France's new ambassador and his traveling companion did not go unobserved however. Undercover agents led by William Clarke, employed by the recently established Home Office, were waiting for them and began their surveillance as soon as the two landed, an indication of English fears and that perhaps the reason for Ternant's presence was already known.[62]

In addition to whatever actions he took regarding his mission, Jean's stay in London was highlighted by two events, his attendance at one of the Queen's Drawing Rooms and presentation to George III and a meeting with one of the leaders of the anti-slave trade movement, Granville Sharp. Neither of these experiences was of much significance to Ternant's career or affected his life in any meaningful manner but they do help illustrate the range of his experiences. The former incident is some indication of how well known Ternant's name had become since the fall of Amsterdam and the latter occasion, evidence that Jean's earlier involvement in his friend John Laurens's efforts to enlist slaves in the Continental army with the promise of emancipation, was not merely the result of war time expediency but reflected Ternant's genuine belief in human dignity and his commitment to cause of abolition.

On a wintry Thursday afternoon in February 1788 Ternant accompanied La Luzerne to Drawing rooms, a regularly scheduled court function hosted by the King and Queen in the Presence room at St. James Palace. Different from the twice weekly royal levees which were restricted to males, required court dress and that only the king attended, the Drawing rooms were less formal, open to both sexes, and attended by both George III and his wife, Sophia Charlotte, and their children.

Drawing rooms took place every Thursday and Sunday, but on the latter day, according to custom, no presentations were permitted.[63] It was customary for foreigners to be presented by their country's ambassador

VII. Versailles—Amsterdam—London • 131

and it was during a Drawing rooms that La Luzerne took the opportunity to present Ternant to the royal couple. As everyone looked upon it as an honor for the person being introduced, the king's response was regarded as an indication of an individual's importance and any failure of the king to speak was seen as a sign of royal disfavor.

According to a report of Ternant's presentation made by Colonel William Stephens Smith, the secretary to John Adams, the American ambassador at the time, Jean's introduction was ignored. "Notwithstanding the most pointed introduction from the Ambassador, both the King and Queen passed him with a glaring and apparently premeditated insult and so strongly marked as to produce a buz of who is it? Do you know him? Does anyone know him?—insomuch that before night his name was writ in every private memorandum book with notes critical and explanatory, and when they found that he had been in service in America and Holland, some were not backward in expressing their astonishment that the Ambassador could introduce a person who had acted so pointedly against the views and interest of the King."[64]

It is impossible to know if the royal couple's failure to engage in conversation with Ternant was a deliberate snub, but Col. Smith's account seems accurate and much more plausible than the more famous but fictional insult supposedly delivered by the royal couple to John Adams and Thomas Jefferson in March 1786.[65] Ternant's response at the time was not noted but he could hardly have been pleased and the event could only have reinforced the anti–English opinion prevalent among French diplomats.

One of Ternant's duties on his visit to England was to deliver a letter from the marquis de Lafayette to Granville Sharp, the chairman of the recently formed Society for effecting the Abolition of the Slave Trade. As had Ternant and many other Frenchmen involved in the war for American independence, Lafayette had come away from the encounter with American slavery a confirmed advocate of emancipation. In 1785 he had even purchased a plantation in Cayenne and begun the process of education and the gradual manumission of its slaves. In his letter to Sharp, Lafayette introduced Ternant and recommended a joint effort on the part of the governments of France and England to suppress the trade in Africans. Sharp used the occasion to begin a correspondence with both Lafayette and Ternant and both were enrolled as honorary and corresponding members of the English society.[66]

Although Jean would continue his interest in the emancipation of slaves and would correspond with Sharp, he remained only marginally involved in the anti-slavery movement. Lafayette, more personally active, would soon join Jacques-Pierre Brissot's *Société des Amis des Noirs*, but

Ternant, even if given the opportunity, never became a member.[67] The importance of Ternant's meeting with Sharp therefore, has less to do with Jean's attitude regarding slavery, than with his growing relationship with Lafayette, an association that would become closer and more significant as time passed.

Ternant returned to France early in March, displeased with his recent experience.[68] His mood however, was immediately brightened when he received notice of his appointment as a *mestre de camp commandant*, signifying the command of a regiment. On 10 March 1788 the secretary of war, Athanase-Louis-Marie de Lomenie, comte de Brienne, proposed Ternant to the King as the replacement for a recent vacancy in the Royal army's newest unit, the foreign infantry regiment, Royal-Liègeois, then in the final stages of its recruitment.[69]

Jean's appointment was more than the fulfillment of his ambition to become an officer in the Royal army; it was also a quite remarkable and unique accomplishment. Out of approximately 35,000 active duty or retired officers in the Royal army in 1788, only 1,750 were *roturiers*, like Ternant, who had never served in the ranks.[70] Ternant's appointment however, was even more of an exception in that he was one of the very few commoners to be appointed to command a regiment during the period. In 1789 there were only six non-titled individuals among the slightly more than 200 colonels serving in the infantry. In one respect however, Jean's nomination did match prevailing norms. In 1788 the average age for colonels commanding infantry regiments, at the time of their appointment was 34; Ternant was 36.[71]

By any measurement Ternant's rise in his chosen profession was spectacular. In the short span of ten years, thanks to his own industry and the influence of his various patrons, he had advanced from being a menial civilian clerk in the Quartermasters department of a foreign army to being a colonel commandant in the army of his King; one promotion away from becoming a general. With his new appointment, the continuing friendship of the marquis de La Luzerne and a growing association with the foreign minister, comte de Montmorin, Ternant's future seemed both secure and bright with promise.

VIII

Paris—Darmstadt—Bitche
March 1788–August 1791

Ternant's good fortune in March 1788 had its beginning four years earlier. On 30 April 1784, while Jean was in Philadelphia preparing for his return to France, an event took place 3,800 miles away that appeared quite unrelated to his future prospects, but which in fact, set in motion a sequence of events that would help launch his career in the Royal army. The Prince-Bishop of Liège, François-Charles de Velbruck, passed away unexpectedly at Hex, his countryside château. The principality of Liège, which shared borders with France, the Dutch Republic, and the Austrian Netherlands, was one of a number of independent church states located on the western border of the Holy Roman Empire, whose archbishops or bishops were secular rulers as well as clerical dignitaries. In as much as the office of Prince-Bishop was an elected position, open to both lay and clerical candidates, the campaign to fill its vacancy stimulated considerable interest, not only among Europe's ecclesiastical officialdom but its foreign ministries as well.[1] Velbruck's sudden death was therefore a political development with substantial international implications. It was also the event that created the circumstances that transformed Ternant's military career.

Immediately following Velbruck's death the campaign to elect a new Prince-Bishop began, one that pitted four clerical candidates from France, Austria and Liège against each other and that generated considerable diplomatic activity. Largely due to the ceaseless activity of the French minister to Liège, Marie-Louis-Henri Descorches, marquis de Sainte-Croix, and considerable financial incentives from Versailles in the form of generous pensions to influence the votes of the canons of the cathedral chapter, when the behind the scenes bargaining and intrigues that characterized the election were finished, one of the local aspirants, Cesar-Constantine-François, comte de Hoensbroeck d'Oost emerged the victor.[2] More ideologically conservative and temperamentally authoritarian than his liberal minded predecessor, the sixty-year-old former chancellor to the comte d'Oultremont, Hoensbroeck, soon clashed with his council of advisors and the Estates of Liège, a political struggle that ultimately led in August 1789 to revolution.

French backing for Hoensbroeck's candidacy and the desire to strengthen the Bourbon monarchy's relationship with the principality of Liège was part of comte de Vergennes's larger effort to limit Hapsburg territorial ambitions and influence and extend French influence within the Empire. The principality, although part of the Empire's Circle of Westphalia, was already a traditional friend, with a long record of providing both financial and military assistance to the French government. Its capital, the city of Liège, was renowned as a center of arms manufacturing and the principality provided a gateway for French trade to northern Germany and the Low Countries.

As part of the French strategy to further improve relations, the marquis de Sainte-Croix proposed the re-establishment of a Liègeois regiment of infantry for French service. The new regiment would serve to provide both a source of much-needed income for the sons of Liègeois nobles and a position worthy of their social standing. At the same time, the regiment would facilitate French military recruitment in the region.[3] The new regiment would also be the means by which Ternant gained his commission in the Royal army.

Sainte-Croix's proposal, although agreeable to the new Prince-Bishop, received a mixed reception at Versailles. Vergennes emphasized the foreign policy advantages of his emissary's plan, but the Secretary of State for War, comte de Segur, had reservations. While not denying the positive aspects of the plan, he argued against the large expenditures a new, and in his opinion, unnecessary, addition to the royal army would entail. According to Segur, the additional regiment would cost France an extra annual expenditure of 335,344 livres, independent of the 22,383 of expense it would cost to clothe and equip.[4] During the next three years, while the French foreign ministry dealt with the international ramifications of Joseph II's territorial ambitions and Prussia's armed intervention in the Dutch Republic, and the various ministers of war struggled to reduce military spending in the face of the monarchy's mounting financial difficulties, discussions between the parties over the proposed new regiment languished.[5]

During this period, the plan's leading proponent and the individual that stood to be the principal beneficiary of any future agreement was a cosmopolitan Savoyard aristocrat, Joseph-Clement Sallier, comte de La Tour. A member of a prominent family in the Kingdom of Piedmont-Sardinia, closely allied with its court, his father had been the Ambassador to Madrid and an older brother, would be appointed ambassador to Versailles in 1789, the forty-six-year-old soldier of fortune had risen to prominence in Liège through an advantageous marriage. In 1779 La Tour married the niece of the Prince-Bishop, Velbruck, Of more importance as it worked out, she was also the widow of La Tour's late colonel, François-Joseph, comte de Hoensbroeck, the older brother of the future Prince-Bishop. In 1786, mostly due to the influence of his "pseudo" brother-in-law, La Tour had been named a chevalier in the Order of Malta. At the same time, he emerged as the most ardent advocate for the proposed new regiment and it was mainly because of his persistent and largely self-serving efforts, that French financial reservations were overcome and an agreement was finally concluded.[6]

On 18 November 1787 terms pertaining to the raising of an infantry regiment in Liège for French service were at last agreed upon and a convention, consisting of 13 articles that thoroughly delineated the respective rights and responsibilities of the King of France and the Prince-Bishop of Liège, was signed. According to the terms of the convention the new regiment received the title, Royal-Liègeois and took the number 107 on the list of infantry units in the Royal army. The new regiment's composition, two battalions, each consisting of five companies, and equipment were to be similar to the other twenty-two foreign regiments in French service. Other articles covered such concerns as discipline, uniforms, the regiment's colors, the respective financial responsibilities of the two states and fixed the percentage of various nationalities for both superior and subaltern officers; at least three quarters of the latter were to come from families of Liègeois nobility and the remaining number, if necessary, from subjects of the French king in either Alsace or German Lorraine. Central to the final agreement were articles that established the prerogatives of the King and Prince-Bishop regarding the appointment of the regiment's commander and regimental staff.[7]

Article two of the convention recognized the Prince-Bishop of Liège as the "perpetual proprietor" of the new unit and gave him the "freedom to propose to his Majesty a subject to represent him in the place of *Mestre-de-Camp Proprietaire* who will be chosen from among the most distinguished persons of his court." Based upon the authority given him in this article, Hoensbroeck, as expected, nominated his friend and his principal representative in the negotiations, the comte de La Tour.

The third article pertained to the right of appointment of the regiment's upper echelon officers and established that "the *mestre-de-camp-commandant* and the other superior officers of the staff will be at the nomination of the King after the fashion of that which is or will be regulated for the other foreign regiments in the service of His Majesty. The choice will fall as much as the circumstances permit upon Liegeois officers who have been found to have the required qualifications." The French ambassador at the Hague, St. Priest, proposed one of either two qualified Dutch officers for the position but Louis XVI relied instead upon the recommendation of La Tour and appointed a forty-five-year-old officer in the Royal army and a member of a distinguished family from Lorraine, Theodore-Charles-Alexandre-Bernard de Raugrave Salm-Salm, as the new regiment's *mestre-de-camp commandant* (in March 1788 the title was changed to colonel-commandant). Although not a native of Liège, de Raugrave's family connections in the principality were substantial. His godfather was a great uncle who had been a canon of the cathedral of Saint Lambert and served in the office of Grand Chancellor for the Prince-Bishop.[8]

Several months after de Raugrave received his appointment however, and before the Royal-Liègeois regiment was completely formed, he was promoted to the rank of *maréchal-de-camp* (Brigadier General) and became ineligible for a regimental command. To fill the vacancy created by de Raugrave's promotion the Prince-Bishop hoped to convince another of his friends, comte Ferdinand d'Oultremont, a Liègeois noble serving in the Dutch army, to accept the appointment, but he declined the offer. It was at this point that the Secretary of State for war, comte Lomenie de Brienne, proposed Ternant for the King's consideration. The nomination was unexpected but for once Jean's timing was perfect. With his recent service in Maillebois's Legion and at Amsterdam to his credit, his membership in the Order of Saint-Louis and his personal links to influential ministers and members of the *corps diplomatique,* Ternant was both qualified and probably a popular choice for the position. It also worked in Jean's favor that he was from Lorraine and that the royal government was attempting at the time to reward French officers for their service in Holland. So, for the second time in his career, Jean benefited from the promotion of another officer.

By the time Ternant received his appointment, the Royal-Liègeois regiment was in the final stage of its formation and it is unlikely that he played any role in the recruitment process. During the winter of 1788, while the regiment's cadre of officers was being formed, a group of professional recruiters, *racoleurs,* had enlisted over 900 rank and file from a variety of nationalities and with varying degrees of military experience. In addition to Liègeois, the regiment included in its ranks Dutch, Germans and Alsatians, Flemings from the Austrian Netherlands, Swiss, Savoyards, Italians and one Spaniard. In addition to being a mixture of nationalities, the regiment was also composed of mostly experienced soldiers. Over 100 of the new enlistees were deserters from other armies; 42 men had combat experience, 163 had between four and eight years of military experience while over six hundred claimed four years or less of service.[9]

Exactly when or where Jean joined the Royal-Liègeois is not known but he was included on the register of the regiment's officers published in *L'État Militaire de France* in June 1788, but that report did not establish his presence with the regiment.[10] In all likelihood Ternant probably joined the regiment at Cambrai immediately after his appointment; he almost certainly was with it during the mandatory period for officers being present, June 1 through October 15, as it moved from one garrison to another across northern and eastern France; first eastward from Cambrai to the fortress of Charlemont at Givet at the end of March, then in June, westward to Valenciennes and Landrecies.[11] During these months Jean devoted himself to the regiment's administration, met most of the regiment's cadre of officers and renewed acquaintances with several that he already knew from his service in the Dutch Republic; among them, Louis-Marie-Gaspard, Godart de la Bardeliere and Jean-Charles, Baron van Lichenberg, two colleagues from Maillebois's Legion and Adrien Van Helden, a Dutch officer of engineers who had served under Jean at Amsterdam.[12]

For much of the next two years however, Ternant was away from the regiment, on furlough or *congé*, an authorized extended leave of absence. From 15 October 1788 until 15 September 1789 he was on an unspecified *"commission particulier,"* special errand, for the king, and then from the fall of 1789 through the summer of 1790, involved in a number of diplomatic endeavors.[13] Jean's experience was not unusual. Between October 1789 and May 1790 almost one half of the officers of the Royal army took their regular seven-month leave of absence in spite of the disorders affecting most of the country. According to Samuel Scott, most colonels were absent during the same period.[14] It was the normal situation in the royal army of the period that colonels usually only presided over their regiments, most of the actual administration (the paper work) was handled by the lieutenant colonel, while the training and day to day activities of the troops were the responsibility of the regiment's major. Jean therefore would have had few responsibilities when present and even fewer if La Tour was with the regiment. Ternant returned to command the Royal Liègeois in person for the last time in November 1790, but again, he only remained with the regiment for a few weeks.

The cold, damp spring of 1789 found Jean in Paris, making every effort to take advantage of the city's many opportunities and attempting to advance his career by improving his standing with influential figures in the government and at the court. He was joined by two old friends from his time in America, the chevalier de Laumoy, like Jean, also a colonel and a member of the Order of St. Louis, and Gouverneur Morris, recently arrived in Paris to represent the interests of his business partner, Robert Morris. In the weeks prior to the opening of the Estates General on May

Gouverneur Morris and Robert Morris by Charles Willson Peale, ca. 1783, oil on canvas, 43.5" × 51.75". Urbane, extremely intelligent and a bon vivant, Gouverneur Morris, shown seated, was a close friend of Ternant during the war for independence and later in Paris during the early years of the French Revolution. He authored the preamble to the Constitution and later served as minister-plenipotentiary to France during the infamous "reign of terror" (courtesy Pennsylvania Academy of the Fine Arts, Philadelphia, Bequest of Richard Ashhurst).

5, the three dined and wined together and the two Frenchmen helped introduce their American colleague to the city.[15] Although Laumoy had been posted to Martinique in February and would soon depart, Ternant and Morris continued as regular companions until the summer of 1791.

Except for Jack Laurens, Ternant had no closer American companion than Gouverneur Morris. In the years immediately following the conclusion of the war, while Jean was pursuing his military career in the United Provinces and gaining notice at Versailles, Morris had been engaged in a variety of private endeavors in Philadelphia. He had established a very lucrative law practice and along with his friend and mentor, Robert Morris, formed a number of profitable partnerships involving trade with China and speculation in western lands. In addition to his personal concerns, Morris in 1787 had also served with considerable distinction as a member of the Pennsylvania delegation to the convention that produced a new constitution for the American Republic.

Armed with letters of introduction from George Washington and the French minister to the United States, Eleonore-François-Elie, comte de Moustier, Morris had arrived in France in January 1789 hoping to organize a group of private investors to purchase the American debt to France, encourage European investment in American back lands and protect Robert Morris's interests as exclusive agent for the French Farmers General's purchase of American tobacco.[16] In each of these endeavors Ternant played an active, if minor, role, using his own connections with government officials to help promote Morris's proposals.

By the spring of 1789 Ternant had become a familiar figure in the ministerial offices at the *Hôtel de la Marine et des Affaires Etrangers* on rue de l'Intendance at Versailles, as well as a frequent guest in the homes of several of the officials on the king's council. He was on terms of familiarity with the Director-General of Finances, Jacques Necker, as well as the minister of the Royal Household and former ambassador to the Hague, comte de St. Priest, and was involved in discussions on a variety of issues that faced the government. Recognized as able and intelligent, Jean was no longer viewed solely as a client of the marquis de La Luzerne. As early as January 1789 it was known that the foreign minister, Montmorin, was considering him for a diplomatic post in the United States.

In an encoded dispatch to John Jay, dated 4 February, Jefferson discussed future changes in personnel at the French legation in New York. The French minister, comte de Moustier, was to be recalled and the legation's long serving principal secretary, Louis-Guillaume Otto, would be sent to London as requested by the marquis de La Luzerne. According to Jefferson, Montmorin had mentioned the possibility of sending Ternant to the United States as *charge d'affaires* and later, pending President Washington's approval, appointing him minister.

In his letter Jefferson admitted that when asked if Ternant would be an agreeable replacement for de Moustier, he was unsure, telling Jay, "At first I hesitated, recollecting to have heard Ternant represented in America as an hypochondriac discontented man, and paused for a moment between him and Barthelemy at London of whom I have heard a great deal of good. However I concluded it safer to take one we knew and who knows us."[17] Notwithstanding Jefferson's lukewarm endorsement, it would take two long years before Ternant finally received his appointment and in the meantime he would have the opportunity to improve his negotiating skills in several other diplomatic endeavors.

Ternant's career advancement depended not only upon his own ability, it also was based upon his relationship with three men at the center of the royal government, three individuals of similar social background and experience, from two military families linked by marriage; his longtime patron, Anne-Cesar, marquis de La Luzerne, serving as ambassador to England, Anne-Cesar's older brother, Cesar-Henri, comte de La Luzerne, the minister of marine and colonies, and most important, the Secretary of State for foreign affairs, Armand-Marc, comte de Montmorin de St. Herem.

Until his death in September 1791 no individual was more steadfast in his support of Ternant than the chevalier, later, marquis de La Luzerne. Beginning in 1780, he befriended Jean, promoted his career and insisted that his young client's services be recognized. It was also primarily through his efforts that Ternant was introduced to many of the leading officials in the government and at court. Without doubt as well, it was La Luzerne who first encouraged Jean to consider a career in the diplomatic corps.

Cesar-Henri-Guillaume, comte de La Luzerne, the minister of the navy and colonies, had been introduced to Ternant by his younger brother in December of 1787, and subsequently employed Jean on an undercover mission to England. During the next several years their mutual interest in natural history and similar travel experiences in the colonies formed the basis for a growing friendship. An amateur but avid botanist who had introduced plants from the Indian Ocean area into the garden of the governor's residence at Port-a-Prince, when he was the governor of Saint Domingue, the fifty-year-old comte de La Luzerne, like his younger brother, had had a successful career as a soldier, rising to the rank of Lieutenant General, before being appointed minister.[18] In 1788 he had been made an honorary member of the *academie royale des sciences* and his son, Cesar-Guillaume, had recently married the eldest daughter of his ministerial colleague, comte de Montmorin. During the period 1789/90 Ternant took advantage of his friendship with La Luzerne to argue for a reduction in trade restrictions that limited commerce between the United States and the French Caribbean Islands. In spite of their friendship however, La Luzerne, as minister of the marine and colonies and mindful of the French mercantile community's attitude, remained unalterably opposed to any liberalization of French trade policy regarding the United States.[19]

The most influential of Ternant's sponsors by 1789 however, was Armand-Marc, comte de Montmorin de Saint Herem, who had replaced Vergennes as foreign minister in February 1787. A member of an old and well-connected family from Auvergne, his mother was the sister of Chretien-Guillaume de Lamoignon de Malesherbes, former minister of the *maison du roi*, Montmorin had been a boyhood companion of Louis XVI when the latter was *dauphin* and remained a trusted friend of the king. He was also related to Ternant's former commander, Maillebois. Montmorin began his public career in the royal army and then, as was quite common, switched to the Foreign Service. During the American conflict he had served as ambassador to Spain and immediately prior to being appointed foreign minister, had been governor of Brittany.[20] Along with Jacques Necker, the Director of Finances, Montmorin was one of the most influential ministers on the royal council and in 1789 was counted among those reform minded, liberal aristocrats that favored doubling the Third Estate for the Estates General.

As Secretary of State for foreign affairs Montmorin proved to be dedicated and diligent, Jefferson thought him "one of the most honest and worthy of human beings," yet Montmorin presided over a series of diplomatic setbacks that called into question both France's position as a great power and his own competence. The failure to resolve to France's advantage the political crisis in the Dutch Republic or to respond to Prussia's military intervention, the collapse of French influence in Eastern Europe and the Ottoman Empire, added to the burden of maintaining the unpopular alliance with Austria and the looming financial crisis confronting the monarchy, undermined Montmorin's confidence and left him feeling trapped by "the rigors of circumstances."[21] By 1789 few at court had any confidence in Montmorin's ability and many in the country agreed that he was ineffective; comte de La Marck, a Belgian aristocrat and a familiar figure at Versailles, considered him slow, indecisive, timid and weak.[22] Gouverneur Morris although more understanding was still critical. In his view Montmorin "means well, very well. But he means it feebly."[23] Much less kindly, Edmund Genet, the Girondist who replaced Ternant in the United States, remembered Montmorin as an "imbecile" engaged in "absurd and fatal putterings."[24] Jean Marat, the radical journalist, later denounced him as a traitor.[25]

The chevalier de La Luzerne had introduced Ternant to Montmorin during the late spring of 1787, and the new foreign minister quickly came to value Jean's pessimistic but clear-eyed reports from the United Provinces and took a personal interest in Jean's career. In late 1789 and early 1790 Montmorin took advantage of Ternant's reputation gained in America and Holland and employed Jean as his representative during negotiations with the Belgian democrats. Later he selected Ternant to serve as a special envoy to the German Princes who held landed estates in Alsace and who's feudal rights the National Assembly had abrogated.

It was also during this period that Ternant began his association with the marquis de Lafayette. Until 1787 Lafayette had shown little interest in his former comrade-in-arms. Jean's induction into the Order of Saint-Louis, his work with the Dutch Patriots and command at Amsterdam, and his reported willingness to serve under Lafayette in the resistance to the Prussian intervention however, encouraged Lafayette's interest and his praise; referring to Ternant's service in Holland, as "grand and noble."[26] Ternant's subsequent appointment as colonel of the Royal-Liègeois regiment, his public association with important members of the royal government and his work as a liaison between the French foreign ministry and the democratic movement in the Austrian Netherlands helped foster both a closer professional relationship with Lafayette and Jean's inclusion in the marquis's circle of liberal friends. Jean was also advised by the marquis de La Luzerne to pay attention to Lafayette. By the fall of 1789 Ternant had become a frequent guest at Lafayette's Paris residence and table.[27]

Notwithstanding their growing professional association and Lafayette's increased appreciation of Jean's talents however, the two men never became intimate friends, and the marquis never acted as Jean's patron. By the fall of 1789 Ternant was already well established in his career and had other individuals, far better placed at court than Lafayette, to promote his interests. There has been a tendency to credit Lafayette for Ternant's appointment as minister, but this was not the case. Lafayette certainly favored and supported Ternant's appointment but he had no hand in the choice. That decision had been made in early 1789, long before Ternant and Lafayette had formed a relationship and it was due to the patronage of Anne-Cesar de La Luzerne and Montmorin.

Although he never achieved great wealth, by the spring of 1789 Ternant's finances were in good order. He had been so successful in his business affairs in fact that by the summer of 1790 there were suspicions that he had, in some mysterious way, used the revolution to amass a small fortune.[28] Ternant's increasing wealth however, was easily accounted for. The income derived from his service in the Dutch Republic had been substantial and included not only his salaries as a colonel in the Maillebois Legion and as a lieutenant general in the Patriot military, salaries that equaled the pay for those grades in the royal army, but also monies he received in payment for information provided to the ministry of foreign affairs.[29]

As colonel commandant of the Royal-Liègeois Ternant's annual salary was 4,000 livres for the four months required service with the regiment, and any additional time spent with his unit would be compensated by an additional 1,000 livres per month.[30] Later, in July 1790, the Constituent Assembly would increase a colonel's annual salary to 6,000 livres.[31] Even without extra pay however, Jean's regular salary represented a substantial level of yearly income as compared with the wages earned by most government employees or the vast majority of French workers. For instance, the yearly salary paid to a *sous-lieutenant,* the lowest commissioned rank in the royal army was 720 livres; sergeants received 276 annually and soldiers 114.³² Ordinary unskilled laborers in Paris, who enjoyed steady employment during the period, earned about 360 livres per annum and most clerks in the ministries received considerably less than 2,500 livres a year.³³ Jacques-Pierre Brissot, a sometime journalist and social critic residing in Paris during the 1780s and later one of the leaders of the Girondins in the Legislative Assembly responsible for Jean's replacement as minister, was able to support a wife and two children in 1786 on 1,384 livres.³⁴ Unmarried and without the expenses of a family, Jean's colonel's salary alone would have allowed him to live in considerable comfort.

Ternant however, had other sources of regular income. In addition to his military pay Jean also received a pension from the Dutch Republic for his service in Maillebois's Legion in the sum of 1,000 florins a year, worth about 2,500 livres. He had as well, the 6 percent per annum interest payment on the pension from his American service (colonel's yearly salary for five years) that amounted to 2,554 livres that he could collect in Paris at the bank of Ferdinand Grand.

In addition to his income Ternant's economic situation was also strengthened by his membership in the Order of Saint-Louis. Often, individuals, at the time of their induction, were awarded a small gratuity. Moreover, if they were commoners, they were also released from the obligation to pay the *taille*, the tax paid by all non-nobles. Both of these benefits would have enhanced Jean's financial well-being.

For the first time Ternant had a substantial amount of disposable income at his command and there is some reason to believe that during this period he began an ongoing and profitable program of regular investment, both in a variety of private commercial ventures and by the purchase of government subscriptions offered on the Paris Bourse or stock exchange. As much as any prudent bourgeois businessman, always sensitive to the state of his finances, Jean was frugal, avoided gambling, only practiced the moderate consumption, *luxe de commodité*, associated with the middle class and was always mindful of his future economic security.³⁵ The few records of his financial dealings that exist from his later years and comments in his correspondence from that same period reveal that he was conservative in his financial transactions and avoided risky short-term investments that promised large profits. He had nothing in common with *agioteurs*, speculators, such as the Genevan banker, Etienne Claviere or the American entrepreneur James Swan, who bought and sold in large volume with borrowed capital and accepted the risk inherent in such operations. Instead, Ternant favored longer-term arrangements that offered a lower but more certain return. Records from the 1820s reveal that he much preferred either bank certificates or government bonds in a class known as *rentes perpetuélles* that promised dividends of between 3 and 8 percent per year on the original investment and that when terminated, returned the principal to the *rentier*.[36]

In addition to his expanding circle of personal relationships with Parisian intellectuals, bankers, wealthy aristocrats and government officials, Ternant also worked to expand his network of acquaintances with members of the American community in Paris and London. In addition to his friend Morris and the diplomats, Thomas Jefferson, minister to the French court, and his young secretary, William Short, Jean also cultivated relations with a number of American businessmen in Europe attempting to increase their fortunes; Daniel Parker, a successful speculator in American paper with a checkered past, James Swan, an entrepreneur included among Lafayette's circle of friends, and the well-connected Anglo-American businessman, John Barker Church, and his wife, the former Angelica Schulyer, an older sister of Alexander Hamilton's wife, Elizabeth.

It may have been at this time that Jean was introduced to Church's ten-year-old daughter, Catherine, a classmate of Jefferson's daughters at the convent school at the Abbaye Royale de Panthemont and a regular weekend guest at the Hôtel de Langsac, Jefferson's Paris residence.[37] Later in life, as the wife of New York businessman, Bertrum Peter Cruger, and the confidant of Gabrielle Josephine Du Pont, Catherine (Kitty to her family and friends) would become a close personal friend of Ternant and a central figure in his social circle. In a codicil attached to his final testament in October 1833, Jean granted Catherine Cruger and her two daughters, Amelia and Henrietta, 2,500 livres as beneficiaries.[38]

Ternant's activities during the summer of 1789 remain a mystery. There is no indication that he witnessed the tumultuous events in Paris and at Versailles that resulted in the collapse of the absolutist monarchy nor is there any information regarding his employment elsewhere on his special mission. He appeared again in Paris however, shortly after the forced return of the royal family during the first week of October.

On the evening of 9 October, Ternant was among a large number of guests at the home of Lafayette where much of the conversation concerned replacing Jacques Necker, the director of finance and his supporters on the king's council, Montmorin, La Luzerne and St. Priest, with individuals more acceptable to the national Assembly.[39] As all those to be removed were close associates of Ternant, he could not have been pleased, but during the course of the evening Jean talked to Gouverneur Morris and limited his remarks to unspecified military matters.

Although in late June the Royal-Liègeois had been notified to hold itself in readiness to reinforce the crown's forces in Paris, Jean's regiment was not among the fifteen infantry units eventually sent for in the weeks leading up to the July crisis.[40] Instead, the Royal-Liègeois, in garrison at

Avesnes-sur-Helpe since March, remained employed in policing rural disturbances associated with what later came to be known as the "Great Fear" and dealing with a dramatic upsurge in desertions, some 205 between June and August, that afflicted many regiments in the second half of 1789. Fortunately for the Royal-Liègeois, most of the individuals attempting to escape were apprehended and returned to duty.[41]

There is some evidence that Ternant was engaged at this time in secretly working to organize a French force, to be commanded by Lafayette, that would act in support of a Belgian revolt against the Hapsburg Emperor.[42] The fact that the Royal-Liègeois was stationed near the border with the Austrian Netherlands and could easily have been made part of Lafayette's proposed army may have been the reason why Jean assured his American friend, Morris, that he was certain of his regiment's loyalty and that, if needed; he could also call upon the service of 600 *chasseurs*, gamekeepers, from the Bois de Boulogne. The secret nature of his activities also caused Ternant to insist that Morris could not mention his name in any third party conversation but could only say that he knew of an officer that could be relied upon.[43]

While the revolution in France continued, a similar upheaval gained strength in the Austrian Netherlands; a resistance movement, that while it drew inspiration from the earlier revolutions in America and the Dutch Republic and was influenced in many respects by the events taking place in Paris, was nevertheless, unique. Unlike the revolution that was unfolding in France, the political revolt that erupted in the late fall of 1789 in the ten mostly independent provinces that made up the Austrian Netherlands began as a conservative reaction *against* the modernizing reforms of Joseph II; a movement for the restoration of ancient corporate and provincial liberties.[44]

In spite of its conservative nature however, the resistance in Brabant and elsewhere soon evolved into a movement for Belgian independence and as such became an international development that concerned the major powers, Prussia, England and especially, France. Belgian patriots soon divided over the question of the future form of political institutions in an independent Belgium. The Statist party, anti–Hapsburg and dedicated to Belgian independence, insisted upon the restoration of the traditional system of political representation and provincial autonomy. The other major group, made up of educated and wealthy individuals historically excluded from the governing class, collected around the leadership of J.F. Vonck, an attorney from Brussels, was more democratic. The Vonckists also called for independence but demanded unification with the Principality of Liège, a national assembly, equal representation and a government based upon the principal of popular sovereignty. Both parties sought to enlist aid from foreign powers; the Statist party looked to Austria's traditional opponent, Prussia, and the Vonskists appealed to France.[45]

Since August Ternant had been involved in talks with a representative from Brussels, in Paris attempting to obtain French support for the Vonckist party. Representing the comte de Montmorin, Ternant assisted Jean-Joseph Torfs, the Vonckist emissary, and Barthelemy Tort de la Sonde, Lafayette's agent, in drawing up a political compromise that would satisfy all parties. The program eventually agreed upon called for an autonomous Belgium within the Austrian empire, a national assembly based upon an enlarged franchise patterned upon the French example and a constitution. It was a plan favored by Lafayette, had the qualified support of Montmorin and accepted by Torfs.[46]

On its part, French support for the Belgian revolution was complicated and ultimately frustrated by the struggle for control of French foreign affairs between the monarchy and the National Assembly. Louis XVI and his ministers remained dedicated to maintaining the alliance with Austria and were unwilling to employ the Royal army to aid or defend an independent Belgium at the expense of Austria. Conversely, in the National Assembly there was little support for the Austrian alliance but considerable interest in promoting democratic reforms in the newly independent Belgium. It was unwilling however, either to assist the Emperor Leopold in restoring Austrian control or to recognize the undemocratic Statist regime.[47]

Through the winter and spring of 1790 Lafayette and Ternant collaborated to advance a more democratic political arrangement in Belgium but to no avail. In January Lafayette, acting independently from the royal government, sent his own agent, Charles-Lous-Hugnet, marquis de Semonville, to Brussels in an effort to persuade the Statist regime to accept the proposals drawn up by Torfs and Ternant. At the same time Ternant met with a Belgian liberal, count Cornet de Grez, in conversations that centered on arranging an international conference to resolve the Belgian question without further fighting. Both efforts failed. In June, against a background of widespread violence directed against the vonckist democrats that drove them into exile, the Statist government in Brussels rejected both the call to include the vonckists in a new government and the proposal to recognize Austrian sovereignty in an autonomous Belgium. Faced with an inevitable Austrian military assault however, and in spite of its unwillingness to accept the French plan, the regime appealed to Lafayette to send "a distinguished officer" to supervise its military preparations and specifically requested the chevalier de Ternant.[48] In his brief response Lafayette informed the Belgian authorities that Ternant was in Germany and unavailable and that the National Assembly refused to recognize the current government.[49] The French foreign ministry also ceased all contact with the Statist dominated government. With the French government unwilling to recognize the regime in Brussels or take any measure to assist it, Ternant's role as a liaison with the Vonckist faction became irrelevant.

Although actively involved in meetings with the Belgian democrats Ternant was not precluded from continuing to look to his own interests. In early February, in a series of meetings at the homes of Montmorin and La Luzerne, Ternant met Morris and discussed a potentially profitable investment opportunity, the sale of lands along the St. Lawrence River, the possibility of stimulating Dutch interest in the project and assisting individuals that might be interested in emigrating. Ternant promised to meet with any interested parties and to keep Morris informed.[50]

One month later Morris was in London, acting as an agent for President Washington, to improve relations and discuss unresolved issues linked to the peace treaty of 1783. In several letters, written in response to a letter from Ternant in late April, Morris reported on the political and economic situation in England, especially its weakened financial condition; "The supposed Prosperity of this Country is a Bubble ... even now in full Peace her Revenue taken at the highest is but barely equal to her Expenditure.... Indeed any serious Blow at the Commerce would give a Shock to Revenue and to every Thing."[51] Morris proposed that France should take advantage of the Nootka Sound crisis and join her ally, Spain, in a war against a financially weakened England. Such a war, in his opinion, would help restore royal authority and distract attention from domestic problems.

On a more personal note, Morris offered Ternant some friendly observations regarding Jean's financial interests. "If your friends speculate in the *Assignats*, I wish them much success, but I incline to think that there will be more loss than gain in such speculations. You and I know a little about *paper money*. There is somewhere on the way towards me a long letter and other documents respecting some lands in America, about which we have had a conversation together. I will write to you about that affair when I receive it. You mistake me if you suppose that I meant to stimulate your endeavors. I was prompted merely by a sense of justice. Why should your time and attention be consumed by the business of other people?"[52]

There is no evidence that Ternant took Morris up on the investment opportunities in the sale of St. Lawrence lands or that he chose to speculate in the lucrative but dangerous area of paper money but such concerns do serve to indicate the diverse nature of Jean's financial interests.

Ternant's next assignment from Montmorin was in response to a dispute with a number of German princes who owned estates in Alsace and his appointment as special envoy reflected both a fundamental change in the nature of his duties and his improved standing in the foreign ministry. Prior to this undertaking, in his work in North America, the United Provinces, his missions to England and as a liaison to the Belgian vonckists, Jean had always been an unofficial agent, working in secret. There was nothing clandestine about this mission however. As emissary of the French government to the German princes his role was both public and official.

During the evening session of the National Assembly on 4 August 1789, in an effort to show support for the wave of peasant riots directed against the seigniorial rights of local landlords, the delegates enthusiastically agreed to surrender personal, municipal and provincial privileges. In the course of a wild meeting, described by one participant as "a moment of patriotic drunkenness" and by a modern historian as a "tidal wave of revolutionary altruism," individual exemption from taxation, ecclesiastical tithes, manorial rights and personal services linked to the ownership of property, the plurality of benefices and the purchase of public office were abolished.[53] Seven days later the National Assembly formally decreed the destruction of the feudal regime in France.

In the course of eliminating the remnants of feudalism in France however, the Assembly made no exception for those feudal rights and legal jurisdictions that belonged to a group of German princes who owned properties in Alsace; rights protected by international treaties. For the National Assembly the issue, although complex, was primarily one of domestic concern and its decree based upon the acknowledged fact of French souvergnity over Alsace. For the German princes however, the issue was viewed in the context of international relations and involved France's unilateral rejection of its treaty obligations.[54]

Separated from the rest of France by the Vosges Mountains, Alsace was both distant and different. From Paris it normally took six days by stagecoach to reach Strasbourg, its largest city. In addition to being remote, Alsace could scarcely be considered French. It was linked to the Rhineland by both culture and commerce. It was German in language and custom, and until the revolution the province had maintained a unique and mostly separate existence. Alsatians insisted upon maintaining their privileges and immunities enshrined in international treaties. Although French sovereignty and control was accepted, fully one-third of the population were inhabitants of 1,442 seigneuries, church properties or villages that continued to pay feudal dues to Bishops and Princes of the Holy Roman Empire.[55]

Even before the night of 4 August however, the issue of financial privileges and tax exemption, including those of foreign princes, was under review in Alsace and it had generally been agreed upon that feudal privileges, either French or German, could only lead to the establishment of a "dangerous aristocracy" and had to be eliminated.[56]

Almost immediately following the French legislation however, Prussia, looking to his own territorial interests, began to stoke the traditional anti–French sentiment among the inhabitants of the Rhineland territories and encouraged the Princes to reject the decrees of the National Assembly. In September 1789 a Prussian envoy urged the Princes to take their complaints to the German Diet and appeal to the Emperor. The Princes need little prodding however. In February 1790 they sent a protest to the National Assembly. By the time Ternant began his journey east, anti- French feelings had been aroused and there was even talk of restoring Alsace to the Empire.[57]

The response to the German protest by both the National Assembly and the foreign ministry was conciliatory and it was generally accepted that some compensation for their respective losses should be offered. Montmorin, as foreign minister, was particularly concerned to quickly resolve the question before anti–French sentiments undermined France's influence among the various member states of the Empire. In June, in response to Prussia's diplomatic effort to organize resistance to the decrees of the National Assembly, he resolved to send an envoy to persuade the German princes to accept the principal of indemnities. To carry out this sensitive mission, one that required tact and a conciliatory manner. Montmorin chose Ternant.

In his instructions Montmorin cautioned Ternant to avoid engaging in discussions over the legal aspects of the international treaties and simply explain to the princes that it was because of its respect for the treaties that France was prepared to offer them a generous compensation for their material losses. He should also emphasize that an acceptance on their part was in their best interests, that after ending the feudal privileges of French landlords, it would be impossible for the princes to maintain their feudal rights; any attempt to do so would only lead to rioting which the French authorities would be unable to prevent or control. Finally Ternant was instructed to explain that it was also in the prince's best interest to treat directly with the French government and not allow either Austria or Prussia to become involved and use the issue to extend their power in the Empire.

Ternant left Paris in early June. In addition to his instructions, he also carried letters of introduction from Lafayette to his cousin, François-Claude-Amour, marquis de Bouille, the military commander at Metz, and the recently elected mayor of Strasbourg, Baron de Dietrich. In both notes Lafayette, who hoped to use Ternant as an intermediary, referred to Jean as "my intimate friend" and he assured Bouille that he could talk to him in confidence on all public affairs.[58] Bouille however, plagued by increasing insubordination among his troops and suspicious of Lafayette's intentions was noncommittal. In his memoirs he later referred to the meeting and described Ternant as "an interesting man, who had acquired a fortune by a variety of means and to whom the revolution furnished new means to raise him higher. I was therefore careful not to enter into any explanations with him."[59]

Ternant spent the months of June and July traveling from court to court through the western areas of the Empire and the Rhineland, endeavoring to convince the various princes to accept the French government's proposal regarding indemnities, but with no success. Beginning first at Strasburg and Karlsruhe, Jean proceeded to visit Stuttgart, Deux-Ponts Heidelberg, Darmstadt, Treves, Bonn and Spire. At each stop his reception was courteous but chilly and his message of compromise and conciliation rejected. Everywhere he was portrayed as an agent of the revolution, working to encourage Germans to resist their rulers.

At Karlsruhe, the Landgrave of Baden, Charles Frederick, refused to send a representative to Paris or act independently of his colleagues. At Stuttgart, the Duke of Wurtemberg, Charles Eugene, expressed some interest in the idea of indemnities but was only interested in acquiring additional territory rather than a cash payment. Charles-Auguste-Chrietien, the Duke of Deux-Ponts was of the same mind. He demanded all the territory in Alsace north of the Querch River and the city of Landau as compensation for his loss of feudal rights. He also indicated that he would not enter into any agreement independent of the other princes.

Ternant's visits to the ecclesiastical rulers at Bonn, Treves and Spire were equally unproductive. The pro–Austria Prince-Bishop of Spire, Damien-August-Philippe-Karl, the most reactionary among the German princes, was adamant in his refusal to accept any compromise with the revolution and Ternant came away convinced that the Prince-Bishop and Prussia controlled the other princes.

By the middle of August Ternant was back in Paris and had submitted his report to Montmorin explaining the mission's failure. In his opinion the German princes had little faith that a constitution would resolve France's political divisions and little confidence in any proposal from the National Assembly. They refused to surrender their traditional rights and incomes that were certain in return for indemnities that were doubtful. The political situation in France was too uncertain; the National Assembly had no international recognition and the king's authority curtailed. They also feared that any indemnity would be paid in *assignats*, paper certificates of uncertain value.[60]

The political situation that Ternant found on his return to Paris was characterized by the continuing erosion of the royal government's authority. The National Assembly remained, as always, suspicious of the king and his ministers, and in the armed forces indiscipline and insubordination were increasing as revolutionary ideology combined with complaints of a purely military nature to form a toxic stew. In fact, 1790 proved to be the year when the longstanding internal problems that plagued the army erupted in a spate of mutinies. In the east, garrisons at Stenay, Longwy, Metz and Sarrelouis were all disrupted by major incidents of insubordination. It was in the mutiny at Nancy, the largest city in Lorraine, however, that the French government faced the most serious challenge to its authority.[61] Throughout August the main concern of the both the National Assembly and the Minister of War was focused on the inability of the city's military and civil authorities to restore order. Finally, on the 31st, after efforts to end the mutiny peacefully had failed, a small force of loyal troops commanded by the marquis de Bouille entered the city in the face of armed resistance and successfully restored order.

No sooner was one mutiny ended however, than another captured the government's attention. In September a mutiny of naval personnel at Brest, that was supported by the city's municipal government, paralyzed much of France's Atlantic fleet and forced the resignation, on 23 October, of Ternant's friend, Cesar-Henri, comte de La Luzerne, the naval minister.[62] La Luzerne's retirement was part of the replacement of most of the ministers, demanded by the National Assembly. With the exception of Montmorin, by the end of January 1791 they had all been replaced. Shortly after La Luzerne's resignation Ternant received orders to rejoin his regiment. His recall to command was the result of an incident in the autumn of 1790 involving the Royal-Liègeois that captured the nation's attention.

During the many months that Ternant was absent from his regiment, the Royal-Liègeois had been exposed to both the professional problems customary to any military establishment of the period and the extraordinary developments associated with the revolution. Since the spring of 1789 the regiment had been garrisoned at Avesnes in Haynaut and on Sunday, 7 March 1790 after the celebration of the Mass, a protest by the rank and file over the right to leave the city when off duty, exploded into a riot that resulted in the desertion of over 200 soldiers, who fled across the border to Mons in the Austrian Netherlands. Fortunately, due to the loyalty of the non-commissioned officers and the majority of the troops, the regiment suffered no long-term adverse effects, but it was Tuesday before order was completely restored.[63]

In early April the Royal-Liègeois was transferred eastward to Sarrelouis, a frontier fortress in a French enclave surrounded by territory belonging to the Empire that guarded the road to Metz and Lorraine.

There, in early August, it witnessed the insurrection of the French regiment, Picardy, against its officers. Fearful of it being influenced by the insubordination of the French regiment, the marquis de Bouille ordered the Royal-Liègeois to the small town, Vic-sur-Seille, and from there elements of the regiment were thought loyal enough to be included in the force he collected to end the summer-long mutiny of the garrison at Nancy.[64]

Bouille's small army entered Nancy on the afternoon of 31 August in the face of armed resistance and it was only after fours hours of combat and numerous casualties that order was restored and the military insurrection ended. Under the command of La Tour, the Royal-Liègeois, was heavily engaged in the street fighting and lost 6 killed and 11 wounded.[65] The suppression of the mutiny at Nancy was the only combat the regiment would experience in its brief existence but the occasion was deemed important enough for the government to recognize the battle as a military campaign and thereby allow deserving participants to be decorated for their efforts. In early September, after a few weeks of rest, the Royal-Liègeois was ordered south to Belfort, a fortress located near the border with the Swiss cantons that guarded the narrow valley passage that separated the Vosges and Jura mountain ranges.

By the time the Royal-Liègeois reached Belfort however, the regiment's status as a foreign regiment was beginning to cause it difficulties. In an environment of increasing political animosity, suspicions regarding the loyalty of the Royal army and especially its foreign units, to the cause of the revolution had gained wide acceptance. Such popular hostility had been aroused by a number of recent well-publicized clashes between foreign troops and civilians. The government's continued use of foreign regiments to police civil disturbances in the countryside, the large number of foreign units summoned to Paris in the summer of 1789 to intimidate the National Assembly, the attack of the Royal-Allemand Cavalry on a crowd in Paris on 12 July, the Swiss regiment, Salis Samade, that defended the Bastille and inflicted numerous casualties on the people gathered beneath its walls and most recently, the "massacre" of patriots at Nancy at the hands of Bouille's Swiss and Liègeois troops confirmed people's worst fears. It was therefore in a poisoned atmosphere of suspicion and hostility on the part of Belfort's inhabitants that the Royal Liègeois arrived, and it was in response to civilian animosity that an altercation occurred that thrust the Royal-Liègeois into the center of the national debate over the trustworthiness of foreign regiments, contributed to the resignation of the minister of war and resulted in Ternant's return to his military duties.

On the Thursday, 21 October 1790 the Lauzun Hussars arrived at Belfort from Troyes and were reunited with several of its squadrons that had participated in the fighting at Nancy. With over 80 percent of its personnel German-speaking troops from Alsace and Lorraine, the regiment was viewed as a foreign unit.[66] Like the Royal-Liègeois, the hussars were also blamed for their part in crushing the mutiny at Nancy and viewed as counter-revolutionaries by many of the city's citizens. As was customary n the Royal army, the officers of the Royal-Liègeois and those attached to the city's citadel, hosted a dinner in honor of the officers of the recently arrived regiment. Held at 3:00 in the afternoon at the café Bechot, an establishment that catered to a middle or upper class cliental, the banquet was a festive but unexceptional occasion for those enjoying the food, drink and camaraderie.[67]

By 4:00 however, a crowd had formed outside the café. For many of those already angry at the two regiments, the occasion brought to mind a similar military banquet at Versailles the previous October, that had scandalized pro-revolutionary sympathizers, led to an assault on the palace and forced the return of the royal family to Paris. The crowd at Belfort was upset that such professional occasions had been forbidden and angry that the local authorities had failed to prohibit it. When the dinner ended and the officers emerged, many of them in high spirits caused by excessive drinking, there was an immediate altercation with the crowd that soon expanded to include troops from the two regiments. Under ordinary circumstances the clash would have been seen as resulting from nothing more than the normal tension between military personnel and civilians. By the time order had been restored however, city officials had been insulted and threatened and civilians injured. The municipal authorities were convinced that the incident had been aimed against the revolution and they demanded the arrest of those individuals it considered most responsible, the colonel proprietor of the Royal Liègeois, comte de la Tour, and the regiment's major, Baron de Grunstein. They also insisted upon the immediate removal of both regiments from the city.[68]

The marquis de Bouille, who conveniently arrived the following day on an inspection of the border in the region, attempted to placate the angry civilians and agreed with the Belfort authorities; La Tour and Grunstein were placed under arrest and the Royal-Liègeois ordered to Sarrebourg in northern Alsace, and then to the small fortress at nearby Bitche. He also immediately informed the minister of war of the incident and his action.

In Paris news of the affair at Belfort quickly became an issue for the competing political factions. The National Assembly launched an investigation and the city's journals carried stories that reflected their political positions. The *L'Ami du Roi*, a conservative paper that catered to the upper classes of society, portrayed the disturbance as little more than the trading of insults produced by overindulgence in wine.[69] The *L'Orateur du Peuple*, on the other hand, a more popular journal described the dinner as an "orgy" and reminded its readers that that both regiments had been at Nancy. Jean Paul Marat in his journal, *L'Ami du Peuple*, used the incident as the basis for a vigorous attack not only on foreign regiments, La Tour and Bouille, but the royal government as well. Marat's view mirrored that of most radicals; foreign regiments were nothing more than mercenaries that Louis would use to "crush the friends of liberty." The king, in being content with only the arrest of the "traitors," had violated his oath to defend the constitution. Marat called Bouille "ferocious, devilish and a hypocrite," and furthermore, an anti-revolutionary, who had slaughtered "peaceful citizens" in the "massacre" at Nancy. La Tour, another aristocrat and therefore an enemy of the people, was likewise thoroughly abused, as being "always a disgraceful subject ... [who] made a profession of roguery, ... a perfect adventurer; he had neither fireside nor place.... He had swindled 30,000 livres.... He sold in open market the potatoes, cucumbers and turnips that the soldiers had grown in the ditches and ramparts at Avesnes. He sold for himself the foals of the regiment's horses. One must say that this cheap rogue is the henchman of the most rabid despotism."[70]

On 29 October, the minister of war, Jean Frederic Gouvernet, comte de La Tour du Pin, informed the Assembly that upon the receipt of General Bouille's report, the king had ordered Colonel La Tour be held under arrest for two months and Major Grunstein for six weeks for their actions. At the Saturday morning session the next day however, members of the Assembly protested the government's handling of the incident. The crimes committed were civil and the regular courts, not a military tribunal, should have conducted the case. Mirabeau insisted that the crimes were not only civil in nature, but also amounted to high treason. At the same time, the minister of war was also attacked for his delay in informing the Assembly.

A few hours later, after considering the report on the disturbance at Belfort from its military and reports committees, the National Assembly decreed that La Tour and Grunstein, as the "principal authors of the crimes at Belfort," should be brought to Paris and incarcerated in the Abbaye de Saint Germain des Pres prison to await civil prosecution for *lèse-nation*. The sieur de Terrnant, as Colonel of the Royal Liègeois, was ordered to return immediately to his regiment.[71]

Responding to his orders, Ternant rejoined the Royal-Liègeois during the first week of November and was received with enthusiasm; the officers met him outside Bitche and provided an escort and the troops illuminated their barracks in his honor.[72] Although the regiment was overjoyed and relieved at his return, Ternant's own attitude was probably more tempered. His prospects for a future career in government service after all, lay in his forthcoming diplomatic appointment, not in the royal army, and his absence from Paris was inconvenient. It was therefore with some sense of resignation that Jean set to work to repair the damage to the regiment's reputation caused by what had been portrayed as a counter-revolutionary demonstration at Belfort. On 7 November he composed an address to the King and National Assembly that assured the government of the regiment's loyalty to the nation, the law and the king, and urged that the criminal activities of La Tour and Grunstein at Belfort and their subsequent dramatic escape from justice should not reflect on the Royal Liègeois' good name. He concluded by insisting that the true sentiments of the regiment were those of admiration for the work of the Assembly and devotion to the principles of a constitution.[73] Shortly after the regiment was transferred to Phalsbourg, where it arrived on 10 November, Ternant turned the command of the Royal Liègeois over to Lieutenant-colonel Ferdinand de Sames de Heidesseim, a long serving veteran and the regiment's normal commander, and returned to Paris.

By early December Jean was once more among his circle of friends, in familiar surroundings and while waiting for his appointment, again actively engaged in discussions pertaining to Franco-American trade and the tobacco question. He also continued to test the political waters regarding a possible appointment as a minister of state. William Short reported in early October that Ternant was attempting to keep his options open. "He is trying to be employed here, and in the mean time keeps the promise of the place to make use of in case of nothing more agreeable being offered."[74] A few weeks later Short commented upon Ternant's almost certain appointment as minister to the United States: "De Moustier's successor is not yet publicly announced, but there is little doubt that it is Ternant. He has been promised the place two years ago. Some of the Americans here think that his appointment will be considered a slight in America. If so it will be without reason. Few people here are better supported by all the ministers than Ternant and besides the marquis de Lafayette is his friend. I think it possible that Ternant's ambition carries his expectations even higher and that he has some hopes of being employed in the administration here."[75] In late January Morris also remarked on Ternant's interest in a ministerial post and his involvement in ministry making intrigues, describing his friend's effort as "play[ing] at heads for kingdoms" and noted regarding the qualifications of a potential candidate, "They want some Person of this Sort of Rank sufficiently elevated to run no Risqué unnecessarily and whose Temper will not avoid any which may be necessary or proper."[76] As a commoner who was also a colonel in the royal army and someone noted for his overall good sense and prudence, Ternant appeared to be an ideal candidate. Even the notification by Montmorin of his appointment as minister to the United States on 16 January did not prevented Ternant from considering a more important position in the government.[77]

As has been noted earlier, Ternant's appointment was the result of the recall of the marquis de Moustier. The same age as Jean, de Moustier had begun his Foreign Service career in 1767 as secretary to his brother-in-law, the Ambassador to Portugal. Following service in a similar role at the embassy at Naples, in 1772 de Moustier was appointed minister to the Elector of Trier and in 1783 he was chosen to head a special mission to London. Appointed to replace La Luzerne, de Moustier arrived in New York in January 1788.[78]

In spite of de Moustier's experience and Jefferson's belief that he would "give the perfect satisfaction in America," the marquis proved to be a poor choice.[79] He suffered in comparison to the popular La Luzerne and by early 1789 his eccentricities had offended American sensibilities. Madison called his appointment "unlucky" and complained to Jefferson that de Moustier was "unsocial, proud and niggardly, and betrays a sort of fastidiousness toward this country. He also suffers from his illicit connection with Madame de Brehan [de Moustier's sister-in-law who accompanied him to the United States] which is universally known and offensive to American manners."[80] In response to numerous complaints the Washington administration requested his recall.

Ternant's subsequent appointment was a reflection of both his good standing with Montmorin and La Luzerne's influence but it was also based upon the recognition that the next minister to the United States must be someone approved of in advance by the American government. Jean's service in the Continental army, his fluency in English, his many acquaintances on Washington's cabinet, Hamilton, Jefferson and Knox, and his familiarity with American customs and manners gave him a considerable advantage and made him a highly suitable candidate for the American post. He was not however, the only individual under consideration. Diplomatic appointments were always much sought after and subject to court intrigue and patronage. François Barthelemy, the secretary of the London embassy was highly regarded and considered for the American position as was Victor-Louis-Charles de Riquet, the son of the comte de Caraman, a Lieutenant-general, former military governor of Provence and the personal friend of both Vergennes and Marie Antoinette. Louis-Guillaume Otto, La Luzerne's former secretary was already in the United States, was experienced and well liked. Finally, even Adele Flahaut, the mistress of Talleyrand and lover of Gouverneur Morris, had suggested her husband Charles, who had succeeded Buffon as keeper of the *Jardins du Roi*, for the position.[81]

At some point between the fall of 1789 and early 1791, most likely at one of Lafayette's gatherings, Ternant was introduced to the liberal economist Pierre-Samuel Du Pont de Nemours and his oldest son, Victor-Marie, beginning a relationship with the Du Pont family that would become the centerpiece of Jean's social network for the remainder of his life. The fifty-two-year-old physiocrat and author was an especially well known and respected intellectual, a friend of Turgot, Voltaire and Victor de Riquetti, marquis de Mirabeau, who had been involved with agricultural improvements in France since the 1760s. In 1783 he had acted as an unofficial advisor to Vergennes and had been honored with a patent of nobility for his services. Later Du Pont gained a reputation for his work on numerous agricultural, manufacturing and trade commissions. As a member of the National Assembly he continued to serve on committees dealing with finances and commerce. He was a close friend of Jefferson, Necker and Lafayette, as well as a financial advisor to Tallyrand. He also served as president of the Assembly during August 1790.[82] This energetic and reform minded intellectual was another of the influential individuals at the center of affairs who was included among Ternant's many acquaintances.

Throughout February Ternant continued to be involved in the discussions regarding the importation of American tobacco and easing trade restrictions between the United States and the French islands in the Caribbean; it was in connection with the latter issue that he began his relationship with Victor-Marie Du Pont, the twenty-three-year-old son of Du Pont de Nemours.[83] Handsome, charming and intelligent, but somewhat dissolute, Victor had begun his career in 1784 as an assistant to his

Victor Du Pont, artist unknown. The eldest son of the renowned economist, Pierre Samuel Du Pont de Nemours, Victor accompanied Ternant to the United States in 1791. Ternant had a long and fatherly relationship with him and made every effort to advance Victor's diplomatic career (courtesy Hagley Museum and Library).

father at the *Bureau du Commerce*. Later he obtained a position as the private secretary to comte de Moustier, the minister to the United States and sailed with him to New York in November 1788. After returning to the family's country estate in December 1789, Victor was elected and commissioned in the local militia but grew bored and returned to Paris in July 1790 with some expectation of using his father's political connections as an aid in continuing a diplomatic career. He wrote his father asking if de Moustier's successor had been named and if the new minister would find place for him. When he failed to gain a post as either the secretary to the National Assembly's *comité diplomatique* or a similar position at a legation in Germany, Victor accepted an appointment as an aide-de-camp to Lafayette, in spite of his father's objections and against Lafayette's advise.[84] Fortunately, and almost certainly due to the influence of both his father and Lafayette; Ternant agreed to include Victor on his staff, but only as an unofficial private secretary, with no promise of a regular appointment.

With his appointment as minister-plenipotentiary now official but his departure delayed, Ternant began the time consuming process of making the necessary arrangements for his journey.[85] On 2 March he was granted official leave from his regiment by the king. He also began to inform friends in the United States of his impending return. He wrote his old friend and mentor, Baron von Steuben, that he hoped to sail in April and renew their friendship in person at the end of June and asked Steuben to engage Otto, the charges d'affaires, to find him a suitable house in Philadelphia.[86] Jean also informed Washington of his appointment.

> I think I cannot, under better auspices, express to your Excellency my heartfelt Satisfaction on being appointed Minister plenipy of France near the United States. It was under your command, I began my public life and learned to value and defend the cause of liberty: and it will be my constant endeavor in the new Station to which the confidence of the king has called me, to render myself particularly agreeable to your Excellency, and by my Steady attention and unremitting zeal in promoting the mutual advantage of France and America, to shew myself Still deserving of your particular approbation and friendship.[87]

There is little doubt that Ternant's appointment was popular among government officials. Lafayette, in particular, was full of praise, informing Washington:

> M. de Ternant has been named Plenipotentiary Minister to the United States. I have warmly wished for it because I know his abilities, his love for liberty, his early, steady and active attachment to the United States, his veneration and love for you. The more I have known Ternant, the more I have found him a man of great parts, a steady virtuous, and faith full friend. He has deserved a great share in the confidence of the National Assembly, the patriotic side I mean, the King has a true regard for him, in a word I hope he will on every account answer your

purposes, and serve America as zealously in the diplomatic line, as he did when in the army.[88]

Three months later, on the eve of Ternant's departure, in another letter to his former commander in chief, Lafayette continued his laudatory comments:

> M. Jefferson and myself had long thought that Ternant was a very proper man to act as French Minister in America. He in a great measure belongs to both countries. He is sensible, honest, well informed, and has a plain and decisive way of doing business which will be very convenient. He has long been an officer under your commands—feeling and acting in an American capacity. He is personally much attached to you, and I had in this Revolution many instances to experience his friendship to me. He might have been a Minister in the Council, but was rather backward on the occasion, and behaved like a prudent, not an ambitious man—so that I take him to be fit to answer your purpose.[89]

Lafayette's remarks clearly indicate that Ternant's failure to press for a higher position in the government was due to his own, very understandable, prudence. Jean was mindful of the forced resignation of his friend, La Luzerne, minister of the navy, and the similar more recent fate of the minister of war, La Tour du Pin; both men among the increasing number of victims of a "politics of paranoia" and of the suspicions of the National Assembly regarding ministerial despotism. He also was all too aware of the increasing incitements to violence against government officials on the part of the radical press. Even Lafayette was being attacked as an aristocrat, and portrayed as a secret servant of the monarchy; untrustworthy and a hypocrite.[90] In this environment, anyone associated with the royal government had to proceed with caution and Jean's decision to accept a foreign service post was an effective way to both escape the dangerous political environment in Paris and advance his career.

The National Assembly's distrust however, was not restricted to royal ministers. It was also directed at the diplomatic corps, dominated by the nobility, whose commitment to the revolution was suspect.[91] In November 1790, the Assembly had mandated that all government official, both civil and military, swear allegiance to the new regime before municipal authorities. The following April a new oath was decreed and it was to comply with this order that Ternant appeared before the head of the *conseil général* of the commune of Paris at the evening session on 10 May. In an unlikely coincidence Jean was accompanied to the bar and took the oath with the recently appointed minister-plenipotentiary to Poland, Louis-Marie-Henri Deschorches, the former marquis de Saint-Croix, a veteran diplomat who had previously served as minister to the Prince-Bishop of Liège and had proposed the raising of the Royal-Liègeois regiment.[92]

In addition to attending to his personal affairs, Ternant was also involved with making the necessary purchases for his journey and bidding farewell to his friends and colleagues. As always, his personal finances were a primary concern. The economy of Paris in the spring of 1791 was unstable and the steady depreciation of the *assignat* made purchasing goods more expensive than usual. Jean later complained that his investments had lost at least 12 percent of their value during the period.[93] Taking advantage of an old colleague, Colonel Benjamin Walker, a former aide-de-camp of both Baron von Steuben and Washington, who was visiting Europe with his wife, Jean requested their assistance in making some purchases in London, to be delivered to Philadelphia.[94]

Ternant was equally concerned with his salary as minister. In 1787 the funds allocated for the operation of the legation in the United States had totaled 72,000 livres, paid in quarterly installments. In 1790 however, as part of his effort to reduce departmental expenses, Montmorin had reduced that amount to 60,000, a sum that included not only the minister's salary, but all ordinary expenses of the legation; the board, lodging and salary of the minister's private secretary, salaries for the domestic staff, travel and supplies.[95] In an effort to increase his compensation Jean asked Morris to discuss his salary needs with Montmorin.[96]

On 25 March, Ternant was a guest at a small dinner hosted by Morris. In addition to Jean the company included the marquis de Lafayette, his longtime friend, the former minister to St. Petersburg, Louis-Philippe, comte de Segur, and their wives. Montmorin's youngest daughter, Pauline, comtesse de Beaumont was present as was the comtesse de Fersensac. William Short, the 32-year-old former secretary to Jefferson, currently serving as the American *charge d'affaires* in Paris, the marquis d'Agout and the abbe de Lisle were also included.[97] It was a gathering of friends to celebrate the recent diplomatic appointments of Ternant as minister-plenipotentiary to the United States and the comte de Segur as ambassador to Rome.[98]

In early June 1791, his preparations complete and his instructions in hand, Ternant departed Paris for the French naval base at Rochefort, the first stop on his return to Philadelphia.[99] He was probably accompanied on the five day journey via Orléans, Tours, Poitiers and La Rochelle, by two of the three other members of his party, Jean-Baptiste Semonet, appointed to serve as the legation's principal secretary, and François-Etienne Kellermann, the twenty-year-old nephew of François Barbe de Marbois, one of Jean's former acquaintances who had served as secretary of the Philadelphia legation under La Luzerne. Young Kellermann was the son of François-Christophe Kellermann, a Brigadier general in the royal army, but it had been decided that he should take advantage of his mother's family's more prominent social status and pursue a diplomatic rather than a military career. Armed with letters of introduction to President Washington from his uncle and Lafayette, the plan called for Kellermann to replace his uncle, Barbe de Marbois's younger brother, as vice consul in New York City. Until that position became available however, Ternant had agreed to employ him as his private secretary.[100] Victor Du Pont, the fourth member of the group, traveled alone and reached Rochefort on 9 June to find Ternant and the others waiting.

It is quite evident that from the very beginning of their relationship Ternant was fond of Du Pont and that the feelings were reciprocated. In Victor's letters to his father from Rochefort, Ternant is revealed as knowledgeable in the ways of the patronage system and willing to advise him on his Foreign Service career. On the 14th Du Pont wrote, "I like M. de Ternant, he treats me kindly and affectionately and I am beginning to hope much from this voyage."[101] Several days later in another note Victor contrasted Ternant's demeanor with that of his former superior, comte de Moustier; "What a difference between this man and the Prussian ambassador [de Moustier had just been appointed minister to Berlin] with all his arrogance and all his pettiness! This one does things liberally and as an ambassador should." In the same letter Dupont related Ternant's advise on the necessity of maintaining multiple options when dealing with one's career. In reference to Victor's earlier desire for a diplomatic post in Germany versus his hope for a post in the United States, Ternant recommended,

Ask your father to urge the Ratisbonne affair or any other on M. de Montmorin. It will be at least six months before M. Herisant retires and you receive official notice of your appointment to the place. It will then be time enough to return or to pretend illness and gain time or to decline altogether if you decide that you can do better in America. It will always help you to have had the appointment even if you refuse it, because your refusal would be supported by a letter from me to M. de Montmorin saying that I need you and cannot spare you. For the rest tell your father that I will do all that is in my power, but it is impossible to tell in advance. We do not know how M. Otto feels about keeping his position in America; since his marriage he may prefer it to advancement in Europe....[102]

For the voyage to Philadelphia, Ternant had been assigned passage on the 22-gun corvette, *Favorite*, under the command of *sous-lieutenant de vaisseau*, François Riviere, a young but experienced officer.[103] Preparations for the voyage completed, *Favorite* left Rochefort on 14 June, but rain, strong head winds and the loss of two anchors and their cables forced delay and the corvette did not reach open water until the 25th.

Once finally at sea, the crossing itself took forty-five days and for the most part was uneventful. The accommodations on board however, were extremely cramped and uncomfortable. A small lightly armed ship used for escorting convoys, scouting or carrying dispatches, the corvette's normal complement was 150 men and eight officers. For its voyage to Philadelphia, the islands of Saint-Pierre and Miquelon and the Antilles however, *Favorite*, in addition to Ternant's party of four, carried a crew of 200 and ten officers; the additional naval personnel most likely were replacements for the West Indies squadron. In addition to the overcrowding, another problem was soon apparent; finding space for Ternant's considerable baggage had caused the removal of a number of water casks and it soon became necessary to ration drinking water.

In spite of the concerns over water, on 14 July in the middle of the Atlantic, the crew marked the anniversary of the Federation with a daylong patriotic celebration that included music, dining and drinking, dancing, the singing of a Te Deum and a twenty-one gun salute. Tables and chairs were set up on the deck, large tarpaulins rigged for shade and everyone participated in the festivities, unaware that shortly before they sailed the attempted escape from Paris by the royal family had caused a political crisis that threatened the monarchy's very existence. Du Pont later admitted in a letter to his brother, that if he had known of the king's flight he would not have left Rochefort.

At last, on Friday, 5 August, *Favorite* reached landfall, entered Delaware Bay and began its slow approach to Philadelphia. Four days later, at 5:00 in the afternoon on 9 August Ternant, accompanied by Louis-Guillaume Otto, the legation's *charge*, landed to the noise of the city's bells ringing in his honor and an official welcome from a group of Philadelphia notables and local dignitaries that included the city's mayor, John Barclay and Pennsylvania's secretary of state, Alexander Dallas.[104] It was a far different reception from the one Jean had experienced thirteen years before in the mud at Valley Forge. On this occasion his arrival was expected and much anticipated and there was no longer any need for letters of introduction. Four months short of his fortieth birthday, Ternant had every right to be pleased with the steady advance of his career and every reason to look ahead with confidence to further success.

IX

Philadelphia— Mount Vernon—Goodstay
August 1791–July 1801

The legation in Philadelphia that Ternant had been appointed to head had been in existence since the treaties of alliance and of amity and commerce between the United States and France signed in 1778 and was one of twenty similarly designated offices maintained by the French Ministry of Foreign Affairs.[1] Because of its geographical isolation and expense however, the American post was viewed as among the least desirable on the list of such positions and was considered of only secondary importance by the Royal government. In the spring of 1791, following the passage of the Residence Act by Congress that called for the creation of a new capital on the banks of the Potomac River, the legation had followed the move of the Federal government from New York City to a temporary home in Philadelphia.

From November 1789 until Jean's arrival the legation had been under the direction of Louis-Guillaume Otto, acting in the capacity of *charges d'affaires*. Born in Baden and educated at the University of Strasbourg, Otto had been a member of the chevalier de La Luzerne's party that had arrived in Philadelphia in August 1779, and by 1791 he had developed into an experienced and respected diplomat with both strong political connections and personal ties in the United States. As La Luzerne's private secretary and attaché from 1779 through 1784, the Protestant, well-educated and socially adept Otto had mixed easily among wealthy Americans and he was already well acquainted with Ternant, the two having met during the period when Jean was a prisoner of war in Philadelphia from the summer of 1780 through January 1782.[2]

In spite of being forced by Ternant's appointment to give up his position as the legation's head, Otto's relationship with his former acquaintance, now his superior, was friendly. Otto returned to France in the fall of 1792 and several years later, as part of a critique written in defense of the American government in its relations with France, he presented a mixed but generally favorable appraisal of Ternant as minister. Though Otto considered Ternant cold and unsociable in comparison to La Luzerne, he nevertheless acknowledged that Jean, unlike de Moustier, had maintained harmonious relations with Americans and that he understood them. Moreover, Ternant had talent, manners and was a highly decent man. In Otto's judgment Ternant's recall had been a disaster for Franco-American relations.[3]

The first several weeks following Jean's arrival were occupied with arranging accommodations, taking up his official duties and attending to numerous social obligations. Immediately upon disembarking Ternant, who was eager to renew his acquaintance with Washington, requested a private meeting with the President prior to the formal presentation of his credentials. Accordingly, the next day Jean was invited to meet with his former commander in chief at 190 High Street, Robert Morris's stately home, serving at the time as Washington's residence. Washington was delighted to welcome a former comrade in arms and old acquaintance and openly expressed his friendship; "You and I are old friends," he said, "and it is a great pleasure to me and Mrs. Washington to see you again among us."[4] For the next half hour the two men reminisced over old times and recalled their long service in a common cause. Two days later, on the 12th, Ternant again visited the President at his residence, this time in an official capacity. In a private audience held in the drawing room of the executive mansion, with little ceremony and with only the President and Secretary of State, Jefferson, present, Jean presented his credentials and officially began his mission.

Ternant also began a minister's obligatory social duties. On Tuesday the 16th he attended the President's weekly afternoon levee and introduced Dupont, Kellermann, and Riviere, the commander of *Favorite*, along with the ship's junior officers. The next evening he dined with Washington, the Spanish *charge d'affaires*, Jose Ignacio de Viar, and a large party of distinguished guests.[5] Jean closed his first seven days of diplomatic socializing by attending Martha Washington's Friday evening reception.

In addition to his meetings with Washington and Jefferson, Ternant also renewed his acquaintance with another old colleague from his days at Valley Forge, Alexander Hamilton, who had been Jack Laurens's best friend, and was now serving as Secretary of the Treasury. Hamilton had only a casual acquaintance with Jean during the war for independence, but reported Ternant's arrival and described him as "a man of easy, pleasing manners and very fit for the objects of his appointment."[6]

At first, finding suitable accommodations proved difficult. In spite of a building boom stimulated by the return of the Federal government, lodging in Philadelphia was in short supply and expensive, and Jean moved temporarily into a small room at the legation. The other members of his party were forced to find quarters elsewhere; Du Pont at the well regarded boarding house of Elizabeth House where James Madison and James Monroe lodged.[7] By early September however, the search for an acceptable site had been successfully completed and Ternant was able to lease one of Philadelphia's newest and most impressive homes, the mansion built in 1790 by John Dunlap, printer and publisher of the daily newspaper, *Pennsylvania Packet*. Located at on the southeast corner of 12th Street and Market, in a rural setting on the western outskirts of the city, the Dunlap property included the entire block between 11th and 12th streets and from Market to Chestnut, and consisted of an imposing three-story main house, stable and numerous outbuildings. In spite of the lack of street paving or sidewalks and its distance from the city's center, the Dunlap house was considered the finest in Philadelphia and in that sense bore the same distinction as the fashionable residence of de Moustier in New York. The Dunlap house was an elegant establishment that reflected the status of the French minister, and provided a suitably impressive facility for hosting the social events that were an important part of Ternant's diplomatic duties. On 10 September Ternant took possession of the mansion that would remain the site of the French legation until 1797.[8]

Jean began his diplomatic duties immediately. Even before presenting his credentials he attempted to draw both Washington and Jefferson into informal conversations regarding a new commercial treaty, a long-standing and contentious issue for the governments of both countries.[9] During the war for independence Franklin and others had hoped that France would replace England as America's most important European trading partner. That dream however, was never realized. After independence was won American consumers resumed their traditional purchasing habits and sought the economic benefits of long established trading links with England. The most serious demand from American merchants, now barred from trade with the British colonies in the Caribbean, was increased access to French colonies in the West Indies, something that both French merchants and the French government were against.[10]

In spite of the failure to increase trade between the two countries, both governments desired to negotiate a new commercial agreement. Three weeks before Ternant sailed, the National Assembly signaled its support for a new treaty in its decree "that the king undertake to cause to be negotiated with the United States a new treaty of commerce which shall multiply relative mutual advantages between both countries."[11] Buoyed by this official assurance, his instructions from Montmorin and his own previous discussions on the subject with Lafayette, Du Pont de Nemours and Gouverneur Morris, Ternant, although not empowered to negotiate a new treaty, was well prepared and eager to discuss details of a new commercial agreement.[12]

Given the demand for increased access to the West Indian market it was not surprising that the Americans took the initiative for trade talks concerning a new commercial treaty. Hamilton, the most engaging and energetic member of Washington's cabinet, visited Ternant in early October and in the course of a four-hour meeting expressed interest in a new trade agreement with France, one based on the principle of reciprocity. Jean agreed. He assured Hamilton that both the king and the National Assembly were also interested in a new treaty, but reminded Hamilton that France had already extended commercial favors and that it was necessary for the United States to respond in kind.[13]

Discussions over a new commercial agreement would continue into the spring of 1792. In April, Secretary of State Jefferson presented Ternant with a proposal to serve as a basis for a new commercial treaty. In his opinion all ports in both countries should be open to citizens of their respective countries; each country should only pay the tonnage duties imposed upon native vessels; agricultural produce and manufactured items from each country should be freely imported and exported without being subject to higher duties than those on native goods and finally, in return for increased access, American ships would only carry American goods to the West Indies and only return with gods for American consumption. Jean's response was noncommittal. With no authority to negotiate a new treaty he only informed Montmorin that President Washington and many members of Congress agreed with Jefferson's ideas.[14]

Notwithstanding their mutual desire for a new commercial treaty and general agreement that it should be based upon the principle of reciprocity, the increasing political turmoil in France proved an obstacle to negotiations. Moreover, by the spring of 1793 a war involving most of the European powers against the French republic had created a situation of considerable commercial advantage to the United States without a new treaty. As the leading neutral, the United States saw its trade to Europe increase dramatically and the young republic experienced an economic boom.

Ternant served as minister for twenty-one months, from 12 August 1791 until 18 May 1793. During this period, in addition to his private correspondence, numerous letters to French consuls and written communications with American officials, Jean sent seventy-seven dispatches covering a wide variety of topics, to eight different French foreign ministers, whose appointments to office and brief terms were a stark reflection of the increasingly unstable political scene in Paris.

IX. Philadelphia—Mount Vernon—Goodstay • 167

As per his instructions, he kept his government informed on the numerous domestic and foreign policy developments in the United States and proved an astute observer. Once more, with the important exception of having his relationship with Thomas Jefferson turn sour, he maintained cordial relations with most American officials throughout his ministry. While the revolutionary upheaval in France turned increasingly radical, resulting in the overthrow of the monarchy and the establishment of a republic, Ternant continued to work diligently, loyally represented whatever government was in power and avoided compromising French national interests.

If any single issue commanded Ternant's attention or caused him more concern and difficulty during his ministry, it was the crisis in Saint Domingue, France's principal colony in the West Indies. The situation in the colony was complicated; one that involved questions of French sovereignty, competing economic interests, changing policy and highly divisive social legislation. In normal times Jean would have had no responsibilities regarding the internal affairs of Saint Domingue, but the political divisions and animosities generated by the revolution in France had been replicated in its colonies, and threatened to end French control. The National Constituent Assembly had struggled without success to reconcile conflicting interests regarding slavery and the political rights of free coloreds in France's colonies with the ideals enunciated in the Declaration of the Rights of Man and the Citizen. The Assembly was also confronted by a growing challenge to its authority from Saint Domingue's assembly; a situation dramatically worsened by the events that occurred on the night of 22/23 August 1791.

Not quite two weeks after Jean arrived in Philadelphia a large-scale slave revolt erupted on the plantations located on Saint Domingue's North Plain, adjacent to the provincial capital, Cap-Français. The size and fury of the insurrection caught the plantation owners by surprise and when initial efforts to restore order failed, the colony's governor and assembly immediately sought foreign assistance.

In addition to threatening the survival of the slave plantations, the uprising also heightened the political divisions that already existed among the colony's white and mulatto populations. Once more, the rebellion encouraged the colony's assembly in its resistance to the authority of both Royal bureaucrats and representatives of the National Assembly.[15] Threatening Saint Domingue's very existence, the growing political instability and slave insurrection combined to cause the flight of increasing numbers of Creole refugees from the colony, many to coastal cities in the United States, an exodus which soon added to Ternant's concerns.[16]

In mid September the first of several groups of agents dispatched by the assembly in Saint Domingue to appeal for assistance against the rebelling slaves, arrived in the United States. Ternant, with no instructions to guide him, and aware of the strong separatist sentiments among the planters and the threat to French national interests posed by the colonial assembly's attempt to deal directly with foreign powers, was initially reluctant to become involved and insisted that all appeals for assistance for aid should be addressed to the proper authorities in France. As the highest ranked French official in the United States, Jean's first concern was to protect French sovereignty in Saint Domingue; the suppression of the slave revolt was a matter of secondary importance.

In spite of his concerns over proper procedures being followed and his own abolitionist sympathies however, Ternant quickly recognized the seriousness of the insurrection. In his first dispatch on the 28th, dealing with what he later described as "a most alarming" slave revolt, Ternant informed Montmorin that he had taken the initiative and requested from the Secretary of War, Henry Knox, 1,000 muskets and cartridge boxes, 50,000 cartridges and 20,000 pounds of powder for Saint Domingue. On the same day he also appealed to Treasury Secretary Hamilton, that $40,000, to pay for the supplies, be deducted from the American debt owed to France. He ended the dispatch with what would be a reoccurring theme in his communications, a request for instructions on how to respond to the situation in the future.[17]

In addition to his letters to Knox and Hamilton, Ternant, in a short note, also informed Washington of his requests. "I hope," he wrote, "the extreme urgency of the case will excuse any irregularity in my applications, and that the President of the United States will not disapprove a measure which may rescue from eminent danger and perhaps from total ruin, an important possession of their first and most attached ally."[18] Two days later, after a thorough interrogation of the colonial agent, Ternant wrote a longer letter to the President describing the complete destruction of more than forty plantations, and the determination of the Negroes to exterminate all whites. He assured Washington, "I have taken the most active measures to forward to the Cape every assistance in my power, and I am waiting anxiously for your approbation of the application I found myself under the necessity of making to Col. Hamilton and General Knox. They are both entitled to my grateful acknowledgement for the zeal and good will they have shown me on this occasion."[19] As much concerned with the effects of the slave revolt as Jean, Washington approved his requests.[20]

The mounting crisis in Saint Domingue that caused Ternant so much concern was also the source of an incident that marked the first stage in the deterioration of Ternant's relationship with Thomas Jefferson. In November another pair of agents arrived in Philadelphia, carrying an appeal from the President of Saint Domingue's Assembly to the Federal government for additional military aid. Embarrassed by their appearance, Ternant once more refused to support their mission or allow any direct communication between the colony's government and that of the United States. Still more concerned with separatist sentiments in the colony than the slave insurrection, Jean feared that the arms would be used against the colony's Royal government instead of the rebelling slaves and that any direct contact might be considered a *de facto* recognition of the colony's independence. Soon however, assured by Jefferson that the agents would only be received as private citizens and not as representatives of the colonial government, Ternant reluctantly consented to their meeting with the American Secretary of State. During the meeting however, Jefferson accepted a letter from them and forwarded it, unopened, to the Congress. When Ternant learned about the letter he confronted Jefferson and accused the Secretary of State of not being straightforward with him.[21] Jefferson, more fearful of the success of the insurrection and the possibility of its spread to the southern states than with questions of French sovereignty, was irritated by Ternant's taking exception to his acceptance of the letter and promises of support for the planters.

Until this incident, and notwithstanding the Secretary of State's usual reserve and reticence to informally discuss diplomatic matters, Ternant had been well disposed toward Jefferson. Now convinced that he had been taken advantage of, Ternant complained to Montmorin of Jefferson's action and appealed again for instructions. Jefferson likewise complained of Ternant's jealousy and rationalized his own behavior.[22]

A policy difference over the slave insurrection in Saint Domingue however, was only the beginning of the gradual estrangement between Ternant and Jefferson. Later, in the spring of 1793 the two would be further alienated by their very different attitudes regarding the radical events in France that had resulted in the overthrow of the monarchy and execution of Louis XVI. Jefferson had little sympathy for Louis' fate and in a letter to Madison, made disparaging remarks about Ternant's monarchist sympathies. "Ternant has at length openly hosted the flag of monarchy by going into deep morning for his prince. I suspect he thinks a cessation of his visits to me a necessary accompaniment to his pious duty. A connection between him and Hamilton seems to be springing up."[23] Later, in a note to James Monroe, Jefferson condemned Jean's changing political loyalties.

> We expect Genet daily. When Ternant received certain account of his appointment thinking he had nothing further to hope from the Jacobins, he that very day found out something to be offended at in me ... attached himself immediately to Hamilton, put on mourning for the king and became a perfect counter-revolutionary. A few days ago he received a letter from Genet giving him hope

that they will employ him in the army. On this he tacked about again, became a Jacobin & refused to present the Viscount Noailles & some French aristocrats arrived here. However, he will hardly have the impudence to speak to me again.[24]

As clearly indicated by Jefferson's letters, it was Jean's association with Alexander Hamilton that more than anything damaged their relationship and gained Ternant Jefferson's ire. Jefferson loathed Hamilton, both personally and everything he represented politically. Consequently, Jean, as a friend to Jefferson's greatest enemy, soon became *persona non grata*. It was only years later, long after Jean had been replaced as minister and Jefferson had gained the presidency that the two were reconciled and reestablished some degree of their former friendship. In June 1801, just prior to his return to France, Ternant wrote to Jefferson.

> Sir
>
> I hope you will not be displeased with an old departing friend taking a private leave of you, and requesting your kind remembrance on the occasion—I had intended going in person, to pay you my last respects before returning to Europe; But with various disappointments, and above all, the bad state of my health, have really put it out of my power to undertake the journey—Being now going off to secure a passage for Havre, I avail myself of M.M. Letombe & Dupont's good offices to get this short valedictory letter put into your hands, and to offer particularly my warmest wishes for your public and private happiness. Remaining very respectfully
>
> > Sir your most obedient and most humble servant
> > Ternant[25]

Two years later from Paris Jean wrote Jefferson again; a short letter of recommendation for a friend, Colonel Jean-Rene Guerin de Foncin, a military engineer emigrating to the United States and seeking a government position. He ended his note to the President, "With heartfelt congratulations on the success of your Louisiana negotiation, and warm wishes for your health, and very paternal administration...."[26] There is no record that Jefferson ever replied.

During the remainder of his ministry, Ternant continued to respond to the needs of Saint Domingue, centering his efforts on obtaining funds to pay for the purchase of provisions and arms for the troubled colony. Throughout 1792 and early 1793 Jean, at first acting without instructions, requested that payments for supplies be deducted from the American debt to France. In March he requested a $400,000 emergency advance, which the Washington administration accepted. In November Jean applied for an additional $326,000. This time his request was rejected, due mostly to uncertainty regarding the possible financial embarrassments caused by the increasing political instability in France and Jean's lack of official authorization from his government.[27]

In early 1793 the scope of Ternant's applications for financial assistance was dramatically expanded to include France. The political situation in France in 1792 had become increasingly chaotic. War against Austria, declared in April, with idealistic optimism and expectations for a brief campaign, had begun with embarrassing military reverses. In August the monarchy had been overthrown and Louis XVI replaced by a provisional executive council. And, by the late summer a combined Prussian and Austrian force had invaded Lorraine, captured Verdun and was preparing to march on Paris. To military defeat had been added the specter of famine. Bad harvests and resulting food shortages in cities had forced the new French government in the fall to instruct Ternant to request 3 million livres from the American debt to be used to purchase of foodstuffs.[28] While waiting for the American response to his petition, Ternant, on his own, applied for an emergency grant of $100,000 and contracted with Coyngham, Nesbit & Co. so that shipments of grain, flour and salted provisions destined for Havre and Nantes could begin without delay.[29] For the remainder of his service as minister Jean's first priority was to insure the steady dispatch of food to France, an effort immediately complicated by the French declaration of war on Britain and the British navy's subsequent blockade of French ports.

The question of whether foodstuffs destined for France could be considered contraband and therefore seized soon became a contentious issue between Britain and the United States involving the trading rights of neutrals. This issue was brought to a head in April 1793 when the American brig, *Sally*, carrying 2,109 barrels of flour destined for Havre was intercepted. Although the cargo was claimed to be American property, documents were discovered that exposed Ternant's negotiations with Americans and his purchase and shipment of the provisions in question.[30] In June a British Order in Council extended the category of contraband to include foodstuffs.

Although extremely conscientious, not all of Ternant's time was taken up with official matters; he had numerous opportunities for activities of a more personal nature. In October 1791 President Washington invited him to spend a weekend at Mount Vernon; a proposal Jean accepted in spite of being preoccupied with the troubles in Saint Domingue. On the 10th he set out by coach for Virginia and arrived on the evening of Friday the 14th.[31] Over the next several days Washington showed Jean his "farms" and at some point on the weekend Thomas Jefferson, on his way to attend the first sale of lots for the new federal city, arrived. Ternant attempted to use the occasion of his visit to discuss business, but neither his host nor Jefferson were so inclined and his stay remained strictly social. Returning to Philadelphia by way of Georgetown, York and Lancaster, Ternant took time to visit the area of the new federal city being laid out by his former comrade in arms, Pierre L'Enfant, and later perhaps paid a return visit to his old encampment at Valley Forge. In Georgetown he roomed at the same inn as Jefferson, but again was unable to get the reserved Secretary of State to discuss common interests.[32]

In Philadelphia there were always social events that required Ternant's presence. On 21 February 1792, for instance, Jean was included among a large gathering of notables at a ball held to honor the President on his sixtieth birthday, and he was frequently invited to the homes of many of Philadelphia's most prominent families, especially those impressed by French culture.[33]

In the summer of 1792 Ternant also took some time to pursue his interest in natural history. In July he planned to explore the mountains west of Philadelphia but his excursion was shortened by a serious fall that forced him to return to the legation.[34] In August Jean traveled to the fashionable spa at Yellow Springs in Chester County, 30 miles west of Philadelphia.[35]

As minister Ternant was often called upon to lend the prestige of his office to unofficial events. One example of his involvement in such events occurred in January 1793. Ternant, in his position as minister, presided over the first manned balloon ascent in the United States. Jean Pierre Blanchard, whose aeronautical feats had delighted Europe, arrived in Philadelphia and Ternant acted as host for the famous Frenchman, providing accommodations at the legation and introducing him to the city's French community. Jean then directed the ceremonies on the day of the launch.[36]

Another instance of Ternant's participation in such affairs was his selection as President of the *Société Française de Bienfaisance de Philadelphie*. Formed to assist the growing number of French refugees from Saint Domingue and modeled on existing societies dedicated to providing financial aid to members of their own nationality in need, the French benevolent society was organized on 6 February 1793 at a meeting of French community leaders at the Sign of the Rainbow, a popular tavern on Race Street.[37] Ternant was given the honor of being named President of the new organization, the French consul general, Antoine de La Forest was selected as Vice-president and Jean's old friend from Valley Forge, Pierre Etienne Du Ponceau, was chosen as one of two secretaries. Other original members of the society included the famous Blanchard, and the brother-in-law of the Girondin leader Brissot, Xavier-François Du Pont, in Philadelphia seeking a position as vice-consul.[38]

Other than matters of policy, the most pressing concerns for Ternant during his tenure were financial difficulties and the continuing absence of official correspondence to guide him in carrying out his duties. As the preeminent foreign dignitary in Philadelphia and the representative of the most important ally of the United States, Jean was sensitive to the need to maintain an establishment that outmatched the expenditures of the other legations. In addition to the expenses for the lease of the Dunlap mansion, Jean found it necessary to maintain a large staff that consisted of thirteen employees; two secretaries, a butler, a *femme de charge* or principal housekeeper, three domestics, two cooks, two coachmen and two servants.[39] In addition to the usual costs of maintaining the legation however, Jean was often confronted by unexpected expenses and complained of his own financial embarrassment. To help resolve his financial problems Ternant asked for and received periodic advances from the United States Treasury. In February 1792 he requested $8,325, in September, $5,445 and in May 1793 shortly before his replacement arrived, a further $3,630; in all Ternant was forced to borrow $17,400 or 95,000 livres.[40]

In February 1793 Ternant was surprised by the news of his replacement as minister. Unbeknownst to him his replacement had been under consideration for over a year and was governed entirely by longstanding political trends that had led to the collapse of the Constitutional Monarchy. The mounting suspicion and hostility directed at the king, his court, his ministers and royal bureaucrats by the Legislative Assembly and encouraged by the political clubs and the radical press made it difficult for the royal government to conduct its affairs. After the king's flight in the summer of 1791 and the declaration of war the following April, it became almost impossible. In less than a year France had four ministers for the navy, four for justice, four for taxation, six ministers each for foreign affairs and interior and seven at the Ministry of War.[41]

There were also demands that the entire diplomatic corps be replaced and the control of French foreign policy assumed by the legislature. Ternant's recall therefore was part of the proposed changes and called for by his being identified with the royal government and his association with Montmorin and Lafayette. His middle class origin, his proven patriotism, his record of loyalty to the revolution, his effectiveness as minister-plenipotentiary and his good standing with American officials were of secondary importance and offered little protection. Similar to so many others during the period, Ternant was guilty by association, but in his case there was no animus against him personally. He simply had no relationship, either personal or professional, with the men who had taken power in France. Finally, Ternant unknowingly contributed to his recall.

After receiving news of the declaration of war Jean had written to the Minister of War volunteering to return to active duty. He was after all, a professional soldier on an open-ended diplomatic assignment and it was difficult for him as an officer in the Royal army who had taken an oath to defend the monarchy, to ignore his duty. A month later Jean wrote to the new foreign minister, Charles-François du Perier Dumouriez, a career soldier with a distinguished combat record, congratulating him on his appointment and after reiterating his dedication to his current duties, added; "permit me to send you a copy of a letter I wrote to the minister of War; if you find my request legitimate, I pray you will be willing to support it; and if you think that my military services in the war in which we presently find ourselves engaged to be useful as those to which you intend me here, I am prepared to fight once again under the banner of liberty."[42]

Dumouriez never responded. One of eight men who acted as Jean's immediate superior, he only served as foreign minister for three months, then briefly as minister of war before returning to a field command. During his short time as foreign minister Dumouriez was far too occupied attempting to influence the king, displaying his commitment to the revolution at the Jacobin Club, instituting a radical reorganization of the foreign ministry and planning a French invasion of the Austrian Netherlands, to pay any attention to Jean's petition.[43]

Four other men followed Dumouriez at the foreign ministry in quick succession during the last two months of Louis XVI's reign. The last of them, Louis-Claude Bigot de Sante-Croix, who only served ten days before the 10 August attack on the Tuileries Palace and the overthrow of the monarchy forced his resignation, had attempted to rid his department of radicals placed there by Dumouriez. As part of his effort, in early August Sante-Croix nominated Guillaume Bonne-Carrere to replace Ternant as minister-plenipotentiary to the United States. Unfortunately for Sante-Croix, Bonne-Carrere, a former secretary of the Jacobin Club and Dumouriez's director-general of the foreign ministry's staff, had a reputation as a gambler and braggart, and all parties opposed his nomination. The Girondin leadership, the American community in Paris and even the Jacobins considered him unfit to serve as minister to the United States, and Sante-Croix's proposal was rejected.[44]

The last foreign minister Ternant served under was Pierre-Henri-Helene-Marie LeBrun-Tondu and it was he and his Girondin allies who would end Jean's diplomatic career. A close friend of Dumouriez and an ardent champion of Belgian independence, LeBrun was an experienced politician acceptable to the radicals in the legislature. In November the Provisional Executive Council, of which he was a member, agreed to replace Ternant with a young diplomat, Edmond Charles Genet, recently expelled from St. Petersburg and the court of the Empress Catherine for his outspoken defense of the revolution. Twenty-nine years old, intelligent, well educated, experienced and charming, Genet on his return to Paris had been befriended by Madam Roland, an influential figure among the Girondins, whose husband also served on the Provisional Executive Council. It was largely due to her, and the fact that Genet had personal connections to the royal family that he was offered the American post.[45] In addition to replacing Ternant, it was planned that Genet would escort the royal family into exile in the United States.

On 30 December the Provisional Executive Council wrote to inform the Washington administration that in accordance with his desire to return to his military career, Ternant was being recalled. "The desire that citizen Ternant, *maréchal de camp* in the armies of the French Republic, witnessed to us of returning to a military career has caused us to recall him and enjoin on him to take leave of you. We are persuaded that he will give to the Republic a new proof of his zeal in fulfilling the last functions near to you."[46]

Two months earlier on 22 October, after the decision for Ternant's recall had been made, LeBrun had written the minister of war, Jean Nicolas Pache, regarding Ternant's status and future service.

> Citizen Ternant, marechal de camp and former minister of France in America has witnessed to me, my dear colleague, to be employed in the armies of the Republic. The distinguished talents of this officer, his profound knowledge of the art of war, his known bravery and the service he has given to the cause of liberty in America are the certificates which cause me to ask you to procure for him the privilege of new service to his country in the career of arms and to award him the promotion of which you think him capable. Citizen Genet who goes to replace him at Philadelphia would be flattered to convey to him this mark of favor and he wishes in consequence as well as me that you will give him very quickly the dispatch relative to the request I make to you.[47]

On 7 January 1793 Pache responded directly to Ternant, informing him that at the present time it would be impossible for him to return to active duty as a *maréchal de camp*. The letter was included among a number addressed to Ternant that Genet carried and which would not be delivered until May.

> The Minister of War to Marechal de Camp Ternant
> The minister of foreign affairs has made known to me your desire to be activated in the rank of marechal de camp and it is with regret that I inform you that this request is not susceptible at this moment to be honored. The number of marechal de camp employed is complete and you will only be able to be one when the National convention will decide an increase of general officers or that there would be a vacancy. Moreover, I urge you to be persuaded that when the occasion presents itself, I will place before the council all the qualifications that you have as a soldier and as a patriot, to be employed in the service and in the defense of the Republic.[48]

Unfortunately for Ternant therefore, everything turned out badly and he lost both his diplomatic and military career. LeBrun conveniently used Jean's petition to return to active duty as the reason for his recall, while Pache at the ministry of war used a technicality to deny his request for a military post. Clearly, the reason for the end of Ternant's public career was the same as for its success; the patronage, or lack there of, of those in power. In spite of the laudatory statements regarding his prior service and military experience and expressions of good will, Jean was not deemed politically acceptable by the idealistic Girondins and therefore was expendable.

Ternant had responded to the unexpected news of his termination as minister by complaining not only of his replacement but also of the manner in which he had been informed. William Stevens Smith, the son-in-law of John Adams acting as a confidential agent of the French government, had returned to the United States in February 1793 with the authority to liquidate the American debt and take charge of the program to purchase food supplies for France, the program that Jean had already put into operation. Before he had received official notification of his replacement Ternant was informed by Smith. His frustration at the continued lack of instructions from the government was heightened by Smith's discussions with Hamilton, Jefferson and Washington that ignored Jean's ministerial authority and in which $200,000 of arrearage was given to the American agent.[49]

In his late February dispatch to Paris, Jean continued to complain of the lack of instructions and reported on Smith's efforts to undermine his position as minister. In spite of his displeasure at being informed of his replacement, he assured the Executive Council that he would continue to fulfill his duties and when replaced would return to France immediately where he hoped to have his record of service vindicated by both the national convention and the executive council. Jean insisted that the written records of the departments of war and foreign affairs would establish his good conduct beyond any doubt. "Born," he declared, "in humble but irreproachable poverty I owe my advance to the services rendered in the army and diplomacy.... I have never made court to nobles with the royal government and I will not either to the powerful under the republican regime. I will favor with these last the same language I always favored with the first; that of truth and honest independence." He concluded by complaining about his "abrupt recall without replacement nor previous notice" and informed Lebrun that his recall would cause him financial loss. It would, he claimed, "force me into a precipitous sale [his personal possessions] which product will not be sufficient to the payment of my current debts and to the cost of my return to Europe."[50]

At the time Ternant had no awareness that his public service career might be permanently ended and in any case he was in no mood to care. One month before Genet arrived at the legation, Jean, frustrated and bitter, complained to the foreign minister: "I am greatly distressed to be left without information with regard to French policy relative to America and to see that my successor, although nominated in November is still not at his post on 18 April. I have sworn to remain at my post and I shall keep that oath religiously, but as soon as I am released by the arrival of citizen Genet, I hope that I will have sufficient resolve, despite my extreme poverty, never again to be the agent of any government whatever."[51]

On 16 May 1793 the long awaited Genet finally arrived in Philadelphia after a month long journey overland from Charlestown, South Carolina. Two days later on 18 May at a quarter till two in the afternoon Ternant met briefly with Washington at the executive mansion, presented his letter of recall and departed. Fifteen minutes later, in a separate and equally brief ceremony, Edmond Genet presented his letter of credence and became the official representative of the French Republic to the United States.[52]

Although Ternant left his diplomatic post disillusioned and angry and with no immediate prospect for employment, there was one positive fact that he took away from his foreign service mission, the increasing intimacy of his relationship with the family of Du Pont de Nemours. Jean's friendship with the patriarch of the family, Pierre-Samuel, his son, Victor, and other members of the extended Du Pont household would in time become the centerpiece of Jean's social network, indeed they would become his surrogate family, both in the United States and in France. As minister and later, Ternant corresponded with Du Pont de Nemours; receiving newspapers along with the patriarch's letters and for as long as he was able Jean used what little influence he had to advance Victor's diplomatic career.[53]

Following his departure from the French legation Ternant moved to the Northern Liberties, a suburb of Philadelphia north of Vine Street characterized by small farms and orchards, where he purchased a small parcel. Although without a source of steady income, Jean's financial situation, in spite of his protests, was adequate for his immediate needs. In the spring of 1792 the Federal government had initiated the process of liquidating the principal owed foreign officers for their service during the war for independence; a program that would continue until 1814. In Jean's case the lump sum payment amounted to $7,885, equal to 42,583 livres; certainly enough to meet his immediate needs and allow for some careful investments.[54] In addition to managing his small estate and tending to an apple orchard Jean also spent time in 1793 and 1794 preparing a manual of cavalry exercises and tactics which was added to the 10th edition of Steuben's *Regulations*.[55]

Unlike the other members of his group, Ternant chose to remain in the United States for what proved to be an unexpectedly extended period. Du Pont, Kellermann and Semonet all returned to France as soon as possible, but Jean for some undetermined reason delayed. In February he had promised to return as soon as Genet arrived, but by May he found it more convenient to remain in the United States. He may have decided to linger over concern for his personal safety. He was all too aware regarding the political turmoil in France and the fate of his colleagues and friends; the La Luzerne brothers dead or in exile, Montmorin, murdered while in prison during the massacres in September 1792 and Lafayette incarcerated in Austria. Perhaps he remained in order to collect his military pension. Whatever the reason, Jean soon found it impossible to return because his name had been included on the list of émigrés. The decree of 28 March 1793 established that all government agents charged with missions to f oreign countries who had not returned to France in three months from the day of their recall would be considered an émigré and declared an enemy of the Republic subject to imprisonment and or death.[56] Ternant would have had to return by 18 August 1793 to avoid being declared an émigré.

Years later during the first Restoration, in an effort to use his lack of military service between 1793 and 1801 as proof of his loyalty to the Bourbon monarchy, Ternant explained his eight-year absence from France by stating that he had been prevented from returning by "a profound feeling of fidelity to the first oath to the king" that made him prefer exile.[57] Many officers in the Royal army during the revolution had refused to swear a new oath of allegiance and had chosen instead to emigrate, so Jean's justification in 1814 was not unique. It was however, disingenuous. In the constantly shifting political environment of the great upheaval Ternant had not hesitated to take whatever oaths were required; even the oath of allegiance to the French Republic. In the summer of 1793, Jean's reasons for remaining in the United States were personal and pragmatic, and had very little to do with his loyalty to the Bourbons.

Similar to others at the time, with money to invest, Ternant was not immune to the lure of real estate. In February 1794 he purchased from Samuel Meredith twelve parcels of land, some 4,772 ½ acres in Wyalusing Township, on the east side of the north-east branch of the Susquehanna River in Luzerne (now Bradford) County, Pennsylvania.[58] Only 140 miles from Philadelphia and located near the recently established French community at Asylum, the property seemed a safe investment. It was close to numerous settlements with easy access via the river and Jean, like other speculators in American backlands, hoped to sell individual parcels at a substantial profit. Congress at the time was selling land in Ohio for $2.00

an acre and Ternant was convinced he could get a higher price due to his property's better location.[59]

In April 1796 Ternant added to his real estate holdings by purchasing at public auction for 2,000 pounds specie, a three-story tenement on the south side of Chestnut Street between 10th and 11th Streets.[60] The boarding house would provide him with a regular and much needed source of income. Finally in November, Jean applied for and was granted title to 450 acres of Ohio land as part of his pension application. Whether he sold his warrant or exchanged it for another part of the public domain is unknown.[61] By the winter of 1797/98 therefore, Ternant had taken considerable steps toward establishing his financial future. However, notwithstanding his success, he was discontented and longed to return to Paris.

Philadelphia in the years immediately following Jean's replacement was inundated with a flood of French refugees fleeing the anarchy in Saint Domingue and a steady stream of individuals escaping from the political terror in France. Between 1793 and 1795 some 25,000 arrived in America ports. Even before the new influx of Creoles and émigrés arrived however, Philadelphia already had a sizable French community that amounted in 1790 to about 5,000 of the city's population of 28,500. It also had the reputation as the center of French culture in the United States and was therefore an attractive destination for many of those seeking either temporary or permanent sanctuary.[62]

Among the new arrivals were a number of Jean's former comrades in arms; returned either to escape arrest in France, to collect their pension or both. Louis le Begue Duportail, the former commandant of engineers in the Continental army and later a minister of war fled to the United States and purchased a farm near the old encampment at Valley Forge. Jean-Baptiste-Joesph de Laumoy, Jean's closest friend and Lafayette's former aide de camp, Louis-Saint-Ange de la Colombe, both of whom had been part of the group of officers that had emigrated with Lafayette in 1792 soon arrived. Later, in the summer of 1798 Thaddeus Kosciusko, now a refugee from his native Poland, also arrived seeking his compensation for service.

In June 1795, two years after he left and much to Ternant's delight, his young friend, Victor Du Pont, returned to Philadelphia; not as an émigré but once again with a diplomatic posting as secretary of legation under the new French minister, Pierre Auguste Adet. He was accompanied by his wife. Following his return to France Victor had served briefly in the consulate division of the *Ministere des Relations Exterieures* and in the spring of 1794 he had married the twenty-three-year-old daughter of a local aristocrat and family friend, Gabrielle Josephine de La Fite de Pelleport.

Unfortunately, Jean had little time to socialize with them, as Victor was sent to Charlestown as consul in July. Nevertheless, in those few short weeks Jean and Josephine began what would become an intimate but platonic friendship that would last for the rest of their lives. The older man with the easy manners of polite society and the young, very conservative wife of his protégé, far from the comforts and culture of her native land, enjoyed each other's company and quickly bonded. So much so that in February 1796 Jean accepted a request to serve as godfather for the young couple's first child, Amelia Elizabeth. "I am a little too fallen from Christianity," he admitted, "to be her godfather in the judgment of the church, but I will be willing in all other senses which would contribute to her happiness and to your satisfaction. Mademoiselle Nixon to whom I have delivered your letter consents to be godmother in every possible sense. She is a zealous Christian, consequently the Catholicism of Madam Du Pont will be entirely reassured."[63] As Amelia's godfather Jean would maintain a continuing interest in her welfare for the remainder of his life and in so doing was accepted as an unofficial member of the Du Pont Family. Over the years Victor, Josephine and their children became a surrogate for the family Jean never had.

Amelia's godmother, Elizabeth (Betsy) Nixon, was one of four daughters of John Nixon, a wealthy Philadelphia merchant and banker. As an occasional guest in the Nixon home Ternant was certainly well acquainted with Betsy and it was he who probably recognized she would make a socially acceptable companion for Josephine and introduced them.[64]

While Victor and Josephine were in Charlestown Jean corresponded with each of them; letters of encouragement and

Gabrielle Josephine (de La Fite de Pelleport) Du Pont by Louis Leopold Boilly, 1798. Convent educated and an ardent opponent of the French Revolution Josephine, as the wife of Victor Du Pont, became Ternant's most intimate and cherished female friend. Ternant served as godfather to Josephine's first child (courtesy Hagley Museum and Library).

advice to Victor and notes of a more informal and personal nature to his wife. It is in the letters to Josephine that we gain some insight to Ternant's situation and his hopes for the future; "... if you choose to return to France, as I would certainly do myself once there is news of peace, one of my first wishes would be to find you there." He describe wishing to retire on the banks of the Loire and imagined the two of them being neighbors and "able to see each other often, which I assure you would give me the greatest pleasure. Meanwhile, wish for the best and come see me in case you pass this way again. If I have not sold my little farm you will find me as before, occupied with rustic work and attending church strictly under compulsion, an experience I have taken the liberty to recommend to Monsieur Du Pont. After the sale of this place, which must take place one day or another I will go live in my small house in town where you will find without any doubt, all the welcome in my power.... Farewell my pretty countrywomen, accept all my wishes for your happiness, as well as the tokens of my tender and respectful attachment."[65]

In May 1797 Victor received a promotion to Consul General and the Du Ponts returned to Philadelphia. Unfortunately, due to worsening relations between France and the United States, President Adams refused to grant the required exequatur and Victor and his family returned to France. In the months that followed Ternant continued his correspondence, informing the young couple of his activities; that he had spent considerable time traveling, of the sale of his small estate in the Northern Liberties, of his desire to return to Europe that proved impossible to effect and of his social isolation. "I am come back to pass my winter here [Philadelphia] where I live as if I was one hundred miles from the city, seeing no one and not going to anyone's home ... and finding in my books, papers and small study all the necessary resources for the enjoyment of family...."[66]

Ternant's social seclusion was entirely self-imposed and would remain the major characteristic of his life style for the next forty years. In a sense his withdrawal from society was the result of his fear that he could not live up to either the social code he practiced or the values of his bourgeois origins. Jean explained his reluctance to pursue an active social life by acknowledging that good manners required him to respond in kind to social engagements; the more invitations he accepted the more similar proposals he was obliged to extend. Equally important, Jean also embodied the middle class values that emphasized family and the avoidance of the unnecessary and expensive expenditures, as well as the bad habits associated with aristocratic behavior. In the end he convinced himself that his financial resources were simply too inadequate to support either an extensive level of social activity or a family.

Ternant never married. It is not known what personal experiences or reservations caused him to remain a bachelor, but judging from his letters it seems to have been the result of a conscious decision to do so. As the French minister to the United States Jean was welcomed into the homes of Philadelphia's elite and certainly had the opportunity to find a socially acceptable wife. He was in his early 40s, handsome, well educated and mannered, with a career. He would have been a good catch. Many of his colleagues in the diplomatic community had found wives during their time in America. Both Otto and Barbe-Marbois married Americans, as did the British minister, George Hammond, the minister representing Spain, Carlos Martinez de Irujo, and Ternant's successor, Edmond Genet. So there was a well-established precedent for such unions. Moreover, Jean liked women. He enjoyed their company, valued their opinions, fashioned numerous long-term friendships with them and was generous to his friends' wives and daughters in his final testament. Women reciprocated his interest and found Jean charming and a good companion.

The only hint in the records of a romantic relationship with a woman is a reference in the 1800 census. Ternant is listed as sharing his accommodations in Southwark, a suburb of Philadelphia, with an unnamed white female between the ages of fifteen and twenty-six. Her status was not described but as she was specifically not listed in the categories of either servant or others, it is possible that Jean was involved in an affair of the heart.[67] How long this relationship lasted or its nature remains a mystery. There is no mention of her in Jean's letters and she did not accompany him when he returned to France.

The extent of Ternant's reluctance to socialize and his absence from Philadelphia's social scene is clearly indicated by statements in his letters from the period and the lack of any mention of him in the journal kept by Moreau de St. Mery. With the exception of Moreau's reference that "M. de Ternant merely passed through the country" in a paragraph that deplored the poor quality of French ministers to the United States, Ternant's lack of social activity in the city and in the French community was confirmed.[68]

At some point Ternant resolved to return to France. Poor health, the lack of future prospects for continuing his career, loneliness perhaps, and a yearning for the familiar surroundings and pleasures of Paris combined to determine his decision. In order to do so safely however, it was necessary to have his name removed from the list of émigrés. For help in this endeavor, Jean turned to two individuals he knew personally that still had influence in the government; Charles-Maurice de Talleyrand-Perigord and François Barthelemy. Talleyrand, a former bishop, member of the Constitute Assembly and one time émigré, had been restored to power as minister of foreign affairs in July 1797. François Barthelemy, the former secretary of the London Embassy and later a member of the Directory, was regarded as one of France's foremost diplomats. Ternant had made the acquaintance of both men during the early years of the revolution and shared their moderate political views. Talleyrand and Ternant had renewed their previous association in person during 1795 and 1796 when the former was in Philadelphia, passing his time in travel and speculation; attempting to replenish his fortune while waiting for the first opportunity to return to Paris.

Although different in status, personality and experience all three men favored a constitutional monarchy, and had had their careers interrupted by the increasing radicalism of the revolution. Ternant had been replaced by the Girondins, Talleyrand had been in England prior to the Terror and was unable to return to France and in the coup of Fructidor (4 September 1797) Barthelemy had been arrested and along with Barbe-Marbois, another one of Ternant's friends, been deported and imprisoned at Cayenne, the capital of French Guiana.

Between 1797 and 1800 Ternant corresponded with both Talleyrand and Barthelemy, describing his predicament, requesting their assistance and in return offering his support. Jean wrote a number of letters to Barthelemy; both to Paris the summer of 1797 after his colleague had been elected a director and again to Guiana, after Barthelemy's deportation. In an April 1799 letter Jean described his desire "more than ever to be able soon to return to the country that saw my birth and to pass there the very few years that remain to me." He explained that although he had given the government of that time his reasons for remaining in America after his dismissal, and there had been no objection, he nevertheless found himself under the restrictions imposed by the decree of 15 November 1794 and could only return in safety if the decree was repealed. "If the natural kindness," he wrote, "which I know you have and the memory of our former close relationship enable you to take any steps favorable to my desires I would be forever obliged to you.... If I am able to be of any service to you in this distant country where I have spent nearly eighteen years in two interesting periods, I will make every zealous effort to comply with your wishes."[69]

Ternant's series of letters to Barthelemy had little effect, but his correspondence with Talleyrand, the minister of foreign affairs, produced the desired result. In December 1800 Jean wrote to thank Talleyrand.

> Citizen Minister, allow a poor old man to thank you especially for the letter which you have been so good to send him on 14 Thermidor last (2 August 1800) to facilitate his return. I already had everything prepared, in spite of the severity of the season, to come myself to show you my great gratitude, when a violent attack of dysentery made impossible my return to New York, where the vessel of which I wrote immediately sailed. But I certainly will take advan-

tage of the first opportunity that presents itself in the spring in one of the other ports. The annoying delay at least allows me the hope of still receiving a passport from the government, which was not attached to the response that you have had the kindness to send me. Citizen Du Pont will, if you permit him, forward the copy in your office and send it by the return of the same vessel. To comply with the wishes that you expressed to me in your letter, I will undertake to offer you the results of some research on my part on our commercial and political relations with the United States ... and their relations with other maritime nations and colonies, if I have not learned of the conclusion of our arrangements with the American plenipotentiaries and if I judge that it is better to still profit from the annoying extension of my stay here during the winter to finish this work and modify it if there is any reason according to the nature of the treaty concluded and the effect it will produce here. Finally, I will neglect nothing to render this report worthy of your notice, and although my infirmities remove any hope of being from now on to be actively useful in any position whatever, I will never place less than all my zeal subject to the government every time that it thinks suitable the fruit of my experience and knowledge acquired in the course of my past service. It is indeed with sincerity that I reiterate to you the homage of my gratitude and the expression of my wishes for your success.[70]

Although as foreign minister Talleyrand's influence was the most important factor in arranging for Jean's return, Lafayette also played a role. The marquis, on his return to France after five years in captivity, urged François Fouche, the minister of police, to remove from the list of émigrés the names of former members of his staff who had fled with him in August 1792, and also Ternant and Duportail, who had been his comrades-in-arms during the American war for independence and had remained loyal to France.[71] In October 1800 Ternant received a short note from Lafayette, dated 9 July. The letter, now lost, was the only communication from Lafayette in more than eight years.[72]

The influence exerted on Jean's behalf by his friends was aided in no small measure by the larger movement in France to resolve the émigré question. Legislation concerning amnesty and repatriation for the 100,000 or so individuals on the list was under consideration. A ministry of justice commission was created to review on an individual basis, applications from émigrés to have their name removed from the government's list. The list itself had been closed but the commission became notorious for being a scene of influence peddling and bribery on a large scale. And after the coup of 18 Brumaire amnesty for the vast majority of émigrés was one of the issues Bonaparte, as First Consul chose to champion; by the spring of 1802 most émigrés had returned. Many however, would remain under police surveillance for a period of ten years and subject to administrative imprisonment.[73]

Ternant's decision to return to France was not due to any dissatisfaction with his experiences in the United States, nor was he prompted by any of the distaste for Americans that was held by so many in the émigré community; who disliked American society for its lack of refinement and all consuming interest in making money at the expense of enjoying life. Moreover, there is nothing in his letters that indicate he perceived himself menaced by either the growing anti–French sentiment in the country, or the anti-alien legislation enacted by the Adams administration in the summer of 1798; the result of a deterioration in relations between the United States and France brought on by attacks on American shipping by ships of the French Republic and the revelations of the XYZ affair.

During the winter of 1799/1800 while preparing for his return to France, Ternant's waiting was made easier by the return to the United States of Victor and Josephine, accompanied this time by his father and the entire Du Pont family. The extended family established itself in a house they called "Goodstay" on Bergen Point, New Jersey, only an hour's sail from New York City.[74] A few months later, Victor moved his family to New York and it was either while visiting Goodstay or Victor's residence in New York that Jean was first introduced to many of the people that would later form his social circle, among them Madame Du Pont, her daughter and Jean-Xavier Bureaux de Pusy. A graduate of Mézières and a captain in the engineers before the revolution, de Pusy had served in the Constitute Assembly, shared Lafayette's captivity and married Julienne Poivre, Du Pont de Nemours' step-daughter. Their daughter, Françoise-Josephine (Sara to her family) would later marry a military engineer and receive 6,000 francs from Jean's testament.[75]

Jean also made the acquaintance of the twenty-year-old Catherine (Kitty) Church, the daughter of Angelica and John Barker Church and a close friend of Josephine Du Pont. Catherine and her family had returned to the United States from England in 1797 and moved into a house on Broadway, close to the home of Alexander Hamilton. Angelica Church and Elizabeth Hamilton, Alexander's wife, were sisters and the two families were thus closely linked. When Victor and Josephine moved to the city in the spring of 1800, they were quickly included in the Hamilton/Church circle.

The Church's were wealthy, extremely well connected and prominent in the Franco-American community. John Church had immigrated to the United States during the war for independence and made a fortune supplying provisions to Rochambeau's expeditionary force. In 1777 he and Angelica, the daughter of Philip Schuyler, a prominent New York landowner, eloped, much to the displeasure of her parents. In addition to being related through marriage to Hamilton, Angelica was a long-time confidante and friend to Thomas Jefferson. Kitty and Jefferson's daughters had attended the same school in Paris and she had been a frequent guest at the Hôtel Langeac, Jefferson's Paris residence. Educated in France, speaking fluent French and sympathetic toward Catholicism, Kitty was the perfect companion for the conservative and religious Josephine. In 1802 Kitty would marry Bertram Peter Cruger, the son of Nicolas Cruger, a wealthy New York merchant, who had hired the young Alexander Hamilton as a clerk in his trading company. Following the collapse of Napoleon's regime, Kitty would return to Paris with her children for an extended stay and Jean, who had maintained a regular correspondence with her, would later bequeath 2,500 francs to her two daughters in his testament.

Writing to Josephine in New York, Jean expressed his delight at her return, his desire to see his goddaughter and excused his failure to visit on his poor health; "My infirmities which allow few trips," he explained, "... have prevented us from being together as often as I would desire." Jean also declined an invitation from Josephine to be a guest in her home when he visited the city. "You are very kind to suggest I lodge at your house. I sense completely the value of this mark of friendship and I would accept it with delight if I had not already declined a similar favor from my friend General Hamilton because of the state of my health that makes me a very troublesome guest. But although lodging elsewhere I will none the less be frequently with you; and at your command for everything." In the same letter he also indicated that if his return to France were postponed any longer he would move to Elizabethtown, New Jersey, to be closer.[76]

In addition to Victor and his father, another of Ternant's old friends reappeared. Gouverneur Morris had returned to the United States in December 1798, after nine years' absence. Following service as American minister-plenipotentiary to France during the Terror and an extended period of travel in Europe afterwards, Morris had returned to the United States prepared to settle into a comfortable retirement. In late April 1799 Ternant visited his fellow diplomat in New York and renewed their friendship. In the spring of 1800 Morris was chosen to fill an un-expired term in the Senate and traveled to Philadelphia. The two old friends from Valley Forge and Paris were again reunited briefly, and when Morris returned to New York he carried Jean's letters to Victor and Josephine.[77]

Although in December Ternant indicated that in the early spring he hoped to visit New York and if the opportunity presented itself, depart from there to France, it was not until the summer that Jean was finally able to secure passage and sail.[78] In brief notes on the eve of his departure Ternant retained George Simpson, the first teller of the Bank of the United States as his financial agent, providing him with a 2 percent commission on all investments; gave Du Pont de Nemours power of attorney over money he had left in Philadelphia and named Pierre-Samuel and Victor as executors of his letters, papers and testament should he meet an untimely death.[79]

On Sunday, 5 July 1801 Jean, accompanied by his old friend and comrade in arms, Jean-Baptiste Joseph de Laumoy, sailed for Nantes on the *Severn*, a 279-ton ship just recently returned from Canton, China, and loaded with a cargo of silks, taffetas, Souchong tea and porcelain for the French market.[80] After a very quick passage of only twenty-nine days, marred only by the "noise and coarse whims" of his fellow passengers, Ternant arrived off the coast of France on 3 August.[81] He was at Nantes by the 5th and immediately reported his safe arrival to Josephine and urged her to write as often as possible. "I will not prolong my stay here beyond tomorrow," he added, "and as I go by post chaise and my health is good, I plan on not stopping until Paris. My first care will be to find Victor there."[82]

That same day Ternant also sent a message to Victor, who had returned to France in January to solicit investments and government support for the family business.

> I am here my dear Du Pont since before yesterday, and not being able to start for Paris before the 22nd.... The *Franklin* not returning till 1 July I decided to leave from New York on the *Severn* which set sail on 5 July and arrived on the lower part of the Loire on 3 August after a rather fortunate crossing. I have left Madame Du Pont, your children and your entire family in perfect health. There is much of interest I have to tell you, we will talk of the rest in Paris where I will arrive by coach next Thursday 25 Thermidor, at five o'clock in the afternoon. If you are able without too much trouble to find a room for me in a hotel in the *quartier central* and leave notice at the office of the coach next Thursday you will oblige me very much. Adieu my dear Du Pont, I embrace you with all my heart.
>
> You will please me by not telling anyone that I have arrived, in order that I will not be obliged to go out before that. M. de Laumoy departs with me. He will need a room in the same hotel as me.[83]

After an absence of almost exactly ten years Ternant was only a short three-day journey from Paris. He was finally almost home.

X

Paris—St. Germain-en-Laye—Contrexéville
August 1801–November 1833

By the time Ternant reached Nantes in the summer of 1801, the Consulate, headed by Napoleon Bonaparte, had been in place for almost two years and France had become a security state, with political authority limited to the government in Paris or its agents and one characterized by expanded police surveillance. Internal travel was closely monitored and registration of residency required at all times; returning émigrés, foreigners or other suspects were under constant surveillance by the authorities and no one, either republican or royalist, was safe from administrative detention. The political instability in the Republic and widespread violence that had marked the authoritarian governments between 1792 and 1799, that Jean had only experienced at second hand, had prepared the way for a dictatorial regime determined to limit political activity and enforce social order at any cost. By 1802 and the acceptance of the consulship for life, Bonaparte had successfully established a personal dictatorship.[1]

Ternant arrived in Paris on Thursday evening, 12 August 1801 and as required by all visitors to the city, reported his presence to the prefecture of police and then to the authorities in the arrondissment where he was staying. There he exchanged his passport for a certificate, signed a register that included a physical description and was issued a *permis de sejour*, permitting his residence. The next day Jean met Victor Du Pont and on the 14th they dined together at Antoine Beauvillier's well-known restaurant on the passage Beauvilliers; an establishment that catered to conservatives and that was also favored by Americans.[2]

After twelve years of revolution Paris was much changed from the city Jean had left. The streets, filthy as ever, were much less crowded but better lit at night. Private carriages that had once dominated traffic had almost disappeared and liveries were nonexistent. Every hat now bore a tricolor cockade and the tricolor flag was prominently displayed.³ Once more, there was now an abundant presence of uniformed personnel, both military and civilian.⁴ Other aspects of the city however, remained unaltered. Paris remained the cultural and political center of the country and living there continued to be expensive. Although food remained relatively cheap, the price for lodging had doubled.⁵ The Palais-Royal, Jean's old haunt, had been stripped of its reputation as a center of revolutionary activity. It nevertheless maintained its status as the center of the city's social life, an "island of pleasure," the "Paris of Paris," and it likely would have been among the first places that he revisited.

Ternant's immediate activities are not recorded but undoubtedly they included a visit to the Ministry of Foreign Affairs in the Hôtel Galliffet, rue du Bac; to pay his respects to Talleyrand and to thank him personally for his help; perhaps also to deliver the report on trade with the United States that he had prepared during his final days in Philadelphia. It would be surprising also if he did not visit Damvillers, but any evidence for such a journey is also lacking; Jean's letters, except for a few comments regarding his brother in Louisiana, are devoid of any mention of the either the city of his youth or his other siblings.

Sometime in September Ternant, in an attempt to maximize his regular income, applied for the pension of a retired general of brigade, formerly *maréchal de camp*. To support his request Jean presented the *Bureau de État-Major* with letters from the minister of foreign affairs in 1793 that recognized him in the grade of *maréchal de camp* and a note from the minister of war at the same time that expressed regret at not being able to employ Jean in that grade, but promised to present his name for consideration for any future vacancy. In spite of the documents supporting his claim, and his explanation that poor health had forced him to remain in Pennsylvania following his replacement as minister, Ternant's request was refused. He was informed that his appointment to the grade of *maréchal de camp* had never been approved and there was no record of any military service to the Republic in that grade.⁶ It was a serious set back for Ternant. The salary for a general of brigade in 1801 was 10,000 francs for active duty and 7,500 if in reserve.⁷ Jean's annual pension would have amounted to 2,500 francs, a considerable sum, and since anyone with excess of that amount could live very comfortably, that sum added to the value his investments would have meant financial security.⁸

In the early fall Jean left Paris, for a brief visit to Holland to inquire into the status of his military pension from the Dutch government and hopefully collect the money due him; by 1801 some 11,000 florins or about 27,500 livres.⁹ In a letter dated 5 November 1802 Jean mentions a meeting with the Dutch ambassador to France and in other letters he alludes to an unspecified legal proceedings, whose success was of paramount importance for his future financial well-being.[10] Whether this case pertained to his financial affairs in Holland is unknown.

Concerning his future, everything hinged upon the state of his financial resources and until they became more certain Jean remained undecided as to where to spend his remaining years. Fifty years old, with all of his former colleagues and friends either dead or removed from power, his military and diplomatic career blocked by poor health and perhaps politics, he wrote to Josephine Du Pont trying to reconcile any future plans with his situation.

> Regarding my plans, they have not changed since the last time I saw you. I am only taking care of my personal matters; I live a simple life, which suits me just fine for the moment, without thinking of anything else other than freely using, in moderation, the varied pleasures of our modern Babylon, which are available to me. Despite the bad air we breath here, I am in good health—even if I am no longer disturbed in the pursuit of my small plans for my future happiness, despite my attachment to the new world, I prefer the old one, even if it is bad and corrupt—I often tell myself as the angel Gabriel said to his fellow angels, if everything is not good, at least it is not too bad. It would be unwise not to take people and things the way they are, and to not make it part of your happiness. I will only be able to make a final decision regarding my future towards the end of winter.

He concluded his letter, "give my best to your children, and remember you can always count on my undying affection."[11]

Most likely under some degree of surveillance by the authorities, Ternant ignored politics and made no attempt either to restart his career or to ingratiate himself with government officials. No ideologue, he had no problem tending only to his private affairs, but as did Lafayette, Jean remained a supporter of a liberal Constitutional Monarchy. Similar to many others of his political persuasion he ignored Napoleon's regime as much as possible. But aware that the government opened his letters, he also avoided any discussion of current events and limited his remarks to personal matters.

In 1802 Ternant's financial situation remained unresolved but he had made a decision on where he would retire. He informed Josephine,

> I am hardly more advanced today with my affairs in France than when I wrote you from Holland. I continue to occupy myself with them and when they are finished I will execute without delay my plan of definite retirement. All chances of preference are still in favor of America and you will see my return next summer. Meanwhile I lead here, with my tolerable health, the life of a good and honest epicurean, sometimes in the city, sometimes in the countryside, often foolish, rarely wise and enjoying without concern or ambition all of the pleasures which are in my reach.[12]

A year later, though Jean's financial situation was still unresolved; his decision to return to the United States remained the same. "I always dream of returning to the hallowed land and I really count on it, if war and the stars don't prevent me from embarking in the course of next summer."[13] It was war.

In December 1804 Napoleon was crowned Emperor, the Peace of Amiens with England had ended and the war of the Third Coalition began. As the momentous events of 1805 occurred that would determine Europe's fate for the next decade, Trafalgar in October and Austerlitz in December, Ternant remained in limbo regarding his future. Once more he assured Josephine, "I still desire to be near you. The legal action that I am still engaged in is finally close to being adjudicated and immediately upon its resolution I certainly will take my leave." He admitted however, having second thoughts. "The truth is that until the present, I have been mostly undecided as to what to do. Sometimes I have wished they would expel me and would gladly do or say anything if I were able to guess the right measure to adhere too in order not to expose myself to the honors of the Temple or an exile to Guyana."[14]

While he waited for his financial situation to be clarified, Jean settled into a regular routine, much of his time traveling in the countryside hoping to preserve his health. By the spring of 1807 however, nothing had changed regarding his future. "I continue in the same arrangements as formerly, always however, with the supposition of winning my cursed legal action. Its loss will necessarily force me to remain where I am and in that case it will probably be a little longer before we meet again, because in the final analysis I count on your return here." He assured her, "My friendship for you will last as long as I do."[15]

In July 1802, much to Ternant's joy, Du Pont de Nemours and his wife had returned to Paris. Included in his baggage the patriarch carried letters from Jefferson to Robert Livingston, the American minister, regarding negotiations for the Louisiana territory. The renowned Physiocrat met with Bonaparte and over the course of the next year was prominent among those advocating Louisiana's sale to the United States.

Unlike Jean, Du Pont de Nemours was able to quickly reestablish his public service career; as a member of the *Chambre de Commerce de Paris,* as an elector in the Department Loiret and in 1814 as Secretary General of the Provisional government. In the last office he was able to survive the regime change and reaffirm his royalist sentiments by supporting Napoleon's abdication and exile. During the years of the Empire Ternant remained in close contact with Du Pont de Nemours, though given Jean's reluctance to socialize on a regular basis, there were frequent periods with little communication.

Finally, in the fall of 1808, after seven years Ternant was at last able to gauge the state of his financial resources and with the apparent loss of his legal suit concluded that he would not be able to retire in the United States; though he continued to harbor hopes of returning for a visit. He advised Josephine however, now living unhappily on a farm in western New York, to forget about returning to France and assured her that life in the United States, in spite of its difficulties was much to be preferred to that in Europe. "If I had children, or if I was young enough to begin a family," he wrote, "America would certainly be the country that I would live in." Regarding his own decision to remain in France rather than to return permanently to the United States he explained,

being neither totally in the one nor the other I remain here and will probably finish my lease on this life here because I am where I have habits which I find most amusing and having become lazy or delirious I fear the financial straits and the embarrassments of the move so far ... you should not be surprised that I have preferred Europe and Paris as a last refuge when you learn that nothing remains to me beyond ten thousand livres in rents. With that I would be much to poor to live agreeably in America.... Moreover, not occupying and neither wishing for nor searching for any post whatever, I enjoy here a completely precious idleness; sometimes in the city sometimes n the countryside, every summer at a spa, Plombieres, Forges or Bourbonne; I have never really been so happy since I am nothing and don't wish to be something. Also my health is very good, it has never been so good.... In spite of all this, my dear friend, I am still very often tempted to cross again the Atlantic and perhaps one day I will surprise you....[16]

During his forays into the surrounding countryside Ternant in all likelihood took the opportunity to visit Lafayette at his country estate, La Grange, located near the small village of Courpalay, southeast from Paris. Refusing to accept Bonaparte's consulship for life in 1802, Lafayette had retired to his chateau, became an apolitical gentleman farmer, but played host to a steady stream of individuals like Jean who were politically liberal or moderate and were opposed to Bonaparte's regime.[17] Given Ternant's modest living arrangements, his perceived inability to entertain and reluctance to make social calls he could not reciprocate, it is not surprising perhaps that the two men never resumed their pre-revolution association. Later, in 1824 when Lafayette was invited to visit to the United States Ternant may have been inclined to accompany him, but due to poor health, could not. He wrote to Victor; "you will see that it is hardly the case of being able to go to America with M. de Lafayette. I am delighted that the congress have shown him so great attention, surely he merits it for all he has given to that country. I don't know if he will profit on that account, because it has been a longtime since I have either visited his home or met him elsewhere."[18]

Ternant also saw less and less of his closest friend and former comrade in arms, Jean-Baptiste Joseph de Laumoy. Following their return to Paris, Laumoy had continued on to his home at Chilleurs-sur-Bois, near Orléans. As Jean, Laumoy did not return to active military duty but in 1803, unlike Jean, he married a young woman thirty years his junior, Agathe-Louise Bocquet de Chantereine. In 1811 Laumoy retired and collected the pension due a Brigadier General. Although well off, Laumoy, again unlike Ternant, chose to work and was appointed a *huissier*, a tipstaff, in the Orléans courts.[19] In addition to his residence in Orléans Laumoy also had an apartment in Paris in the hôtel de Rosambo, No. 64 rue de Bondy, 5th arrondissement (today rue Rene-Boulanger, 10th arrondissement). After Laumoy's death in January 1832 his widow remained in Paris and was named as one of the principal beneficiaries in Jean's testament.[20]

No longer a participant in the great affairs of his time Ternant became instead an informed but uninvolved spectator, only a witness to events. No longer involved with military duties, meetings with heads of state or associating with the leading figures of his day, the hectic pace and excitement of his military and diplomatic careers was replaced by the quiet of his study, leisurely visits to the countryside, hunting on occasion and preoccupation with his own strictly personal affairs. Jean made this change in lifestyle with little regret. Armed with his intellectual interests in natural history and art, and his disillusionment with his treatment at the hands of the revolutionary government, he slipped into retirement with ease and a sense of relief. "I continue to vegetate here in my corner, the most agreeable possible," he wrote, "finding myself furthermore passably content."[21] His only concern continued to be if he would be able to husband his financial resources to lead a comfortable existence.

In socio-economic terms Ternant was a *rentier*, an individual who lived off unearned income; either an annuity, dividends from shares of stock, a government pension or a combination thereof. It was a traditional dream of every bourgeois to live "nobly," in other words, to avoid having to work for a living. Ternant's military and foreign service careers had been taken up with the expectation that they would provide a substantial pension for his old age and allow him the leisure time to follow his interests.

Ternant's correspondence during the period 1809–1812, the high point of Napoleon's imperial regime, continued the same themes as his earlier letters; filled with comments on his health, "passably good"; his travels, "each summer I make a little journey to the waters to strengthen"; his financial worries, "Paris is so expensive that when one is not very wealthy one finds oneself concerned without ceasing after his finances" and concerns for the well being of Josephine and her friends.[22] He also paid particular attention to his goddaughter, Amelia, corresponding with her directly.

> I have perused with great satisfaction, my dear Amelia, your two letters of March and July last. The handwriting style and sentiments espoused deserve much praise, and are promising forerunners of greater accomplishment. It is a fortunate thing for you to have experienced the effects of Mrs. Cruger's friendship for your dear mama. A young lady must feel proud to have such a protector. Continue your efforts to deserve her kindness and as she has already spoken handsomely of you, I am in hopes you will derive essential advantages from her benevolent patronage. I have been particularly much pleased with your disinterestedness and ready compliance with your good parent's disposal of the little sum sent you. That is very laudable on all sides. But when I send again another such token of my remembrance, I shall insist on the money being lodged in your private purse and left entirely at your disposal for such little purchases as may best suit your age and fancy.... Believe me my dear Amelia, your most affectionate godfather.[23]

The major events of the time—the war with Austria in 1809, the recession of 1810 and 1811, the economic hardships that stemmed from Napoleon's continental system, unending military operations in Spain with their attendant difficulties, Napoleon's marriage to a Hapsburg princess or the drift toward a war with Russia—were ignored. It was during this period that Ternant began a program of regular investment. In 1811 he purchased seventeen shares in the Bank of France and a year later, in January 1812, he purchased three more. By 1830 Jean had accumulated sixty-nine shares. Later, in the 1820s, he would add to his investment portfolio with the purchase of government bonds.[24]

For the first nine years following his return to France there is no information regarding where in Paris Ternant lived. In September 1810 however, after spending two months at the seashore "taking baths and breathing the salt air which has strengthened me very much" he reported moving to a new lodging at No. 12 rue Mesle, *quartier marais*, 8th arrondissement (today rue Meslay in the 3rd arrondissement), an inexpensive residential district on the east side of Paris filled with *hôtels particuliers* of the old aristocracy dating primarily from the seventeenth century.[25] He would remain there until the spring of 1814.

With the end of his public service career Ternant's financial well-being depended upon two factors, first, obtaining the largest military pension possible and second, managing his investments to insure the highest possible dividends. Together, his pension and dividends would provide for Jean's everyday needs and be the measure for his standard of living. His working capital was to be protected from loss and if possible, increased. Living modestly therefore was essential to both Jean's financial health and his peace of mind. His failure to obtain a general of brigade pension has been noted but his pension amounting to 666.13 florins from the Dutch government continued and in late January 1812, after the Kingdom of Holland had been annexed to France, it was converted into a *solde de retraite* of 1,400 francs.[26]

Some idea of Ternant's financial situation at the time is illustrated by a comparison of incomes. The salaries of government officials in 1810 were liberal, a Prefect of a department received 20,000 francs per annum; a Bishop 10,000, the Chief Engineer of Bridges and Roads 5,000, and a parish priest 1,500. The yearly income for an average worker was about 500 francs.[27] It was largely because his efforts to maximize the financial benefits of his military and foreign service career had proved unsuccessful therefore that Jean became preoccupied with the necessity for increasing the return from his investment holdings; an effort that while ultimately successful was initially plagued by bad luck and disappointment.

In September 1811 Ternant experienced a serious financial setback regarding his American investments, one that caused him briefly to consider an immediate return to the United States in spite of the late season. In November 1810, after only receiving a partial return on the 6 percent interest on his holdings, Jean had exchanged them for shares in the Bank of the United States that were paying 8 percent at the time.[28] Now, less than a year later, he had been informed that the bank's charter had not been renewed and that for the next twenty months no dividends would be paid to shareholders on either principal or interest and the principal would only be repaid after the liquidation of the bank's assets. Confronted by the loss of what he estimated to be one-third of the value of his holdings, Jean admitted to being worried that his means of existence would be so reduced that he would be compelled to lower his standard of living by reducing his needs to match his means.[29] Fortunately, the liquidation process was rapid and successful. During the first six months the bank paid off almost all of both its public and private deposits.[30]

The threat of investment reverses in the United States was not the only financial difficulty that Ternant faced. Like many speculators in undeveloped lands he had had no luck selling tracks from his more than 4,000 acres in Luzerne County and whose taxes further depleted his available funds. Anxious to receive any money from his American investments he instructed his agent, George Simpson, to use his discretion in either keeping or selling Jean's 3 percent notes.[31]

While Jean settled into his routine of summer visits to the surrounding countryside and worried over being able to tailor his expenditures to his revenues, the French Empire collapsed. The twenty-two months between June 1812 and March 1814 were filled with military defeats that culminated on 31 March with the surrender of Paris and Napoleon's abdication and exile. A month later, to large crowds of enthusiastic but war weary Parisians; Louis XVIII entered Paris after having agreed to restore the constitutional monarchy. Ternant was among the many that welcomed the return of the king and he later openly expressed his feelings about the course of recent events to his American agent. "Luckily we have at last got rid of Bonaparte's horrid tyranny, and the Bourbons are recalled to the throne of France—A general peace with all the European powers is to be the immediate consequence and most probably England and America will at the same time put an end to the war between them."[32] He expressed the same sentiments to Josephine.

> I don't know, my dear friend, if the last two letters I have written you since the arrival of your last of March 1813 have been more successful than yours. Absolutely nothing has reached me from you since that time. That is not surprising. We were by that time in the thick of the great confused follies and frightful tyranny of Bonaparte. Behold, we are delivered at last and the Bourbons are again, and I hope rightly forever, in possession of the French monarchy.[33]

At some point during the early days of the first restoration, Ternant moved again to new lodgings, taking a more expensive room or a small apartment at No 34 rue Quiberon, 2nd arrondissement (today rue Montpensier in the 1st arrondissement) directly above the café de Foy on the western side of the Palais-Royale.[34] It was an ideal location; down a fight of stairs to a café that catered to a wealthy and mostly royalist cliental and that was considered one of the best in the city, and only a short walk from the Tuileries Palace, its gardens and government offices.[35]

As most former public servants who depended upon government pensions as an important source for their livelihood, Ternant, once the court had been reestablished, attended the king's Sunday levees in the state apartments of the Tuileries Palace and ministerial receptions, assuring the king and his ministers of his unwavering devotion to the monarchy and hoping thereby to obtain recognition as a general of brigade with its attendant pension. Jean had no more success with the Bourbon bureaucrats however, than he did with Napoleon's, but he did succeed in getting his pension of 1,400 francs from his Dutch service recognized.[36]

During his discussions with officials Ternant mentioned, as proof of his loyalty, having among his possessions an engraving of Louis XVI. In 1791, for his mission to the United States, he had included in his baggage twenty prints of Clement Bervie's engraving of François Callet's full length portrait of Louis XVI in his coronation robe.[37] The pictures had originally been intended either as gifts for members of the American government or for display in the legation and various consulates. In December 1791,

Jean sent one of the engravings to Washington, as a personal token of his admiration, assuring the President that it was "a feeble mark of my lively and respectful attachment for your person...."[38] Enclosed in a gilt frame that bore the coats of arms of both Washington and the king, Washington was most appreciative of the gift, and displayed the engraving in the executive mansion. "I accept with great pleasure, the new and elegant print of the King of the French," he wrote in reply, "which you have been so obliging as to send me this morning as a mark of your attachment to my person."[39] Ternant also probably presented one to Jefferson at the same time.

Ternant's copy of the engraving now assumed significance far above its original importance. When Louis XVIII learned of the engravings existence, he requested its return. Unfortunately Jean had left the print with Victor in New York prior to his return to France, and now almost fourteen years later, he wrote to his young friend, requesting its immediate return for presentation to the king.

> Monsieur and good friend, the king desiring that I return to him, the portrait of Louis XVI deposited by me in your home in New York in July 1801, you without doubt share my eagerness to fulfill at the earliest the wishes of his Majesty. I beg you then on receiving this letter to carefully pack and load the picture on board a vessel of your choice, preferably French, if there are any in your place, in case the war with England has not yet ended. One must write on the bill of consignment as well as on each of the large sides of the crate "Picture of Louis XVI, King of France belonging to Monsieur the chevalier de Ternant, former minister-plenipotentiary to the United States, at Paris." It also will be necessary to privately address the crate to a reliable correspondent at the port of destination, with a request to send it to Paris as promptly and as carefully as possible and giving me notification.... I already have made known in my official communication on this subject that I preferred to entrust this painting to your care, as having been attached to the legation for a long time and having always manifested for the King and his august family sentiments most deserving of praise. Be convinced that I will take great pleasure subsequently to make the most of your care and zeal on this occasion. Your father, worshipped by all men of good will here, warned by me, also has written you on this subject; and I hope that our joint effort will not be without useful results for our common interests.... If there is a vessel of the French navy at your port you should be able to entrust to it the picture addressed then to the Department of Foreign Affairs, rue du Bac.[40]

In addition to his letter to Victor, Jean also wrote a number of times to Josephine, urging the prompt return of the engraving. "The King having desired, my dear friend, that I recover and return to him the picture portrait of his unfortunate brother, left with you in 1801 and become very rare today, you should know that I have hastened to write to Monsieur Du Pont to entreat him to send it to me as soon as possible."[41]

In August however, Ternant was informed that the picture was now in the possession of Bertram Peter Cruger, and as there is no further mention of the engraving in Ternant's letters; if and when it was ever returned remains unknown.

The Bourbon restoration, won with so much effort and expense, lasted less than a year. In March 1815 Napoleon returned from exile, determined to restore the Empire. Supported by a largely disaffected army, both rank and file and officers, and by a good deal of popular discontent with the Louis XVIII's regime, in less than a month he had regained the Tuileries, resumed his rule in France and begun a three-month reign that was ended by his defeat at Waterloo.

Napoleon's march on Paris threw many royalists and liberal moderates into a panic; some like Ternant's friend, Du Pont de Nemours, quickly fled the country. Others resisted. Ternant hoped to leave but was forced to stay.

> We are on the verge of suffering more strongly than ever all the scourges of war, at once both foreign and domestic. There has been fighting already in some provinces and foreign armies have perhaps at this moment begun hostilities on our borders. What will be the results in the final analysis of this frightful war? It is really impossible to foretell. Being too old, too sick and too near my end to be able to take an active part in this fight, I have resolved to steal away from its consequences returning to the United States. I would have departed long ago if I had been able to carry out my small fortune, which is entirely in the public funs of France. But their very considerable fall in price prevented me, and consequently I have had to postpone my departure.[42]

On 15 June, as Napoleon's army was posed for the invasion of Belgium, Jean reiterated his intentions regarding his future. He also did not intend to allow events, no matter their consequence, disrupt his usual routine.

> Our sad position has not changed since that moment [Napoleon's return] Always the same fear and uncertainty regarding the future. Nevertheless, there is reason to believe that since the 12th Napoleon has departed for the army, that finally our destiny will not be slow in unfolding, well or ill. Probably the family will inform you of the first results, their parcels will definitely be ready in four or five days. I will send them presently and within ½ hour leave to spend a week or two in the country, fifteen leagues from here. If these events are likely to significantly increase [the value of] our public funds, I will quickly sell mine and immediately make arrangements to return to the United States. If it is otherwise it will be necessary to wait longer because my small fortune, being entirely in these public funds and shares of the Bank of France, I am not able to think of leaving, without carrying with me this last resource for my old age.[43]

Ternant was not mistaken in thinking that the results of events in Belgium would effect the value of his portfolio; the news of Napoleon's defeat caused the value of government bonds on the Bourse, the French stock exchange, to increase 5 percent.[44]

X. Paris—St. Germain-en-Laye—Contrexéville • 199

With the defeat of Napoleon, his exile to St. Helena and the return to the throne of Louis XVIII, France settled into an uneasy thirty-year Second Restoration, marked by ministerial instability and increasing public discontent. Between July 1815 and July 1830, indeed for a hundred years thereafter, French politics would be a contentious and often bloody competition between royalist, republican and bonapartist factions. With the exception of the adverse effects of political crises on the value of French stock, Ternant remained above the fray, concerned only with his private interests, resigned to his retirement from the world of public events.

Ternant's concern for the well being of Victor and his family however, remained constant over the years; early on, advising and encouraging Victor in his diplomatic career, later, counseling and consoling Josephine during her frequent bouts of homesickness and financial difficulties and finally, establishing a personal, albeit long-distance, relationship with his beloved goddaughter, Amelia. With the restoration of the monarchy Victor made an attempt to restart his diplomatic career. After a series of business failures that had culminated in the humiliation of being forced to declare bankruptcy Victor had moved his family to western New York and tried to make a go of farming and shop keeping. Unhappy and with little to show for his effort, in August 1809, Victor and his family returned to Delaware. Faced with few prospects he hoped to use his numerous contacts to resume his Foreign Service career as Consul-General of France in the United States.[45] He naturally turned to Ternant as both a friend and mentor for help, but unfortunately Jean had little influence and in a letter to Josephine, explained even efforts to help himself had proved unavailing.

> ... as far as I am concerned there is nothing more I can do for him, which I greatly regret. Once we leave the world and business behind, as in my case, we do not have any more power, even when it comes to our own interests. And this is so true that I was unable to get a retirement pension for my past service and sacrifice, not even the least sign of generosity from the King, it spite of the last resounding proof of my zeal [the return of the picture of Louis XVI?]. That is why I have stopped going to Court, as well as visiting ministers, where I have nothing to do, a role that has always been odious to me. Leading a simple and independent life has become so important to me that I went back to it without regret and with strong determination. Despite my tight budget, it is easier for me to provide for all my needs than to try to increase my budget by asking others for money, which disgusts me because I find it humiliating. Nevertheless, I am happy with what I have and I have decided to make the best of it, in order to contribute to my happiness in old age. The only thing that I am worried about is that almost my entire fortune is in public funds. This casts doubt on the future of my fortune.[46]

At some point in the September 1821 Ternant abandoned Paris and moved to the nearby village of St. Germain-en-Laye, about twelve miles west of Paris, where the air was much cleaner and healthier and where he would reside until May 1826. The exact reason or circumstances that prompted his move are not clear but in his letters Jean explained that one factor was his failing health, which at times even prevented him from writing. He informed Josephine, "It is necessary before ending [this letter] that I tell you a word about my health and my situation. The first is in a state of decay accompanied by great suffering, gout, rheumatism, irritability, for which there is no cure at seventy-one years of age, except patience and resignation. As for the second, it is even worse than before, not having obtained since the royal restoration either a retirement pension or indemnities for all my former sacrifices."[47] The move to the country may just as well have been caused by the expense of living in Paris and his continuing fear of poverty. In St. Germain-en-Laye Ternant purchased a small house and continued his reclusive lifestyle, shunning even his closest friends. His mobility reduced by his infirmities and his inability to reciprocate social calls, Jean ignored invitations and reduced his social activity.

In spite of his advancing years and the infirmities of old age Ternant's financial situation during the decade of the 1820s improved. Monies from his American investments were transferred to France, he was relieved from the tax burden on his property on the Susquehanna, and his portfolio of French government and Bank of France bonds gradually increased in value. Two old friends that Jean respected and trusted managed his financial interests in the United States. His agent from July 1801 until his death in 1822 was George Simpson, the first teller of the Bank of the United States and later chief cashier of Stephan Girard's Bank. After Simpson's death Stephan Girard acquired Jean's power of attorney and managed the liquidation of Jean's holdings.

Of the two, Simpson is less well known but few men of his time were more knowledgeable regarding the world of banking and international finance. He had a reputation for honesty and was particularly respected in Europe. For many years Simpson acted as an agent for a number of the most important European banking interests and his letters of introduction insured a person a warm reception. During the war for independence Simpson had served in the commissary department and later was appointed an officer in the Bank of North America. He was also well connected, and included Washington, Hamilton and Robert Morris among his friends. From its inception in 1792 until 1811 when its operations were terminated, Simpson served as the first teller for the Bank of the United States and when Stephen Girard purchased the bank building in 1812 and launched his own private bank, Simpson was continued as chief of operations in the new enterprise, responsible the bank's daily operations.[48] Ternant could not have chosen a more reliable and effective financial advisor.

Stephen Girard was a prominent Philadelphia merchant who created one of the largest fortunes in the early period of the Republic. Engaged primarily at first in trade with St. Domingue and the Antilles and then later with Marseilles, Girard, as a member of an international network of commerce and later finance, became the richest merchant in Philadelphia and with the possible exception of John Jacob Astor, the wealthiest man in the United States. Unlike so many other successful merchants of the time Girard avoided dissipating his fortune on speculation in undeveloped backlands. He also differed from other successful businessmen in his decision to live modestly and not allow ostentatious living to erode his hard earned savings. During the yellow fever epidemic in the fall of 1793, when most other wealthy Philadelphians fled, Girard remained and courageously supervised the operation of a hospital at Bush Hill to aid victims of the disease.[49]

Exactly when Ternant made Girard's acquaintance and became friends is unknown but most likely it occurred when Jean was minister and as leading members of the French community, both were involved with the philanthropic efforts to aid refugees from St. Domingue. After learning of Simpson's death, and not receiving any information for over a year on his American interests Jean turned to his old friend Girard for assistance.

> Dear Sir,
>   I was greatly afflicted by the death of Mr. George Simpson mentioned in the New York papers of last December, and as he had the management of my concerns ever since July 1801, I expected to have received a few lines from his sons on that subject. Their continued silence of nine months, obliges me at last to have them called upon for the account of the year 1822, and the delivery of the certificate of public funds purchased for me by their father, as well as the deeds of my back lands of Luzerne county and of all other papers left in his hands relative to my interests.
>   I hope your old acquaintance and your laudable disposition to oblige, will excuse my begging of you a friendly assistance in the present case—under a persuasion that you will not refuse that service. I shall herewith enclose two powers of attorney with names in blank and a memorandum to guide in the business after closing with the heirs of our deceased friend. I shall beg of you to have my public funds sold off, and the proceeds along with the balance due for 1822 transmitted to me here, when as you think best for my interests. As to the back lands, I wish they will be sold in a block for cash, either by private sale or at auction if practical, and the proceeds also transmitted. If such a sale be impossible or unadvised, be so good as to keep by you the deeds and other papers therein relating, until I can otherwise determine.
>   I forgot to mention the dividends on my public stocks for the present year 1823, the mount of which is also to be transmitted.

I hope you will not decline rendering that service to an old friend who will ever be grateful for that kindness, and who with ardent wishes for your health and happiness remains ... your most obedient servant.[50]

Along with his letter, as indicated, Ternant included a memorandum that provided Girard with a complete listing and value in dollars of his American investments.

> The late Mr. Simpson who managed Mr. Ternant's concerns from July 1801, having from time to time transmitted regular accounts, and remitted the balance up to the 9th of March 1822, his heirs will only have to account for the proceeds and expenses of the year 1822 and pay the balance.
> They will have at the same time to deliver the certificates of eight purchases into the public funds of the U.S. made for Mr. Ternant, by Mr. Simpson, out of the dividends received from the liquidation of the former Bank of the United States.

6330	dollars	6 June	1812
6211	"	12 June	"
1600	"	12 Feb.	1813
2550	"	16 Feb.	"
1500	"	23 Apr.	"
750	"	28 Feb.	1814
18,941	"	in the three percent	
1400	"	2 July	1816
900	"	16 Feb.	1817
2,300	"	in the six percent.	

> These public funds produce an annual revenue of 706 dollars and twelve cents.
> The same heirs will have also, to return the deeds of the back lands of Luzerne County with all the papers thereto relating, such as receipts of monies paid for taxes, resurvey and other charges; and in the case of a sale of the whole or part of the same lands, to which purpose the late Mr. Simpson had been duly authorized, the monies received in consequence are to be accounted for; and proper documents of what remain due are to be furnished.
> Finally, all papers left to the care of Mr. Simpson in a red Moroccan portfolio and also a will sent a few years ago under the sealed cover of Claudius Vincent Ternant of Louisiana are likewise to be returned and then full discharge of the question may be given if required.
> The proceeds or dividends on the public stocks before mentioned for the year 1823 are to be received and remitted. Paris, 18 Sept. 1823. J.Ternant

The memorandum also includes several marginal notes that add detail to Jean's American holdings.

> There were originally twelve tracts of those lands, one of which was made over to Miss Amelia Dupont and the rest amount to 4772 acres, standing now with taxes and incidental charges, exclusive of interest on purchase money to about 4,500 dollars.

The condition of that agency [Mr. Simpson's salary] was two percent on all monies received as a full compensation, which was accepted by a letter of 29 June 1801.[51]

Throughout the late teens and early 20s Ternant continued to hope that a profit might be gained from his investments in the property on the Susquehanna; basing his hopes on emigrants from Europe to provide him with the opportunity to dispose of the remaining eleven tracts.[52] Such however, was not the case and by the time of Simpson's death in 1822 none of the property had been sold. In March 1823 Girard wrote to Benjamin Laporte, an officer of the Asylum Land Company residing in the area, for information regarding the condition and value of Ternant's property. Laporte responded: "As to the quality, it is what would be called on an average the 2nd rate of wild land and I suppose it would be worth from $2 to $3 per acre. That is to dispose of it in small quantities of one or two hundred acres to purchasers." Laporte also informed Girard that purchasing practices in the region worked against selling the eleven parcels as a whole. "There is no other way of selling, but in small quantities to suit the convenience of settlers. The manner of selling all land in this county is something owing to the situation. I sell land for different landholders. Some I sell to be paid in five or six equal annual payments, and the first payment to be made in one year from the date of the contract, others in two years from the date of the contract and generally two years without interest. The sales are commonly made by contract, but sometimes by giving deeds and taking land as mortgages.... As to selling for cash only, or part down, such sales cannot be made in this county. I suppose that some part of Mr. Ternant's land could be sold on the above terms." Finally, Laporte informed Girard that timber had been cut on Jean's property by trespassers, who ignored Laporte's order to cease. He also reported that two of Ternant's parcels had settlers living on them without authorization, who however paid the taxes.[53]

Having held title to his Susquehanna property for thirty years that had cost him over $12,000 in purchase price, interest and "very arbitrary" taxes and with little chance to sell the whole for cash, Ternant, in July 1824, disposed of his unproductive burden by deeding the remaining eleven tracts to his goddaughter as a gift.[54]

Although Ternant's speculation in back lands had proved both unprofitable and costly, his other American investments were a success. In 1823 and 1824, with Girard's assistance, Jean sold his American stocks and withdrew the money to France. In June he received from Girard a bill of exchange for the sum of 95,344 francs 78 sou in his favor, on James Lafitte & Co. of Paris, to be paid in sixty days.[55] In early 1825 he received a further 1093 francs 43 sou, again on Lafitte & Company.[56] In addition to his American monies Jean's French government bonds in 1824 were selling above par. Here at last were the funds to support him for the remainder of his life; the nest egg to free him from the constant fear of a poverty stricken old age.

In 1814 Ternant, thanks to Victor, Josephine and Kitty Cruger, added a new couple to his circle of friends. Jean Guillaume Hyde de Neuville and his wife, Henriette, returned to France after spending seven years in exile in the United States. Forced to leave France by Napoleon because of Hyde's involvement in royalist plotting during the Directory and Consulate, the couple had become an important addition to the Franco-American community in New York. They were an engaging couple. Jean Gillaume was a physician with an interest, like Ternant, in natural history, and was known personally to Louis XVIII. His wife, fifteen years his senior, was a strong-willed and capable woman who had shared the hardship and dangers of her husband's clandestine and conspiratorial life.

Unlike many French emigrants in the United States, Hyde and his wife did not remain aloof, but mixed freely and happily in American society. Most importantly, they became friends with Philip Church, Kitty Cruger's brother and through him were introduced to the elite of New York society. Through Kitty and Philip, Hyde and his wife were also introduced to Victor and Josephine Du Pont and it was Hyde that had encouraged Victor to move his family to western New York. The two families became fast friends, so much so that in 1808 Josephine sent her daughter Amelia to New York City to stay with the Hydes in order to complete her education.[57]

With the news of the fall of Napoleon and the Bourbon restoration, Hyde and his wife returned immediately to Paris, where Hyde had expectations of being rewarded for his previous service to the king. During the Hundred Days, he joined Louis XVIII at Ghent and in January 1816, was appointed minister-plenipotentiary to the United States.[58] In spite of the twenty-five year difference in their ages, Hyde's royalist convictions, his loyalty to the Bourbons and his appointment as minister to the United States helped foster a close relationship with Ternant. Like other members of Ternant's circle the Hydes were named beneficiaries in Jean's testament.[59]

In the spring of 1825, Ternant's health had not improved and when Kitty Cruger, who had been living in Paris since 1819, returned to New York she carried what proved to be the last existing letter from Jean to Josephine. He regretted not being strong enough to accompany their friend. "My health," he explained to Josephine, "is declining and my life so frail that it would probably be necessary to throw my cadaver into the sea, very shortly after I embarked." In spite of his failing heath Ternant informed Josephine that he had returned to Paris. He urged her to write more often and assured her that she could always count on his "inviolable attachment."[60]

Sometime in March 1826 Jean purchased for 45,000 francs, a substantial three-story town house in one of the new residential developments near Montmarte, in the city's northern suburbs; No. 28 rue des Petits-Hôtels, Nouveau Quartier Poissonnaire, 3rd arrondissement (today the 10th). Carved out of the enclosed land formerly part of the St. Lazare convent, the area was open, less congested and had better air to breathe.[61] With two live-in servants, a cook and a factotum, for assistance and company, Jean's new home became a comfortable and pleasant retreat and despite his increasing infirmity, he was able to continue his well established routine of quiet evenings in his study and summer excursions to various spas.

It is not surprising perhaps, given Ternant's increasing reclusion and the fact that his papers have not survived, that there is little information regarding his activities from 1826 until 1833, the year of his death. How he managed the terrible winter of 1829–1830, his reaction to the riots in July that ended the Bourdon dynasty or if he was among the 80 guests at the 4th of July dinner hosted by the American community in Paris and which honored his friend, Lafayette, there is no record. In the summer of 1833 however, Ternant was still able to travel and he and Louis Martin, his valet/coachman, made a leisurely journey to Contrexéville, a fashionable spa located on the Vair River south of Vittel in the western Vosges. One of the *villes d'eaux,* Contrexéville was famous for its cold saline waters, which when consumed was thought to relieve the discomfort of gravel and gout; the very afflictions from which Jean suffered.

While he was at Contrexéville Ternant wrote the Mayor of Damvillers, M. Gerard-Lenfant, requesting his assistance in locating members of his family still living in the area, and indicated that he planned to visit his hometown in the near future.[62] Since the spring Jean had been engaged in the task of putting his affairs in order and was searching for any relatives prior to preparing his last testament. Whether the Mayor responded or Jean ever traveled to Damvillers is not known but by August he was back in Paris and had drawn up his will. Written by himself in a legible script that did not betray either his eighty-one plus years or his rheumatism, the document included twenty-seven individuals as beneficiaries; fourteen of whom were related to him either by blood or marriage, but none of them were named Ternant and none resided in Damvillers.[63] In September Jean added a codicil to his will, a bequest of 300 francs to the commune of Damvillers to aid the indigent of the local parish, and still later, on 10 October he attached a final addition that dealt with the dispensation of any additional funds.

Throughout the fall Ternant's condition steadily weakened and by early November the end was near and a physician summoned. Finally, at 3:00 o'clock in the morning on Friday the 15th Jean died, in the comfort of his bed, in his own home, in the city he loved; tended to in his final hours by his housekeeper Anne Bardou. He was only a month shy of his eighty-second birthday. Following funeral services at the church of St. Vincent de Paul, Ternant was laid to rest; most likely in one of the nearby cemeteries, either that of the recently opened St. Vincent or that of Montmartre.[64]

Adhering to the legal requirements and standard practice, it was a month and a half after Ternant's death that the legal procedures regarding his estate began, headed by his notary and executor, M. Alexandre Marie Delamotte.[65] At the request of the principal beneficiaries, on Monday 30 December an inventory and appraisal of Jean's chattel and financial holdings was begun that was finally completed, after several interruptions, on Wednesday 9 January 1834. Conducted by the commissioner appraiser, M. Bichellerie, from the Department of the Seine, and the attorneys representing Jean's beneficiaries, the inventory numbered thirty-three pages and provided a description of all movables and assigned a price to each item, and as was customary in most cases much lower than their market value or real worth. The total appraised value of Ternant's movables amounted to 8,971.90 francs. There was also an additional 104 francs worth of coins.[66]

Ternant's financial records were grouped together according to subject matter; the deed for his house and related papers, his investments in the Bank of France, certificates of government bonds and documents pertaining to his purchase of three annuities. The total worth of Ternant's yearly income at the time of his death amounted to 13,838 francs.

Without a wife or children of his own, the beneficiaries of Ternant's last testament were selected from distant relatives or close friends, their widows and children. The principal financial beneficiaries were his ten surviving great nieces and nephews, the children of his brother's daughter, Marie-Basilee Fuselier, residing in Louisiana. Eighty thousand francs in cash were to be divided among them and in 1835 the Fuseliers acknowledged the receipt of 76,460.19 francs.[67] Another great nephew received 3,000 francs in cash and an additional 2,200 francs from Jean's investments.

To Jacques-Louis Lamacq, a former captain in the army and a maternal relative still residing near Verdun, Ternant bequeathed his hunting rifle and regimental sword, plus 2,000 francs from his investments. To Jean-Antoine Gillant, another veteran and a nephew of his stepmother, Jean gave 2,000 francs from his income, a pair of pistols and all his documents and certificates relative to his public service, as well as his personal papers. Finally, an unmarried female relation from his mother's family, Marguerite Claudine Lamarre, was given 2,000 francs from Jean's investments and the choice of either half of all his silverware collection or an extra 1,500 francs.

From among his friends Jean gave Catherine (Kitty) Cruger, a central figure in Josephine Du Pont's social circle, 2,500 francs from his income for her and her two daughters. Two thousand four hundred francs were awarded to the minor children and widow of Judge Maugis, another personal friend. The Baron Hyde de Neuville and his wife were permitted to select four pieces from among Jean's collection of paintings and objets d'art and Henriette, in addition, was presented a gold snuffbox containing a diamond worth 2,000 francs. The daughter of Bureaux de Pusy, Madame de Cossigny, and the widow of his friend Laumoy, Agathe Louise Bocquet de Chantereine, received 6,000 francs each. Madame Laumoy, in addition, received the title to Jean's town house. Finally, it is noteworthy that noticeably absent from Jean's testament was any mention of the Du Pont family. In spite of deep affection for them and his many years of correspondence, neither Josephine nor his goddaughter, Amelia, were included among his heirs.

Lastly, although Ternant ignored the Du Ponts, he did not forget his servants. Louis-Paul Martin and Anne-Elizabeth Bardou were both generously rewarded for their loyalty and service. Martin was awarded 500 francs above his yearly salary of 4,000 francs and given all of Jean's shirts. Mademoiselle Bardou received three years of wages and given all the domestic clothes and aprons.[68]

Ternant's advanced age at the time of his death meant that he had been preceded in death by most of his former colleagues and friends. Jean's closest American comrade in arms, Jack Laurens, had been dead for forty years. His best friend, Laumoy, had passed away in 1832. Duportail, who had fled to the United States and owned a farm near Valley Forge had taken ill during his return to France in the summer of 1801, died at sea and had been buried there. Bureaux de Pusy, after having returned to government service as a prefect, had died in 1806. Gouvenur Morris, Jean's American friend for more than two decades, had died in 1816. Du Pont de Nemours had passed away a year later and even dear Victor was gone, dying in the summer of 1827 at the age of fifty-nine; the same year as another of Jean's circle of Parisian friends, the engineer and dramatist, Reveroni de Saint-Cyr. Ternant's patrons, of course, were all long since departed; Anne-Cesar de La Luzerne, in 1791, comte de Montmorin and Henry Laurens a year later and Jean's military mentor, Steuben, in 1794. Only Lafayette, the "apostle of liberty" remained, and he also soon followed the others, in May 1834. Josephine Du Pont died in 1837.

Like most other men Ternant was as obscure at the end of his life as he had been in his youth, and apparently was content to be so. It is doubtful that even his neighbors on the rue des Petits-Hôtels paid him much attention. But as a young man Ternant had traveled far and his involvement in the armed struggles of the age of revolution in both America and Europe, his membership in the American Philosophical Society and his support for the ending of the slave trade are testaments to his commitment to the political and social ideals of the Age of Enlightenment. He experienced in full measure a life of adventure and exemplified Justice Holmes's later insistence that only those who shared the passion and action of their time could be considered to have lived.

Chapter Notes

The following abbreviations are used throughout the notes.

ADM Archives départementales de la Meuse, Bar-le-Duc
AG   Archives de la Guerre
AN   Archives nationales de France
CFM "Correspondence of the French Ministers to the United States, 1791–1797," *The Annual Report of the American Historical Association for the Year 1903* (Washington, D.C., 1904).
HML Hagley Museum and Library
SP   Friedrich Wilhelm von Steuben, *The Papers of General Friedrich Wilhelm von Steuben 1777–1794*, edited by Edith Von Zemensky (Millwood, NY: Kraus International Publishing, 1976–1984).

Introduction

1. AN, Minutier Central des Notaires LXXXVII 1469, Succession & Partage de Jean Ternant.
2. American Philosophical Society Minutes, 18 April 1834, 22.
3. Notable biographies include A.E. Zucker, *Général de Kalb, Lafayette's Mentor* (Chapel Hill, 1966); Francis Kajencki, *Casmir Pulaski, Cavalry Commander of the American Revolution* (El Paso, 2001); Alex Storozynski, *The Peasant Prince: Thaddeus Kosciuszko* (New York, 2009); Kenneth R. Bowling, *Peter Charles L'Enfant: Vision, Honor and Male Friendship in the Early American Republic* (Washington, D.C., 2002); Elizabeth S. Kite, *Brigadier Général Louis Lebgue Duportail, Commandant of Engineers in the Continental Army 1777–1783* (Baltimore, 1937); Serge Le Pottier, *Duportail ou le Génie de George Washington* (Paris, 2011); Frederick Kapp, *The Life of Frederick William von Steuben* (New York, 1859); John McAuley Palmer, *Général von Steuben* (New Haven, 1937); Maurice de la Faye and Emile Babeau, *The Apostle of Liberty: A Life of Lafayette* (New York, 1958); Lloyd Kramer, *Lafayette in Two Worlds: Public Culture and Personal Identification in an Age of Revolutions* (Chapel Hill, 1996).
4. Francis Drake, *Dictionary of American Biography* (Boston, 1879); James Grant Wilson and John Fiske, eds., *Appleton's Cyclopedia of American Biography* (New York, 1889), 6, 64; Asa Bird Gardiner, *The Order of the Cincinnati in France* (Newark, 1905), 160–162; Baron Ludovic de Contenson, *La Société des Cincinnati de France et la Guerre d'Amérique 1778–1783* (Paris, 1934), 270; Andre Lasseray, *Les Française sous Le Trieze Étoiles 1775–1783* (Paris, 1935), 2, 433–436; Gilbert Bodinier, *Dictionnaire des Officiers de l'Armée Royale que ont combatton aux États-Unis pendant la Guerre d'Amérique 1776–1783* (Vincennes, 1983), 524; John C. Fredricksen, *Revolutionary War Almanac* (New York, 2006), 664–665; Douglas N. Adams, "Jean Baptiste Ternant, Inspector General and Advisor to the Commanding Generals of the Southern Forces 1778–1782," *South Carolina Historical Magazine* 86 (October 1985): 221–40.

5. Joseph Addison, *Cato*, act IV, scene 4, cited in Jack Rakove, *Revolutionaries: A History of the Invention of America* (Boston, 2010), 166.
6. George Washington to Arthur Young, 4 December 1788, Letter Book 16, *The George Washington Papers at the Library of Congress*, Manuscript Division.
7. Nicolas Govin Dufief to T. Jefferson, 22 Oct. 1801, Barbara B. Oberg, ed., *Papers of Thomas Jefferson* Vol. 35 (Princeton, 2008), 483.
8. AN, Minutier Central des Notaires LXXXVII, 1469. Succession & Partage de Jean Ternant.
9. Louis-Guillaume Otto, *Considerations sur la Conduire du Gouvernement Americain envers la France, depuis le commencement de la Revolution jusqu'en 1797*, Gilbert Chinard, ed. (Princeton, 1945), 10.
10. Jefferson to John Jay, 4 February 1789, Julian Boyd et al., eds. *Papers of Thomas Jefferson* Vol. 14 (Princeton, 1950-), 520.
11. Charles Coleman Sellers, *The Artist of the Revolution: The Early life of Charles Willson Peale* (Hebron, 1939).
12. Charles Coleman Sellers, *Portraits and Miniatures by Charles Willson Peale*, Vol. 42, Part 1 of the Transactions of the American Philosophical Society Philadelphia, 1952, 208; Doris Devine Fanelli, *History of the Portrait Collection, Independence National Historical Park*; and catalog of the Collection by Karie Diethorn, ed. (Philadelphia, 2002), 303.
13. Elizabeth (Betsy) Nixon to Josephine du Pont, 3 September 1796, HML, Papers of Gabrielle Josephine, wife of Victor Du Pont, Series D, W3-5322.

Chapter I

1. AG, 2Ye Dossiers d'officiers supérieurs et subalternes 1791-1847, Extrait des Registres de Baptême de la paroisse de Damvillers, diocese de Verdun sur Meuse. Jean Ternant dated 13 December 1787.
2. ADM, Series 2E Registres Paroissiaux et d'État Civil, Marriage certificate of Claude Ternant and Marie Lamarre dated 12 January 1751.
3. http://www.familysearch.org, genealogical information on Ternant family.
4. John McManners, *Death and the Enlightenment* (Oxford, 1981), 5-23; Jacques Geliset, *Entrer dans la Vie: Naissances et enfances dans la France Traditionnel* (Paris, 1995).
5. http://www.familysearch.org, 1759-1777, Batch C817261, source call no. 1226846, microfilm.
6. *Ibid*.
7. https://commons.wikimedia.org/wiki/File:Blason_de_la_ville_de_Damvillers_(55).svg. The blazon of Damvillers combines the arms of Luxembourg, a red lion on a field of ten alternating stripes of silver and blue with the arms of the Count of Clermont, the father of Beatrix de Bourbon; a blue field with gold fleur d'lis and a red bar superimposed on an angle.
8. P.M. Bonnabelle, "Notice Historique et Statistique sur la Ville de Damvillers, Meuse," *Memoires de la Société des Lettres, Sciences et Arts de Bar-Le-Duc*, 1871, 209-211; Lucien de Chardon, *Damvillers et son Canton: Vingt Siècles d'Histoire* (Verdun, 1973); Christopher Duffy, *Siege Warfare: The Fortress in the Early Modern World 1494-1660* (New York, 1979), 49-51, 138.
9. Christopher Duffy, *The Fortress in the Age of Vauban and Frederick the Great 1660-1789* (New York, 1985), 90.
10. ADM, Series 2E Registres Paroissiaux et d'État Civil. Marriage certificate of Claude Ternant and Marie Lamarre dated 12 January 1751.
11. ADM, Series C Administrations provinicales. Famille Lamarre or de Lamarre, 146 & 287.
12. Jean François Louis Jeantin, *Manuel de la Meuse Histoire de Montmédy et de localities meusiennes de l'ancien comte de Chiny* (Nancy, 1862), 1298-1300.
13. Louis Leconte, *Le Regiment Royal-Liègeois au service du Roi de France 1787-1792* (Moulins, 1937), 284. Leconte confused Philibert-Jean Dubard de Ternant (1753-1800?) with Jean Ternant. Dubard was born at Beaune in Burgundy into a recently ennobled family. His father purchased the seigneurie of Ternant in 1757. Dubard was a student at the school for engineers at Mézières 1775-76 and was a *lieutenant en premier* stationed at St-Omer in 1789. At that time Jean Ternant was Colonel in the Royal Liègeois regiment. For Dubard see Anne Blanchard, *Dictionnaire des Ingénieurs Militaires 1691-1791* (Montpellier, 1981), 230; also *L'État Militaire de France pour l'ànee 1789*, seconde partie, troups, Chapitre II, Corps Royal du Génie; AG, l'École du Génie establie a Mézières puis a Metz Material et Personnel 1748-1783, Carton No. 1, Mézières état de génie 1775.
14. Peter C. Welsh, *Tanning in the United States to 1850* (Washington, D.C., 1964) 13-21.
15. Robert Parisot, *Histoire de Lorraine (Duche de Lorraine, Duche de Bar, Trois-Eveches)* Vol. II. 1552-1789 (Paris, 1922), 218.

16. Roland Mousnier, *The Institutions of France under the Absolute Monarchy 1598–1789: Society and State* Vol. I. Trans by Brian Pearce (Chicago, 1979), 50.
17. Daniel Roche, *France in the Enlightenment*, Trans. Arthur Goldhammer (Cambridge, 1998), 163–165; Parisot, *Histoire de Lorraine*, 239–240.
18. Ternant to G. Washington, 29 September 1778, Series 4, General Correspondence 1697–1799, *The George Washington Papers at the Library of Congress 1741–1799*, Manuscript Division.
19. David M. Hopkin, *Soldier and Peasant in French Popular Culture 1766–1870* (Rochester, NY, 2003), 2–6. Also Jean-Denis G.G. Lepage, *Vauban and the French Military under Louis XIV: An Illustrated History of Fortifications and Strategy* (Jefferson, NC, 2010), 170–187.
20. Christopher Duffy, *The Fortress in the Age of Vauban and Frederick the Great 1660–1789* (Boston, 1985), 116. Also Bonnabelle, 211.
21. Gilbert Bodinier, *Les Officiers de l'Armée Royale combatants de la guerre d'Indépendance des États-Unis de Yorktown a l'an II* (Vincennes, 1983), 139. Also Robert Palmer, *The Age of Democratic Revolution: A Political History of Europe and America, 1760–1800, The Struggle*, Vol. I (Princeton, 1959), 67–70.
22. Marcel Reinhard, *Le grand Carnot: Lazare Carnot, 1753–1823* (Paris, 1950), Vol. 1, 46.
23. Anna Blanchard, *Les Ingénieurs du Roy de Louis XIV a Louis XVI* (Montpellier, 1981), 236.
24. Janis Langins, *Conserving the Enlightenment: French Military Engineers from Vauban to the Revolution* (Cambridge, 2004), 26.
25. Rene Taton, "L'École Royale du Génie de Mézières" in Rene Taton ed., *L'Enseignement et Diffusion des Sciences en France au XVIII Siècle* (Paris, 1964), 586–596.
26. *Ibid.*, 581.
27. *Ibid.*, 589.
28. Pierre Chalmin, "La Formation des Officiers des Armes Savantes sous l'Ancien Régime," *Actes du Soixante-seizieme Congress des Sociétés Savantes* (Paris, 1951), 168.
29. Claude Manceron, *The French Revolution*, vol. III, *Their Gracious Pleasure*, trans. Nancy Amphoux (New York, 1980), 369.
30. AG, Series 2Ye, Dossiers d'officiers supérieurs et subalterns 1791–1847—Jean Ternant, Pour le Croix de St. Louis, 24 June 1787.
31. Bodinier, *Les Officiers de L'Armée Royale*, 269.

32. Talon, "L'École Royale du Génie de Mézières," 593. The following list contains the names, social status and age (if known) at the time of their examination of successful candidates for Mézières in 1772, cited in Blanchard, *Dictionnaire*.
Jean-Baptiste-Brice Bizot, commoner, 18
Dominique-Andre de Chambarlhac, noble, 18
François-Joseph Chaussegros
Pierre-Augustin-François Corporandy, commoner
Jean Crublier, commoner
Charles-Gaspard Galbaud du Fort, commoner, 18
Charles-Martin de Boisville et Valandre, noble, 21
Jacques-Paul de Vergnes, noble, 17
Charles-Humbert-Marie Vingot, noble, 19
33. Langins, *Conserving the Enlightenment*, 187. Only a third of engineers had reached the rank of captain after 30 years of service. For Mathieu Dumas see Count Mathieu Dumas, *Memoirs of His Own Time* Vol. 1 (Philadelphia, 1839).
34. Blanchard, *Dictionnaire des Ingénieurs Militaires 1691–1791*, 353–354. See also Historic American Buildings Survey: Fort McHenry, HABS No. MD-63.

Chapter II

1. Ternant to B. Franklin, 15 Jan. 1777, in William B. Wilcox et al., eds., *The Papers of Benjamin Franklin*, Vol. 23 (New Haven, 1983–), 191–192.
2. For Floridablanca see Richard B. Morris, *The Peacemakers: The Great Powers and American Independence* (New York, 1965), 48–49; John Lynch, *Bourbon Spain 1700–1808* (London, 1989), 252–253, 295, 297; Claude Manceron, *Their Gracious Pleasures 1782–1785* (New York, 1980), 299.
3. Voltaire to Comte d'Argental, 1 Nov. 1760 cited in E. Wilson Lyon, *Louisiana in French Diplomacy 1759–1804* (Norman, 1974), 35. "You should inspire the Duke of Choiseul with my taste for Louisiana ... the most beautiful climate of the earth, from which one may have tobacco, silk, indigo and a thousand useful products.... I declare to you that if I had not built Ferney, I would go establish myself in Louisiana."
4. For Spanish Louisiana see Jack L. Holmes, "Some Economic Problems of Spanish Governors of Louisiana" in *Hispanic American Historical Review* XLII, 1962, 521–543; Lawrence Kinnaird, ed., *Spain in the Mississippi Valley, 1765–1794*, Vol. 1, *Annual*

Report of the American Historical Association, 1945 (Washington, D.C., 1949) xv-xxxi; Ameda Ruth King, "Social and Economic Life in Spanish Louisiana, 1763–1783," Ph.D. Dissertation (University of Illinois, 1931).

5. *The Correspondence of the Right Honorable Sir John Sinclair*, Vol. 2 (London, 1831), 132.

6. Helen Auger, *The Secret War of American Independence* (Boston, 1955), 65.

7. AG, Series 2Ye, Dossiers d'officiers supérieurs et subalterns—Jean Ternant, Pour le Croix de St Louis, 24 June 1787 and Rapport fais au ministre le 12 vendemaire l'an 10 (4 October 1801) 3rd Division Bureau des États Major.

8. Josephine F. Pacheco, "French Secret Agents in America 1763–1778," unpublished Ph.D. Dissertation (University of Chicago, 1950), 79–80.

9. *Ibid.*, 122–141.

10. For French foreign policies regarding England and its North American colonies from 1758 through 1777 see Colin Jones, *The Great Nation; France from Louis XV to Napoleon 1715–99* (New York, 2002), 241–259; Jonathan R. Dull, *The French Navy and the Seven Years War* (Lincoln, 2005), 245–254.

11. Richard W. Van Alstyne, *Empire and Independence: The International History of the American Revolution* (New York, 1965), 83–85.

12. Hilliard d'Auberteuil, *Essais Historiques et Politiques sur la Revolution de l'Amerique* (Paris, 1782); List of French officers who served in the American armies with commissions prior to the treaties made between France and the Thirteen United States of America reprinted in *The Magazine of American History* Vol. III (New York, 1879), 364–369.

13. Information on Franklin's experiences during his first weeks in France was taken from Stacy Schiff, *Dr. Franklin Goes to France* (London, 2005).

14. Catherine M. Prelinger, "Less Lucky than Lafayette: A Note on the French Applicants to Benjamin Franklin for Commissions in the American Army, 1776–1785," *Proceedings of the Western Society for French History*, No. 4, 1976, 263–270.

15. Ternant to B. Franklin. 15 Jan. 1777, op cit.

16. On travel from Paris to Bordeaux see Victor Marie Du Pont, *Journal to France and Spain 1801*, Charles W. David, ed. (Port Washington, 1972), 66–68. Two months after Ternant, on 16 March 1777, Lafayette and de Kalb made the trip from Paris to Bordeaux in three days, but they hired a private conveyance and traveled day and night. See Claude Manceron, trans. Patricia Wolf, *The French Revolution*, Vol. I, *Twilight of the Old Order 1774–1778* (New York, 1977), 398.

17. For Bordeaux see Paul Butel, *Le Negociants Bordleais: L'Europe et les Îles au XVIIIe Siècle*, Paris, 1974.

18. Pecholier Freres to B. Franklin 18 January 1777, *The Papers of Benjamin Franklin* Vol. 23. 210. In the 1770s Pecholier and Co. were involved in the London trade. See Françoise Giteau and others, *Repertoire numerique de fonds des Negociants* (Bordeaux, 1979) 7B 1455 Londres (Angleterre) 83. The firm may have employed Ternant during the period 1773–1776.

19. Archives départementales de la Gironde, Registres de l'Amiraute de Guyenne, series 6B 55 Certificate d'identité et de catholique 1774–1777, 140.

20. *Ibid.*, series 6B 109 Sousmissions des captaines de 1775–1777, 174. The 330-ton *le Prudent* was typical of French merchant vessels engaged in trade with the West Indies.

21. For details regarding voyages to the West Indies see Jean Cavignac, *Jean Pellet commercant de gros 1694–1772* (Paris, 1967), 49–51 and Victor Marie Du Pont, op cit., 116–118; Average crossing time between Bordeaux and the West Indies was 60 to 70 days in the second half of the eighteenth century, although some voyages took as many as 120 days. Paul Butel, *Les Negociants Bordelais, l'Europe et les Îles au XVIII siècle*, 226.

22. For Cap-Français see David Geggus, "The Major Ports of Saint Domingue in the Later Eighteenth Century" in Franklin W. Knight and Peggy K. Liss, Eds., *Atlantic Port Cities: Economy, Culture and Society in the Atlantic World* (Knoxville, 1991), 87–116.

23. Raymond W. Logan, "Saint Domingue: Entrepôt for Revolutionaries" in Charles W. Toth, ed., *The American Revolution in the West Indies* (Port Washington, 1975), 101–111; Elizabeth M. Nuxoll, *Congress and the Munitions Merchants: The Secret Committee of Trade during the American Revolution 1775–1777* (New York, 1985), 456–466.

24. Gregory D. Massey, *John Laurens and the American Revolution* (Columbia, 2000), 71.

25. John Laurens to Henry Laurens, 25 March 1778, *The Army Correspondence of Colonel John Laurens in the Years 1777 and 1778* (New York, 1969), 147–148.

26. For Franco-Spanish diplomacy regarding Louisiana see John Walton Caughey, *Bernardo de Galvez in Louisiana 1776–1783* (Berkeley, 1934); E. Wilson Lyon, *Louisiana in French Diplomacy 1759–1804* (Norman, 1934); Light Townsend Cummins,

Spanish Observers of the American Revolution 1775–1783 (Baton Rouge, 1991).
27. Ternant to George Simpson, 21 April 1816, Library of Congress, Manuscript Division. See also Ternant to George Simpson, 20 October 1820, Alexander Autographs.
28. Winston De Ville, *Colonial Louisiana Marriage Contracts 1736–1803* Vol. III, Post of Pointe Coupee, Book 1778 No. 951 (Baton Rouge, 1962), 27.
29. *Ibid.*, Book 1784 No. 1370, 38. Information on Claude Vincent Ternant, his career and family is taken from Brian J. Costello, *From Ternant to Parlange: A Creole Plantation through Seven Generations* (Baton Rouge, 2002).

Chapter III

1. P.E. Duponceau, *Diary, Sojourn at Camp Valley Forge 24 Feb.–25 April 1778.* Entry for Friday, 6 March, The Delaware Historical Society.
2. Wayne K. Bodle and Jacqueline Thibaut, *Valley Forge Historical Research Report* Vol. 1 (Valley Forge, 1980), 314.
3. Louis Phillip de Segur, *Memoires ou Souvenirs et Anecdots*, Vol. 1 (Paris, 1825), 108. Segur claimed Ternant was one of Lafayette's companions. Louis Gottschalk, *Lafayette Comes to America* (Chicago, 1935), 165.
4. Caroline Cox, *A Proper Sense of Honor: Service and Sacrifice in George Washington's Army* (Chapel Hill, 2004), 45.
5. John Laurens to Henry Laurens, 25 March 1778, *The Army Correspondence of Colonel John Laurens, 1777–1778* (New York, 1969), 147–148.
6. Helen F. Jones, "James Lovell in the Continental Congress 1777–1782," Unpublished Ph.D. Dissertation (Columbia University, 1968), 45.
7. Jonathan G. Rossie, *The Politics of Command in the American Revolution* (Syracuse, 1975), 188–202.
8. Durand Echeverria, *Mirage in the West: A History of the French Image of American Society to 1815* (New York, 1966), 79–115.
9. Elizabeth Kite, *Brigadier Général Louis Lebegue Duportail, Commandant of Engineers in the Continental Army 1777–1783* (Baltimore, 1933); Bodinier, *Dictionnaire des Officiers de l'Armée Royale*, 290; Blanchard, *Dictionnaire des Ingénieurs Militaires 1691–1791*, 440.
10. Langins, *Conserving the Enlightenment*, 216; Arthur S. Lefkowitz, *George Washington's Indispensable Men; The Thirty-Two Men Who Helped Win the American Revolution* (Mechanicsburg, 2003), 350.
11. Duportail to Washington, 18 January 1778 cited in Kite, *Brigadier Général Duportail*, 49–50.
12. Bodinier, *Dictionnaire des Officiers de l'Armée Royale*, 213.
13. Duportail to Washington, 23 February 1778 cited in Kite, *Brigadier Général Duportail*, 51–52.
14. In February 1763 Duportail played a prominent role in a student demonstration aimed at two students who were not nobles. For his part in the affair Duportail was suspended from Mézières and imprisoned at Bouillon for a year. He was later pardoned and permitted to resume his studies. Similar to many members of the provincial nobility, Duportail exhibited a heightened class-consciousness and was unprepared to see the distinctions between nobles and commoners ignored or diluted. The fact that his mother was the daughter of a merchant may well have made him sensitive to his own social status. See Blanchard, *Dictionnaire des Ingénieurs Militaires 1691–1791*, 440; Serge Le Pottier, *Duportail ou le Génie de George Washington* (Paris, 2011), 40.
15. John Laurens to Henry Laurens, 25 March 1778, *The Army Correspondence of Colonel John Laurens in the Years 1777 and 1778*, 147–148.
16. Arthur S. Lefkowitz, *George Washington's Indispensable Men*, 13.
17. Washington to Steuben, 21 March 1778, John C. Fitzpatrick, ed., *The Writings of George Washington* (Washington, D.C., 1934) Vol. 11, 122–23.
18. Saffell, W.T.R. *Records of the Revolutionary Army containing the Military and Financial Correspondence of distinguished Officers* (Philadelphia, 1860), 374–376.
19. Washington to Jean Ternant, 26 March 1778, Fitzpatrick, ed., *The Writings of George Washington*, Vol. 11, 153.
20. Washington to the President of Congress, 30 April 1778, *ibid.*, 330.
21. For most recent study of Steuben's career see Paul Lockhart, *The Drillmaster of Valley Forge: The Baron de Steuben and the Making of the American Army* (New York, 2003).
22. Frederick Kapp, *The Life of Frederick William von Steuben* (New York, 1859), 144.
23. Duponceau, *Sojourn at Camp Valley Forge 24 Feb–25 April 1778.*
24. Washington to Lt. Cols. Barber and Brooks, SP, roll 1:74.
25. Samuel Davies Alexander, *Princeton College during the Eighteenth Century*, for

214 • Notes—Chapter III

Francis Barber, 117–118; for William Davies, 96; for John Brooks see John R. Galvin, *The Minute Men: The First Fight, Myth and Reality in the American Revolution* (Washington, D.C., 2006), 163.

26. *Baron von Steuben's Revolutionary War Drill Manual: A Facsimile Reprint of the 1794 Edition* (Dover Publications, 1985), 13.

27. Christopher Duffy, *The Army of Frederick the Great* (Chicago, 2000), 118–120; Brent Nosworthy, *The Anatomy of Victory: Battle Tactics 1689–1763* (New York, 1990), 183–197.

28. Maurice de Saxe, *Mes Rêveries* cited in Nosworthy, 160.

29. Michael Lee Lanning, *African Americans in the Revolutionary War* (New York, 2000), 112–113; William Wood and Ralph Henry Gabriel, *The Winning of Freedom* (New Haven, 1927), 119.

30. For description of de Steuben's program of instruction and development of Inspectorship see David A. Clary and Joseph W. A. Whitehorne, *The Inspector General of the United States Army 1777–1903* (Washington, D.C., 1987), 26–51; Lockhart, *The Drillmaster of Valley Forge*, 95–116.

31. Cox, *A Proper Sense of Honor*, 21–29.

32. Pete Maslowski, "National Policy Toward the Use of Black Troops in the Revolution," *South Carolina Historical Magazine* (January 1972), 1–17. See also Gregory D. Massie, "Slavery and Liberty in the American Revolution: John Laurens's Black Regiment Proposal," *Early America Review*, 2003.

33. For Morris see William Howard Adams, *Gouverneur Morris: An Independent Life* (New Haven, 2003).

34. Kapp, *The Life of Frederick William von Steuben*, 472–473.

35. George Barrie, *The Army and Navy of the United States from the Period of the Revolution to the Present Day* (Boston, 1889–1895), 15 of supplement.

36. John W. Jackson, *With the British Army in Philadelphia 1777–1778* (San Rafael, 1979), 226–229.

37. Henry Laurens to John Wells, 31 May 1778, Paul H. Smith and Gerard W. Gawait, eds., *Letters of Delegates to Congress, 1774–1789* (Washington, D.C., 1976–) Vol. 9, 788–790.

38. Steuben to H. Laurens, 27 May 1778, Philip M. Hamer and others, eds. *The Papers of Henry Laurens*, Vol. 13 (Columbia, 1992), 353–354.

39. Oaths of Allegiance and Fidelity, 1778, certificate #43, John Ternant, May 23, 1778, War Department Records, Vol. 165A. National Archives and Records Administration, Washington, D.C.

40. H. Laurens to John Wells, 31 May 1778, Smith, *Letters of Delegates to Congress, 1774–1789*, Vol. 9, 788–790.

41. J. Laurens to H. Laurens, 27 May 1778, *The Papers of Henry Laurens*, Vol. 13, 354.

42. H. Laurens to Baron Steuben, 4 June 1778, Smith, *Letters of Delegates to Congress 1774–1789*, Vol. 10, 21.

43. Steuben to Board of War, 27 May 1778, cited in Kapp, 144.

44. Board of War to Baron Steuben, 2 June 1778, cited in Kapp, 144.

45. General Orders 4 June 1778, Fitzpatrick, ed., *The Writings of George Washington*, Vol. 12, 15–16.

46. Unpublished "Opinion at Council of War" attributed to Ternant but unsigned and undated, American Historical Autographs catalog "The American Revolution" list 125, No. 9, cited in Theodore J. Crackel ed., *The Papers of George Washington Digital Edition* (Charlottesville: Rotunda, 2007). Crackel suggests that Steuben based his reply to Washington on opinions expressed by Ternant. If in fact the piece reflects Ternant's views it most likely would have been written in French rather than English which Steuben had difficulty understanding. A more plausible explanation is that the document represents a preliminary draft of Steuben's response composed by Ternant, reflecting Steuben's opinion regarding future operations.

47. Steuben to Washington, 18 June 1778, *The Papers of George Washington Digital Edition*, Theodore J. Crackel, ed. (Charlottesville: University of Virginia Press, Rotunda, 2007).

48. William S. Stryker, *The Battle of Monmouth* (Port Washington, 1927; republished 1970), 209–210.

49. General Orders, 23 July 1778, *The Papers of George Washington Digital Edition*.

50. Erna Risch, *Supplying Washington's Army* (Washington, D.C., 1981), 44–45.

51. *Ibid.*, 47.

52. Greene to Washington, 21 July 1778, *The Papers of George Washington Digital Edition*.

53. General Orders, 23 July 1778, *ibid*. Born in Ireland and three years younger than Ternant, Forsythe had joined the army in Virginia in 1775 and in 1778 was an aide to General Greene. He resigned his office as deputy Quartermaster general at the same time as Ternant and later served in Virginia in the commissary department. In 1789 Washington appointed him Federal Marshal in Georgia. He was killed in 1794, the first such officer to die while performing his duty.

54. Ternant to de Steuben, 11 August 1778

cited in Kapp, 621–622; Letters in Kapp are abridgments. For complete letters see Von Zemenszky, SP, roll 1, 210.
55. Ternant to Washington, 29 August 1778, *The Papers of George Washington Digital Edition*.
56. Washington to Ternant, 2 September 1778, *The Papers of George Washington Digital Edition*.
57. Ternant to Washington, 4 September 1778, *The George Washington Papers at the Library of Congress 1741–1799*, Manuscript Division, Series 4, General Correspondence 1697–1799.
58. Steuben to Laurens, 5 September 1778, *Papers of the Continental Congress 1774–1789*, microfilm, M247, roll 181, I164, 146.
59. H. Laurens to J. Laurens, 17 September 1778, Smith, *Letters of the Delegates to Congress, 1774–1789*, Vol. 10, 655–656.
60. Laurens to Steuben, 17 September 1778, *ibid.*, 657.
61. *Journals of the Continental Congress*, Vol. 12, September 2–December 31, 1778, 952.
62. Kapp, *The Life of Frederick William von Steuben*, 188.
63. Ternant to Washington, 29 September 1778, *The Papers of George Washington Digital Edition*.
64. Ternant to H. Laurens, 29 September 1778, *Papers of the Continental Congress 1774–1789*, microfilm, M247, roll 105, i78.
65. *Journals of the Continental Congress 1774–1789*, Vol. 11, 293.

Chapter IV

1. George Washington, *The Diaries of George Washington*, Vol. VI, January 1790–December 1799 (Charlottesville, 1979), 96.
2. Ternant to H. Laurens, 9 October 1778, Frederic R. Kirkland, *Letters on the American Revolution in the Library at Karolfred* (Philadelphia, 1941) Vol. 2, 55–56.
3. Ternant to H. Laurens, 29 October 1778, *Emmet Collection*, # 7670, New York Public Library.
4. H. Laurens to Rawlins Lowndes, 6 October 1778, *Letters of Delegates to Congress 1774–1789*, Vol. 10, 34.
5. C. Gadsden to Samuel Adams, 4 April 1779, Richard Walsh, ed. *The Writings of Christopher Gadsden 1746–1805* (Columbia, 1966), 161.
6. L'Enfant to M. de Gerard, 8 August 1779, H. Paul Caemmerer, *The Life of Pierre Charles L'Enfant* (Washington, D.C., 1950), 416.

7. Daniel J. McDonough, *Christopher Gadsden and Henry Laurens, The Parallel Lives of Two American Patriots* (Sellingsgrove, 2000), 237–239.
8. Mabel Louise Webber, ed., "Order Book of John Faucheraud Grimke, Aug. 1778 to May 1780," *The South Carolina Historical and Genealogical Magazine* 13 (1912), 205.
9. Ternant to H. Laurens, 23 November 1778, Hamer, ed., *The Papers of Henry Laurens*, Vol. 14, 530.
10. Ternant to de Steuben 28 November 1778, Kapp, 657–659.
11. Details of the Battle of Savannah and Ternant's role in it can be found in David K. Wilson, *The Southern Strategy: Britain's Conquest of South Carolina and Georgia 1775–1780* (Columbia, 2005), 65–80; Charles E. Bennett and Donald R. Lennon, *A Quest for Glory: Major General Robert Howe and the American Revolution* (Chapel Hill, 1991), 85–99; *Proceedings of a General Court Martial Held at Philadelphia ... for the Trial of Major General Howe, December 7, 1781* (Philadelphia: Hall and Sellers, 1782).
12. Ternant to Steuben, 30 December 1778, Von Zemensky, E. *The Papers of General Friedrich Wilhelm von Steuben 1777–1794*, microfilm reel 1, 279.
13. R. Howe to B. Lincoln and the President of Congress, 30 December 1778, *Papers of the Continental Congress*, M247, r163, i149, v2, p599.
14. Clifford L. Shipton, "Benjamin Lincoln" *Sibley's Harvard Graduates*, Vol. XII (1962), 416–458, condensed in Frederick S. Allen Jr. and Wayne A. Frederick, *Guide to the Microfilm Edition of the Benjamin Lincoln Papers* (Boston, 1967), 11.
15. Ternant to de Steuben, 20 January 1779 reproduced in Kapp, 661.
16. *Ibid.*
17. Steuben, *Regulations*, 75–79.
18. Ternant to de Steuben, 6 March 1779, reproduced in Kapp, 662–663.
19. *Ibid.*
20. David B. Mattern, *Benjamin Lincoln and the American Revolution* (Columbia, 1995), 92; see also Lanning, *African Americans in the Revolutionary War*, 69.
21. A. Hamilton to J. Laurens, 11 Sept. 1779, Harold Syrett and Jacob E. Cooke, eds., *The Papers of Alexander Hamilton* (New York, 1961–87), Vol. 2, 166.
22. Caemmerer, *L'Enfant*, 411–419.
23. Kenneth R. Bowling, *Peter Charles L'Enfant: Vision, Honor and Male Friendship in the Early American Republic* (Washington, D.C., 2005).
24. Bodinier, *Dictionnaire*, 87.
25. Blanchard, *Dictionnaire*, 433–434;

216 • Notes—Chapter IV

Bodinier, *Dictionnaire*, 286–287; see also Kite, *Duportail*, 272.
26. Ternant to Steuben, 4 June 1779, SP, reel 1: 398.
27. De Pontiere to Steuben, 12 July 1779, SP, reel 1: 446; L'Enfant to Steuben, 6 July 1779, SP, reel 1: 438; Bretigney to Steuben, 25 July 1779, Reel 1:457
28. John Laurens to Alexander Hamilton, 14 July 1779, *Hamilton Papers*, Vol. 2, 102–103.
29. Ternant to Steuben, 28 August 1779, Kapp, 66.
30. Sarah Bache to B. Franklin cited in Frederick D. Stone, "Philadelphia Society One Hundred Years Ago or the Reign of Continental Money," *Pennsylvania Magazine of History and Biography* Vol. 3 (1879): 373.
31. For Philadelphia's economic crisis see Ray Raphael, *Founders: The People Who Brought You the Revolution* (New York, 2000), 339–340, 344–349; Charles Rappleye, *Robert Morris: Financier of the American Revolution* (New York, 2010), 173–197.
32. For details of Arnold's legal troubles see Clare Brandt, *The Man in the Mirror: A Life of Benedict Arnold* (New York, 1994), 148–195.
33. Ternant to John Jay, 4 Sept. 1779, *Papers of the Continental Congress*, M247, r103, i78, v22, p641; Ternant memorandum of accounts, 20 Sept. 1779, *ibid.*, M247, r103, i78, v22, p645.
34. Ternant to Steuben, 28 August 1779, SP, reel 2, 29.
35. Ternant to Steuben, 30 September 1779, Kapp, 664–665.
36. Francy to Steuben, 25 May 1779, SP, reel 1:382.
37. Washington to Steuben, 1 July 1779, *Writings of George Washington*, Vol. 12, 352–354. William Galvin, a native of Martinique, entered service in September as a lieutenant in the 1st South Carolina Regiment; arrived in Philadelphia in August 1778. In 1780 promoted to major but left the line due to health but served at Yorktown as an inspector under Steuben's command.

Chapter V

1. Wilson, *The Southern Strategy*, 133–192.
2. Journals of the South Carolina General Assembly 1776–1780, 254, 269, cited in Hamer et al., eds., *The Papers of Henry Laurens*, Vol. 16, 239.
3. Wilson, *The Southern Strategy*, 195.
4. *Ibid.*, 196.

5. Light Townsend Cummins, *Spanish Observers and the American Revolution 1775–1783* (Baton Rouge, 1991), 157.
6. Johann Ewald, *Diary of the American War*, ed. Joseph P. Tustin (New Haven, 1979), 240.
7. For fortifications at Charlestown see George C. Rogers Jr., *Charleston in the Age of Pinckneys* (Norman, 1968), 59; Ferdinand de Brahm, Plan of Charlestown Defenses, Engineer Museum, Fort Belvoir, Virginia, cited in Paul K. Walker, *Engineers of Independence: A Documentary History of the Army Engineers in the American Revolution 1775–1783* in (Washington, D.C., 1981), 272.
8. Lincoln to Steuben, 8 January 1780, Kapp, 666.
9. Washington to Lincoln, 26 October 1779, *The Writings of George Washington from the Original Manuscript Sources*, Internet resource, http://etext.virginia.edu.
10. Ternant to Steuben, 7 January 1780, Kapp, 665–666.
11. Ternant to Steuben, 26 January 1780, Kapp, 666–667.
12. Cummins, *Spanish Observers*, 154.
13. Lincoln to Ternant, 2 February 1780, National Archives, *Papers of the Continental Congress*, M247, r177, i158, 355.
14. Lincoln to Ternant, 4 February 1780, *ibid.*, M247, r177, i158, 357.
15. Ministerio de Asuntos Exteriores, *Docmentos Relativos a la Independencia de Norteamerica existentes en Archivos Espanoles* (Madrid, 1976-) I, 205, Doc. No. 511.
16. Allen J. Kueth, "Havana in the Eighteenth Century," 13–25 in Franklin W. Knight and Peggy K. Liss, eds., *Atlantic Port Cities: Economy, Culture and Society 1650–1850* (Knoxville, 1991); see also Allan J. Kuethe, *Cuba, 1753–1815 Crown, Military and Society* (Knoxville, 1986).
17. Cummins, *Spanish Observers*, 105, 126–129; Rappleye, *Robert Morris*, 206–208.
18. Cummins, 60.
19. David Humphreys to Sec. of State, Pickering, 30 March 1798 in Holmes, "Some Economic Problems of Spanish Governors of Louisiana," 529.
20. Richard Morris, *The Peacemakers: The Great Powers and American Independence* (New York, 1965), 218–223.
21. Ternant to Lincoln, 23 March 1780, *Papers of the Continental Congress*, Microfilm, M247, r177, i158, p365; see also Ternant to Luzerne, 23 March 1780, Archives du Ministere des Affaires Etranges, *Correspondance Politique, États-Unis, Supplement*, vol. XII fol. 128; Keuthe, *Cuba, 1753–1815*, 98; Buchanan Parker Thomson, *Spain: Forgotten Ally of the*

American Revolution (North Quincy, 1976), 205–216.
22. Lincoln to Ternant, 23 March 1780, *Papers of the Continental Congress*, microfilm, M247, r177, i158.
23. J.D. Lewis, "The American Revolution in South Carolina-Gibbe's Plantation," http://www.carolina.com/SC/Revolution/revolution_gibbes_plantat... See also Diary of Captain Johann Hinrich, 30 March 1780, Bernhard A. Uhlendorf, trans. & ed., *The Siege of Charleston* (Ann Arbor, 1938), 225–229.
24. Benjamin Taliaferro, *The Orderly Book of Captain Benjamin Taliaferro, 2nd Virginia Detachment, Charleston, South Carolina 1780*, Lee A. Wallace, ed. (Richmond, 1980), 113.
25. For details on siege see Carl P. Borick, *A Gallant Defense: The Siege of Charleston, 1780* (Columbia, 2003); see also Wilson, *The Southern Strategy*, 193–241; and Richard Murdock, "A French Account of the Siege of Charlestown 1780," *South Carolina Historical Magazine*, 67 (July 1966), 138–154.
26. Ternant to Lincoln, 24 May 1780, *Benjamin Lincoln Papers*, Emmet Collection #7726, Manuscript and Archive Division, New York Public Library. For a detailed review of American and British troop strength during the siege see Wilson, *Southern Strategy*, 315–317.
27. Franklin B. Hough, ed., *The Siege of Charlestown 1780* (Spartanburg, SC, 1975), 47–48.
28. Ibid., 51–52.
29. Lincoln to Clinton and Clinton to Lincoln 12 May 1780, *ibid.*, 55.
30. For career of Major John Andre see Robert McConnell Hatch, *Major John Andre: A Gallant in Spy's Clothing* (Boston, 1986).
31. Hamilton to John Laurens, 11 October 1780, Harold C. Syrett et al., eds., *The Papers of Alexander Hamilton* (New York, 1961) Vol. 2, 467.
32. Joseph P. Tustin, trans and ed., *Diary of the American War: A Hessian Journal by Captain Johann Ewald* (New Haven, 1979), 238.
33. W.C. Houston to William Livingston, 16 June 1780, *Letters to Delegates of Congress*, Vol. 15, 332: "It appears that every idle excuse and unfair contrivance has been used to detain Mr. Ternant, and as to the vessel stipulated to General Lincoln and in which he comes himself, we have heard nothing of it."; W.C. Houston to John Jay, 10 July 1780, *ibid.*, 419: "the Enemy after the capitulation, interposed every means by dilatory and frivolous Pretenses, by what candour will probably decide to be a breach of the spirit of their engagements to delay the dispatches General Lincoln had stipulated should be forwarded immediately to Congress."
34. John Ternant's parole, *Clinton Papers*, William L. Clements Library, Manuscripts, University of Michigan.
35. James Custer to Henry Laurens, June 1780, Hamar, *Papers of Henry Laurens*, Vol. 15, 301–303.
36. James Lovell to Baron Steuben, 15 June 1780, SP, reel 2, 350; William C. Houston to William Livingston, 16 June 1780, *Letters of Delegates to Congress*, Vol. 15, 332.
37. Lincoln to Samuel Huntington, 24 May 1780, *Papers of the Continental Congress*, microfilm, M247, r177, i158, 373.
38. Description by Ezra Stiles quoted in William E. O'Donnell, *The Chevalier de la Luzerne: French Minister to the United States 1779–1784* (Louvain, 1938), 43.
39. Betsy Knight, "Prisoner Exchange and Parole in the American Revolution," *The William and Mary Quarterly*, 3rd Ser., Vol. 48, No. 2 (April, 1991), 208–210.
40. J. Laurens to Washington, 25 May 1780, Massie, *John Laurens and the American Revolution*, 167.
41. Hamilton to John Laurens, 30 June 1780, Syrett, *The Papers of Alexander Hamilton*, Vol. 2, 147.
42. La Luzerne to Steuben, 27 July 1780, SP, reel 2, 429; Ternant to Steuben, 23 August 1780, SP, reel 2, 466.
43. Library of Congress, *Papers of the Continental Congress, 1774–1789*, Vol. 17, 703; Vol. 18, 932; Vol. 21, 1027.
44. John Adams, Diary for 21 July 1779, quoted in O'Donnell, *The Chevalier de La Luzerne*, 109.
45. For Chevalier d'Annemours see Kathryn Sullivan, *Maryland and France 1774–1789* (Philadelphia, 1936), 39–45.
46. D'Annemours to Jefferson, 27 February 1782, *Papers of Thomas Jefferson Digital Edition*, Barbara B.Oberg and J. Jefferson Looney, eds. (Charlottesville: Rotunda, 2008), 161.
47. For John Holker see Abraham P. Nasatir and Gary Elwyn Monell, *French Consuls in the United States: A Calendar of Their Correspondence in the Archives Nationales* (Washington, D.C., 1967), 561–563.
48. Marquis de Chastellux, *Travels in North America in the Years 1780, 1781 and 1782*, trans. Howard C. Rice Jr. (Chapell Hill, 1963) Vol. 1, 130–131.
49. AG, 2Ye, Dossiers d'officiers supérieurs et subalterns—Jean Ternant, Letter of Marquis de Chastellux to Sec of War, 26 September 1783.
50. Bodinier, *Les Officiers de L'Armée Royale*, 266.

218 • Notes—Chapter V

51. Armand biography and request for Ternant's services see Asa Bird Gardiner, *The Order of the Cincinnati in France* (Rhode Island State Society of the Cincinnati, 1905), 157–158; Armand to Washington, 11 January 1781, Fitzpatrick, *Writings of George Washington*, Vol. 21, 92; Washington to Armand, 12 January 1781, *ibid.*, 93–94.

52. Ternant to John Laurens, 29 January 1781 "The Mission of Col. John Laurens to Europe in 1781," *South Carolina Historical and Genealogical Magazine*, Vol. 2 (April, 1901), 27–28.

53. Ternant to Washington, 30 May 1781, *The George Washington Papers at the Library of Congress, 1741–1799*, Manuscript Division, Series 4, General Correspondence 1697–1799; see also Ternant to Steuben, 4 May 1781, SP, roll 4, #20.

54. Washington to Ternant, 8 June 1781, *The George Washington Papers at the Library of Congress, 1741–1799*, Series 4, General Correspondence.

55. Sir Guy Carleton to Comte de Rochambeau, 1 August 1782 cited in Kite, *Diportail*, 235–236. See also Rochambeau to Sir Henry Clinton, 29 April 1782 and Rochambeau to Carleton, 29 June 1782, H.J. Brown, ed., *Report on American Manuscripts in the Royal Institutions of Great Britain* (Boston, 1972) Vol. 2, 473, 547–548.

56. Ternant to Galvez, 4 October 1781, Ministerio de Asunto Exteriores, *Documento Relativos a la Independencia de Norteamerica existents en Archivos Espanoles*, I, 2, 1.892.

57. Galvez to Ternant, 15 October 1781, *ibid.*, 1.895.

58. Rochambeau to Sir Henry Clinton, 9 November 1781, H.J. Brown, ed., *Report on American Manuscripts in the Royal Institutions of Great Britain* (Boston, 1972) vol. 2, 347–348 and 362; for Doyle see also Colonel Alfred Doyle, *A Hundred Years of Conflict: Being Some Records of the Service of Six Generals of the Doyle Family 1756–1856* (London, 1911).

59. *Proceedings of a General Court Martial Held at Philadelphia... for the Trial of Major General Howe*, December 7, 1781 (Philadelphia, 1782), 3.

60. Ternant to Washington, 11 December 1781, *George Washington Papers at the Library of Congress, 1741–1799*, Manuscript Division, Series 4, General Correspondence 1697–1799.

61. Washington to Benjamin Walker, 13 December 1781, Fitzpatrick, *Writings of George Washington*, Vol. 22, 384–385.

62. Washington to Rochambeau, 14 January 1782, *Writings of George Washington from the Original Manuscript Sources*, University of Virginia Library, http://etext.virginia.edu/etcon.

63. Diary, 23 January 1782, E.J. Ferguson, ed., *Papers of Robert Morris 1781–1784* (Pittsburgh, 1973–1988), Vol. 4, 98.

64. Robert Morris, *Diary*, 12 February 1782, *ibid.*, 216.

65. Morris to Washington, 18 October 1781, *ibid.*, Vol. 3, 79; 18 February 1782, *ibid.*, Vol. 4, 249.

Chapter VI

1. John H. Stutesman, "Colonel Armand and Washington's Cavalry," *New York Historical Society Quarterly*, Vol. XLV, No. 1 (January 1961): 5–42.

2. Chevalier d'Annemours to T. Jefferson, 27 February 1782, *Papers of Thomas Jefferson Digital Edition*.

3. Ternant to Washington, 5 March 1782, *The George Washington Papers at the Library of Congress*. See also Washington to Charles Armand Tuffin, 13 February 1782, *The Writings of George Washington from the Original Manuscript Sources*, Electronic Text Center, University of Virginia Library.

4. Armand to Washington, 8 March 1782, *The George Washington Papers at the Library of Congress, 1741–1799*, Manuscript Division, Series 4, General Correspondence, 1697–1799.

5. Walter Edgar, *Partisans and Redcoats* (New York, 2001), 3. Ternant would have been encouraged by Jefferson to visit the Natural Bridge south of Staunton, located on land purchases by Jefferson in 1774.

6. N. Greene's Orders, Headquarters near Bacon's Bridge, S.C., 2 April 1782, Dennis M. Conrad and Roger Parks, eds., *The Papers of General Nathanael Greene* (Chapel Hill, 1976–) Vol. 10, 574.

7. For operations in the southern theater see Introductions by Dennis M. Conrad, *The Papers of General Nathanael Greene*, Vols. 10, December 1781–April 1782, xi-xv; Vol. 11, April–September 1782, xi-xv; and Vol. 12, October 1782–May 1783, xi-ix.

8. April 1782 report of muster and inspection by Lieutenant Colonel J. Ternant, cited in Kapp, 675–678; see also Josiah Harmar, Remarks on Southern Army, 5 February 1782, *Papers of General Nathaniel Greene*, Vol. 10, 319–320; Ternant to Greene, 26 October 1782, Greene Papers, No. 40139, William L. Clements Library, University of Michigan; Ternant to Steuben, 22 April, 26 April and 19 May 1782 in SP, roll #5436, 442 and 459.

Notes—Chapter VI • 219

9. A. Wayne to N. Greene, 18 April 1782, *Papers of General Nathanael Greene*, Vol. 11, 75–76.
10. Peter Maslowski, "National Policy Toward the Use of Black Troops in the American Revolution," *South Carolina Historical Magazine* (January 1972): 15.
11. Thaddeus Kosciuszko to N. Greene, 5 September 1782, note no. 4, *Papers of General Nathanael Greene*, Vol. 11, 629–630.
12. John Mathews to Greene, *ibid.*, 353.
13. Abstract of the Muster of the Several Corps and Detachments composing the Southern Army, from the 1st April to the 19th September 1782, Kapp, 708–709.
14. Mordecai Gist to Greene, 27 August 1782, *Papers of General Nathanael Greene* Vol. 11, 579.
15. For Kosciusko's career see Paul Walker, *Engineers of Independence: A Documentary History of the Army Engineers in the American Revolution 1775–1783*, Washington, D.C., 1981); Miecislaus Haiman, *Kosciuszko in the American Revolution* (New York, 1943) and M.K. Dziewanowski, "Tadeusz Kosciuszko and Kazimierz Pulaski and the American War of Independence: A Study in National Symbolism and Mythology" in Jaroslaw Pelenski, ed., *The American and European Revolutions 1776–1848: Sociopolitical and Ideological Aspects* (Iowa City, 1980).
16. For details of the incident concerning Mrs. Fuller's boat see Metchie J.E. Budka, *Autograph Letters of Thaddeus Kosciuszko* (Chicago, 1977), 105–106 and *Papers of General Nathanael Greene*, Vol. 11, 629–630.
17. Greene to Charles Pettit, 2 November 1782, *Papers of General Nathanael Greene*, Vol. 12, 398.
18. Ternant to Greene, 27 September 1782, Nathaneal Greene Papers, William L. Clements Library, University of Michigan.
19. Ternant to Greene, 26 October 1782, *Papers of General Nathaneal Greene*. Vol. 11, 701–702.
20. Greene to Ternant, 4 November 1782, *ibid.*, 142–143.
21. Southern Army's General Orders, 4 November 1782, *Papers of General Nathanael Greene*, Vol. 12, 144.
22. Ternant to Steuben, 12 November 1782, SP, reel 6, #25.
23. Ternant to Greene, 25 December 1782, Greene Papers, William L. Clements Library, University of Michigan.
24. Ternant to Steuben, 21 December 1782, SP, reel 6, # 48.
25. Ternant to Greene, 25 December 1782 *Papers of General Nathanael Greene*, Vol. 12, 348.

26. Steuben to Ternant, 3 March 1783, SP, reel No. 6.
27. Ternant to Washington, 20 May 1783, *The George Washington Papers at the Library of Congress*.
28. Ternant to Josiah Harmar, 3 April 1783, *Papers of Josiah Harmar*, William L. Clements Library, University of Michigan.
29. For Armand's Legion during the years 1782–1783, see "Letters of Col. Armand (Marquis de la Rouerie) 1777–1792," *Collections of the New York Historical Society for 1878* (New York, 1879), 289–396.
30. Resolution, 26 March 1783, *Journals of the Continental Congress 1774–1789*.
31. Armand to Washington, 20 May 1783, "Letters of Col. Armand (Marquis de la Rouerie) 1777–1791," 360–361.
32. Ternant to Lincoln, 14 May 1783, *Papers of the Continental Congress 1774–1789*, M247, r163, i149, v.2, 603–04.
33. Ternant to Washington, 20 May 1783, *The George Washington Papers at the Library of Congress*, Manuscript Division, Series 4, General Correspondence 1697–1799.
34. Washington to Ternant, 28 May 1783, *Papers of the Continental Congress 1774–1789*, microfilm, N247, r163, i149, v. 2, 601.
35. Lincoln to Pres. of Congress, 14 May 1783, *ibid.*, 531.
36. Lincoln to Thomas Mifflin, 17 June 1783, *ibid.*, 535.
37. Congress, Committee report, 23 July 1783, *ibid.*, 605.
38. Kite, *Duportail*, 292 and note.
39. Ternant to Luzerne, 8 September 1783, AG, Series 2Ye Dossiers d'officiers superieus et subaltern—Jean Ternant.
40. Luzerne to Minister of War, 14 September 1783, *ibid.*
41. Ternant to Jacob Reed, 18 October 1783, Library of Congress, Manuscript Division.
42. Armand to Washington, 29 November 1783, "Letters of Col. Armand (Marquis de la Rouerie, 1777–1791)," *Collection of the New York Historical Society for the Year 1878: Revolutionary Papers*, Vol. 1, 366–368.
43. Ternant to Lincoln, 10 February 1784, Massachusetts Historical Society, Benjamin Lincoln Papers, M-3784 microfilm 1–527, reel 7. Exactly which member of the Vaughan family Ternant refers to has not been identified, but it was most likely either John Vaughan (1756–1841) or his brother Charles (1759–1839). Their mother, Sarah Hallowell Vaughan, was Boston born and her family owned considerable property in Maine. Benjamin Lincoln also owned land in the same region and this probably explains Ternant asking for Lincoln's assistance for Mr.

Vaughan. In the 1790s several of the Vaughans would move to Maine and establish their home there. Ternant's recommendation may also have been helped by the fact that another brother, Benjamin Vaughan, had married Sarah Manning. She was a sister of Martha Manning who had wed Jack Laurens. John and Charles Vaughan therefore had been brothers-in-law to Ternant's best friend.

John Vaughan was a business partner with Robert and Gouverneur Morris and in 1783 was sent to England to raise capital. In January 1784 Samuel Vaughan and his son John were elected to the American Philosophical Society, and John served as the Society's secretary and was a friend of Peter Duponceau, Ternant's friend from Valley Forge.

44. Duportail to Washington, 16 June 1784, Serge Le Pottier, *Duportail ou le génie de George Washington*, 252.

45. Congress, Report of Committee re Jean Ternant, 22 April 1784, *Papers of the Continental Congress 1774–1789*, microfilm, M247, r28, i19, v5, p302.

46. Thomas Mifflin to Ternant, 26 April 1784, *ibid.*, M247, r24, i16, p302.

47. Letter of Duportail, 29 October 1783, see *Journal of Cont. Congress*, XXVI, 43.

48. Debt due to Foreign Officers, 3 February 1784, Harold C. Syrett and Jacob E. Cooke, eds., *The Papers of Alexander Hamilton* (New York, 1961–) Vol. 23, 540–541.

49. Thomas J. Schaeper, *France and America in the Revolutionary Era: The Life of Jacques-Donatien Leray de Chaumont, 1725–1803* (Oxford, 1995), Appendix, "Eighteenth-Century Currencies," 348.

50. Bryce Metcalf, *Original Members and Other Officers Eligible to the Society of the Cincinnati, 1783–1938* (Strasburg, 1938), 307; see also Minor J. Myers, *Liberty without Anarchy: A History of the Society of Cincinnati* (Charlottesville, 1983); also Baron Ludovic de Contenson, *La Société des Cincinnati de France et La Guerre d'Amérique 1778–1783* (Paris, 1934), 270.

51. O'Donnell, *The Chevalier de la Luzerne*, 247–248.

52. Ibid.

Chapter VII

1. AG, Series 2Ye, Dossiers d'officers supérieurs et subalterns 1791–1847, Jean Ternant, Pour le Croix de Saint-Louis, 24 June 1787.

2. Bodinier, *Les Officiers de l'armée Royale*, 147–157.

3. *Ibid.*, 150; see also Samuel F. Scott, "Strains in the Franco-American Alliance: The French Army in Virginia, 1781–1782" in Richard A. Rutyna and Peter C. Stewart, eds., *Virginia in the American Revolution: A Collection of Essays* (Norfolk, 1983), 93–94: Lee Kennett, *The French Forces in America, 1780–1783* (Westport, 1978), 158.

4. Bodinier, *Les Officers de l'armée Royale*, 103; see also Monro Price, *Preserving the Monarchy: The Comte de Vergennes, 1774–1787* (Cambridge, 1995), 168.

5. For military reforms see Rafe Blaufarb, *The French Army 1750–1820: Careers, Talent, Merit* (Manchester, 2002), 30–45; for reglement of 22 May 1781 (Segur Law) see David D. Bien, "The Army in the Enlightenment: Reform, Reaction and Revolution," *Past and Present* 85 (1979): 68–98.

6. Steuben to Vergennes, December 1782, SP, reel 6, #59.

7. Alfred Cobban, *Ambassadors and Secret Agents: The Diplomacy of the First Earl of Malmesbury at the Hague* (London, 1954), 211–212.

8. Major studies on the democratic revolution in the United Provinces are R.R. Palmer, *The Age of Democratic Revolution: A Political History of Europe and America, 1760–1800*, Vol. 1, The Challenge (Princeton, 1959): Simon Schama, *Patriots and Liberators: Revolution in the Netherlands, 1780–1813* (London, 1977); Jan Willem Schulte Nordholt, *The Dutch Republic and American Independence*, trans. Herbert H. Rowen (Chapel Hill, 1982); Margaret C. Jacob and Wijnand W. Mijnhardt, Eds., *The Dutch Republic in the Eighteenth Century: Decline, Enlightenment and Revolution* (Ithaca, 1992).

9. Munro Price, *Preserving the Monarchy*, 189–190; Cobban, 48–70.

10. Cobban, *Ambassadors and Secret Agents*, 20–25, 42, 43; see also Price, 191, 212.

11. Henri de Peyster, *Les Troubles de Hollande a la veille de la Revolution Français 1780–1795* (Paris, 1905), 127–128; see also Price, 212–221; Cobban, *Ambassadors and Secret Agents*, 42–44; and for Angelique-Dorothee de Cassini, see www.catnaps.org/cassini/babaud.html.

12. Cobban, *Ambassadors and Secret Agents*, 43.

13. Joep van Hoof, *Military Uniforms in the Netherlands 1752–1800* (Vienna, 2011), 8, 150–157, 160–167; see also Louis Leconte, *Le Régiment Royal-Liègeois au service du Roi de France, 1787–1792* (Moulins, 1937), 62.

14. David M. Hopkin, *Soldier and Peasant in French Popular Culture 1766–1870* (Rochester, NY, 2003), 249–250; see also John Mollo and Malcolm McGregor, *Uni-*

forms of the Seven Years War 1756–1763 (New York, 1977), 191.

15. Liliane and Fred Funcken, *The Lace Wars*, Part II (London, 1977), 40; Terry Crowdy, *French Revolutionary Infantry 1789–1802* (Oxford, 2004), 4; see also John Mollo and Malcolm McGregor, *Uniforms of the American Revolution* (London, 1975), 216.

16. R. Grouvel, Baron, "La Legion de Maillebois 1784–1786," *Le Passepoil*, 12th Annee, No. 2, 33–34.

17. Blanchard, *Dictionnaire*, 55–56.

18. Grouvel, 33–37; see also Leconte, 60–61.

19. Peter Reaveley, "Chapter IV: The Battle" in Jean Boudriot, *John Paul Jones and the Bonhomme Richard*, trans. David H. Roberts (Annapolis, 1987), 69, 74.

20. Bodinier, *Dictionnaire*, 430. See also T.E. Crowdy, *Incomparable: Napoleon's 9th Light Infantry Regiment* (Oxford, 2012), 33–34.

21. Grouvel, 36; for Lajard see M.M. Arnault, Jay, Jouy, et al. eds., *Biographie Nouvelle des Contemporains* (1820–1835), 355–356; for Dupont de l'Etang see Georges Six, *Dictionnaire Biographique des Genereux et Amiraux Français de la Revolution et de l'Empire 1792–1815* (Paris, 1934) Vol. 1, 404–406; and for Macdonald see Alan Hankinson, "His Outspokenness"—Macdonald in David G. Chandler, ed., *Napoleon's Marshals* (New York, 1987), 236–253.

22. Grouvel, 33.

23. Leconte, 60.

24. For Frederick III, Rhinegrave of Salm-Kryburg see Cobban, *Ambassadors and Secret Agents*, 44–47, 120 and Price, 208; see also Howard C. Rice Jr., *Thomas Jefferson's Paris* (Princeton, 1976); Henry de Peyster, *Les Troubles de Holland a la veille de la Revolution Française*, 113, 114.

25. Cobban, *Ambassadors and Secret Agents*, 120.

26. Cobban, 46; see also *Papers of Thomas Jefferson*, Vol. 12, 77.

27. Grouvel, 35; Leconte, 63.

28. AG, Series 2Yf, Dossiers de Pensions Militaires 1801–1817, Jean de Ternant, Control du Ministere de la Guerre, No. 10,260. Pension Militaire de la Holland.

29. Cobban, *Ambassadors and Secret Agents*, 143, 160.

30. *The Correspondence of the Right Honorable Sir Jon Sinclair Bart* (London, 1831) Vol. 2, 182.

31. Cobban, *Ambassadors and Secret Agents*, 105, 145–146.

32. Cobban, *ibid.*, 143.

33. Victor L. Belhomme, *Histoire de l'In-fanterie en France* (Paris, 1895–1905) Vol. III, 392.

34. AG, series 2Ye, Dossier d'Officiers et Subalternes 1791–1847, Jean de Ternant, 24 June 1787, Pour la Croix de St-Louis.

35. Ternant to unidentified recipient, most likely La Luzerne, 29 June 1787, AG, series 2Ye, dossiers de'officiers supérieurs et subalternes, 1791–1847, Jean de Ternant.

36. Harvey Chisick, *The Production, Distribution and Readership of a Conservative Journal in the Early French Revolution, The Ami Royale of the Abbe Royou* (Philadelphia, 1992), 182–183; see also Mousnier, *Institutions of France under the Absolute Monarchy*, Vol. 1, 131 and 196.

37. David Hackett Fischer, *Champlain's Dream* (New York, 2008), 643.

38. Cobban, *Ambassadors and Secret Agents*, 148–153.

39. Cobban, 185; Geert van Uythoven, "The Dutch during the Revolutionary Wars: The Prussian Campaign in Holland, 1787," *First Empire* Nos. 45, 46 & 47. For van Rijssel see Six, *Dictionnaire Biographique des Generaux et Amiraux 1789–1815*, Vol. 2, 531.

40. For Ternant's support for Lafayette see Louis Gottschalk, *Lafayette between the American and French Revolutions*, 1783–1789 (Chicago, 1950), 33. From 2 August until 18 September 1787 Lafayette was in Auvergne. He received notification of Dutch interest at some point and was attempting to reach Amsterdam when news of the city's fall interrupted his journey. See also Lafayette to Washington, 9 October 1787, Louis Gottschalk, ed., *The Letters of Lafayette to Washington, 1777–1789* (New York, 1944), 331.

41. Cobban, *Ambassadors and Secret Agents*, 143, 185.

42. Simon Schama, *Patriots and Liberators: Revolution in the Netherlands 1780–1813* (New York, 1977), 76, 119; see also Wayne PH. TE Brake, Provincial Histories and National Revolution in the Dutch Republic in Jacob and Mijinhardt, eds., *The Dutch Republic in the Eighteenth Century: Decline, Enlightenment and Revolution*, 64–82.

43. Cobban, *Ambassadors and Secret Agents*, 119, 143.

44. Louis Philippe de Segur, *Tableau Historique et Politique de l'Europe depuis 1786 jusqu'en 1796* (Paris, 1830), 133.

45. Cobban, *Ambassadors and Secret Agents*, 158, 177–179, 184.

46. Unless otherwise noted all material relating to the military events in September and October 1787 is taken from Van Uythoven, *The Dutch during the Revolution-*

222 • Notes—Chapter VII

ary Wars; The Prussian Campaign in Holland.
47. Ternant to Bourgoing, 23 September 1787, H. T. Colenbrander, De Patriottenjid, Vol. 3, 214–215.
48. Ibid.
49. Ibid.
50. Cobban, 192–193.
51. Memoirs of His Own Time, Lieu-General Count Mathieu Dumas, trans. (Philadelphia, 1839) Vol. 1, 89–94.
52. Conrad de Mandach, Un Gentlehomme Suisse au service de la Hollande et de la France: Le Comte Guillaume de Portes 1750–1823 (Paris, 1904), 116–125.
53. Orville T. Murphy, The Diplomatic Retreat of France and Public Opinion on the Eve of the French Revolution 1783–1789 (Washington, D.C., 1998), 80–96.
54. Montmorin to Verac, 20 August 1787, cited in Cobban, 164.
55. Six, Dictionnaire, Vol. 2, 531. And van Uythoven, First Empire Magazine, 46.
56. Blanchard, Dictionnaire, 55–56, 89–90.
57. AG, Series 2Ye, Dossier individual officiers supérieur et subaltern 1791–1847, Jean de Ternant.
58. AG, Series 2Yf, Dossier de pensions militaires 1801–1817, Jean de Ternant, Precis des services du Colonel Ternant.
59. Barthelemy to Montmorin, 26 September 1787 and 15 September 1787, cited in Cobban, 189.
60. Montmorin to Barthelemy, 13 September 1787, cited in Cobban, 190.
61. Montmorin to La Luzerne, January 1788, cited in Cobban, 213.
62. Ronald Ray Nelson, The Home Office, 1782–1801 (Durham, 1969), 90.
63. John Brooke, George III (New York, 1972), 294–298, for description of royal levees and drawing rooms.
64. William S. Smith to William Short, 17 February 1788, The Papers of Thomas Jefferson, Vol. 8, 621.
65. Charles R. Ritcheson, "The Fragile Memory: Thomas Jefferson at the Court of George III," Eighteenth Century Life, Vol. 6 (1981): 1–16.
66. Melvin D. Kennedy, Lafayette and Slavery from His Letters to Thomas Clarkson and Granville Sharp (Easton, 1950).
67. AN, AD, XVIII, C, 115, List of Members of the Société des Amis des Noirs, in Eloise Ellery, Brissot de Warville: A Study in the History of the French Revolution (Boston, 1913), appendix B.
68. William Short to T. Jefferson, 17 March 1788, Papers of Thomas Jefferson, Vol. 8, 676–677.

69. AG, Series 2Ye, Dossier individual officiers supérieur et subaltern 1791–1847, Jean de Ternant.
70. Blaufarb, The French Army 1750–1820: Careers, Talent, Merit, 49.
71. Bodinier, Les Officiers de l'Armée Royale, 58.

Chapter VIII

1. Derek Beales, Joseph II: In the Shadow of Maria-Theresa, 1741–1780 (Cambridge, 1987), 118; Patricia Chastain Howe, Foreign Policy and the French Revolution: Charles-François Dumouriez, Pierre LeBrun and the Belgian Plan, 1789–1793 (New York, 2008), 8–15.
2. Pierre Doyon, "Marie-Louis d'Escorches, marquis de Sainte-Croix: Sa mission Diplomatique a Liège 1782–1791," Revue d'Histoire Diplomatique, XXXVII (1923): 89–113, 208–235. The candidates for the office of Prince-Bishop of Liège in 1784 were Ferdinand-Maximillien Meriadec, Prince de Rohan-Guemenee, Archbishop of Cambrai; Wilhelm Florentin, Prince of Salm-Salm, Bishop of Tournai; Charles-Alexandre, comte d'Arberg, Bishop of Ypres; and Cesar-Constantine-François, comte d'Hoensbroeck d'Osst; N.F. Magnette, "Les dessous d'une election episcopale sous l'ancien régime," Bulletin de l'Academie Royale des Sciences des Lettres et des Beaux-Arts de Belgique (1896): 163–206.
3. Leconte, Le Régiment Royal-Liègeois as service du Roi de France 1787–1792, 15; Doyon, 212.
4. Leconte, 20.
5. Ibid., 21–52.
6. Ibid., 311–317.
7. "Convention faite entre sa Majeste Tres Christienne et la Monsieur le Prince-Eveque de Liège relativelle a l'etablissment du régiment Royal-Liègeois," reproduced in Leconte, 53–57.
8. Leconte, 101, 272–274.
9. Ibid., 272–274.
10. L'État Militaire 1788, cited in Leconte, 101.
11. Leconte, 98–112; for officers annual leave see Samuel F. Scott, From Yorktown to Valmy: The Transformation of the French Army in an Age of Revolution (Niwot, 1998), 143.
12. Leconte, 257–58, 297–98, 322.
13. AG, Series 2Ye, dossiers d'officiers supérieurs et subalterns 1791–1847, Jean Ternant, Request for relief, October 1789 and marginal note by Montmorin to the minister

for war, comte de la Tour du Pin, explaining Ternant's absence.
14. Samuel F. Scott, *The Response of the Royal Army to the French Revolution*, 33.
15. G. Morris, *Diary*, 10 April 1789, Beatrix Cary Davenport, ed., *A Diary of the French Revolution* (Boston, 1939), Vol. I, 36.
16. William Howard Adams, *Gouverneur Morris: An Independent Life* (New Haven, 2003), 167–168; Melanie Randolph Miller, *Envoy to the Terror: Gouverneur Morris & the French Revolution* (Dulles, VA, 2005), 44–47.
17. Jefferson to Jay, 4 February 1789, *Papers of Thomas Jefferson*, Vol. 14, 520.
18. McClellan, James E., III, *Colonialism and Science: Sainte Domingue and the Old Régime* (Chicago, 2010), 157–158.
19. G. Morris, *Diary*, 27 December 1789, ed. Davenport, Vol. I, 346. See also Alec Dun, "What avenues of commerce, will you Americans, not explore." "Philadelphia's commercial vantage on St Domingue, 1789–1793," The Atlantic Economy in the Eighteenth Century revolutions, Program in Early American Economy and Society Conference, 19 September 2003, 8.
20. Frederic Masson, *Les Department des Affaires Étrangères pendant la Revolution, 1787–1804* (Paris, 1877), 50–56.
21. Orville T. Murphy, *The Diplomatic Retreat of France and Public Opinion on the Eve of the French Revolution, 1783–1789* (Washington, D.C.), 1–2.
22. Linda Frey and Marsha Frey, *"Proven Patriots": The French Diplomatic Corps, 1789–1799* (St. Andrews, 2011), 12, note 53.
23. Morris to Washington, 24 January 1790, *The Papers of George Washington, Presidential Series*, eds. W.W. Abbot, Dorothy Twohig and Philander Chase, Vol. 5, 48–57.
24. Genet to Jefferson, 4 July 1797, cited in Meade Minnigerode, *Jefferson Friend of France 1793: The Career of Edmund-Charles Genet* (New York, 1928), 414.
25. Marat, *L'Ami du Peuple* 5 No. 296 (30 November 1790), 5, 6.
26. St. Priest to Lafayette, 26 September 1787, Marquis de Lafayette, *Memories*, Vol. 2, 498–499; Lafayette to Washington, 9 October 1787, *ibid.*, 206–216; see also Louis Gottschalk, *Lafayette between the American and French Revolution 1783–1789* (Chicago, 1950), 339.
27. G. Morris, *Diary*, 11 December 1789, Davenport, Vol. I, 329–330; and 27 December 1789, 346.
28. François-Claude-Armour, Bouille, marquis de, *Memoires relating to the French Revolution* (London, 1797), 163–164.

29. Cobban, *Ambassadors and Secret Agents*, 143.
30. Bodinier, *Les Officiers de l'Armée Royale*, 139.
31. Etienne Chavaray, *Les Grades Militaries sous la Revolution* (Paris, 1894), 18.
32. Bodinier, *Les Officiers de l'Armée Royale*, 139; Claude C. Sturgill, "Observations of the French War Budget, 1781–1790," *Military Affairs*, 48 (October 1984): 187.
33. Louis Gottschalk and Margaret Maddox, *Lafayette in the French Revolution: From the October Days through the Federation* (Chicago, 1973), 318; for ministerial staff salaries see Clive H. Church, *Revolution and Red Tape: The French Ministerial Bureaucracy 1779–1850* (Oxford, 1981), 37.
34. Robert Darnton, *George Washington's False Teeth: An Unconventional Guide to the Eighteenth Century* (New York, 2003), 139.
35. Garrioch, *The Making of Revolutionary Paris* (Berkeley, 2002), 274.
36. George V. Taylor, "The Paris Bourse on the Eve of the Revolution, 1781–1789," *American Historical Review*, 67 (1962): 959–960.
37. William Howard Rice, Jr., *The Paris Years of Thomas Jefferson* (Princeton, 1976).
38. AN, LXXXVII, 1468, 10 October 1833, Testament of Jean Ternant.
39. Gottschalk and Maddox, *Lafayette in the French Revolution: From the October Days through the Federation*, 28–33.
40. Pierre Caron, "La tentative de contre-revolution de juin-juillet 1789," *Revue d'histoire et contemporaine*, Vol. 8 (1907–1907): 13.
41. Leconte, 122.
42. Gottschalk and Maddox, 276.
43. G. Morris, *Diary*, 9 October 1789, Davenport, Vol. 1, 251.
44. R.R. Palmer, *The Age of Democratic Revolution: A Political History of Europe and America, 1769–1800*, Vol. 1, 341–357.
45. Janet Polasky, *Revolution in Brussels, 1787–1793*; see also Howe, *Foreign Policy and the French Revolution: Charles-François Dumouriez, Pierre LeBrun and the Belgian Plan, 1789–1793*.
46. Gottschalk and Maddox, 278.
47. Ibid., 284.
48. Lafayette, *Memoires*, Vol. 3, 43–44.
49. Ibid., 44.
50. G. Morris, *Diary*, 10, 11, 12 February 1790, Davenport, Vol. 1, 408–409.
51. Morris to Ternant, 7 May 1790, G. Morris, *Diary*, Davenport, Vol. 1, 508.
52. Morris to Ternant, 4 May 1790, Jared Sparks, *The Life and Correspondence of Gouverneur Morris* Vol. 2 (Boston, 1832), 112–113.

53. Simon Schama, *Citizens: A Chronicle of the French Revolution* (New York, 1989), 439.
54. Pierre Muret, "L'Affaire des princes possessionnes d'Alsace et les origins du conflit entrée la Revolution et l'Empire," *Revue d'Histoire Moderne et Contemporaire*, 1899–1900, 433–456 & 566–593. Unless otherwise noted, all material pertaining to the affair with the German princes and Ternant's mission is taken from Muret's article.
55. Ruth Strong Hudson, "Conrad-Alexandre Gerard and the Coming of the Revolution in Alsace," in Morris Slavin and Agnes Smith, eds., *Bourgeois, Sans-culottes and Other Frenchmen: Essays on the French Revolution in Honor of John Hall Stewart* (Waterloo, 1981), 26.
56. *Ibid.*, 34.
57. Sidney Seymour Biro, *The German Policy of Revolutionary France: A Study in French Diplomacy during the War of the First Coalition 1792–1797* (Cambridge, 1957), Vol. I, 39–42.
58. Lafayette to Bouille, 20 May 1790, Lafayette, *Memoires*, Vol. 2, 461–62; see also Gottschalk and Maddox, *Lafayette in the French Revolution: From the October Days until the Federation*, 360.
59. François-Claude-Amour, marquis de Bouille, *Memories Relating to the French Revolution*, 163–164.
60. Resume des demarches faites, par ordre du roi, aupres des princes d'empire Possessionnes en France (October, 1790, Aff. Etr., Allemagne, 662), cited in Muret, 571–572.
61. Scott, *The Response of the Royal Army to the French Revolution*, 89–91.
62. For details of naval mutinies and La Luzerne's resignation see William S. Cormack, *Revolution and Political Conflict in the French Navy 1780–1794* (Cambridge, 1995); see also Samuel Anderson Covington, "The comité militaire and the Legislative Reform of the French Army 1789–1791," Ph.D. Diss. (University of Arkansas, 1970), 132–135.
63. Leconte, 122–128; see also T.L.J. Pillot, "Les consequences d'une Mutinerie Militaire a Avesnes en 1790," *Société Archeologique & Historique de arrondisement d'Avesnes (Nord) Memoires*, Vol. XV, 1935, 17–22; see also Jean Mossay, *Histoire de la Ville Avesnes* (Avesnes-sur-Help, 1969), 173–174.
64. Leconte, 128–134.
65. William Clinton Baldwin, "The Beginnings of the Revolution and the Mutiny of the Royal Garrison in Nancy: L'Affaire de Nancy, 1790," Ph.D. Diss. (University of Michigan, 1973); see also Charles Berlot, *La Revolte de la Garrison de Nancy en 1790* (Nancy, 1943), 149–164; and Leconte, 134–149.
66. Samuel F. Scott, *Yorktown to Valmy*, 153.
67. Henri Bardy, "Une insurrection a Belfort (21 Octobre 1790)," *Revue d'Alsace* Juillet 1851, 304–321; and "La Place de Belfort au commencment de la Revolution 1788–1792," *Bulletin de la Société Belfontaine d'emulation* No. 24 (1905): 87–88; Leconte, 155–158; Thomas Brennan, *Public Drinking and Popular Culture in Eighteenth Century Paris* (Princeton, 1988), 157.
68. Bardy, 308–309; Earl Gower to Lord Grenville, 29 October 1790, in Oscar Browning, ed., *The Dispatches of Earl Gower, English Ambassador at Paris from June 1790 to August 1792* (Cambridge, 1885), 40–41.
69. Harvey Chisick, *The Production, Distribution and Readership of a Conservative Journal in the Early French Revolution. The Ami du Roi of the Abbé Royou* (Philadelphia, 1992), 217.
70. Jean Paul Marat, *L'Ami du Peuple*, Vol. 6, No 271, 14 October 1790 to December 1790, Society for the Reproduction of Rare Books, 1967.
71. Muguet de Nanthou, "Rapport fait a l'assemblee nationale dans le séance du samedi 30 Octobre, au nom des comités militaries et des rapports sur les evenemens arrives le 21 Octobre a Belfort," Maclure Collection of French Revolutionary Material (University of Pennsylvania), 832.
72. Leconte, 174.
73. "Addresse presentee a l'Assemblee Nationale et au Roi par tous les officiers, sous-officiers et soldats du Régiment Royal-Liègeois," in Leconte, 175–178. Soon after the regiment arrived at Bitche and after receiving notice of the order for their transportation to Paris for trial, La Tour and Grunstein fled across the border to the Principality of Deux-Ponts thereby avoiding prosecution and a possible death sentence. Both men served in émigré units during the wars of the revolution and Grunstein was later arrested as a companion of the Duc d'Euigen in 1804. In 1814 after the fall of the First Empire La Tour returned to France seeking compensation. He succeeded in obtaining the cross of the newly restored Royal and Military Order of Saint-Louis and in March of 1815 a pension of 4000 francs. In 1816 he was named an honorary brigadier général. La Tour died at Chambrey in 1822.
74. William Short to Jefferson, 3 October 1790, *The Papers of Thomas Jefferson*, Vol. 17, 558.
75. William Short to Jefferson, 21 October

1790, *ibid.*, 616; see also David Humphreys to Jefferson, 20 October 1790, *ibid.*, 603.
76. G. Morris, *Diary*, 26 January 1791, Davenport, Vol. II, 108.
77. G. Morris, *Diary*, 21 January 1791, Davenport, Vol. II, 103. See also Montmorin to William Short, 24 January 1791, *Papers of Alexander Hamilton*, 176.
78. en.wikipedia.org/wiki/Elenor-François-Elie_comte_de_Moustier.
79. Jefferson on de Moustier, P.L. Ford, *The Works of Thomas Jefferson*, Vol. 5 (New York, 1905), 257.
80. Madison to Jefferson, 8 Dec. 1788, Boyd, *The Papers of Thomas Jefferson*, Vol. XIV, 340–341; Stephen Decatur, Jr., *The Private Affairs of George Washington* (Boston, 1933), 18.
81. For comte de Caraman see fr.wiki pedia.org; for Flahaut see Morris's *Diary*, 12 November 1789, Davenport, Vol. I, 298.
82. John Beverley Riggs, *A Guide to the Manuscripts in the Eleutherian Mills Historical Library, Accessions through the Year 1965* (Greenville, 1970), Chronology and biographical note, 2–10.
83. Victor Du Pont to Ternant, 15 February 1791, HML, Correspondence of Victor Du Pont 1767–1827, W3-204.
84. Marc Bouloiseau, *Bourgeoisie et Revolution; Les Du Pont de Nemours (1788–1799* (Paris, 1972), 61–69; Riggs, chronology and biographical Note on Victor Du Pont, 14–18.
85. Earl Gower to Lord Grenville, 4 March 1791, Oscar Browning, ed., *Dispatches of Earl Gower, English Ambassador at Paris from June 1790 to August 1792* (Cambridge, 1885), 69.
86. Ternant to Steuben, 8 March 1791, SP, microfilm reel #7, and Jan. 1786–Dec. 1794, #325.
87. Ternant to Washington, 8 March 1791, *The Papers of George Washington Digital Edition*, Theodore J. Crackel ed. (Rotunda, 2007).
88. Lafayette to Washington, 7 March 1791, *ibid.*
89. Lafayette to Washington, 6 June 1791, *ibid.*
90. George A. Kelly, *Victims, Authority and Terror: The Parallel Deaths of d'Orléans, Custine, Bailly and Malsherbes* (Chapel Hill, 1982), 181.
91. See Linda S. Fred and Marsha L. Frey, *"Proven Patriots": The French Diplomatic Corps, 1789–1799* (St. Andrews, 2011).
92. Sigismond Lacroix, ed., *Actes de la Commune de Paris pendant la Revolution 1789–1794* (Paris, 1894–98), Vol. 4, 210–211.
93. Ternant to Montmorin, 1 March 1792, Frederick J. Turner, ed., "Correspondence of the French Ministers to the United States, 1791–1797," *The Annual Report of the American Historical Association for the Year 1903* (Washington, D.C., 1904), 87–88. Hereafter CFM.
94. Ternant to Benjamin Walker, 24 August 1791 and 30 September 1791 Emmet Collection Manuscript Division, New York Public Library, No. 3680.
95. Masson, 48, 72.
96. G. Morris, *Diary*, 25 January 1791, Davenport, Vol. II, 107.
97. G. Morris, *Diary*, 25 March 1791, Davenport, Vol. II, 146.
98. For list of diplomatic appointments submitted by Montmorin on 27 March 1791 see Frey, *"Proven Patriots": The French Diplomatic Corps, 1789–1799*, 16–17.
99. Lord Gower to Lord Grenville, 3 June 1791, Browning, *Dispatches of Earl Gower*, 93. In 1903, the copyist who prepared the abridged transcripts of the Ministers of France to the United States from 1791 to 1797 was unable to locate Ternant's instructions. The "Memoire pour servir d'instructions au S. de Ternant, ch. De l'Ordre royal et militaire de St. Louis, Colonel commandant du Regt. Royal-liègeois, allant en Amerique en qualite de Ministre-plenipot. Du Roi pres le Congres des États-Unis" was issued on 29 May 1791 and is contained in Ministere des Affaires Étrangères, correspondence politique, États-Unis, sup. 2, 18.
100. Lafayette to Washington, 25 January 1791; Barbe-Marbois to Washington, 28 May 1791, Theodore J. Crackel, ed., *The Papers of George Washington Digital Edition* (Rotunda, 2007).
101. Victor Du Pont to Pierre Samuel Du Pont de Nemours, 14 June 1791, *Life of Eleuthere Irenee Du Pont from Contemporary Correspondence, 1778–1791*, trans. Bessie Gardiner Dupont (Newark, 1923–1928), 147.
102. Victor Du Pont to P.S. Du Pont de Nemours, 18 June 1791, *ibid.*, 149.
103. *La Favorite* was one of four corvettes of the *Fauvette* (Warbler) class constructed in the mid 1780s. Built at Bayonne, the 430-ton *La Favorite* was part of the French West Indies squadron. It was captured on 5 March 1796 off Cape Finisterre by H.M.S. *Alfred*. See Jean Michel Roche, *Dictionnaire des Batiments de la flotte de guerre Française de Colbert a nos jours*, Vol. 1, 1671–1870, 490.
104. Information on the voyage to America is taken from Victor Du Pont, "Journal de mon voyage d'Amérique, annee 1791," HML, Papers of Victor Du Pont 1767–1827, Series B, W3-3573. In his journal Du Pont mentioned the presence of a secretary of state but did not identify the individual. It is cer-

226 • Notes—Chapter VIII

tainly possible that Jefferson was among the officials that greeted Ternant, but his presence seems unlikely.

Chapter IX

1. Jean Baillou, Charles Lucet and Jacques Vimont, eds., *Les Affaires Étrangères et le corps diplomatique française*, Vol. I, *De l'Ancien Régime au Second Empire* (Paris, 1984), 305.
2. Margaret M. O'Dwyer" "Louis Guillaume Otto in America (1779–1791)," unpublished Ph.D. Diss. (Northwestern University, 1954); also Peter P. Hill, *French Perceptions of the Early American Republic, 1783–1793* (Philadelphia, 1988), 10–12.
3. Gilbert Chinard, ed., "Considerations sur la Conduite du Gouvernement americain envers la France, depuis le commencement de la Revolution jusqu'en 1797, par Louis-Guillamue Otto," *Bulletin de l'Institut Française*, No. XVI (Dec. 1943), 10–11.
4. Frederick J. Turner, ed., "Correspondence of the French Ministers to the United States, 1791–1797," *Annual Report of the American Historical Association for the Year 1903*, Vol. II (Washington, 1904), 44.
5. *Dunlap's American Daily Advertiser*, 18 August 1791.
6. Conversation with George Beckwith, Harold C. Syrett and others, ed., *The Papers of Alexander Hamilton*, Vol. IX (New York, 1965), 29.
7. Victor Dupont, Journal de mon second voyage d'Amérique, commence en juin 1791, Correspondence of Victor Du Pont (1767–1827), HML, series A, W3–3573. See also Kenneth R. Bowling, "The Federal Government and the Republican Court Move to Philadelphia, November 1780–March 1791," in Kenneth R. Bowling and Donald R. Kennon, eds., *Neither Separate Nor Equal, Congress in the 1790s* (Athens, OH, 2000), 14.
8. Henry A. Boorse, "Barralet's the Dunlap House, 1807, and Its Associates," *Pennsylvania Magazine of History and Biography*, Vol. 99, No. 2 (April 1975): 131–155. For a discussion of de Moustier's residence in New York see Margaret W. O'Dwyer, "Louis-Guillaume Otto in America," 13–14.
9. George F. Zook, "Proposals for New Commercial Treaty between France and the United States, 1778–1793," *South Atlantic Quarterly*, VIII (July 1909): 267–283.
10. Ibid.
11. Archives Parlementaire, XXVI, 710, cited in Zook, 278.
12. Memoire pour servir d'instructions au S. de Ternant, 29 May 1791, Ministere des Affaires étrangères, Correspondence politique, États-unis, sup. 2, 18.
13. Ternant to Montmorin, 9 October 1791, CFM, 57–58.
14. Ternant to Lessart, 8 April 1792, Turner, CFM, 111–112.
15. Standard account of slave insurrection and related developments in St. Domingue see C.L.R. James, *The Black Jacobins, Toussaint L'Ouverture and the San Domingo Revolution*, 1963; see also, Roger F. Kennedy, *Orders from France*.
16. See R. Darrell Meadows, "Engineering Exile: Social Networks and the French Atlantic Community 1789–1809," *French Historical Studies*, Vol. 23, No. 1 (Winter 2000): 67–102; and Allan Potofsky, "The Non-Aligned Status of French Emigres and Refugees in Philadelphia, 1793–1798," *Transatlantica* (2006): 2, Revolution, [En Ligne], Mis en ligne le 7 juillet 2006, reference du 11 juillet 2009, URL:http://Transatlantica.revues.org/document1147.html.
17. Ternant to Montmorin, 28 September 1791, CFM, 45–51.Ternant's neglect by the French government was his principal complaint. During one period he received only one letter in reply to the sixty that he had sent.
18. Ternant to President of the United States, 22 September 1791, State Department, *Notes from the French Legation, to the Department of State, 1789–1906*, vol. 1.
19. Ternant to Washington, 24 September 1791, ibid.
20. Washington to Ternant, 2 October 1791, Jared Sparks, ed., *The Writings of George Washington* (Boston, 1834–1837), vol. 10, 95.
21. Ternant to Montmorin, 24 November 1791, CFM, 76–79.
22. Jefferson to William Short, 24 November 1791, Andrew A. Lipscomb and Albert E. Bergh, eds., *The Writings of Thomas Jefferson* (Washington, D.C., 1907), vol. 7, 260–263.
23. Jefferson to Madison, March 1793, Paul L. Ford, ed., *The Works of Thomas Jefferson* (New York, 1904), vol. 6, 193.
24. Jefferson to Monroe, 5 May 1793, *ibid.*, 240.
25. Ternant to Jefferson, 21 June 1801, Barbara B. Oberg, ed., *The Papers of Thomas Jefferson* (Princeton, 2007), vol. 34, 400.
26. Ternant to Jefferson, 18 August 1803, *ibid.*, Vol. 35. Foncin first visited the United States in January 1796. He arrived from Cayenne and met with Moreau de St. Mery in Philadelphia. Kenneth Roberts and Ann M. Roberts, eds. and trans., *Moreau de St.*

Mery's American Journey 1793–1798 (Garden City, NY, 1947), 277.
27. For a study on the Washington administration's response to the crisis in Saint Domingue and Ternant's role see Tim Matthewson, *A Pro-slavery Foreign Policy: Haitian-American Relations during the Early Republic* (Westport, 2003), 19–55; see also Dorothy Twohig, ed., *The Journal of the Proceedings of the President 1793–1797* (Charlottesville, 1981), notes 17, 46.
28. Frederick A. Schminke, *Genet: The Origins of his Mission to America* (Toulouse, 1929), 45; see also Twohig, note 1, 46; also, Ternant to the Secretary of State, 8 February 1793, State Department, Notes from the French Legation to the Department of State 1789–1906.
29. Ternant to Lebrun, 13 February 1793, CFM, 170–175; Ternant to Minister of Foreign Affairs, 25 February 1793, *ibid.*, 176–179.
30. Charles R. Ritcheson, *Aftermath of Revolution: British Policy toward the United States 1783–1795* (Dallas, 1969), 277–278; Ternant to Minister of Foreign Affairs, 6 March 1793, CFM, 183–186; see also Ternant to Mayor of Harve, 25 February 1793, Ministere des Affaires Étrangères, Correspondence politique: États-Unis, Vol. 37, microfilm, reel 3, #71.
31. Tobias Lear to Washington, 9 October 1791, Theodore J. Crackel, *The Papers of George Washington* (Rotunda, 2007).
32. Ternant to Montmorin, 24 October 1791, CFM, 60–65.
33. Scott W. Berg, *Grand Avenues: The Story of the French Visionary who Designed Washington, D.C.* (New York, 2007), 188.
34. Ternant to Dumouriez, 28 July 1792, CFM, 146–147.
35. Department of State, *Notes from the French Legation to the Department of State 1789–1906*, Ternant to Secretary of State, 8 August 1792.
36. Jean-Pierre Blanchard, Journal of my Forty-Fifth Ascension and the First in America in *The First Air Voyage in America* (Philadelphia, 1943), 13, 27.
37. Francis James Dallet, "The French Benevolent Society of Philadelphia and the Bicentennial," an Address to the *Assemblee General* of the Society, 15 November 1976, printed in *Records of the American Catholic Historical Society of Philadelphia* (Philadelphia, 1977), Vol. 88, 61–68.
38. C. Perroud, ed., *J.P. Brissot: Correspondance et Papiers* (Paris, 1912), 324.
39. Department of State, *Notes from the French Legation to the Department of State, 1789–1906*, "Fiat des personnel attacher a la maison du minister-plenipotentiare de France a Philadelphie, 3 July 1792."
40. Commissioners to Minister of Foreign Affairs, 20 April 1794, CFM, 326–327.
41. C.J. Mitchell, *The French Legislative Assembly of 1791* (Leiden, 1988), 174.
42. Ternant to Dumouriez, 17 June 1792, CFM, 132–133.
43. For Dumouriez's career, his involvement in the Belgian revolution and his service as Foreign Minister see Patricia Chastain Howe, "Charles-François Dumouriez and the Revolutionizing of French Foreign Affairs in 1792," *French Historical Studies*, No. 14 (1986): 366–390 and her study *Foreign Policy and the French Revolution: Charles-François Dumouriez, Pierre LeBrun and the Belgian Plan, 1789–1793* (New York, 2008).
44. Linda S. Frey and Marsha L. Frey, *"Proven Patriots": The French Diplomatic Corps, 1789–1799* (St. Andrews, 2011), 34–49.
45. Meade Minnigerode, *Jefferson Friend of France, 1793, The Career of Edmond Charles Genet* (New York, 1928) and Schminke, *Genet: The Origins of His Mission to America.* Also Maude H. Woodfin, "Citizen Genet and His Mission," Unpublished diss. (University of Chicago, 1928).
46. Provisional Executive Council of France to Washington, 30 December 1792, Lettre de rapport de M. de Ternant, AG, Series 2Ye Dossiers d'officiers supérieurs et subalterns 1791–1847.
47. Minister of Foreign Affairs to the Minister of War, 22 December 1792, AG, Series 2Ye, Dosiers d'officiers supérieurs et subalterns 1791–1847.
48. Minister of War to Maréchal de Camp Ternant, 7 January 1792, AG, *ibid.*
49. Charles R. Ritcheson, *Aftermath of Revolution: British Policy toward the United States 1783–1795*, 277.
50. Ternant to Minister of Foreign Affairs, 28 February 1793, CFM, 180–183.
51. Ternant to Minister of Foreign Affairs, 18 April, CFM, 193–194.
52. Maude H. Woodfin, "Citizen Genet and his Mission," 227. Ternant to Jefferson, 18 May 1792, Misc. Letters, 11.
53. Ternant to P.S. Du Pont de Nemours, 15 June 1792, HML, Papers of Pierre Samuel Du Pont de Nemours, 1739–1817, W3–1025 and Ternant to P.S. Du Pont de Nemours, 10 April 1793, W2–2096.
54. Ternant to Lessart, 6 April 1792, CFM, 105–108.
55. "Regulations for the Order and Discipline of the Volunteer Army of the United States of America ... to which is added, instructions for the exercise of the light horse, never before published." The cavalry

drills may be from a previously unpublished manuscript prepared by Ternant. Library of Congress, Rare book/Special Collections Reading Room.
56. Marcel Ragon, *La Legislation sur les Émigrés 1789–1825* (Paris, 1904), 44.
57. Ternant to Marshal and Duke of Dalmata, Minister Secretary of State for War, 1815, AG, Series 2Ye, Dossiers d'officiers supérieurs et subalternes 1791–1847.
58. Deed recorded 27 February 1794 in Luzerne County Deed Book No. 6 beginning on page 170. In 1795 Lafayette's wife agreed to purchased 1,000 acres in Luzerne County on the Susquehanna for 40,000 livres payable in six years.
59. Ternant to Victor Du Pont, 20 February 1796, HML, Correspondence of Victor Du Pont 1767–1827, Series A, W3–1109.
60. City of Philadelphia, Deed book 57, 139.
61. National Archives and Records Administration Washington, D.C., Bounty Land Warrant 2241–450 issued 26 November 1796. Revolutionary War Pension Applications and Bounty Land Warrants, microfilm 804, roll 2358.
62. Figures cited in Potofsky, "The Non-Aligned Status of French Émigrés and Refugees in Philadelphia, 1793–1798," 1. See also Anne Catherine Bieri Hebert, "The Pennsylvania French in the 1790s: The Story of their Survival," Unpublished diss. (University of Texas, 1981).
63. Ternant to Victor Du Pont, 20 February 1796, HML, Correspondence of Victor Du Pont 1767–1827, Series A, W3–1109.
64. For John Nixon and his daughter Elizabeth see Charles H. Hart, "Colonel John Nixon," *Pennsylvania Magazine of History and Biography*, 1 (1877): 188–203.
65. Ternant to Josephine Du Pont, 15 January 1797, HML, Correspondence of Josephine du Pont, Series D, W3–5328.
66. Ternant to Victor Du Pont, 15 February 1798, HML, Correspondence of Victor Du Pont, 1767–1827, Series A, W3–1356.
67. U.S. census, 1800, Schedule of the second census of the United States, Vol. 5, microfilm reel 9, 88. National Archives. For Ternant's later residence at No. 7 North Street see Letombe to Jefferson, 16 June 1801, *The Papers of Thomas Jefferson*, Vol. 35, 358–359.
68. Roberts and Roberts, eds. and trans., *Moreau de St. Mery's American Journey 1793–1798*, 275.
69. Ternant to Barthelemy, 30 April 1799, Ministere des Affaires etrangers, Correspondence politique: États-Unis, vol. 42, microfilm reel 13, 24.
70. Ternant to Talleyrand, 11 December 1800, *ibid.*, vol. 42, microfilm reel 14, 436.

71. *Memoires, Correspondance et Manuscrits du Général Lafayette* (Paris, 1837–1838), Vol., 5, 162.
72. Ternant to Victor Du Pont, 30 October 1800, HML, Correspondence of Victor Du Pont 1767–1827, Series A, W3–1490.
73. Howard Brown, *Ending the French Revolution: Violence, Justice and Repression, from the Terror to Napoleon* (Charlottesville, 2006), 344–345.
74. Ambrose Saricks, *Pierre Samuel Du Pont de Nemours* (Lawrence, 1965), 281. See also Mack Thompson, "Causes and Circumstances of the Du Pont Family's Emigration," *French Historical Studies*, Vol. 6 No. 1 (Spring 1969): 59–77; and Roger G. Kennedy, *Orders from France: The American and the French in a Revolutionary World 1780–1820* (New York, 1989).
75. Archives Nationale, Ternant's Final Testament.
76. Ternant to Josephine Du Pont, 30 March 1800, HML, Correspondence of Victor Du Pont 1767–1827, Series A, W3–5350.
77. Adams, *Gouverneur Morris: An Independent Life*, 270–271.
78. Ternant to Josephine Du Pont, 19 December 1800 and Ternant to Victor Du Pont, 23 December 1800, HML, Papers of Victor Du Pont and his Wife W3–1504 and W3–1507.
79. Ternant to Pierre Samuel Du Pont de Nemours, 4 July 1801, HML, Papers of Pierre Samuel Du Pont de Nemours, W2–2628: for appointment of George Simpson see Ternant to Stephen Girard, Memorandum, 18 September 1823, American Philosophical Society.
80. Greg H. Williams, *The French Assault on American Shipping, 1793–1813* (Jefferson, NC, 2009), 124; Eric Hornberger, *The Historical Atlas of New York City: A Visual Celebration of Nearly 400 Years of New York City's History* (New York, 2005), 67; Axel Madsen, *John Jacob Astor: America's First Multimillionaire* (New York, 2001).
81. Ternant to Josephine Du Pont, 5 August 1801, HML, Correspondence of Josephine Du Pont, Series D, W3–5355.
82. *Ibid.*
83. Ternant to Victor Du Pont, 5 August 1801, HML, Correspondence of Victor Du Pont, Series A, W3–1533.

Chapter X

1. Howard G. Brown, "The Search for Stability," in Howard G. Brown, ed., *Taking Liberties: Problems of a New Order from the*

Notes—Chapter IX • 229

French Revolution to Napoleon (Manchester, 2002), 20–50; see also Howard G. Brown, *Ending the French Revolution: Violence, Justice and Repression from the Terror to Napoleon* (Charlottesville, 2006), 14–15.

2. Victor Marie du Pont, *Journey to France and Spain 1801*, Charles W. David, ed. (Port Washington, NY, 1972), note 39 and pages 50, 104.

3. Francis William Blagdon, *Paris as It Was and as It Is; or a Sketch of the French Capital...During the Years 1801–2* (London, 1815), Vol. 1, 13–15.

4. Victor Marie du Pont, *Journey to France and Spain 1801*, 25.

5. Blagdon, 19.

6. AG, Series 2Yf, dossier des pensions militaries 1801–1817, Jean Ternant, Bureau des État-Major, 3rd division, Rapport fais au Ministre le 12 Vendemiaire L'an 10 (4 October 1801).

7. Etienne Charavay, *Les Grades Militaires sous la Republic*, 9.

8. Hugh Brogan, *Alexis de Tocqueville, A Life* (New Haven, 2006), note page 240. An income of 8,000 to 10,000 francs enabled an individual to live very well.

9. Ternant to Josephine du Pont, 10 August 1802, HML, Correspondence of Josephine du Pont, Series D, W3–5363.

10. Ternant to Du Pont de Nemours, 5 November 1802, HML, Correspondence of Du Pont de Nemours 1780–1817, Series A, W2–4535.

11. Ternant to Josephine du Pont, 17 October 1801, HML, Correspondence of Josephine Du Pont, Series D, W3–5358.

12. Ternant to Josephine du Pont, 10 August 1802, *ibid.*, W3–5363.

13. Ternant to Josephine du Pont, 19 August 1803, *ibid.*, W3–5367.

14. Ternant to Josephine du Pont, 10 October 1805, *ibid.*, W3–5374.

15. Ternant to Josephine du Pont, 18 May 1807, *ibid.*, W3–5387.

16. Ternant to Josephine du Pont, 25 November 1808, *ibid.*, W3–5393. The reference to spas in Ternant's letter reveals the range of his travels. Plombieres-Les-Bains is located in the Vosges, Forges-les-Eaux, in Haute Normandie and Bourbnne-lea-Bains in Haute Marne.

17. For Lafayette's post-revolutionary career see Lloyd Kramer, *Lafayette in Two Worlds* (Chapel Hill, 1996).

18. Ternant to Victor du Pont, 15 April 1824, HML, Correspondence of Victor Dupont, Series A, W3–3372.

19. Blanchard, *Dictionnaire des Ingénieurs Militaires 1691–1791*, 233–234; see also Bodinier, *Les Officiers de l'Armée Royale*, 223.

20. AN, Minutier Central des Notaires LXXXVII, 1469, Succession et Partage de Jean Ternant.

21. Ternant to Josephine du Pont, 10 June 1809, HML, Correspondence of Josephine du Pont, Series D, W3–5396.

22. Ternant to Josephine du Pont, 14 November 1809, *ibid.*, W3–5398.

23. Ternant to Amelia du Pont, 6 September 1810, HML, Letters to Madame Amelia du Pont, Series A, Box 2, 5/A.

24. AN, Minutier Central des Notaires, Inventory of Jean Ternant' estate.

25. Ternant to Josephine du Pont, 6 September 1810, HML, Correspondence of Josephine du Pont, Series D, W3–5404.

26. AG, Series 2Yf Dossiers des pensions 1801–1817, Jean Ternant. Controle du Ministere de la guerre, No. 10,260, Pension Militaire de la Holland inscrite sur les controles des Soldes de retraite de France. The document indicates that Jean's original pension in 1786 had been for 1,000 florins. How it came to be reduced to 666.13 florins in 1811 is unknown.

27. Louis Bergeron, *L'Episode Napoleonien 1799–1815*, Vol. 1, *Aspects Interieurs* (Paris, 1972), 150–151.

28. John Thom Holdsworth and Davis R. Dewey, *The First and Second Banks of the United States* (Washington, D.C., 1910), 122.

29. Ternant to Josephine du Pont, 10 September 1811, HML, Correspondence of Josephine Du Pont, Series D, W3–5410 and 15 March 1812, W3–5413.

30. Holdsworth and Dewey, 107.

31. Ternant to George Simpson, 15 May 1814, New York Public Library, Miscellaneous Personal Name File, Emmet Collection, 170.

32. *Ibid.*

33. Ternant to Josephine du Pont, 20 May 1814, HML, Correspondence of Josephine du Pont, Series D, W3–5435.

34. Ternant to Victor du Pont, 15 May 1814, HML, Correspondence of Victor du Pont, Series A, W3–2827. See also Jacques Hillairet, *Dictionnaire Historique des Rues de Paris* (Paris, 1963), 160.

35. Philip Mansel, *Paris between Empires: Monarchy and Revolution 1814–1852* (New York, 2001), 45.

36. AG, Series 2Yf Dossier des pensions militaries 1801–1817, Jean Ternant. Demande en etablissement d'une solde de retraite de holliand, en faveur de Ternant (Jean), 5th Division, Bureau des retraites, No. 137255.

37. Gilbert T. Vincent, "Fine Arts: A collection fitting a Nation," Wendell Garrett, ed., *George Washington's Mount Vernon* (New

York, 1998), 176. Today the print hangs in the large dining room at Mount Vernon.
38. Ternant to Washington, 22 December 1791, *The Papers of George Washington Digital Edition*, ed. Theodore J. Crackel.
39. Washington to Ternant, 22 December 1791, *ibid.*
40. Ternant to Victor du Pont, 15 May 1814, HML, Correspondence of Victor du Pont, Series A, W3–2827.
41. Ternant to Josephine du Pont, 20 May 1814, Correspondence of Josephine du Pont, Series D, W3–5435, and 1 June 1814, W3–5438.
42. Ternant to Josephine du Pont, 26 May 1815, *ibid.*, W3–5452.
43. Ternant to Josephine du Pont, 15 June 1815, *ibid.*, W3–5454.
44. Edgar Leon Newman and Robert Lawrence Simpson, *Historical Dictionary of France from the 1815 Restoration to the Second Empire* (New York, 1987), 1142.
45. For a review of Victor du Pont's business interests see Roger G. Kennedy, *Orders From France: The Americans and French in a Revolutionary World, 1780–1820*, 189–195, 201–293 and 210–211; see also Chronology of Victor du Pont, 1767–1827 in John Beverly Riggs, *A Guide to the Manuscripts in the Eleutheran Mills Historical Library, Accessions through 1965* (Greenville, 1970), 14–18.
46. Ternant to Josephine du Pont, 21 April 1816, HML, Correspondence of Josephine du Pont, Series D, W3–5463.
47. Ternant to Josephine du Pont, 1 February 1822, *ibid.*, W3–5537.
48. Henry Simpson, *The Lives of Eminent Philadelphians* (Philadelphia, 1859), 890–893.
49. Donald R. Adams, *Finance and Enterprise in Early America: A Study of Stephen Girard's Bank* (Philadelphia, 1978), 4–6; see also Harry Emerson Wildes, *Lonely Midas* (New York, 1943); and relevant sections in Kennedy's *Orders from France*.
50. Ternant to Stephen Girard, 18 September 1823, Papers of Stephen Girard, American Philosophical Society.
51. Memorandum from Ternant to Girard attached to the above.
52. Ternant to George Simpson, 15 May 1814, New York Public Library, Miscellaneous personal name file, Emmet Collection, N. 170.
53. Barthelemy Laporte to Stephen Girard, 1 April 1824, HML, Box 22, W3–3965.
54. Land Title, Jean Ternant to Angelica Elizabeth du Pont, 1 July 1824, Deed Records, Bradford County, Pennsylvania, Vol. 5, 456–460
55. Ternant to Stephen Girard, 1 March 1824, Papers of Stephen Girard, American Philosophical Society.
56. Ternant to Stephen Girard, 28 March 1825, *ibid.*
57. Françoise Watel, *Jean-Guillaum Hyde de Neuville (1776–1857) Conspirateur et Diplomate* (Paris, 1987), 81.
58. James K. Kieswetter, "Hyde de Neuville, Jean Guillaume, Baron," Neuman and Simpson, *Historical Dictionary of France from the 1815 Restoration to the Second Empire*, 503–504.
59. Testament of Jean Ternant, 19 November 1833, AN, LXXXVII, 1468.
60. Ternant to Josephine du Pont, 20 May 1826, HML, Correspondence of Josephine du Pont, Series D, W3–5559.
61. Bernard Rouleau, *Memoires et Documents: Le Trace des Rues de Paris, Formation, Typologie, Fonctions* (Paris, 1967), 95–97.
62. Lucien de Chardon, *Damvillers et son cantons: Vingt siècles d'histoire*, 170.
63. Testament of Jean Ternant.
64. AN, Minutier Central des Notaires, LXXXVII, 1469, Succession & Partage de Jean Ternant; Archives de Paris, Prefecture du Department de la Seine, Ville de Paris, Extract du register des Actes de Deces de l'An 1833, 695.
65. See Pierre Chaunu, La Mort a Paris: XXVIIe et XXVIIIe siècles, Paris, 1978.
66. For the military careers of Jean-Antoine Gillant and Jacques-Louis Lamacq see AN, Base Leonore, dossier LH-1133/74 and dossier LH 1453/8.
67. Conveyance book 1835–1836, Civil records, Pointe Coupee Clerk of Courts cited in Costello, *From Ternant to Parlange*, 2.
68. Testament of Jean Ternant.

Bibliography

Archival and Manuscript Sources

American Philosophical Society, Philadelphia. Correspondence and Papers of Stephen Girard.
Archives de la Guerre (AG)
 Series 2Ye Dossiers d'officiers supérieurs et subalterns, 1791–1847—Jean de Ternant.
 Series 2Yf Dossiers de pensions militaries, 1801–1817—Jean de Temant.
Archives départementales de la Gironde
 Registres de l'amiraute de Guyenne, sous-series 6 B 109, Sousmissions des captaines, 1775–1777.
 Sous-series 6B 55,Certificate d'identité et de catholique, 1774–1777.
Archives départementales de la Meuse, Bar-le-Duc (ADM)
 Series 2E, Registres paroissiaux et d'État civil, 1759–1791.
 Series C, Administrations provincials.
Archives de Paris
 Actes d'État civil, reconstitution.
 Declarations de Deces, DQ7 3557 Jean Ternant.
 Declarations de Successions, DQ8 619 Jean Ternant.
Archives Nationales de France (AN)
 Minutier Central des Notaires, Inventory of Jean Ternant's estate.
 Base Leonore.
Hagley Museum and Library (HML)
 Longwood Manuscripts. Series A. Correspondence of Du Pont de Nemours, 1780–1817.
 Papers of Pierre Samual Du Pont de Nemours, 1739–1817.
 Winterthur Manuscripts. Personal papers of Victor Du Pont, Series B, W3–3573. Journal de mon voyage d'Amérique, June–Nov. 1791.
 Winterthur Manuscripts. Correspondence of Victor Du Pont. Series A, W3. Letters from Jean Ternant, 1792–1824. Letters to Jean Ternant, 1791–1814.
 Correspondence of Gabrielle Josephine, wife of Victor Du Pont. Series D, W3 Letters from Jean Ternant, 1797–1826.
 Betsey Nixon Letters.
 Papers of Amelia Elizabeth Du Pont. Series A.
Library of Congress (Manuscript Division) Washington, D.C.
 Affaires Etrangères, Correspondence politique, États-unis.
Maclure Collection of French Revolutionary Materials (University of Pennsylvania). Vol. 832.
Massachusetts Historical Society, Boston. Benjamin Lincoln Papers.

232 • Bibliography

National Archives and Records Administration, Washington, D.C.
  Revolutionary War Pension Applications and Bounty-Land Warrant Application Files.
  Papers of the Continental Congress.
  Records of the Department of State (RG59), Notes from the French Legation in the United States to the Department of State, 1789–1906.
  U.S. Census, 1800.
  War Department Records (RG93), Oaths of Allegiance and Fidelity, 1778.
New York Public Library
  Benjamin Lincoln papers, Thomas Addis Emmet Collection.
  Miscellaneous Personal Names File.
Pennsylvania Land-Title Records
  Bradford County, Deed Book No. 5.
  Luzerne County, Deed Book No. 6.
  City of Philadelphia, Deed Book No. 57.
William L. Clements Library (University of Michigan)
  Henry Clinton Papers.
  Nathanael Greene Papers.
  Josiah Harmar Papers.

Published Primary Sources

Actes de la Commune de Paris pendant la Revolution, 1789–1794. Sigismond Lacrois, Ed. 7 Vols. Paris: L. Cerf, 1894–98.
Blagdon, Francis William. *Paris As It Was and As It Is; or a Sketch of the French Capital during the Years 1801–02.* 2 Vols. London: C and R Baldwin, 1803.
Blanchard, Jean-Pierre. "Journal of My Forty-Fifth Ascension, Being the First Performed in America, on the Ninth of January 1793." In *The First Air Voyage in America.* Philadelphia: The Penn Mutual Life Insurance Company, 1943.
Bouille, François-Claude Amour, Marquis de. *Memoires Relating to the French Revolution.* London: Cadell and Davies, 1797.
Brissot, J.P. *Correspondence et Papiers.* C. Perroud. Paris: A. Picard & Fils, 1912.
Chastellux, Marquis de. *Travels in North America in the Years 1780, 1781 and 1782.* Edited and translated by Howard C. Rice Jr. 2 Vols. Chapel Hill: University of North Carolina Press, 1963.
Dunlap's American Daily Advertiser, Philadelphia (1791–1793).
Duponceau, P.E. *Diary: Sojourn at Camp Valley Forge, 24 Feb.–25 April 1778.* Delaware Historical Society.
DuPont, Bessie Gardner, ed. *Life of Eleuthere Irenee Du Pont from Contemporary Correspondence, 1778–1791.* Newark: University of Delaware Press, 1923–28. Microfilm.
Du Pont, Victor Marie. *Journey to France and Spain 1801.* Edited by Charles W. David. Port Washington: Kennikat Press, 1972.
Ewald, Johann, Captain. *Diary of the American War.* Edited and trans. by Joseph P. Tustin. New Haven: Yale University Press, 1979.
Franklin, Benjamin. *The Papers of Benjamin Franklin.* Edited by William B. Wilcox et al. 18 Vols. New Haven: Yale University Press, 1959–.
Gadsden, Christopher. *The Writings of Christopher Gadsden, 1746–1805.* Edited by Richard Walsh. Columbia: University of South Carolina Press, 1966.
Gower, Earl. *The Dispatches of Earl Gower, English Ambassador at Paris from June 1790 to August 1792.* Edited by Oscar Browning. Cambridge: Cambridge University Press, 1885.
Greene, Nathanael. *The Papers of General Nathanael Greene.* Edited by Denis Conrad and Roger Parks. 13 Vols. Chapel Hill: University of North Carolina Press, 1976–.
Hamilton, Alexander. *The Papers of Alexander Hamilton.* Edited by Harold Syrett et al. 27 Vols. New York: Columbia University Press, 1961–1987.

Huth, Hans, and Wilma J. Pugh, eds. and trans. *Talleyrand in America as a Financial Promoter 1794–96*. Vol. II. Washington, D.C.: United States Government Printing Office, 1942.
Jefferson, Thomas. *The Papers of Thomas Jefferson*. Edited by Julian Boyd et al. Princeton: Princeton University Press, 1950–.
Jefferson, Thomas. *The Papers of Thomas Jefferson Digital Edition*. Edited by Barbara B. Oberg and J. Jefferson Looney. Charlottesville: University of Virginia Press, Rotunda, 2008–2015.
Jefferson, Thomas. *The Works of Thomas Jefferson*. Edited by Paul L. Ford. 12 Vols. New York: G.P. Putnam's Sons, 1904–05.
Jefferson, Thomas. *The Writings of Thomas Jefferson 1767–1827*. Edited by Albert E. Bergh and Andrew A. Lipscomb. 20 Vols. Washington, D.C.: Thomas Jefferson Memorial Association of the United States, 1907.
Lafayette, Marie-Paul-Joseph-Roch-Ives-Gilbert de Motier, marquis de. *Lafayette in the Age of the American Revolution: Selected Letters and Papers, 1776–1790*. Edited by Stanley J. Idzerda et al. 5 Vols. Ithaca: Cornell University Press, 1979–1983.
Lafayette, Marie-Paul-Joseph-Roch-Ives-Gilbert de Motier, marquis de. *Memoires, Correspondance et manuscripts du général LaFayette, publies par sa famille*. 6 Vols. Paris: H. Fournier Aine, 1838–39.
La Tour-du-Pin Governnet, Henriette Lucie Dillon, marquise de. *Memoirs of Madame de La Tour du Pin*. Edited and trans. by Felice Harcourt. New York: McCall, 1971.
Laurens, Henry. *The Papers of Henry Laurens*. Edited by Philip M. Hamer et al. 16 Vols. Columbia: University of South Carolina Press, 1968–.
Laurens, John. *The Army Correspondence of Colonel John Laurens in the Years 1777–8*. New York: Arno Press, 1969.
Marat, Jean-Paul. *L'Amie du Peuple*. Society for Reproduction of Rare Books, 1967.
Morris, Gouverneur. *The Diary and Letters of Gouverneur Morris*. Edited by Anne Cary Morris. 2 Vols. New York: Scribner's, 1888.
Morris, Gouverneur. *A Diary of the French Revolution*. Edited by Beatrix Cary Davenport. 2 Vols. Boston: Houghton Mifflin, 1939.
Morris, Robert. *The Papers of Robert Morris, 1781–1784*. Edited by E.J. Ferguson. 9 Vols. Pittsburgh: University of Pittsburgh Press, 1973–1988.
Order Book of John Faucheraud Grimke, Aug. 1778 to May 1780. Edited by Mable Louise Webber. *The South Carolina Historical and Genealogical Magazine*, 13 (1912).
Otto, Louis Guillaume. *Considerations sur la conduire du government American envers la Française, depuis le commencement de la Revolution jusqu'en 1797*. Edited by Gilbert Chinard. Princeton: Princeton University Press, 1945.
Pennsylvania Archives. Edited by Thomas Lynch Montgomery. Harrisburg Publishing Co., 1906.
Proceedings of a Court Martial Held at Philadelphia... for the Trial of Major General Howe, December 7, 1781. Philadelphia: Hall & Sellers, 1782.
Report on American Manuscripts in the Royal Institutions of Great Britain. Edited by H.J. Brown. 4 Vols. Boston: Gregg Press, 1972.
Roussel, M. de. *État Militaire de France pour l'annee 1789*. Paris: Chez Onfroy, 1789.
Sinclair, John. *Correspondence of the Right Honorable Sir John Sinclair, Bart*. 2 Vols. London: H. Colburn & R. Bentley, 1831.
Smith, Paul H., et al., eds. *Letters of Delegates to Congress, 1774–1789*. 26 Vols. Washington, D.C.: Library of Congress, 1976–2000.
Steuben, Friedrich Wilhelm von. *Baron von Steuben's Revolutionary War Drill Manual*, 1794. Reprint, New York: Dover, 1985.
Steuben, Friedrich Wilhelm von. *The Papers of General Friedrich Wilhelm von Steuben, 1777–1794*. Edited by Edith Von Zemenszky. Millwood, NY: Kraus International Publishing, 1976–1984. Microfilm. 7 rolls.
Taliaferro, Benjamin. *The Orderly Book of Captain Benjamin Taliaferro*. Edited by Lee A. Wallace. Richmond: Virginia State Library, 1980.
Tuffin, Armand-Charles. *Letters of Col. Armand (Marquis de la Rourerie) 1779–1792*.

234 • Bibliography

Revolutionary Papers, Vol. 1. Collections of the New York Historical Society for 1878, New York, 1879.
Turner, Frederick Jackson, ed. "Correspondence of the French Ministers to the United States, 1791–1797." *The Annual Report of the American Historical Association for the Year 1903*. Vol. II. Washington, D.C.: Government Printing Office, 1904.
Uhlendorf, Bernhard A., ed. and trans. *The Siege of Charleston*. Ann Arbor: University of Michigan Press, 1938.
Washington, George. *The Diaries of George Washington*. Edited by Donald Jackson and Dorothy Twohig. 6 Vols. Charlottesville: University Press of Virginia, 1976–1979.
Washington, George. *The George Washington Papers at the Library of Congress, 1741–1799*. Manuscript Division.
Washington, George. *The Papers of George Washington Digital Edition*. Edited by Theodore J. Crackel. Charlottesville: University of Virginia Press, Rotunda, 2002.
Washington, George. *The Papers of George Washington: Presidential Series*. Edited by W.W. Abbot, Dorothy Twohig and Philander Chase. 11 Vols. Charlottesville: University Press of Virginia, 1981.
Washington, George. *The Writings of George Washington*. Edited by Jared Sparks. 10 Vols. Boston, 1834–1837.
Washington, George. *The Writings of George Washington from the Original Manuscripts, 1746–1799*. Edited by J.C. Fitzpatrick. 39 Vols. Washington, D.C.: U.S. Government Printing Office, 1931–1944.

Secondary Sources: Books

Adams, Donald R., Jr. *Finance and Enterprise in Early America: A Study of Stephen Girard's Bank 1812–1831*. Philadelphia: University of Pennsylvania Press, 1978.
Adams, William Howard. *Gouverneur Morris: An Independent Life*. New Haven: Yale University Press, 2003.
Adams, William Howard. *The Paris Years of Thomas Jefferson*. New Haven: Yale University Press, 1997.
Alder, Ken. *Engineering the Revolution: Arms and Enlightenment in France 1763–1815*. Princeton: Princeton University Press, 1997.
Alexander, Samuel Davies. *Princeton College during the Eighteenth Century*. New York: A.D.F. Randolph, 1872.
Allen, Rodney. *Threshold of Terror: The Last Hours of the Monarchy in the French Revolution*. Sparkford: J.H. Haynes & Co., 1999.
Apt, Leon. *Louis-Philippe de Segur, an Intellectual in a Revolutionary Age*. The Hague: Martinus Nijhoff, 1969.
Aries, Philippe. *L'Enfant et la vie familiale sous l'ancien régime*. Trans. by Robert Baldick. New York: Alfred A. Knopf, 1962.
Augur, Helen. *The Secret War of American Independence*. Boston: Little Brown, 1955.
Baillou, Jean, et al. *Les Affaires Étrangères et le Corps Diplomatique Française*. Vol 1. De l'Ancien Régime au Second Empire. Paris: Editions du Centre National de la Recherche Scientifique, 1984.
Barrie, George. *The Army and Navy of the United States from the Revolution to the Present Day*. Boston: William Walton, 1889–1895.
Beales, Derek. *Joseph II in the Shadow of Maria Theresa 1741–1780*. London: Cambridge University Press, 1987.
Belhomme, Victor L. *Histoire de Infantrie en France*. Vol. III, Paris: Charles Lavauzelle, 1893–1905.
Bennett, Charles E., and Donald R. Lennon. *A Quest for Glory: Major General Robert Howe and the American Revolution*. Chapel Hill: University of North Carolina Press, 1991.
Berg, Scott W. *Grand Avenues: The Story of the French Visionary Who Designed Washington, D.C.* New York: Pantheon Books, 2007.

Bergeron, Louis. *L'Episode Napoleonien 1799–1815*. Vol. 1 *Aspects Interieurs*. Paris: Editions du Sevil, 1972.
Beriot, Charles. *La Revolte de la Garnison de Nancy en 1790*. Nancy: Bailly & Wettstein, 1943.
Bertier de Sauvigny, Guillaume de. *Nouvelle Histoire de Paris: La Restauration 1815–1830*. Paris: Hachette, 1977.
Biographie Nouvelles des Contemporains. 20 Vols. Paris: Librarie Historique, 1820–1825.
Biro, Sydney Seymour. *The German Policy of Revolutionary France*. 2 vols. Cambridge: Harvard University Press, 1957.
Blanc, Olivier. *Last Letters: Prisons and Prisoners of the French Revolution 1793–1794*. Trans. by Alan Sheridan. New York: Farrar, Straus and Giroux, 1987.
Blanchard, Anne. *Dictionnaire des Ingénieurs Militaires 1691–1791*. Montpellier: 1981.
Blanchard, Anne. *Les Ingénieurs du Roy de Louis XIV a Louis XVI: Etude du Corps des Fortifications*. Montpellier: Centre d'histoire militaire d'etudes de defense nationale, Universite Paul Valery, 1979.
Blaufarb, Rafe. *The French Army 1750–1820: Careers, Talent, Merit*. New York: Manchester University Press, 2002.
Bodinier, Gilbert. *Dictionnaire des Officers de l'armée royal qui ont Combattu aux États-Unis pendant la Guerre d'independence 1776–1783*. Vincennes: Archives de Guerre, 2005.
Bodinier, Gilbert. *Le Officiers de l'Armée Royale, combatants de la guerre d'independence des États-Unis de Yorktown a l'an II*. Vincennes: Archives de Guerre, 1983.
Bodle, Wayne. *The Valley Forge Winter: Civilians and Soldiers in War*. University Park: Pennsylvania State University Press, 2002.
Bodle, Wayne, and Jacqueline Thibaud. *Valley Forge Historical Research Project*. 3 Vols. Valley Forge, PA: U.S. Dept. of the Interior, National Park Service, 1980.
Borick, Carl P. *A Gallant Defense: The Siege of Charleston 1780*. Columbia: University of South Carolina Press, 2003.
Bouloiseau, Marc. *Bourgeoisie et Revolution: Les Du Pont de Nemours 1788–1799*. Paris: Biblotheque Nationale, 1972.
Bowling, Kenneth R. "The Federal Government and the Republican Court Move to Philadelphia, November 1790–March 1791." In *Neither Separate nor Equal: Congress in the 1790s*, edited by Kenneth R. Bowling and Donald R. Kennon. Athens: Ohio University Press, 2000.
Bowling, Kenneth R. *Peter Charles L'Enfant: Vision, Honor and Male Friendship*. Washington, D.C.: Printed for the Friends of George Washington Libraries, 2002.
Boyle, Joseph Lee. *Writings from the Valley Forge Encampment of the Continental Army*. 5 Vols. Bowie, MD: Heritage Books, 2003.
Brandt, Clare. *The Man in the Mirror: A Life of Benedict Arnold*. New York: Random House, 1994.
Brennan, Thomas. *Public Drinking and Popular Culture in Eighteenth-Century Paris*. Princeton: Princeton University Press, 1988.
Brogan, Hugh. *Alexis de Tocqueville: A Life*. New Haven: Yale University Press, 2006.
Brooke, John. *George III*. London: Constable & Company, 1972.
Brown, Howard G. *Ending the French Revolution: Violence, Justice and Repression from the Terror to Napoleon*. Charlottesville: University of Virginia Press, 2006.
Brown, Howard G. "The Search for Stability." In *Taking Liberties: Problems of a New Order from the French Revolution to Napoleon*, edited by Howard G. Brown and Judith A. Miller. Manchester: Manchester University Press, 2002.
Bruckman, Peter. *Lafayette: A Biography*. New York: Paddington Press, 1977.
Budka, Metchie J. E. *Autograph Letters of Thaddeus Kosciuszko in the American Revolution*. Chicago: The Polish Museum of America, 1977.
Butel, Paul. *Les Negociants Bordelais: l'Europe et les Îles au XVIII Siècle*. Paris: Auber, 1974.
Caemmerer, H. Paul. *The Life of Pierre Charles l'Enfant, Planner of the City Beautiful, the City of Washington*. Washington, D.C.: National Republic Publishing Co., 1950.

Carp, E. Wayne. *To Starve the Army: Continental Army Administration and American Political Culture, 1775–1783*. Chapel Hill: University of North Carolina Press, 1984.
Caughey, John Walton. *Bernardo De Galvez in Louisiana 1776–1783*. Berkley: University of California Press, 1934.
Cavignac, Jean. *Jean Pellet commerciant de gros 1694–1772*. Paris: S.E.V.P.E.N., 1967.
Censer, Jack R. *Prelude to Power: The Partisan Radical Press 1789–1791*. Baltimore: Johns Hopkins University Press, 1976.
Chardon, Lucien de. *Damvillers et son Canton: Vingt Siècles d'Histoire*. Verdun: Cogerex, 1972.
Chaunu, Pierre. *La Mort a Paris: XVIIe et XVIIIe siècles*. Paris: Fayard, 1978.
Chavaray, Etienne. *Les Grades Militaries sous la Revolution Française*. Paris: Société de L'Histoire de la Revolution Française, 1894.
Chisick, Harvey. *The Production, Distribution and Readership of a Conservative Journal in the Early French Revolution, The Ami du Roi of the Abbe Royou*. Philadelphia: American Philosophical Society, 1992.
Choppin, Henri. *Insurrections Militaires en 1790*. Paris: Librairie J. Rothschild, 1910.
Chorley, Katherine. *Armies and the Art of Revolution*. London: Faber and Faber, 1943.
Church, Clive H. *Revolution and Red Tape: The French Ministerial Bureaucracy 1779–1850*. Oxford: Clarendon Press, 1981.
Clarke, T. Wood. *Émigrés in the Wilderness*. New York: Macmillan, 1941.
Clary, David A., and Joseph W.A. Whitehorne. *The Inspectors-General of the United States Army, 1777–1903*. Washington, D.C.: Office of the Inspector General and Center of Military History, U.S. Army, 1987.
Cobban, Alfred. *Ambassadors and Secret Agents*. London: Jonathan Cape, 1954.
Colenbrander, H.T. *De Patriottentjid*. 3 vols. s'Gravenhage: M. Nijhoff, 1897–99.
Contenson, Ludovic, baron de. *La Société des Cincinnati de France et la Guerre d'Amérique 1778–1783*. Paris: Auguste Picard, 1934.
Cooling, Benjamin F. "The Militant Dr. Franklin." In *Soldier-Statesmen of the Enlightenment, International Colloquy on Military History* Age, edited by Abigail T. Siddall. Manhattan, KS: Sunflower Press, 1984.
Cormack, William S. *Revolution and Political Conflict in the French Navy, 1789–1794*. New York: Cambridge University Press, 1995.
Costello, Brian. *From Ternant to Parlange: A Creole Plantation through Seven Generations*. Baton Rouge: Franklin Press, 2002.
Cox, Caroline. *A Proper Sense of Honor: Service and Sacrifice in George Washington's Army*. Chapel Hill: University of North Carolina Press, 2004.
Crowdy, T.E. *French Revolutionary Infantry Uniforms 1789–1802*. Oxford: Osprey Publishing, 2004.
Crowdy, T.E. *Incomparable: Napoleon's 9th Light Infantry Regiment*. Oxford: Osprey Publishing, 2012.
Cummins, Light Townsend. *Spanish Observers and the American Revolution, 1775–1783*. Baton Rouge: Louisiana State University Press, 1991.
Darnton, Robert. *George Washington's False Teeth: An Unconventional Guide to the Eighteenth Century*. New York: W.W. Norton, 2003.
Davis, Joseph Stancliff. *Essays in the Earlier History of American Corporations*. New York: Russell & Russell, 1917; reprint, 1965.
Decatur, Stephen, Jr. *The Private Affairs of George Washington from the Records of Tobias Lear Esquire, His Secretary*. Boston: Houghton Mifflin, 1933.
DeConde, Alexander. *Entangling Alliances: Politics & Diplomacy under George Washington*. Durham: Duke University Press, 1958.
Doyle, Alfred. *A Hundred Years of Conflict: Being Some Records of the Service of Six Generals of the Doyle Family*. London, 1911.
Doyle, William. *Officers, Nobles and Revolutionaries: Essays on Eighteenth-Century France*. London: The Hambledon Press, 1995.
Drake, Francis Samuel. *Dictionary of American Biography*. Boston: Houghton, Osgood and Company, 1872.

Duffy, Christopher. *The Army of Frederick the Great*, second edition. Chicago: The Emperor's Press, 1996.
Duffy, Christopher. *The Fortress in the Age of Vauban and Frederick the Great, 1660–1789.* Boston: Routledge & Kegan Paul, 1985.
Duffy, Christopher. *Siege Warfare: The Fortress in the Early Modern World, 1494–1660.* New York: Barnes & Noble, 1979.
Dull, Jonathan R. *The French Navy and the Seven Years' War.* Lincoln: University of Nebraska Press, 2005.
Dumas, Guillaume-Mathieu. *Memoirs of His Own Time.* 2 Vols. Philadelphia: Lea & Blanchard, 1839.
Dziewanowski, M.K. "Tadeusz Kosciuszko and Kazimierz Pulaski and the American War of Independence: A Study in National Symbolism and Mythology." In *The American and European Revolutions, 1776–1848: Sociopolitical and Ideological Aspects*, edited by Jaroslaw Pelenski. Iowa City: University of Iowa Press, 1980.
Echeverria, Durand. *Mirage in the West: A History of the French Image of American Society to 1815.* Princeton: Princeton University Press, 1957.
Edgar, Walter. *Partisans and Redcoats: The Southern Campaign that Turned the Tide in the American Revolution.* New York: Morrow, 2001.
Egret, Jean. *The French Prerevolution, 1787–1788.* Trans. by Wesley D. Camp. Chicago: University of Chicago Press, 1977.
Ellery, Eloise. *Brissot de Warville: A Study in the History of the French Revolution.* Boston: Houghton Mifflin, 1915.
Fanelli, Doris Devine. *History of the Portrait Collection Independence National Historical Park and Catalog of the Collection.* Edited by Karie Diethorn. Philadelphia: American Philosophical Society, 2002.
Fay, Bernard. *The Revolutionary Spirit in France and America.* Trans. by Ramon Guthrie. New York: Cooper Square Publishers, 1966.
Fischer, David Hackett. *Champlain's Dream.* New York: Simon & Schuster, 2008.
Fredricksen, John C. *Revolutionary War Almanac.* New York, 2006.
Freedeman, Charles E. *Joint-Stock Enterprise in France 1807–1867.* Chapel Hill: University of North Carolina Press, 1979.
Frey, Linda, and Marsha Frey. *"Proven Patriots": The French Diplomatic Corps, 1789–1799.* Saint Andrews: Center for French History and Culture at the University of Saint Andrews, 2011.
Funcken, Liliane, and Fred Funcken. *The Lace Wars.* 2 Vols. London: Ward Lock Limited, 1977.
Furet, François, and Mona Ozouf, eds. *A Critical Dictionary of the French Revolution.* Trans. by Arthur Goldhammer. Cambridge: Harvard University Press, 1989.
Galvin, John R. *The Minute Men, The First Fight: Myths and Realities of the American Revolution.* Washington, D.C.: Pergamon-Brassey's International Defense Publisher, 1989.
Gardiner, Asa Bird. *The Order of the Cincinnati in France.* The Rhode Island State Society of the Cincinnati, 1905.
Garrioch, David. *The Making of Revolutionary Paris.* Berkeley: University of California Press, 2002.
Geggus, David. "The Major Port Towns of Saint Domingue in the Later Eighteenth Century." In *Atlantic Port Cities: Economy, Culture and Society in the Atlantic World*, edited by Franklin W. Knight and Peggy K. Liss. Knoxville: University of Tennessee Press, 1991.
Gelis, Jacques, Mireille Laget, and Marie Morel. *Entrer dans la Vie: Naissances et enfances dans la France Traditionelle.* Paris, 1978.
Giteau, Françoise, et al., eds. *Reperotire Numerique du fonds des Negociants.* Bordeaux: Archives Départementales, 1979.
Gottschalk, Louis. *Lafayette between the American and French Revolutions, 1783–1789.* Chicago: University of Chicago Press, 1950.
Gottschalk, Louis. *Lafayette Comes to America.* Chicago: University of Chicago Press, 1935.

Gottschalk, Louis. *Lafayette Joins the American Army.* Chicago: University of Chicago Press, 1937.
Gottschalk, Louis. *The Letters of Lafayette to Washington, 1777–1799.* Philadelphia: American Philosophical Society, 1944.
Gottschalk, Louis, and Margaret Maddox. *Lafayette in the French Revolution: From the October Days through the Federation.* Chicago: University of Chicago Press, 1973.
Hampson, Norman. *Prelude to Terror: The Constituent Assembly and the Failure of Consensus 1789–1791.* Oxford: Basil Blackwell, 1988.
Hankinson, Alan. "'His Outspokenness'—Macdonald." In *Napoleon's Marshals* edited by David G. Chandler. New York: Macmillan, 1987.
Hardman, John. *Louis XVI.* New Haven: Yale University Press, 1993.
Harsanyi, Doina Pasca. *Lessons from America: Liberal French Nobles in Exile, 1793–1798.* University Park: The Pennsylvania State University Press, 2010.
Hartmann, Louis. *Les Officiers de L'armée Royale et la Revolution.* Paris: Librairies Felix Alcan et Guillaumin Reunies, 1910.
Hatch, Robert McConnell. *Major John Andre: A Gallant in Spy's Clothing.* Boston: Houghton Mifflin, 1986.
Hill, Peter P. *French Perceptions of the Early American Republic, 1783–1793.* Philadelphia: American Philosophical Society, 1988.
Hillairet, Jacques. *Dictionnaire Historique des Rues de Paris.* 2 Vols. Paris: Edition de Minuit, 1963.
Historic American Building Survey: Fort McHenry, HABS No. MD-63.
Holdsworth, John Thom, and David R. Dewey. *The First and Second Banks of the United States.* Washington, D.C.: Government Printing Office, 1910.
Homberger, Eric. *The Historical Atlas of New York City: A Visual Celebration of Nearly 400 Years of New York City's History.* New York: Henry Holt, 2005.
Hoof, Joep van. *Military Uniforms in the Netherlands, 1752–1800.* Vienna: Verlag Militaria, 2011.
Hopkin, David M. *Soldier and Peasant in French Popular Culture 1766–1870.* Rochester, NY: Boydell Press, 2003.
Hough, Franklin B. *The Siege of Charleston.* Spartanburg: The Reprint Company, 1975.
Howe, Patricia Chastain. *Foreign Policy and the French Revolution: Charles-François Dumouriez, Pierre LeBrun and the Belgian Plan, 1789–1793.* New York: Macmillan, 2008.
Hudson, Ruth Strong. "Conrad-Alexandre Gerard and the Coming of the French Revolution to Alsace." In *Bourgeois, Sans-culottes and Other Frenchmen: Essays on the French Revolution in Honor of John Hall Stewart,* edited by Morris Slavin and Agnes Smith. Waterloo, Ontario, Canada: Wilfrid Laurier University Press, 1981.
Jackson, John W. *With the British Army in Philadelphia, 1777–1778.* San Rafael, CA: Presidio Press, 1979.
Jacob, Margaret C., and Wijnard W. Mijnhardt. *The Dutch Republic in the Eighteenth Century: Decline, Enlightenment and Revolution.* Ithaca: Cornell University Press, 1992.
James, C.L.R. *The Black Jacobins: Toussaint L'Ouverture and the San Domingo Revolution.* New York: The Dial Press, 1938.
Jeantin, M. *Manuel de la Meuse Histoire de Momtmedy et les localites Meusiennes de l'Ancien Comte de Chiny.* Nancy: Veuve Raybois, 1861.
Jones, Colin. *The Great Nation: France from Louis XIV to Napoleon, 1715–99.* New York: Columbia University Press, 2002.
Kapp, Frederick. *The Life of Frederick William von Steuben.* New York: Mason Brothers, 1859.
Kelly, George A. *Victims, Authority and Terror: The Parallel Deaths of d'Orléans, Custine, Bailly and Malsherbes.* Chapel Hill: University of North Carolina Press, 1982.
Kelly, Joseph J., Jr. *Life and Times in Colonial Philadelphia.* Harrisburg: The Stackpole Company, 1973.
Kennedy, Melvin D. *Lafayette and Slavery from His Letters to Thomas Clarkson and Granville Sharp.* Easton: The American Friends of Lafayette, 1950.

Kennedy, Roger G. *Orders from France: The Americans and the French in a Revolutionary World, 1780–1820*. New York: Alfred A. Knopf, 1989.
Kennett, Lee. *The French Forces in America, 1780–1783*. Westport, CT: Greenwood, 1977.
Kinnaird, Lawrence, ed. "Spain in the Mississippi Valley 1765–1794." Vol. I, *Annual Report of the American Historical Association for the Year 1945*. Washington, D.C.: U.S. Government Printing Office, 1949.
Kirkland, Frederic R. *Letters on the American Revolution in the Library at "Karolfred."* 2 Vols. Philadelphia: Private Printing, 1941.
Kite, Elizabeth S. *Brigadier-General Louis Lebegue Duportail, Commandant of Engineers in the Continental Army, 1777–1783*. Baltimore: Johns Hopkins University Press, 1933.
Kohn, Richard H. *Eagle and Sword: The Federalists and the Creation of the Military Establishment in America, 1783–1802*. New York: Macmillan, 1975.
Kramer, Lloyd. *Lafayette in Two Worlds: Public Cultures and Personal Identities in an Age of Revolutions*. Chapel Hill: University of North Carolina Press, 1996.
Kuethe, Allan J. *Cuba, 1752–1815: Crown, Military and Society*. Knoxville: University of Tennessee Press, 1986.
Kuethe, Allan J. "Havana in the Eighteenth Century." In *Atlantic Port Cities: Economy, Culture and Society*, edited by Franklin W. Knight and Peggy K. Liss. Knoxville: University of Tennessee Press, 1991.
Kund, J.V. Jespersen. "Claude-Louis, Comte de Saint-Germain (1707–1778). Soldier-Statesmen of the Age of Enlightenment." *International Colloquy of Military History*, edited by Abigail T. Siddall. Manhattan, KS: Sunflower Press, 1984.
Langins, Janis. *Conserving the Enlightenment: French Military Engineering from Vauban to the Revolution*. Cambridge: The MIT Press, 2004.
Lanning, Michael Lee. *African Americans in the Revolutionary War*. New York: Citadel Press, 2000.
Lasseray, Andre. *Les Françaises sous le Treize Étoiles 1775–1783*. 2 Vols. Paris: Protat, 1935.
Leconte, Louis. *Le Régiment Royal-Liègeois au service du Roi de France 1787–1792*. Moulins: Crepin-Leblond, 1937.
LeDiberder, Georges, ed. *Les Armées Françaises a la Epoque Revolutionaire 1789–1804*. Vol 8. Paris: Les Collections Historique du Musee de l'armée, 1989.
Lefkowitz, Arthur S. *George Washington's Indispensable Men: The Thirty-two Aides de Camp Who Helped Win American Independence*. Mechanicsburg, PA: Stackpole Books, 2003.
Lepage, Jean-Denis G.G. *Vauban and the French Military under Louis XIV: An Illustrated History of Fortifications and Strategies*. Jefferson, NC: McFarland, 2010.
Le Pottier, Serge. *Duportail ou le Génie de George Washington*. Paris: Economica, 2011.
Lockhart, Paul. *The Drillmaster of Valley Forge: The Baron de Steuben and the Making of the American Army*. New York: HarperCollins, 2008.
Logan, Raymond W. "St. Domingue: Entrepôt for Revolutionaries." In *The American Revolution in the West Indies*, edited by Charles W. Toth. Port Washington, NY: Kennikat Press, 1975.
Lonchay, Henri. *La Principaute de Liège, la France et les Pays-bas aux XVII et XVIII siècle*. Bruxelles, 1891.
Lynch, John. *Bourbon Spain, 1700–1808*. Cambridge, MA: B. Blackwell, 1989.
Lyon, E. Wilson. *Louisiana in French Diplomacy, 1759–1804*. Norman: University of Oklahoma Press, 1934.
Madsen, Axel. *John Jacob Astor: America's First Multimillionaire*. New York: John Wiley & Son, 2001.
Manceron, Claude. *The French Revolution, Vol. I, The Twilight of the Old Order*, Trans. by Patricia Wolf. New York: Alfred A. Knopf, 1977.
Manceron, Claude. *The French Revolution, Vol. III, Their Gracious Pleasure*. Trans. by Nancy Amphoux. New York: Alfred A. Knopf, 1980.
Mandach, Conrad de. *Le Comte Guillaume de Portes: Un Gentilhomme Suisse au service de la Hollande et de la France, 1750–1823*. Paris: Perrin et C., 1904.

240 • Bibliography

Mann, Bruce H. *Republic of Debtors: Bankruptcy in the Age of American Independence.* Cambridge: Harvard University Press, 2002.
Mansel, Philip. *Paris Between Empires: Monarchy and Revolution, 1814–1852.* New York: St. Martins Press, 2001.
Massey, Gregory D. *John Laurens and the American Revolution.* Columbia: University of South Carolina Press, 2000.
Masson, Frederick. *Le Department des Affaires Étrangères pendant le Revolution 1787–1804.* Paris: E. Pion, 1877.
Mattern, David B. *Benjamin Lincoln and the American Revolution.* Columbia: University of South Carolina Press, 1995.
Matthewson, Tim. *A Proslavery Foreign Policy: Haitian-American Relations during the Early Republic.* Westport, CT: Praeger, 2003.
McClellan, James E., III. *Colonialism and Science: Saint Domingue in the Old Regime.* Chicago: University of Chicago Press, 2010.
McCrady, Edward. *The History of South Carolina in the Revolution, 1775–1780.* 2 Vols. New York: Russell & Russell, 1901.
McDonough, Daniel J. *Christopher Gadsden and Henry Laurens: The Parallel Lives of Two American Patriots.* Sellinsgrove: Susquehanna University Press, 2000.
Metcalf, Bryce. *Original Members and Other Officers Eligible to the Society of the Cincinnati.* Strasburg, VA: Shenandoah Publishing House, 1938.
Michaud, J. F. *Biographie Universelle ancienne et moderne.* 45 vols. Paris: Delagrave et Cie., 1854.
Miller, Charles A. *Jefferson and Nature: An Interpretation.* Baltimore: Johns Hopkins University Press, 1988.
Miller, Melanie Randolph. *Envoy to the Terror: Gouverneur Morris & The French Revolution.* Dulles: Potomac Books, 2005.
Minnigerode, Meade. *Jefferson Friend of France 1793: The Career of Edmond-Charles Genet.* New York: G.P. Putnam's Sons, 1928.
Mitchell, C.J. *The French Legislative Assembly of 1791.* Leiden: E.J. Brill, 1988.
Mollo, John, and Malcolm McGregor. *Uniforms of the American Revolution.* New York: Macmillan, 1975.
Mollo, John, and Malcolm McGregor. *Uniforms of the Seven Years War 1756–1763.* New York: Hippocrene Books, 1977.
Morris, Richard B. *The Peacemakers: The Great Powers and American Independence.* New York: Harper & Row, 1965.
Mossay, Jean. *Histoire de la Ville d'Avesnes.* Avesnes-sur-Helpe: Imp. de l'observateur.
Mousnier, Roland. *The Institutions of France under the Absolute Monarchy 1598–1789.* Trans. by Brian Pearce. 2 Vols. Chicago: University of Chicago Press, 1979.
Muirhead, Findlay, and Marcel Monmarche, eds. *The Blue Guides: North-Eastern France.* London: Macmillan, 1922.
Murphy, Orville T. *The Diplomatic Retreat of France and Public Opinion on the Eve of the French Revolution, 1783–1789.* Washington, D.C.: The Catholic University of America Press, 1998.
Myers, Minor, Jr. *Liberty without Anarchy: A History of the Society of the Cincinnati.* Charlottesville: University Press of Virginia, 1983.
Nasatir, Abraham, and Gary Elwyn Monel, eds. *French Consuls in the United States: A Calendar of the Correspondence in the Archives Nationales.* Washington, D.C.: Library of Congress, 1967.
Nelson, Ronald Roy. *The Home Office, 1782–1801.* Durham, NC: Duke University Press, 1969.
Newman, Edgar Leon, and Robert Lawrence Simpson, eds. *Historical Dictionary of France from the 1815 Restoration to the Second Empire.* New York: Greenwood Press, 1987.
Nordholt, Jan Willem Schulte. *The Dutch Republic and American Independence.* Trans. by Herbert Rowen. Chapel Hill: University of North Carolina Press, 1982.
Nosworthy, Brent. *The Anatomy of Victory, Battle Tactics 1689–1763.* New York: Hippocrene Books, 1992.

Nuxoll, Elizabeth Miles. *Congress and the Munitions Merchants: The Secret Committee of Trade during the American Revolution.* New York: Garland Publishing, 1985.
O'Donnell, William Emmett. *The Chevalier de la Luzerne: French Minister to the United States, 1779–1784.* Louvain: Bibliotheque de l'Universite, 1938.
Palmer, John McAuley. *General Von Steuben.* Port Washington, NY: Kennikat Press, 1937.
Palmer, R.R. *The Age of Democratic Revolution: A Political History of Europe and America 1760–1800.* 2 vols. Princeton: Princeton University Press, 1964.
Pancake, John S. *This Destructive War: The British Campaign in the Carolinas 1780–1782.* Tuscaloosa: University of Alabama Press, 1985.
Pardailhe-Galabrun, Annik. *The Birth of Intimacy: Privacy and Domestic Life in Early Modern Paris.* Trans. by Jocelyn Phelps. Philadelphia: University of Pennsylvania Press, 1991.
Parisot, Robert. *Histoire de Lorraine (Duche de Lorraine, duchy de Bar, Trois Eveches).* 4 Vols. Paris: A. Picard, 1922–1925.
Peyster, Henri de. *Les Troubles de Hollande a la veille de la Revolution Français 1780–1795.* Paris: A. Picard, 1905.
Phillips, Kevin. *1775: A Good Year for Revolution.* New York: Viking, 2012.
Pirenne, Henri. *Histoire de Belgique.* Brussels: Maurice Lamertin, 1926.
Polasky, Janet. *Revolution in Brussels, 1787–1793.* Hanover: University Press of New England, 1987.
Powell, J. H. *Bring Out Your Dead: The Great Plague of Yellow Fever in Philadelphia in 1793.* Philadelphia: University of Pennsylvania Press, 1949.
Price, Monro. *Preserving the Monarchy: Vergennes 1774–1787.* Cambridge: Cambridge University Press, 1995.
Ragon, Marcel. *La Legislation sur les Emigres 1789–1825.* Paris: Librairie Nouvelle de Droit & de Jurisprudnce, 1904.
Rakove, Jack. *Revolutionaries: A New History of the Invention of America.* Boston: Houghton Mifflin Harcourt, 2010.
Raphael, Ray. *Founders: The People Who Brought You the Revolution.* New York: The New Press, 2000.
Rappleye, Charles. *Robert Morris: Financier of the American Revolution.* New York: Simon & Schuster, 2010.
Reaveley, Peter. "Chapter IV: The Battle." In *John Paul Jones and the Bonhomme Richard,* edited by Jean Boudriot, trans. by David H. Roberts. Annapolis: Naval Institute Press, 1987.
Reinhard, Marcel. *Le Grand Carnot: Lazare Carnot 1753–1823.* 2 Vols. Paris: Hachette, 1950 and 1952.
Rice, Howard C. Jr. *Thomas Jefferson's Paris.* Princeton: Princeton University Press, 1972.
Risch, Erna. *Supplying Washington's Army.* Washington, D.C.: Center of Military History, United States Army, 1981.
Ritcheson, Charles R. *Aftermath of Revolution: British Policy toward the United States, 1783–1795.* Dallas: Southern Methodist University Press, 1969.
Roberts, Kenneth, and Anna M. Roberts, eds. and trans. *Moreau de St. Mery's American Journey (1793–1795).* Garden City, NY: Doubleday, 1947.
Roche, Daniel. *France in the Enlightenment.* Trans. Arthur Goldhammer. Cambridge: Harvard University Press, 1998.
Roche, Jean-Michel. *Dictionnaire des batiments de la Flotte de guerre française de Colbert a nos jours.* Vol. 1, 1671–1870. France: Groupe Rezotel, 2005.
Rogers, George C., Jr. *Charleston in the Age of the Pinckneys.* Norman: University of Oklahoma Press, 1969.
Rosengarten, J. G. *French Colonists and Exiles in the United States.* Philadelphia: J.B. Lippincott, 1907.
Rossie, Jonathan G. *Politics of Command in the American Revolution.* Syracuse, NY: Syracuse University Press, 1975.
Rouleau, Bernard. *Memoires et Documents: Le Trace des Rues de Paris, Formation, Typologie, Fonctions.* Paris: Centre de Recherches et Documentation Certographiques et Geographiques, 1967.

Rutyna, Richard A., and Peter C. Stewart. *Virginia in the American Revolution: A Collection of Essays.* Norfolk: Old Dominion University, 1977.
Ruwet, Joseph. *Soldats des Régiments nationaux au XVIII siècle.* Brussels: Palais des Academies, 1962.
Saffell, W.T.R. *Records of the Revolutionary Army Containing the Military and Financial Correspondence of Distinguished Officers.* Philadelphia: G.G. Evans Publisher, 1860.
Saricks, Ambrose. *Pierre Samuel Du Pont de Nemours.* Lawrence: University of Kansas Press, 1965.
Schaeper, Thomas J. *France and America in the Revolutionary Era: The Life of Jacques-Donatien Leray de Chaumont, 1725–1803.* Oxford: Berghehn Books, 1995.
Schama, Simon. *Citizens: A Chronicle of the French Revolution.* New York: Alfred A. Knopf, 1989.
Schama, Simon. *Patriots and Liberators: Revolution in the Netherlands, 1780–1813.* New York: Alfred A. Knopf, 1977.
Schiff, Stacy. *Dr. Franklin Goes to France.* London: Bloomsbury, 2005.
Schminke, Frederick A. *Genet: The Origins of His Mission to America.* Toulouse: Lion et Fils, 1937.
Scott, Samuel F. *From Yorktown to Valmy: The Transformation of the French Army in the Age of Revolution.* Niwot: University of Colorado Press, 1998; reissue, 1978.
Scott, Samuel F. *The Response of the Royal Army to the French Revolution: The Role and Development of the Line Army, 1787–1793.* Oxford: Clarendon Press, 1978.
Scott, Samuel F. "Strains in the Franco-American Alliance: The French Army in Virginia, 1781–1782." In *Virginia in the American Revolution 1780–1783,* edited by Richard A. Rutyan and Peter C. Edwards. 2 Vols. Norfolk: Old Dominion University, 1983.
Segur, Louis Philippe. *Memoires: Ou Souvenirs et anecdotes.* 3 Vols. Paris: A. Eymery, 1824–1826.
Segur, Louis Philippe. *Tableau Histoirque et Politique de l'Europe depuis 1786 jusqu'en 1796.* Paris: A. Bertrand, 1830.
Sellers, Charles Coleman. *The Artist of the Revolution: The Early Life of Charles Willson Peale.* Hebron, CT: Feather and Good, 1939.
Sellers, Charles Coleman. *Portraits and Miniatures by Charles Willson Peale.* Philadelphia: American Philosophical Society, 1952.
Shapiro, Barry M. *Revolutionary Justice in Paris, 1789–1790.* Cambridge: Cambridge University Press, 1993.
Simpson, Henry. *The Lives of Eminent Philadelphians Now Deceased.* Philadelphia: W. Brotherhead, 1859.
Six, Georges. *Dictionnaire biographique des Generaux et amiraux français de la Revolution et l'Empire 1792–1815.* 2 Vols. Paris: Georges Saffroy, 1934.
Smith, Jay M. *The Culture of Merit: Nobility, Royal Service and the Making of Absolute Monarchy in France, 1600–1789.* Ann Arbor: University of Michigan Press, 1996.
Spalding, Paul S. *Lafayette: Prisoner of State.* Columbia: University of South Carolina Press, 2010.
Sparks, Jared. *The Life of Gouverneur Morris.* 3 Vols. Boston: Grey & Bollen, 1832.
Stryker, William S. *The Battle of Monmouth.* Port Washington: Kennikat Press, 1970.
Sullivan, Kathryn. *Maryland and France 1774–1789.* Philadelphia: University of Pennsylvania Press, 1939.
Taton, Rene. "L'École Royale du Génie de Mézières." In *L'Enseignement et Diffusion des Sciences en France au XVIII Siècle,* edited by Rene Taton. Paris: Hermann, 1964.
Te Brake, Wayne Ph. "Provincial Histories and National Revolution in the Dutch Republic." In *The Dutch Republic in the Eighteenth Century: Decline, Enlightenment and Revolution,* edited by Margaret C. Jacob and Wijnand W. Mijnhardt. Ithaca: Cornell University Press, 1992.
Thomson, Buchanan Parker. *Spain: Forgotten Ally of the American Revolution.* North Quincy: Christopher Publishing House, 1976.
Townsend, Sara Bertha. *An American Soldier: The Life of John Laurens.* Raleigh: Edwards & Broughton, 1958.

Van Alstyne, Richard W. *Empire and Independence: The International History of the American Revolution.* New York: John Wiley & Sons, 1965.
van Sas, Nicolas C.F. "The Patriot Revolution: New Perspectives." In *The Dutch Republic in the Eighteenth Century: Decline, Enlightenment and Revolution,* edited by Margaret C. Jacob and Winjnand W. Mijnhardt. Ithaca: Cornell University Press, 1992.
Vincent, Gilbert T. "Fine Arts: A Collection fitting a Nation." In *George Washington's Mount Vernon,* edited by Wendell Garret. New York: Monacelli Press, 1998.
Walker, Paul K. *Engineers of Independence: A Documentary History of the Army Engineers in the American Revolution 1775–1783.* Washington, D.C.: Historical Division, Office of Administrative Services, Office of the Chief of Engineers, 1981.
Ward, Harry M. *The Department of War 1781–1795.* Pittsburgh: University of Pittsburgh Press, 1962.
Watel, Françoise. *Jean-Guillaume Hyde de Neuville (1776–1857) Conspirateur et Diplomate.* Paris: Direction des Archives et de la Documentation Ministere des Affaires Etrangers, 1987.
Welsh, Peter C. *Tanning in the United States to 1850: A Brief History.* Washington, D.C.: Museum of History and Technology, Smithsonian Institution, 1964.
Wildes, Harry Emerson. *Lonely Midas: The Story of Stephen Girard.* New York: Farrar & Rhihart, 1943.
Williams, Greg H. *The French Assault on American Shipping, 1793–1813.* Jefferson, NC: McFarland, 2009.
Wilson, David K. *The Southern Strategy: Britain's Conquest of South Carolina and Georgia 1775–1780.* Columbia: University of South Carolina Press, 2005.
Wilson, James Grant, and John Fiske, eds. *Appleton's Cyclopaedia of American Biography.* 6 Vols. New York: D. Appleton and Company, 1886–1891.
Witt, Pierre de. *Une Invasion Prussienne en Hollande en 1787.* Paris: E. Plon, Nourrit et cie, 1886.
Wood, William, and Ralph Henry Gabriel, eds. *The Winning of Freedom.* New Haven: Yale University Press, 1927.
Wright, Robert K., Jr. *The Continental Army.* Washington, D.C.: Center of Military History, U.S. Army, 1983.
Zucher, A.E. *Général de Kalb, Lafayette's Mentor.* Chapel Hill: University of North Carolina Press, 1966.

Secondary Sources: Articles

Adams, Douglas N. "Jean Baptiste Ternant, Inspector General and Advisor to the Commanding Generals of the Southern Forces, 1778–1782." *South Carolina Historical Magazine* 86 (October 1985): 221–240.
Baradel, Yvette. "Belfort place de guerre et ville frontier dans la revolution 1791–1794." *Actes de la Société Jurassienne d'emulation* No. 92 (1989): 319–332.
Baradel, Yvette. "La Grande Peur a Belfort." *Saisons d'Alsace* 104 (1989): 265–267.
Bardy, H. "La Place de Belfort au commencement de la Revolution 1788–1792." *Bulletin de la Société Belfortaine d'emulation* No 24 (1905): 81–108.
Bardy, H. "Une Insurrection a Belfort (21 Octobre 1790)." *Revue d'Alsace* Juillet (1851): 304–321.
Bertrand, A. "Les États-unis et la Revolution Française." *Revue des deux-monds* XXXIII (May 1906): 392–430.
Bien, David D. "The Army in the French Enlightenment." *Past and Present* No. 85 (Nov. 1979): 68–9.
Bonnabelle, M. "Notice Historique et Statistique sur la Ville de Damvillers, Meuse." *Memoires de la Société des letters, sciences et Arts de Bar-le-Duc* (1871): 203–221.
Boorse, Henry. "Barralet's 'The Dunlap House' and Its Associates." *The Pennsylvania Magazine of History and Biography* Vol. 99, issue 2 (April 1975): 131–155.

244 • Bibliography

Caron, Pierre. "Tentative de counter-revolution de juin-juillet 1789." *Revue Histoire Moderne* VIII (1906–07): 5–34 and 649–678.
Chalmin, Pierre. "La Formation des Officiers des Armies savantes sous l'ancien Régime." *Actes du Soixante-seizieme Congres des Sociétés Savantes,* Paris (1951): 165–182.
Dallettt, Francis James. "The French Benevolent Society of Philadelphia and the Bicentennial: An Address to the *Assemblee Général* of the Society." *Records of the American Catholic Historical Society of Philadelphia* Vol. 88 (1977): 61–68.
D'Auberteuil, Hillard. "List of French Officers Who Served in the American Armies with Commissions from Congress Prior to the Treaties Made between France and the Thirteen United States of America." *Magazine of American History* 3 (1879): 364–69.
De Ville, Winston. " Post of Pointe Coupee." *Colonial Louisiana Marriage Contracts,* Vol. III: 1–67.
Doyon, Pierre, "Marie-Louis d'Escorches, Marquis de Sainte-Croix sa mission diplomatique a Liège 1782–1791." *Revue d'Histoire Diplomatique* XXXVII (1923): 89–113 and 208–235.
Dun, Alec. "'What avenues of commerce will you, Americans not explore!' Philadelphia's Commercial Vantage on St. Domingue, 1789–1793." *The Atlantic Economy in the Era of Eighteenth-Century Revolutions,* Program in Early American Economy and Society Conference, The Library Company of Philadelphia, September 19, 2003.
Fortune, Brandon B. "Charles Willson Peale's Portrait Gallery: Persuasion and Plain Style." *Word and Image* (Oct.–Dec. 1990): 308–324.
Grouvel, R. "La Legion de Maillebois, 1784–1786." *Le Passepoil* Year 12, No. 2: 33–37.
Hart, Charles Henry. "Colonel John Nixon." *Pennsylvania Magazine of History and Biography* 1 (1877): 188–202.
Holmes, Jack L. "Some Economic Problems of Spanish Governors of Louisiana." *Hispanic American Historical Review* XLII (1962): 521–543.
Kite, Elizabeth S. "Lafayette and His Companions on the Victoire." *Record of the Catholic Historical Society* Vol. XLV, No 1 (March 1934): 1–32, 144–178, 212–245.
Knight, Betsy. "Prisoner Exchange and Parole in the American Revolution." *William and Mary Quarterly,* 3rd Series, Vol. 48, No. 2 (April 1991): 201–222.
Lewis, J.D. "The American Revolution in South Carolina—Gibbe's Plantation." www. carolina.com/SC/Revolution/revolution_Gibbe's_ plantation.
Magnette, M.F. "Les Dessous d'une Election Episcopale sous l'ancien régime." *Bulletin de l'Academie Royale des Sciences, des Lettres et des Beaux-arts de Belgique* (1896): 163–206.
Maslowski, Pete. "National Policy toward the Use of Black Troops in the Revolution." *South Carolina Historical Magazine* (January 1972): 1–17.
Massie, Gregory D. "Slavery and Liberty in the American Revolution: John Laurens's Black Regiment Proposal." *Early America Review,* Spring 2003.
Meadows, R. Darrell. "Engineering Exiles Social Networks and the French Atlantic Community 1789–1809." *French Historical Studies* Vol. 23, No. 1 (Winter 2000): 67–102.
"Mission of Col. John Laurens to Europe 1781." *South Carolina Historical and Genealogical Magazine* Vol. 2 (April 1901): 27–28.
Murdock, Richard. "A French Account of the Siege of Charlestown 1780." *South Carolina Historical Magazine* 67 (July 1966): 138–154.
Muret, Pierre. "L'Affaire des princes possessiones d' Alsace et les origines du conflict entre la Revolution et l'Empire." *Revue d'Histoire Moderne et Contemporaire* 1899–1900: 433–456 and 566–59.
Pillot, Theodore-Louis-Joseph. "Les consequences d'une mutinerie militaire a Avesnes en 1790." *Société Archeologique Historique de l'arrondissement d' Avesnes. Memoires Avesnes* XV (1935): 17–22.
Potofsky, Allan. "The 'Non-aligned' Status of French Emigres and Refugees in Philadelphia 1793–1798." *Transatlantica* [En ligne] 2 (2006).
Prelinger, Catherine M. "Less Lucky than Lafayette: A Note on the French Applicants to Benjamin Franklin for Commissions in the American Army 1776–1785." *Proceedings of the Western Society for French History* 4 (1976): 263–271.

Richards, Rhys. "United States Trade with China, 1784–1814." *American Neptune* 54 (1994): Special Supplement 1.
Ritcheson, Charles R. "The Fragile Memory: Thomas Jefferson at the Court of George III." *Eighteenth Century Life* Vol. 6 (1981): 1–16.
Simpson, Clifford L. "Benjamin Lincoln." *Sibley's Harvard Graduates* Vol. XII (1962): 416–458. Condensed in Frederick S. Allen Jr. and Wayne A. Frederick. *Guide to the Microfilm Edition of the Benjamin Lincoln Papers.* Boston: 1967.
Stone, Frederick D. "Philadelphia Society One Hundred Years Ago, or the Reign of Continental Money." *Pennsylvania Magazine of History and Biography* Vol. 3 (1879): 361–394.
Sturgill, Claude C. "Observations of the French War Budget 1781–1790." *Military Affairs* 48 (October 1984): 180–187.
Stutesman, John H. "Colonel Armand and Washington's Cavalry." *New York Historical Society Quarterly* Vol. XLV, No. 1 (January 1961): 5–42.
Taylor, George. "The Paris Bourse on the Eve of the French Revolution, 1781–1789." *American Historical Review* 67 (1962): 951–977.
Thompson, Mack. "Causes and Circumstances of the Dupont Family's Emigration." *French Historical Studies* Vol. 6, No. 1 (Spring 1969): 55–77.
Van Uythoven, Geert. "The Dutch during the Revolutionary Wars: The Prussian Campaign in Holland, 1787." *First Empire Magazine* Nos. 45, 46 and 47.
Wrong, Charles John. "The Officiers de Fortune in the French Infantry." *French Historical Studies* 9 (1976): 400–431.
Zook, George. "Proposals for a New Commercial Treaty between France and the United States, 1778–1793." *South Atlantic Quarterly* Vol. 8 (1909): 267–283.

Unpublished Sources

Baldwin, William. "The Beginning of the Revolution and the Mutiny of the Royal Garrison in Nancy: L'Affaire de Nancy 1790." Ph.D. Dissertation, University of Michigan, 1973.
Chase, Philander Dean. "Baron Von Steuben in the War of Independence." Ph.D. Dissertation, Duke University, 1972.
Coulet du Gard, Rene. "Les Français exiles, emigres, refugies en Pensylvanie de 1789 a 1800." Ph.D. Dissertation, L'universite de Besancon, 1966.
Covington, Samuel Anderson. "The 'Comité Militaire' and the Legislative Reform of the French Army, 1789–1791." Ph.D. Dissertation, University of Arkansas, 1976.
Cyphers, Mary Ann. "The Diplomatic Career of Victor Marie Du Pont, 1795–1800." Masters Thesis, University of Delaware, 1969.
Eaton, Reed R. "The Public Life of Stephen Girard." Ph.D. Dissertation, Kent State University, 1971.
Hebert, Anne Catherine Bieri. "The Pennsylvania French in the 1790s: The Story of Their Survival." Ph.D. Dissertation, University of Texas at Austin, 1981.
Howe, Patricia Chastain. "French Revolutionary Foreign Policy and the Belgian Project, 1789–1793." Ph.D. Dissertation, University of North Carolina, 1982. 2 vols.
Jones, Helen F. "James Lovell in the Continental Congress 1777–1782." Ph.D. Dissertation, Columbia University, 1968.
King, Amanda Ruth. "Social and Economic Life in Spanish Louisiana 1763–1783." Ph.D. Dissertation, University of Illinois, 1931.
O'Dwyer, Margaret W. "Louis-Guillaume Otto in America." Ph.D. Dissertation, Northwestern University, 1954.
Pacheco, Josephine Fennell. "French Secret Agents in America, 1776–1778." Ph.D. Dissertation, University of Chicago, 1950.
Woodfin, Maude H. "Citizen Genet and His Mission." Ph.D. Dissertation, University of Chicago, 1928.

Bibliographical Sources

Breton, Arthur. *A Guide to the Manuscript Collections of the New-York Historical Society.* 2 Vols. Westport, CT: Greenwood Press, 1972.

Butler, John P. *Index of the Papers of the Continental Congress, 1774–1789.* 5 vols. Washington D.C: National Archives and Records Service, 1978.

Catlett, J. Stephen, ed. *A New Guide to the Collections in the Library of the American Philosophical Society.* Philadelphia: American Philosophical Society, 1987.

Documentos Relativos a la Independencia de Norteamerica existents en Archivos Espanoles. 11 Vols. Madrid: Ministerio de Asuntos Exteriores, Direccion Général de Relacions Culturales, 1976–.

Gottschalk, Louis, Phyllis S. Pestieau, and Linda J. Pike. *Lafayette: A Guide to the Letters, Documents and Manuscripts in the United States.* Ithaca: Cornell University Press, 1975.

Hardy, James D., Sr., John H. Jensen and Martin Wolfe, eds. *The McClure Collection of French Revolutionary Materials.* Philadelphia: University of Pennsylvania Press, 1966.

Riggs, John Beverley. *A Guide to the Manuscripts in the Eleutherian Mills Historical Library, Accessions through the Year 1965.* Greenville: Eleutherian Mills Historical Library, 1970.

Surrey, N.M. Miller, ed. *Calendar of Manuscripts in Paris Archives and Libraries Relating to the History of the Mississippi Valley to 1803.* 2 vols. Washington, D.C.: Carnegie Institution of Washington, 1928.

Tourtier-Bonazzi, Chantal de. *Lafayette: Documents Conserves en France.* Paris: Archives Nationales, 1976.

Index

Adams, John 131, 176, 181
Adams, Samuel 62
Adet, Pierre-Auguste 179
Agioteurs 143
American Philosophical Society 1, 208
Amiens, Peace of 191
Amsterdam 20, 26, 120, 126–128, 130, 131, 136, 137, 141, 142
Andre, John 82
Armand's Legion 88, 92–94, 106, 117; *see also* First Partisan Legion; Legionary Corps
Arnold, Benedict 70
Ashley Hill plantation 96, 100
Asylum Land Company 178, 203
Austerlitz, battle of 191
Austrian Netherlands (Belgium) 3, 114, 118, 133, 145, 151, 174
Avesnes-sur-Helpe 145, 151, 154

Bache, Sarah 69
Baden, Charles-Francis 150
Bank of France 194, 100, 106
Bank of North America 200
Barbe-Marbois, François 5, 87, 160, 182, 183
Barber, Francis 44
Barclay, John 162
Bardou, Anne Elizabeth 1, 206, 207
Barren Hill, skirmish at 48, 49
Barthelemy, François 5, 129, 156, 182, 183
Beaumarchais, Pierre-Augustin Caron de 29, 31
Beaumont, Pauline, comtesse de 160
Beauvillier, Antoine 188
Béchet de Rochefontaine, Étienne-Nicolas-Marie 105, 112
Belfort 152, 154, 155

Belle-Isle, Charles Fouquet, marquis de 16
Bellefonds, Louis-Charles 117
Bellonet, Henri-Marie 116, 128
Bert, Claudius de 105
Bervie, Charles-Clement 196
Bichellerie, M. 206
Bigot de Saint-Croix, Louis-Claude 174
Bingham, William 87
Bitche 153, 154
black project 67, 96; *see also* enlistment of slaves
Blanchard, Jean-Pierre 172
Bland, Humphrey 44
Board of War 49, 50, 58, 59, 70, 71
Bocquet de Chantereine, Agathe-Louise 20, 193, 207
Bonaparte, Napoleon 184, 186, 188, 190–193, 196, 198, 199, 204
Bonne-Carrère, Guillaume 174
Bonvoulior, Julian-Alexandre Archard de 28
Bordeaux 22, 29, 32, 34, 39
Bosquillon, Finnin-Paul-François de 128
Bossut, Abbe Charles-François 19
Bouille, François-Claude Amour, marquis de 149–151, 154
Bourbon, Beatrix de 12
Brissot, Jacques-Pierre 131, 143, 171
Broglie, Charles-François, comte de 31
Brooks, John 44, 55
Brun de Bellecourt 105
Brunswick, Charles-William-Ferdinand, duke of 125, 126
Brunswick-Wolfenbuttel, Louis-Ernest, duke of 115, 119, 125
Buffon, George-Louis Leclerc, de 7, 94, 156
Bureaux de Pusy, Françoise-Josephine 185

247

Bureaux de Pusy, Jean-Xavier 20, 185, 207
Café de Foy, Paris 196
Callet, François 196
Calonne, Charles-Alexandre de 119
Cambray-Digny, Louis-Antoine 67, 68, 75, 90, 95, 104, 105, 109
Campbell, Archibald 63, 64
Cap Français 32–34, 37, 39, 167, 168
Capellen tot den Pol, Joan-Derk van der 114
Carrot, Lazare 18, 19
Cassini, Angélique-Dorothée de 115
Cassini, Dominique-Joseph, de 116
certificat d'identité et de catholique 23, 32
Charles IV, king of Spain 79
Charles V, Holy Roman Emperor 13
Charlestown 59–62; siege of 79–84
Chastellux, François-Jean de Beauvoir, marquis de 88, 111, 119
Choiseul, Étienne-François, duc de 28
Church, Catherine (Kitty) 144, 185, 186; *see also* Cruger, Catherine
Church, John Barker 144, 185
Church, Philip 204
Clarke, William 130
Clavière, Étienne 143
Clinton, Henry 52, 73, 74, 81–83, 91
Clymer, George 87
Committee of Foreign Applications 38
Committee of Secret Correspondence 28, 30, 31
Contrexéville 205
Conway, Thomas 38
Cornwallis, Charles 74, 90
Corps du Génie 19–21, 39
Côte-d'Or 14
Coyngham, Nesbit & Company 171
Cruger, Amelia 144
Cruger, Bertrum Peter 186, 198
Cruger, Catherine 185, 186; *see also* Church, Catherine
Cruger, Henrietta 144

d'Agout, marquis 160
Dallas, Alexander 162
Damvillers 11–15, 17, 21, 27, 101, 113, 189, 205
d'Angély, François-Marie 117
d'Annemours, Charles-François-Adrien le Paulinier, chevalier 87, 93
Davies, William 44, 55
Deane, Silas 29–52
de Brahm, Ferdinand 75
de Grasse, François-Joseph Paul, comte 78
Delamotte, Alexandre-Marie 206
de Ponthiere, Louis 69
de Riquet, Victor-Louis-Charles 156
de Saxe, Maurice 44
d'Estaing, Charles-Henri Hector, comte 73
Deux-Ponts, Charles-Auguste-Chrietien, duke of 150
de Viar, José Ignacio 164
de Wailly, Charles 7
Doyle, Welborn Ellis 91
Dubard de Ternant, Philibert-Jean 210*chln*13
Dumas, Guillaume-Mathieu 20, 90, 127
Dumouriez, Charles-François de Perier 174
Dunlap, John 165
Duponceau, Pierre-Étienne 1, 42, 43, 45, 171
Du Pont, Amelia 180, 194, 199, 202, 204
Du Pont, Gabrielle-Josephine 6, 179, *180*, 181, 186, 187
Du Pont, Victor-Marie 157, 158, 160–162, 164, 165, 177, 179–181, 185–187, 190, 192, 196, 200, 204, 207
Du Pont, Xavier-François 172
Du Pont de l'Étang, Pierre-Antoine 117
Du Pont de Nemours, Pierre-Samuel 6, 157, 166, 177, 186, 191, 193, 207
Duportail, Louis le Begue de Presles 2, 32, 38, 39, 40, 43, 68, 81, 84, 86, 89, 108, 109, 179, 184, 207
Dutch Patriots 113, 114, 129, 121, 125, 126, 128, 141
Dutch Republic 113, 114, 119, 122, 128, 129, 133, 141–132; *see also* United Provinces

Eagle 77
l'Écolé du Génie 16, 37
enlistment of slaves 46, 70, 74, 97; *see also* black project

Favorite 161, 162, 164
Fersensac, comtesse de 160
First Bank of the United States 186, 195
First Partisan Corps 102, 108; *see also* Armand's Legion; Legionary Corps
Fischer, Jean-Christian 116
Flahaut, Adélaide-Marie-Émile, comtesse de 156
Flahaut, Charles, comte de 156
Floridablanca, Don Jose de Monino, conde de 22, 23, 79

Fontainebleau, Treaty of 119
Fontevieux, Jean-Georges de 105
Forsythe, Robert 55
Fort Moultrie 76, 81
Franklin, Benjamin 5, 22, 23, 29–32, 34, 42, 113
Fuller, Catherine 96, 98
Fuller, Thomas 96
Fuselier, Marie-Basilee 206; *see also* Ternant, Marie-Basilee

Gadsden, Christopher 62
Galvez, Don Bernardo Vicente 34, 78, 79, 91
Galvin, William 70, 71
Gates, Horatio 98
Genêt, Edmund-Charles 141, 174, 175, 177, 178, 182
Genton de Villefranche, Jean-Louis-Ambrose de 40, 104
George III, king of England 6, 130
Gerard, Conrad-Alexandre 29, 58
Gerard-Lenfant, M. 205
Gibbes' plantation 80
Gillant, Anne-Marguerite 11, 12
Gillant, Jean-Antoine 206
Girard, Stephen 5, 200–203
Girondins 174–176, 183
Givet 16, 124, 137
Godart de Bardeliere, Louis-Marie-Gaspard 137
Goodstay house 185
Gouvion, Jean-Baptiste 39, 109
Grand, Ferdinand 29, 108, 143
Great Wagon road 94
Greene, Nathaneal 54–56, 86, 92, 93, 97, 99, 100, 106
Gribeauval, Jean-Baptiste Vaquette de 29
Gruillocheau, Louis 32
Grunstein, Louis-Auguste de Schwengsfeld, baron de 153–155
Guerin de Foncin, Jean-Rene 20, 170
Guyana 133, 191

Hamilton, Alexander 5, 42, 44, 69, 82, 84–86, 156, 164, 1666, 168, 170, 176, 185, 186
Hammond, George 182
Harmar, Josiah 101
Havana 77–79, 86, 87, 110
Hesse-Darmstadt, Christian-Louis, prince of 115
Hoensbroech, François-Joseph 135
Hoensbroech d'Ost, Cesar-Constantine-François-Charles, comte de 133–135

Holker, John 87
Holmes, Oliver Wendell, Jr. 1, 208
Holtzendorff, Louis-Casimir, baron de 71, 118
Howe, Robert 61–65, 91, 92
Howe, William 48
Hundred Days 204
Huntington, Samuel 78, 84
Hyde de Neuville, Henriette 204, 207
Hyde de Neuville, Jean-Guillaume 204, 207
Hyrne, Edmund 80

Inspectors General Department 8, 36, 49, 59, 60, 72
Iujo, Carlos Martinez de 182

Jacobin Club 174
James LaFitte & Company 203
Jean, King of Bohemia 12
Jefferson, Thomas 5, 7, 87, 93, 113, 119, 139, 141, 156, 157, 164–171, 176
Jones, John Paul 117
Joseph II, emperor of Austria 114, 115, 120, 134, 145

Kalb, Johann, baron de 2, 31, 38
Kellermann, François-Christophe 160
Kellermann, François-Étienne 160–161, 164
Knox, Henry 91, 156, 168
Kosciusko, Tadeusz 2, 98, 179

La Colombe, Louis-Saint-Ange de 179
Lafayette, Marie-Paul-Yves-Roch-Gilbert du Motier, marquis de 2, 5, 8, 31, 36, 38, 46, *47*, 48, 51, 53, 55, 63, 88, 112, 113, 119, 125, 131, 141, 142, 144–146, 149, 158–160, 173, 178, 184, 190, 192, 205, 207
LaForest, Antoine de 172
Lajard, Pierre-Auguste 117
La Luzerne, Anne-Cesar, chevalier de 3, 5, 7, 84, *85*, 86–88, 96, 105–107, 109–111, 118, 120–124, 128–132, 139, 140, 142, 147, 156, 163, 164, 178
La Luzerne, Cesar-Henri-Guillaume, comte de 129, 178
Lamacq, Jacques-Louis 206
La Mark, Auguste-Marie-Raymond, prince d'Arenberg, comte de 141
Lamarre, Marguerite-Claudine 207
Lamarre, Marie 11
Lamarre, Pierre 11
Lambert, Henri-Joseph, marquis de 127
Laporte, Benjamin 203

la Prade, Jean-Baptiste-Raymond de Fenis, comte de 117
la Radière, Louis-Guillaume-Servais Deshayes de 39
la Rouerie, Armand-Charles Tuffin, marquis de 88, 90, 94, 100, 102, 107
La Tour, Joseph-Clement Sallier, comte de 134–136, 153–155
La Tour du Pin, Jean-Frederic Gouvernet, comte de 154, 159
Laumoy, Jean-Baptiste-Joseph de 20, 39, 67–70, 75, 90, 104, 108, 109, 112, 137, 179, 187, 193
Laurens, Henry 5, 37, 49, *50*, 57–59, 61, 62, 75, 88, 95
Laurens, John (Jack) 5, 33, *34*, 37, 41, 42, 46, 48, 50, 55, 61, 66, 67, 73–75, 80, 84–86, 88, 89, 95–98, 130, 138, 164, 207
Lauzun, Charles-Armand de Goutant-Biron, duc de 116
Lauzun hussars 152
Law, John 24
LeBrun-Tondu, Pierre-Henri-Helene-Marie 174, 176
Legionary Corps 103, 104; *see also* Armand's Legion; First Partisan Legion
L'Enfant, Pierre-Charles 2, 53, 67–69, 73, 90, 95, 104, 106, 171
Leray de Chaumont, Jacques-Donatien 29
letter d'exame 18, 40
Liège 26, 124, 133–146, 145
Lincoln, Benjamin 8, 62, 65–68, 70, 73–85, 97, 103, 104, 106
Linnaeus, Carolus 94
Livingston, Robert 191
livre de raison 15
Lolot, Therese 12
Lomenie de Brienne, Athanase-Louis-Marie de 132, 136
Lotbinière, Michel-Chartier 28
Louis XVI, king of France 6, 16, 27, 84, 115, 117, 119, 129, 140, 146, 169, 171, 196
Louis XVIII, king of France 196–199, 204
Louisiana 23–27, 31, 32, 34, 35, 93
Lovell, James 38
Lowndes, Rawlin 62

Macarthy, Eugene 117
Macdonald, Joseph-Alexandre 117
Madison, James 156, 165, 169
Maillebois, Yves-Marie Desmarets, comte de 115–117, 119, 121, 141
Maillebois legion 116–118, 120, 136, 142, 143

Malmady, François-Lellorquis, comte de 74
Marais quarter 194
Marat, Jean-Paul 141, 154
Martin, Louis 1, 205, 207
Mattha, Jean-Alexandre, baron de 115
Matthews, John 97
Maugis, M. 207
Maurepas, Jean-Frederic Phelypeaux, comte de 27, 28, 30, 123
Mentges, Francis 99
Mepkin plantation 75, 110
Meredith, Samuel 178
Mezieres 16–20, 40, 68, 185
Mifflin, Thomas 102, 107
Mirabeau, comte de 154
Miralles, Don Juan de 74, 77, 78
Monmouth, battle of 53
Monroe, James 165
Monticello 93, 94, 110
Montmorin de St Herem, Armand-Marc, comte de 5, 121, 129, 130, 132, 139–141, 144, 146, 147, 149, 150, 155, 156, 160, 165, 166, 168, 169, 173, 178
Moreau de Saint-Mery, Mederic-Louis-Elie de 182
Morris, Gouverneur 5, 46, 87, 88, 137, *138*, 139, 140, 141, 144, 145, 147, 155, 156, 160, 166, 186, 207
Morris, Robert 70, 78, 87, 92, 108, 137, *138*, 139, 200
Mount Vernon 171
Moustier, Eleonore-François Elie, comte de 139, 156, 158, 161, 164, 165
Murnan, Jean-Bernard-Bourg Gauther de 40, 41

Nancy, Mutiny at 151–154
Navarro, Don Diego Joseph 78, 79
Necker, Jacques 139, 41, 144, 157
New Orleans 24, 25, 27, 78, 87, 110
Nicola, Lewis 44
Nixon, Elizabeth (Betsy) 8, 180
Nixon, John 6, 8, 87
Northern Liberties 177, 181

Orange, Frederika-Sophia-Wilhelmia, princess of 124
Order of Saint Louis 1, 19, 28, 111, 112, 122–125, 136, 141, 143
Otto, Louis-Guillaume 5, 7, 86, 87, 139, 156, 158, 162–163, 182
Overijssel 114, 120, 125, 126

Pache, Jean-Nicolas 175
Palais Royal 189, 196

Parker, Daniel 144
Peale, Charles Willson 8, 84
Pennsylvania packet 165
Peters, Richard 50, 58
Petits-Hotels, rue des 1, 205, 208
Pickering, Timothy 45
Pierponts plantation 96
Pierre, Jeanne 11
Pointe Coupee 25, 35
Providence 75
Provisional Executive council 175
Prudent 32, 33
Pulaski, Kazimierz 2, 73
Pyrenees, Treaty of 13

Quartermasters General department 54, 56–58

Raad van state 115
Raugrave de Salm, Theodore-Charles-Alexandre Bernard de 136
Rawdon, George Augustus Francis 91
Rayneval, Joseph-Mathias Gerard de 5, 121, 129
Reed, Joseph 105
Regulations for the Order and Discipline of the Troops of the United States 44, 71, 75
rentes perpetuelles 143, 177
rentiers 12, 144, 193
Reveroni de Saint-Cyr, Jacques-Antoine de 20, 207
Riviere, François 161, 162, 164
Rochambeau, Jean-Baptiste-Donatien de Vimeur, comte de 20, 86, 88, 92, 111, 112, 127, 185
Roland de la Platiere, Marie-Jeanne 175
roturier 13, 17, 41, 132
Rouget de l'Isle, Claude-Joseph 19
Rousseau, Jean-Jacques 6, 7
Royal-Liègeois regiment 129, 132, 135–137, 142, 144, 145, 151–155, 159
Rutledge, James 78

Saint-Croix, Louis-Henri Descorches, marquis de 133, 134, 159
Saint-Domingue 6, 33, 35, 167–169, 170, 172, 179
Saint-Germain, Claude-Louis, comte de 27, 28, 30, 32, 39, 42, 123
St. Gettnain-en-Laye 199, 200
St Priest, François-Emmanuel Guignard, comte de 127, 136, 144
Sally 171
Salm-Krynburg, Frederick-Johan Otto, rhinegrave of 115, 118, 125, 127

Sames d'Heidesseim, Ferdinand de 155
Savannah: battle of 63–65; siege of 73–74
Schulyer, Angelica 144
Schulyer, Elizabeth 144, 185
Segond de Sederon, Marie-Blaise-Jacques 117
Segur, Louis-Philippe, vicomte de 160
Segur, Philippe-Henri, marquis de 88, 105, 112, 134
Semonet, Jean-Baptiste 160
Semonville, Charles-Louis Hugnet, marquis de 146
Sevelinges de Bretigny, Charles-François 69, 75
Seven Years' War 16, 24, 28
Severn 187
Sharp, Granville 131
Short, William 144, 155, 160
Simpson, George 6, 35, 186, 195, 200, 202
Sinclair, Sir John 120
Smith, William Stevens 131, 176
Société des Amis des Noirs 131
Société française de bienfaisance de Philadelphie 172
Society of the Cincinnati 1, 109
Sonnerat, Pierre 6
Southern Department 8, 60, 63, 76, 89, 94, 98
Spire, Damien-August-Philippe Karl, prince-bishop of 150
Statist Party 146
Steele, Archibald 96
Stendhal (Marie-Henri Beyle) 7
Steuben, Friedrich-Wilhelm, baron von 2, 5, 8, 36, 37, 41, 42, 43, 44–47, 50–53, 55, 57–59, 60, 63, 65, 66, 70–72, 74, 74–77, 86, 89, 91, 95–97, 100, 112, 153, 160, 207
Stono Ferry, battle of 67
Swan, James 143, 144

Tabouillot, Claude 14
Tabouillot, Hubert 14
Tabouillot, Jeanne 11, 13
Talleyrand-Perigord, Charles-Maurice de 157, 182–184, 189
Ternant, Claude (father) 11, 14
Ternant, Claude-Vincent (half-brother) 12, 27, 35
Ternant, Claude-Vincentfi/s (nephew) 35
Ternant, Marie-Basilee (niece) 35; *see also* Fuselier, Marie-Basilee
Theveneau de Franey, Lazare-Jean-Baptiste 49, 58, 71

Third coalition 191
Three Bishoprics 16
Torfs, Jean-Joseph 146
Tort de la Sonde, Barthelemy 146
Trafalgar, battle of 191
Tronson du Coudray, Philippe-Charles-Jean-Baptiste 29, 31, 38, 40, 67

United Provinces 3, 25, 75, 113, 114, 119, 120, 124, 128; see also Dutch Republic
Unzaga, Don Luis de 78

Valley Forge encampment 2, 23, 25, 33, 36–38, 42, 44, 46–50, 53, 60, 62, 67, 69, 72, 87, 91, 172, 179, 186, 207
Valmont-Bomare, Jacques-Christophe 7
van Helden, Adrien 137
van Lichtenberg, Jean-Charles, baron 137
van Rijssel, Albertus 125, 128
Velbruck, François-Charles 133, 135
Verac, Chartles-Olivier de St George, marquis de 128, 129
Verdier, Baptiste 105
Vergennes, Charles Gravier, comte de 5, 28, 29, 112, 114, 115, 121, 129, 134, 156, 157
Vernier, Pierre-François 75
Versailles 27, 89, 111, 119, 122, 124, 128, 129, 134, 125, 138, 139, 141, 144, 153

Voltaire (François-Marie Arouet) 4, 6, 7, 24, 40, 157
Vonck, J.F. 145
Vonckists 145–148
Vrijkorpsen 114

Walker, Benjamin 91, 160
Walton, Col. George 64
Washington, George 4, 5, 36–39, 41, 43, 47, 48, 51, 56, 59, 71, 85, 88–92, 101–104, 107, 111, 139, 147, 158, 160, 164–166, 168, 171, 176, 177, 197
Waterloo, battle of 198
Wayne, Anthony 96
William V, prince of Orange and stadholder of the Dutch Republic 113, 115, 119, 120, 127
Willing, Thomas 87
Wilson, Robert 70
Wurttenberg, Charles-Eugene, duke of 150
Wyahusing Township 178

XYZ Affair 185

York, Pennsylvania 49, 102
Yorktown, siege of 2, 86, 90, 92, 94, 96
Young, Arthur 4